D0330438

Exploring the
APPALACHIAN TRAIL™

THE SERIES

HIKES IN THE SOUTHERN APPALACHIANS
Georgia North Carolina Tennessee

HIKES IN THE VIRGINIAS
Virginia West Virginia

HIKES IN THE MID-ATLANTIC STATES
Maryland Pennsylvania New Jersey New York

HIKES IN SOUTHERN NEW ENGLAND
Connecticut Massachusetts Vermont

HIKES IN NORTHERN NEW ENGLAND
New Hampshire Maine

Exploring the
APPALACHIAN TRAIL

HIKES in the
MID-ATLANTIC STATES

Maryland Pennsylvania New Jersey
New York

GLENN SCHERER
DON HOPEY

STACKPOLE BOOKS

Mechanicsburg, Pennsylvania

Exploring the Appalachian Trail™ Series Concept: David Emblidge

Series Editor: David Emblidge

Managing Editor: Katherine Ness

Researcher and Editorial Assistant: Marcy Ross

Copy Editor: Susannah Driver

Book design and cover design: Walter Schwarz, of Figaro, Inc.

Page make-up: Figaro, Inc.

Cartography: Jean Saliter and Lisa Story, of Figaro, Inc. (topo maps); Peter Jensen, of OpenSpace (trail drawing); Kevin Woolley, of WoolleySoft, Ltd. (trail profiles)

Cover photograph: Delaware Water Gap, Pa.-N.J., by Michael Warren

Page xii: photograph of Springer Mt. AT plaque (southern terminus) by Doris Gove

Page 26: photograph by David Emblidge

Interior photographs: See credits with each image.

Proofreader: Rodelinde Albrecht

Indexer: Letitia Mutter

Library of Congress Cataloging-in-Publication Data

Scherer, Glenn.
    Hikes in the Mid-Atlantic states / Glenn Scherer, Don Hopey.— 1st ed.
        p. cm. — (Exploring the Appalachian Trail)
    ISBN 0-8117-2666-5
    1. Hiking—Middle Atlantic States—Guidebooks. 2. Middle Atlantic States—Guidebooks. 3. Appalachian Trail—Guidebooks. I. Hopey, Don. II. Title. III. Series
GV199.42.M5S35
917.404 '43—dc21   97-50082
                                                    CIP

Printed in the United States
10 9 8 7 6 5 4 3 2

Mt. Katahdin

VT
ME
NY
NH
MA
CT
PA
NJ
MD
WV
VA
TN
NC
Springer Mt.
GA

Thousands of feet elev.

6
5
4
3
2
1

Northern New England

Southern New England

Mid-Atlantic States

The Virginias

Southern Appalachians

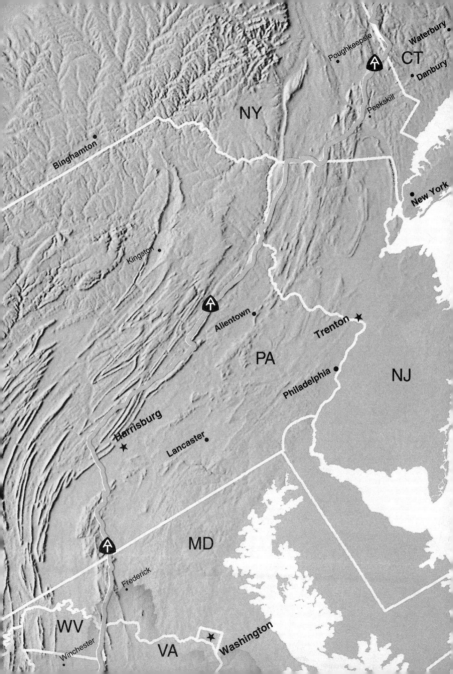

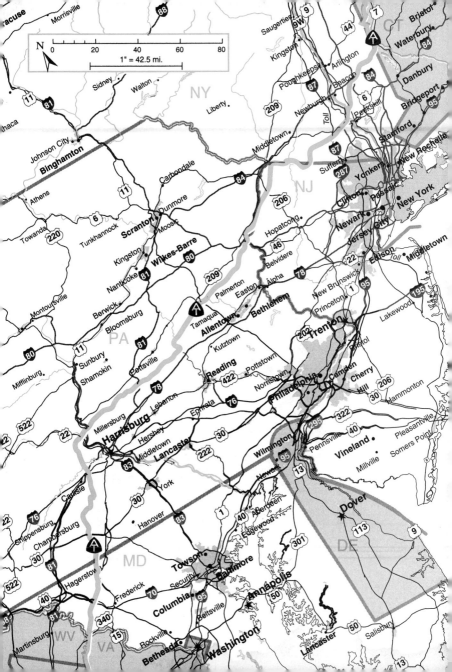

Contents

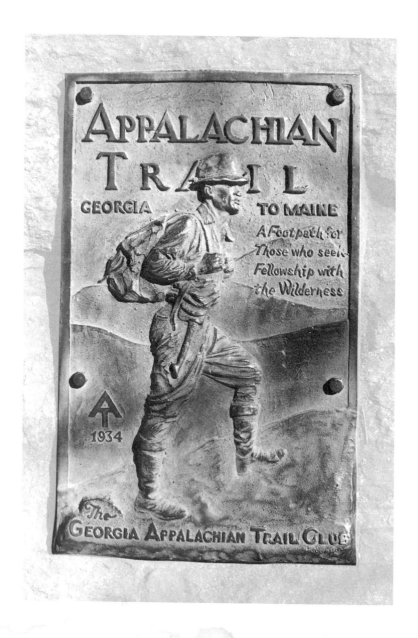

Introduction

Welcome to *Exploring the Appalachian Trail*. We're glad to have you join us for what promises to be a fine outdoor adventure. In this volume, Glenn Scherer was the lead author, covering Maryland, New Jersey, and New York; Don Hopey was co-author, covering Pennsylvania.

You may not have realized it when you bought or borrowed this book, but if the truth be told, it's all about a long-standing love affair. The authors of the hiking guides in this series have been in love with the Appalachian Trail since before we can remember. And we've come to believe that if you truly love something, you will probably act positively to protect it. So when we invite you to join us in walking on the trail, we're also inviting you to let yourself be seduced, indeed to go ahead and take the leap into a sweet and enduring love affair of your own. But then be sure to act on the responsibility created as a by-product of that love. It's called service and support. In the section below called "Joining Up," you can read more about how each of us can contribute to the health and continuing life of the trail. The Appalachian Trail will give you many gifts. Be sure you give some back.

Unlike other good books about walking the Appalachian Trail, this one will encourage you to slow down, to yield to the many temptations offered up freely by nature and by the social-historical world along the trail. Benton MacKaye, considered by most to be the chief visionary of the early Appalachian Trail, once defined the purpose of hiking on the AT as "to see, and to *see* what you see." MacKaye was something of a romantic, and we know he read Emerson, who instructs us all to "Adopt the peace of Nature, her secret is patience." We can't improve on that.

Our intention is to help you plan and carry out a wide variety of hikes on the nation's longest continuously marked footpath, surely one of the most famous walking trails in the world. We'll guide you from point A to point B, to be sure, but as far as this book is concerned, it's what happens for you *between* points A and B that counts the most.

If the goal of hiking on the Appalachian Trail is to come home refreshed in body, rejuvenated in mind, and renewed in spirit, then along with the fun of being outside in the mountains, a little work will be required. The most obvious work is of the muscular variety. Less obvious but just as rewarding is the mental kind, and it's here that the books in this series will help you the most. The famous world traveler Sven-Olof Lindblad said, "Travel is not about where you've been but what you've gained. True travel is about how you've enriched your life through encounters with beauty, wildness and the seldom-seen."

In these AT hiking books, we'll pause to inspect the rocks underfoot and the giant folding and crunching of the entire Appalachian landscape. We'll take time to listen to birds and to look closely at wildflowers. We will deliberately digress into the social history of the area the AT passes through, thinking sometimes about industry, other times about politics, and now and then about a well-known or an obscure but colorful character who happened to live nearby. We'll explore trail towns and comment on trail shelters and campsites (they're not all alike!). And to help make you a savvy hiker (if you aren't already), we will offer up some choice bits of hiker wisdom that just might get you out of a jam or make your load a bit lighter to carry.

This is a participatory book. You will enjoy it and profit from it most if you carry a small notebook and a pen or pencil, if you bring along a camera and perhaps a birding book or a wildflower guide or a guide to some other aspect of the natural world (see the Bibliography for suggestions). Bring a compass and use our maps, or better yet, supplement the maps in this book with the more detailed ones available from the Appalachian Trail Conference and other local sources (see page 8 and the Bibliography).

Chatting with your walking companions is a delightful thing to do some of the time while out on the trail, but the more noise you make, the less wildlife you'll see, and besides, it's hard for anyone to be both in conversation and simultaneously in close observance of the real details of the natural realm. Try hard to make some part of every hike a *silent walk*, during which you open all your senses and your imagination to drink in the marvelous environment of the Appalachian Trail.

The Appalachian Trail in the Mid-Atlantic States: Landscape and Environment

The states covered by this volume of Exploring the Appalachian Trail™ — Maryland, Pennsylvania, New Jersey, and New York—make up the Mid-Atlantic section of the Appalachian Trail. There are about 433 miles of the AT in these states, walked here in 41 hikes. Altitudes on the trail range from 124 feet above sea level at the Hudson River in New York to 1940 feet at Chimney Rock, Pennsylvania. Some hikes are benign enough for a toddler, while others challenge the most robust hiker (Pennsylvania is particularly infamous for its relentless rockiness). The Mid-Atlantic AT and hundreds of miles of side trails create a vast web of hiking possibilities, rich in natural and cultural history. A billion years of geologic change—proof of continental collisions, volcanism, and glaciation—lie at hikers' feet. A seasonal procession of wildflowers—purple trillium, pink lady's-slippers, and asters—is captivating. Bear, coyote, and deer share trail lands with walkers, as do songbirds and raptors. Human history has left its mark, too. The trail passes Native American rock shelters, iron and coal industry ruins, farm sites, stagecoach stops, canals, abandoned railroads, resorts from a bygone era, and Civil War battlefields. Mid-Atlantic AT hikers pass through forests, fields, and wetlands, and along country roads into hiker-friendly villages where services, supplies, and diversions are plentiful. The landscape offers a pleasing rural contrast to cliches of an overcrowded metropolitan Northeast. In this series, Volume #2 (*Hikes in the Virginias*) covers states to the south (Virginia and West Virginia) while Volume #4 (*Hikes in Southern New England*) walks north through Connecticut, Massachusetts, and Vermont. For those new to the Mid-Atlantic region, a colorful armchair traveler's introduction is *The Mid-Atlantic States* in The Smithsonian Guide to Historic America series.

Joining Up

We urge you, our fellow hikers, to honor the thousands of volunteers and paid workers who built and who nowadays maintain the Appalachian Trail by becoming a volunteer and a financial supporter yourself. Join your local hiking club and join any or all of the following organizations, each of which contributes to the survival of the Appalachian Trail:

Appalachian Trail Conference, P.O. Box 807, Harpers Ferry, WV 25425

Appalachian Mountain Club, 5 Joy St., Boston, MA 02108

American Hiking Society, 1422 Fenwick Lane, Silver Spring, MD 20910

New York-New Jersey Trail Conference, 232 Madison Ave., Suite 802, NY, NY 10016

Keystone Trails Association, Box 251, Cogan Station, PA 17728-0251

Potomac Appalachian Trail Club, 118 Park St. SE, Vienna, VA 22180-4609

Walking Lightly on the Land

On behalf of the hiking community, we urge all hikers to manage their behavior in the woods and mountains so as to have a minimal impact on the land. The old adages are apt: Take only pictures, leave only footprints. Pack out whatever you pack in. Leave no trace. Indeed, be a sport and pack out some other careless hiker's garbage if you find it along the trail. The National Park Service, which maintains a protective corridor along the Appalachian Trail, estimates that between 3 and 4 million people use the trail every year, and the numbers are growing. In many places the ecology of the AT landscape is fragile. But fragile or not, every one of its 2150 miles is subject to abuse, even if unintended. Leave the trail a better place than you found it, and you'll take home better memories.

Soft Paths: *How to Enjoy the Wilderness Without Harming It* is a good general introduction to the principles of leave-no-trace hiking and camping. See the Bibliography.

We wish you good weather, warm companionship, and a great adventure, be it for 6 hours, 6 days, 6 weeks, or 6 months on the trail. The Appalachian Trail belongs to all of us. Treat it as you would something precious of your very own.

Reader Participation

Readers are invited to respond. Please correct our mistakes, offer your perspectives, tell us what else you'd like to see in the next edition. Please also tell us where you bought or borrowed this book. Write to: Editors, Exploring the Appalachian Trail™, Stackpole Books, 5067 Ritter Rd., Mechanicsburg, PA 17055.

Acknowledgments

Information and help on this project came from many quarters. We are grateful to Series Editor David Embledge for involving us as writers in this ambitious project. The authors and editors of each of the volumes in the series have helped strengthen and enrich our own book. Many others have our sincere thanks: Susannah Driver, Volume 3 Editor, whose painstaking questions and fastidious attention to detail kept us both honest and accurate. For dogged research with good humor, we salute Marcy Ross.

Carolyn Golojuch provided efficient keyboarding. Walter Schwarz of Figaro completed the book design, directed map and trail profile production, designed covers, and directed typesetting. He is a master. At his studio we particularly thank Jean Saliter. Map maker (and trail planner) Peter Jensen, of OpenSpace Management, drew the corrected AT on our maps. Emilie Jeanneney produced early drafts of the Maryland, New Jersey, and New York maps. Thanks to each photographer, and to proofreader Rodelinde Albrecht and Indexer Letitia Mutter, both of whom did a fine job.

The trail clubs provided important assistance. At the Appalachian Trail Conference, we thank Judy Jenner, *Appalachian Trailway News* Editor, and Karen Lutz, Mid-Atlantic Regional Director, for their knowledge of the trail community; at the New York-New Jersey Trail Confer-ence, Ron Rosen (Dutchess/Putnam County New York AT Management Committee Chair), Paul DeCoste (New Jersey AT Management Committee Chair), Jane and Walt Daniels, Jim Palmer, and Dan Chazin for reading portions of the manuscript; at the Potomac Appalachian Trail Club, Pat Frankhauser and Paula Strain for reviewing the Maryland hikes; and we thank the members of the Keystone Trails Association. Special thanks go to Ron Dupont, Jr., Ed Lenik, Jane Geisler, Paul Kuznia (Taconic Education Center), and John Gebhards and John Yrizarry of the Sterling Forest Partnership, Inc., for their generously shared knowledge of natural and cultural history. Thanks goes to all of the National Park Service, National Wildlife Refuge, and state parks personnel who assisted us with information gathering, plus all the "ridge-runners" and club volunteers we met on the trail and who freely gave of their time. Thanks finally to our hiking companions and trailhead shuttlers: Don Owen (ATC), George Lightcap, Marty Fletcher, and Len Clifford. Every step of Don's was made easier by his wife, Carol, and daughter,

Coyne. Even when his pack is light he is thankful for their love.

This book was a vast undertaking and involved help from many others. For our errors (there will be some in such a complex work) and for our omissions, we apologize. In the writing of this volume, both of us gained a deeper appreciation of the natural world, strengthening our desire to preserve it. Our greatest hope is that this book will inspire similar feelings in others and enrich the walks of all those who read it.

HOW TO USE THIS BOOK

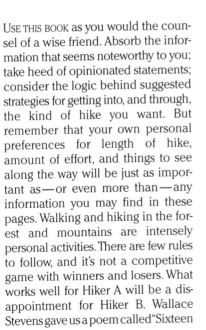

USE THIS BOOK as you would the counsel of a wise friend. Absorb the information that seems noteworthy to you; take heed of opinionated statements; consider the logic behind suggested strategies for getting into, and through, the kind of hike you want. But remember that your own personal preferences for length of hike, amount of effort, and things to see along the way will be just as important as—or even more than—any information you may find in these pages. Walking and hiking in the forest and mountains are intensely personal activities. There are few rules to follow, and it's not a competitive game with winners and losers. What works well for Hiker A will be a disappointment for Hiker B. Wallace Stevens gave us a poem called "Sixteen

Ways of Looking at a Blackbird." This book should indicate that there are at least that many ways to complete and enjoy a hike on the AT.

How Hike Information Is Displayed Here

INFORMATION BLOCK: The hike's first page, a snapshot of the hike in the form of data and directions. Here you'll find road access information, elevation gain, distance to be walked, names of shelters, and so on. This first section gives an objective overview of the hike.

NARRATIVE: The full story—the hike you're likely to have on this section of the AT. Conditions vary widely depending on season and weather,

depending on whether you're a robust 18-year-old, a tottering little kid, or a slow-but-steady octogenarian. Our description of the hike aims for a middle-range hiker, in good shape, with modestly ambitious goals but not with an eye on the stopwatch or the pedometer.

Throughout the hike's narrative we cite mileages at the major waypoints and landmarks. Occasionally we indicate the amount of time needed to go from one point to another. Generally, however, we stick to mileage as a reference point because each hiker's pace is different.

The narrative also pauses to describe rocks, plants, animals, vistas, and social history seen along the way. . . and then picks up the hike again with further directions toward its destination.

TRAIL PROFILE: A rendering of the trail's up-and-down travels over the landscape, suggesting graphically how easy or challenging sections may be. The profiles are based on USGS digital elevation maps and were created via cartography software called WoolleySoft created by Kevin Woolley, of Scotland. The linear scale on the profiles does not match the scale on the hike's topographic map (see below). Instead, the profile gives a cross-section view of the mountains and valleys with the trail running up and down as if on a straight line across the landscape. Trail profiles entail a certain degree of vertical exaggeration to make the rendering meaningful, and

they do not show every hill or knob in the path.

TOPOGRAPHIC MAP: Based on USGS 1:100,000 scale maps, the hike topo map also draws on information provided on AT maps published by the Appalachian Trail Conference and its member trail clubs. Our scale is usually 1 inch to 1 mile — or as close to that as the page trim size and length of the hike will allow. These maps show actual elevations (read about contour lines on page 8), usually in feet. They also show the compass direction (north) and important waypoints along the trail. See the map legend on page 7. For most day hikes, the maps in this book will serve well. For extended backpacking in the wild backcountry or high mountains, we recommend using Appalachian Trail Conference or Appalachian Mountain Club maps.

Note: Some USGS maps have not been updated for several years and may not show recent trail relocations. Follow the dark green line of the AT on the maps in this book. You may see the old AT outlined in gray on the map. In some cases the old path is open and usable, but in many it's not. Check the narrative and consult local trail clubs before hiking on discontinued sections of the AT.

ITINERARY: A summary of the hike in table format, listing important waypoints noted in the narrative and shown on the topo map and/or the trail profile. Both the narrative and the itinerary describe the hike as either a south-to-north (most common) or north-to-south walk. Thus, in a S-N itinerary, directions to turn left (L) or right (R) mean "left when walking northward on the trail" and "right when walking northward on the trail," respectively. On a N-S itinerary, the reverse is true.

Bear in mind that "north" and "south" as used along the AT are not always literally true. The trail is said to run north from Georgia to Maine, but at any given point, even if you're walking "northward toward Maine," the footpath may veer to the west or east, or even southward to skirt a difficult mountain before resuming its generally northward direction. That's why in the narrative and itinerary we generally use "left" and "right" rather than compass directions. Inexperienced AT hikers simply have to orient themselves correctly at the start of the hike: Make sure you know whether you're following the trail to the north or south, and keep that in mind as you proceed. Then, "left" and "right" in the narrative and itinerary will be easy to follow. In any case, always carry a compass.

Note: In keeping with the tradition of showing north at the top of maps, we structure the itineraries with north always at the top of the table, south at the bottom. Thus, for a S-N hike, you will find the "Start" at the bottom (south) end of the itinerary, and you should read upward. "End" will be at the top (north) end of the table. We give mileage in both direc-

tions: the left-hand column goes S-N; the right-hand column goes N-S. Remember that *access trail* mileage must be added to miles walked on the AT itself. We total both mileages for you on the itinerary. Elevations are given in both feet and meters (feet elsewhere in this book). To construct our itineraries, we relied on walking the trail, taking careful notes, and then verifying by reference to other trail guides, especially the Appalachian Trail Conference and member club trail guides. Published trail guides, USGS maps, and ATC maps sometimes disagree by as much as a few tenths of a mile (distance) or a few feet (elevation).

SIDEBAR: In some hikes, special topics are discussed in a box set off from the narrative. The sidebars are listed in the table of contents.

Abbreviations

Abbreviations commonly used in this book:

AHS, American Hiking Society

AMC, Appalachian Mountain Club

ATC, Appalachian Trail Conference

CCC, Civilian Conservation Corps

KTA, Keystone Trails Association

NY-NJTC, New York–New Jersey Trail Conference

PATC, Potomac Appalachian Trail Club

SP, State Park

USFS, U.S. Forest Service

USGS, U.S. Geological Survey

Geographic Organization

The hikes included in this volume follow the Appalachian Trail from south to north. Most of the hikes are described as south-to-north walks, but many are suitable to walking the opposite way, too. A few hikes are best done from north to south. Pay attention to the suggested direction. We have avoided some wicked climbs by bringing you down, rather than up, certain nasty hills.

Maps: Legends, Skills, Sources

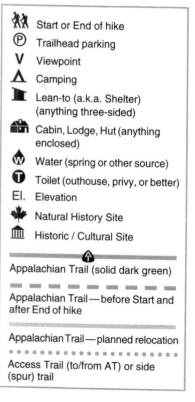

Start or End of hike

Trailhead parking

V Viewpoint

Camping

Lean-to (a.k.a. Shelter) (anything three-sided)

Cabin, Lodge, Hut (anything enclosed)

Water (spring or other source)

Toilet (outhouse, privy, or better)

El. Elevation

Natural History Site

Historic / Cultural Site

Appalachian Trail (solid dark green)

Appalachian Trail — before Start and after End of hike

Appalachian Trail — planned relocation

Access Trail (to/from AT) or side (spur) trail

SCALE — Unless otherwise noted, approximately 1 inch = 1 mile.

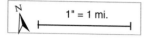

COMPASS DIRECTION AND DEVIATION — The scale bar shows the compass direction North. The north shown on the map is "true" or "grid" north, essentially a straight line to the north pole, whereas the north you see on your compass is "magnetic" north, usually a few degrees different due to the earth's magnetic field. Along the AT, magnetic north deviates from true or grid north by several degrees *west*. The farther north one goes, the greater the deviation. At the Vermont/New Hampshire state line the deviation is 15.5° west; throughout Maine it is about 18°.

CONTOUR INTERVAL — See "Contour Lines" below. Contour intervals on the USGS topographic maps used as the base for the hiking maps in this book are either 10 meters (32.8 ft.) or 20 meters (66 ft.) depending on the map (see "List of Maps" under "Useful Information").

Reading and planning your hikes with topographic maps can be fun and is certainly useful. Every hiking party should have at least one competent map reader. Often, if there are children aboard, they will be eager to follow the hike's progress on the topographic map. Here are a few pointers for beginning map readers.

CONTOUR LINES—All the hiking maps in this series of guides are based on official topographic maps which represent the three-dimensional shape of the land with contour lines (CLs). Typically, CLs are drawn at fixed intervals, for example, 20 meters, meaning that between each pair of lines in our example there is a rise or fall of 20 meters in the landscape.

In this example, the CLs are close together, suggesting a steep climb or descent:

In this example, the CLs are farther apart, suggesting a gently sloping or nearly flat landscape:

LINEAR SCALE—To understand CLs fully, they must be related to the *linear scale* of the map. This relationship gives a sense of vertical rise or fall as it spreads out horizontally across the landscape. Thus, if 1 inch = 1 mile and if there are many CLs clustered in, say, a ½-inch section of trail, then it's safe to assume that this ½-mile section of the trail will be steep, going up or down depending on your direction.

MAP SOURCES—All maps in this series are derived from United States Geological Survey topographic maps. Each of our maps is a small slice of a USGS topo map. We have updated relevant AT information (some USGS maps are 10 or more years old; the AT has moved at several points). The original map scale of 1:100,000 is enlarged here generally to about 1:62,000 (around 1 inch = 1 mile) for readability. A 1:100,000-scale map is not practical to carry on the trail. USGS maps scaled at a more convenient 1:62,000 are easy to read as trail maps, but a day's hike may cut across several maps or use only a tiny portion of one large map, an unwieldy affair when hiking.

For short day hikes, we recommend using the maps in this book. For longer hikes, overnight trips, or serious backpacking, we advise using official AT maps from the Appalachian Trail Conference or supplementary maps from the Potomac Appalachian Trail Club, Keystone Trails Association, and New York-New Jersey Trail Conference (see below for information).

Bookstores and outdoor outfitters in towns near the Appalachian Trail usually stock the USGS quadrangles (1:62,500) for the local area. USGS maps can also be ordered by telephone (see "Useful Information" and the Bibliography). If you do not know the USGS map number (see the "Useful Information" list for maps used in this book), be sure to indicate (a) the portion of the AT you want to hike by providing nearby cities, towns, rivers, or other landmarks and (b) the scale you prefer. Anything over 1 inch = 1 mile will be impractical for hiking.

The Appalachian Trail Conference publishes a set of color-shaded topographic hiking maps for almost the entire length of the trail (excluding the national parks through which the AT passes). The scale is generally 1:38,750. This translates to about 1⅝ inches = 1 mile. In other words, much more detail than on the USGS quadrangles and more than we can show in a book of this size. See your local bookseller or outdoor outfitter, or call the ATC (see "Useful Information"). A catalogue is available. For serious hikers and for any overnight or backcountry hiking on the Appalachian Trail, we strongly recommend these fine maps.

The Appalachian Mountain Club publishes hiking guides and nature walk books, including a few titles on the northern part of the mid-Atlantic region. See your local bookseller or outdoor outfitter, or contact the Appalachian Mountain Club (see "Joining Up," page 3).

For the AT in the Mid-Atlantic states, you'll want the fine trail guides and maps developed by the New York-New Jersey Trail Conference, Keystone Trails Association, and Potomac Appalachian Trail Club. The guides give the AT route and natural and cultural history. The three clubs also offer fine maps and books detailing the AT side trail network (indispensable in planning loop hikes and overnight trips). Of special note are: NY-NJTC maps of Kittatinny Mt., northern New Jersey, Bear Mt.-Harriman State Parks, East Hudson Trails, Fahnestock State Park, and southern Taconics; PATC maps of South Mt. Recreation Area, Cunningham Falls State Park, and Catoctin Mt. Park; and KTA's *Pennsylvania Hiking Trails* (a guide to 2000 miles of trails). The maps come in various scales and contour intervals and are waterproof and tear resistant. To order them, see your local bookseller or outdoor outfitter, or contact the individual clubs (see "Joining Up," page 3).

Driving Time to the Trailhead

A factor frequently overlooked when planning a hike is the driving time required to reach the trailhead or to get back to civilization at day's end. When a substantial number of miles must be traveled from a major highway or town to get up into the mountains to the trailhead, we tell you in the information block. You must be sure to leave sufficient time to get to the starting point. Positioning two cars (finish and start) takes even longer.

Remember that many Appalachian Trail access roads are "secondary" at best. Some are decidedly unkind to low-chassis, two-wheel-drive cars. Some are impassable in wet weather (the entire spring mud season). Travel to the trailhead can be slow and dicey. Read our instructions carefully. Plan ahead.

Choosing Your Hike / Effort Required

In this book we rate hikes by three levels of "effort required": easy, moderate, and strenuous. Some hikes are a mix of easy, moderate, and strenuous sections.

If little kids or folks with disabilities might find a hike too rugged, we tell you. If there are difficult water crossings, perhaps varying seasonally, we say so.

But remember, our judgments are somewhat subjective.

Easy: gentle ups and downs, fairly smooth path, few obstacles

Moderate: elevation gain or loss of up to 1000 feet; narrower, rocky path; some obstacles (for example, brook crossings with no bridge).

Strenuous: elevation gain or loss of more than 1000 feet; steep ups and downs; difficult, challenging path; numerous obstacles; possibly unsuitable for young children or the infirm.

Blazing

A "blaze" (from the Old English blœse, meaning "torch") is a bright painted mark (about 6 inches x 2 inches) on a tree, post, or rock indicating the path of a hiking trail. The Appalachian Trail is blazed in white (rather easy to see even in fog, though tough to follow in brightly dappled sunlight), all the way from Georgia to Maine. It's the same in each direction, south–north or north–south.

Side trails are often but not always blazed in a different color — generally blue, orange, or yellow. AT blazes are usually spaced 30 to 50 yards apart. In some sections overzealous trail maintainers have blazed at shorter intervals, while in other areas blazing has faded and may be hard to follow. If you haven't seen a white blaze for several minutes, backtrack and make sure you're still on the white-blazed AT, not an unmarked side trail or logging road.

Two blazes, one above the other, indicate a turn coming in the trail. In some states, if the upper blaze is positioned to the left, look for a left turn, and vice versa.

Estimating Hiking Times

An average adult hiker's pace is about 2.0 miles per hour on the flat. For every 1000-foot gain in elevation, add 30 minutes of time to your estimate. Thus an 8-mile hike up a 2500-foot mountain might take you 5¼ hours. This formula does not account for rests, mealtimes, or lollygagging to smell the flowers or talk to the bears. With a full backpack, little kids in tow, or slippery conditions, obviously you would add more time.

We recommend that you keep a record of your time and distance and the hiking conditions for a half dozen hikes, and then compare your averages to ours. You'll soon see whether our numbers match yours and if not, how much time you need to add or subtract from our estimates.

Day Hikes / Overnight Backpacking Hikes

The majority of the hikes in this book can be done as day hikes. Some day hikes can be conveniently strung together to make overnight backpacking trips of 2 or more days' duration. And some hikes are manageable only as overnight backpacking trips. The general rule: the more wilderness there is to traverse, the less likely it is that you can pop in and out for a day hike only. Read the information block carefully, and look at the hike south or north of the one you're considering to see whether a linkage is feasible.

Avoiding the Crowds

A great debate is raging: Is the AT now overused, too busy to be enjoyable, too tough on the land to be justifiable? Are we approaching, or are we already at, the point where reservations will have to be made for floor space in an AT shelter? (In fact, in some southern sections — Great Smoky Mts. National Park, for example — shelters are reserved for thru-hikers or other long-distance hikers only, not the casual weekender.) We don't mean to equivocate, but the answer seems to be yes and no. Collectively, the authors of this series have hiked thousands of AT miles over several decades. Far more often than not, we have had the trail essentially to ourselves, passing only a few people per day. Inevitably, however, certain sites on the trail (beautifully located shelters, or summits with great views or symbolic significance, for example) attract crowds, especially on weekends, and most especially in midsummer or at fall foliage time. The southern section of the AT is busy with hundreds of would-be thru-hikers in early spring. Don't expect to be alone on Springer Mt. in April.

It does not require a graduate degree in engineering to figure out a plan to avoid these crowds or to avoid swelling them yourself. The best times to be alone on the trail are midweek. No offense to kids or parents (we love 'em all), but June, before the kids leave school, and September, after they're back in, are great times to find warm-weather solitude on the AT. If you can swing it, why not work on Saturday (or even Sunday) and hike on Sunday and Monday (or better yet Monday and Tuesday). We've tried it with success. The most popular shelter in Connecticut is Riga: fantastic cliffside sunrise view. We had it all to ourselves on a Sunday night in mid-August, in good weather.

If you cannot hike midweek and are headed for peaks or shelters likely to be overcrowded, start out early enough to permit you to move on to another site in daylight if your first target has already hung out the "No Vacancy" sign. When the shelter or official tent sites are full, accept the bad news and walk on. Carving out an impromptu tent site is generally forbidden except in extremely bad weather. Carry a detailed map. Study it carefully before leaving home to find the alternative site you may need in a pinch.

Circuit or Loop Hikes / Shuttle Services

Ideally you have a limousine with built-in hot tub and cold drinks awaiting you at the end of the trail. Short of that, you may have to improvise a way to get back to your starting point. Whenever it's convenient and sensible from a hiking viewpoint, we have suggested how to make the hike into a circuit or loop, bringing you back, on foot, to your car or pretty close to it. There are many hikes, however, especially those in wilderness areas, where this is simply not feasible.

It's usually best if you can work out a two-car team for your hike, with one car dropped at the finish line and another driven to the starting trailhead.

Out and back: Most of our hikes are described as linear—from A to B to C. Hikers with only one car available can make many fine hikes, however, by simply going out to a well-chosen point (the mountaintop, the pond) and then reversing direction to the starting point. The mileage indicators in the Itineraries will help you decide on a turn-around point. You may be pleasantly surprised to find that when walked in the opposite direction, the same section of trail yields a very different experience—especially if one direction is steeply up and the other sharply down.

Shuttles: In some areas, and through the auspices of some local hiking clubs, shuttle services are available. For example, the Green Mountain Club in Vermont provides to its members a list of shuttle drivers, although they are few in number and require early notice and modest fees. In this book, when we know there is a reliable shuttle service that is useful on a particular hike, we tell you. If we don't make a shuttle suggestion, it's often worth asking your motel or bed-and-breakfast keeper, or calling the local Chamber of Commerce or even the local taxi company. A hunting-lodge manager helped us one time at a good price. Ask around, make new friends.

Some hikers like to position a bicycle (locked) at the end of a hike so they can ride back to their car at the starting point.

If your hiking group consists of, say, four or more people and two cars, you might swap extra car keys at the beginning of the day and send people, a car, and a key for the other car to each end of the trail. You all meet somewhere in the middle of the hike, trade stories, and perhaps share lunch. And each group finds a car waiting at day's end. Depending on roads and distances to trailheads, this system can shave a good deal of time off the car travel at the start and end of your hiking day. This is especially helpful for very long day hikes and even more so in early spring or late fall when days are short. Besides, meeting friends deep in the forest or on a mountaintop is great fun.

Early Exit Options
Our hikes range from 5 to 15 miles per day. When road crossings and parking facilities permit, we indicate points where you could leave the AT before finishing the entire hike. Sometimes such exits are convenient and safe; sometimes they should be used only for emergencies. Heed our advice. If we do not say good parking is available, don't assume there's a parking lot.

The Early Exit Options can often be used to make a loop hike out of an otherwise longish linear hike. To see your options clearly, study a good local road map.

Camping
Camp only in designated camping areas unless you know for sure that free-for-all camping is permitted. In most sections of the AT the land is too heavily used to permit improvisatory camping. We indicate official camp campgrounds. Each state has its own camping rules. Open fires, for example, are illegal along the trail in New Jersey. In Pennsylvania, there are designated camping areas in state parks, as in the other Mid-Atlantic states, but there are also stretches through private game reserves and the Cumberland Valley where camping is prohibited. The rules may vary as you pass through state forest, national forest, or national park. In some areas, especially national parks, camping permits may be required and campsite reservations may be possible. See "Shelter and Campsites" in "Useful Information."

Shelters
The names may vary but the accommodations are much the same: Along the AT, about every 10 to 15 miles, you'll find three-sided lean-tos with minimalist interior decorating. Bunk beds or no beds at all, just floor space. Possibly a picnic table, a fire ring, an outhouse, a water source nearby. Many of these shelters have well-maintained facilities, charming names, and equally charming views. Some you wouldn't let your dog sleep in. We tell you which ones we like. Shelters usually have a few tent sites surrounding them.

Except in the two national parks through which the AT passes (Great Smoky Mts., Shenandoah) and in New Hampshire's White Mt. National Forest, where shelters are reserved for thru-hikers (for a fee), the "reservations policy" is first come, first served. Certain rules apply, however: Maximum stay, 3 nights. If it's raining, squeeze in and make room for late arrivals. Clean up after yourself, and respect others' needs for quiet and privacy.

Trail Registers

At shelters and occasionally at trail junctions, you'll find notebooks where you can, and should, write a few words for posterity and for practicality's sake. Logging in your arrival and departure time will help searchers find you if, unluckily, you get lost or hurt on the trail. But the real fun of the trail registers is adding your own thoughts to the collective wisdom and tomfoolery other hikers have already scribbled in the notebooks. The registers make great reading. A whole new literary genre! Go ahead, wax poetic or philosophical. Surely there's at least one haiku in you to express your joy at the view from the mountaintop or the first time you shook hands with a moose. . . .

Trail registers also sometimes provide helpful warnings about trail conditions (recent mud slides or bridge washouts, for example). If the weather has been wild of late, read back a few days in the register to see what previous hikers may have said about what lies ahead of you.

HIKING: THE BASICS

WHILE IT'S TRUE that we go to the woods and the mountains to get away from the trappings of civilization, few of us really want to put our lives in jeopardy. Here are some recommendations every adult hiker (and Boy or Girl Scout–age youngster) should follow.

When the subject is equipment, we suggest you visit your outdoor outfitter to ask for advice or that you read back issues of *Backpacker* magazine, in print or on-line (see "Useful Information"). *Backpacker*'s annual "gear guide" sorts through hundreds of choices and makes useful recommendations. For the truly hiking/camping gizmo-obsessed, there are on-line chat rooms (again, see *Backpacker*) where you and other similarly gadget-crazed friends can compare notes.

Boots / Shoes

Nothing is more important to a hiker than the condition of his or her feet. From this axiom derives an important rule: Wear the right boots or shoes for hiking, or stay home. Some of the easier sections of the AT can be hiked in firm running shoes or high-top basketball sneakers, but most sections require a tougher, waterproof or water-resistant boot providing nonslip soles, toe protection, and firm ankle support. Shop carefully. Go to an outdoor outfitter rather than a regular shoe store. Try on several pairs of boots, with the actual socks you intend to wear (two pair: one thin, one thick). If you buy boots by mail, trace your foot size with those socks on your feet. Save your pennies and buy the best you can afford. Gore-Tex or one of its waterproofing clones is worth the money. Check the hiking magazines' annual gear reviews (in print or on-line) for ratings of comfort, weight, durability, and price. Think of the purchase as a multiyear investment. Shop long before the hiking season starts, and wear your boots for a good 10 to 20 miles of everyday walking before hitting the trail. Your feet will thank you.

Caveat for kids: The better discount stores carry boot brands that are quite sufficient for a season of hiking by young people whose feet are still growing. Parents, buy your own boots first and then use your shopper's savvy to find inexpensive boots for the kids.

Clothing

Bring sufficient clothes, appropriate for rain and cold. Layers work best. Gore-Tex and other waterproof fabrics are miraculous, but a $3 emergency poncho will do in a pinch. Think about what you would need to get through a rainy night, even if you're just out for a short, sunny day hike.

A visored hat. The top of your head is the point of major heat loss, whether you're bald or not. Inexpensive Gore-Tex hats can be found. Cruise the catalogues.

Sunglasses, in a protective case. Rhinestone decorative motif not required.

Cotton socks, sweatshirts, and T-shirts: avoid them. Blue jeans (essentially cotton): avoid them. Cotton is comfortable until it gets wet (from rain or perspiration). Then it's your enemy. It dries slowly and does not wick away perspiration. There are extraordinary synthetic fabrics nowadays for shirts, underwear, and long johns that will keep you warm or cool and will let the moisture leave your body. Visit your outdoor outfitter for a wardrobe consultation. Money well spent.

Wool is a miracle fabric from nature. Especially good for socks and gloves. Polartec is a miracle fabric from the high-tech world (recycled plastic bottles!). Jackets and pull-overs in these miracle fabrics are what you want.

Food

Hiking eats up calories. Cold weather demands body heat, which demands calories. Diet at home. Eat high-energy foods on the trail. Carbohydrates are best. Sweets are less helpful than you might think, though a chocolate or energy bar to help you up the hill is sometimes right. It's better to eat several smaller meals en route than to gorge on a big one, unless you plan for a siesta. Digestion itself takes considerable energy. You'll find it hard to climb and digest at the same time. The hiker's fallback snack plan: (1) "Gorp," a mix of nuts, granola, chocolate chips, dried fruit, and whatever else you like. Mix it yourself at home —much cheaper than the ready-made variety at the store. (2) Peanut butter on anything.(3) Fruit. Heavy to carry but oh so refreshing. The sugar in fruit is fructose, high in energy but it won't put you to sleep.

And remember the miracle food for hikers, the humble banana. Or dried banana chips (crunch them or add water). High in potassium, bananas are your muscles' best friends because the potassium minimizes aches and cramps.

Planning menus and packing food for extended backpacking trips is a subject beyond the scope of this book. Several camping cookbooks are available, and *Backpacker* frequently runs how-to articles worth reading. Search their Web site for articles you can download. Advice: Whatever you plan to cook on the trail, try it out first, on the backpacking stove, at home. Make a list of cooking gear and condiments needed, and if the list looks long, simplify the menu unless you have willing friends along who will carry a gourmet's kitchen for you. Over time you'll find camp food tricks and tastes to add to your repertoire, such as bagging breakfast granola with powdered milk in self-seal bags (just add water and stir), or choosing tough-skinned veggies like carrots, celery, or snow peas that can be eaten cooked or raw and won't turn to mush in your pack. The ever popular macaroni and cheese (available nowadays in many fancy permutations from Lipton, Kraft, et al.) can be dressed up in countless lightweight, quick-cook ways. The camper's most important kitchen tool is imagination.

Whatever you plan to eat or cook on the trail, be prepared to clean up spotlessly. Leave no mess—indeed, no trace.

Food Storage

You're not the only hungry critter in the woods. Everyone from the bears to the squirrels and mice would like to breakfast on your granola and snack on your Oreos. Never keep food in your tent overnight. It's an invitation for unwanted company in the dark. Use a drawstring food sack, wrapped in a plastic garbage bag, which you hang from a sturdy branch on a nearby tree, keeping the sack several feet out on the branch, about 10 feet off the ground and several feet below the branch. Obviously this means you must carry about 50 feet of lightweight cord (useful in emergencies too)..

Don't store your food in your backpack, either, indoors or out. Those cute little chipmunks and their bigger friends will eat a hole right through that expensive high-tech fabric.

Water

Keep drinking a little at a time all day while you hike. Dehydration is the major cause of hiker fatigue. Double or triple your normal daily intake of water.

Sadly, most of the water flowing in streams the AT crosses is polluted to one degree or another, sometimes by industry or agriculture, often by wild animals such as beavers upstream. The most common problem is a nasty protozoan known as giardia from which we get stomach cramps, fever, and the runs. Trust us: you don't want it. The rule is, unless an official sign says the water has been tested and is pure, assume the water must be treated with either iodine tablets or a water filter. Iodine is cheap and lightweight but slow, and it leaves a somewhat unpleasant taste in the treated water (Potable Aqua is an iodine treatment that minimizes the bad taste). Hiker water filters are faster-acting but more cumbersome. They are useful elsewhere too — on boats, at freshwater beaches, and so forth. A good investment. Look for one that screens out most bacteria, is lightweight, and pumps quickly. The most convenient water bottles are (a) wide-mouth, facilitating refill and filter attachment, and (b) equipped with a drinking tube or nipple, eliminating the need to open the bottle itself.

When Nature Calls

Every hiker — day only or overnight backpacker — must come prepared to deal appropriately with disposal of human waste in the woods. At most shelters and many campsites along the AT there are outhouses. Please help to keep them clean. Gentlemen especially are encouraged to urinate in the woods, a few hundred feet off the trail. Urine in the outhouse pit adds to the bad aroma.

Believe it or not, there's an entire book on the subject of defecating in the woods (see the Bibliography). Good reading on a slow day in camp, perhaps. This much you must know to do: Bring biodegradable white single-ply toilet paper in a plastic bag. Bring a little shovel (a plastic garden trowel will do). Bring a strong self-seal plastic bag to carry out used toilet paper, tampons, etc. If the woods is your toilet, get at least 100 feet off the trail and at least 200 feet away from any water. Dig a hole at least 8 inches deep, and cover your waste firmly. A squat is the time-tested position.

Weather

Basic precautions include a careful review of weather forecasts and typical conditions in the area you're hiking — before you pack your pack or leave home. See "Useful Information" for a weather Web site. If you go adventuring outdoors frequently, you'll enjoy and benefit from a lightweight battery-operated weather radio that provides access to several NOAA (National Oceanic and Atmospheric Administration) channels, offering detailed forecasts 24 hours a day, with special recreational forecasts emphasizing conditions at elevations of 3000 feet and above.

Learn to forecast weather yourself by reading the clouds (particularly cumulous clouds with towering thunderheads) and by noticing changes in animal and plant behavior that may telegraph the advent of a storm. Make it a habit to do a 360-degree sky check every hour or so to see what's coming and from which direction. If trouble is heading your way, plan ahead for emergency shelter. Get off the mountaintop or exposed ridge, where high winds and lightning are most likely to hit. Don't sit under a big rotting tree with branches waiting to clunk you on the head. When lightning is likely, avoid all metal objects (fire towers, tent poles, pack frames, etc.). Do find a dry, wind-protected spot (the downwind side of overhanging boulders is good), and lay a plan to make it your home for a few hours.

Wet weather often brings cool or cold temperatures. Wet clothing or a wet sleeping bag can exacerbate your sense of chill. Hypothermia can set in quickly, especially if you're fatigued or anxious. Even day hikers should carry extra clothing and something, if only a big plastic garbage bag, to cover themselves and their pack. Overnight backpackers, anywhere on the AT, must be ready for the worst. Keep rainwear light and simple so you won't resent carrying it on a sunny day.

See "Unfriendly Weather," page 60.

First Aid

Outfitters such as Campmor and REI (excellent catalogues) offer first-aid kits for everyone from the day hiker to the Mt. Everest climber. Buy from them or patch together your own kit, based on the contents listed in the catalogues. A waterproof container is a must. Be prepared for cuts, scrapes, burns, blisters, sprains, headache. Sunscreen if exposure is likely. A very lightweight first-aid manual is not a bad idea either.

One essential is moleskin, a skin-covering adhesive, thicker than a Band-aid but soft enough to wrap around an unhappy toe. Many a hike has been ruined by blisters. At the first sign (heat, burning, tingling feelings on toes or heels), slap on the moleskin and leave it there until you're back home. Insurance against blisters is cheap: two pairs of (dry!) socks. And break in your new hiking boots *thoroughly* before you hit the trail.

Further insurance: bring a few feet of dental floss. If your teeth don't use it, a sewing job might.

Include a little but loud whistle in your first-aid kit. You might need to call for help.

If first aid is foreign to you, by all means take a course, with CPR (artificial respiration) training, from the local Red Cross. For parents hiking with kids, this is a must. For kids, join the Scouts and earn that First Aid merit badge.

Hiking Alone

There are real pleasures to be had from hiking alone. Generally, however, it's not recommended. Whether you hike alone or in a group, take pains to let someone know your plans (route, estimated times of departure and arrival, what to do if you don't check back in). Often a hiker who wants to walk alone can have that pleasure, letting fellow hikers know that by day's end he or she will rejoin the group.

Hiking in Groups

Keep your group size down to fewer

than ten people. Even that many is stretching what the trailside facilities can bear. Large groups tend to overwhelm smaller ones, yet everyone has the same rights to enjoy the space and the quiet on the trail. Don't take a busload of kids on the trail. Find volunteers who will lead sections of a group with at least a mile or 30 minutes between them.

Women Hikers

Statistically, the Appalachian Trail is one of the safest places a woman (or a man) can be in the United States. But there have been some problems with harrassment, and there have been some cases of violence, even a few tragic murders. Play it safe. Don't hike alone. Be sensible—inappropriate clothing may attract the wrong kind of attention. Avoid the rowdy set sometimes found at shelters near road crossings or towns. If you arrive at a shelter and find suspicious people there, move on.

Taking Children on the Trail

By all means, do take the kids. The environment of the Appalachian Trail and the activities of climbing, exploring, and camping will engage the imagination and channel the energies of almost every kid, including those whose regular turf is the city street. Adult hikers just need to remember that a few things are different about kid hikers. Kids' attention spans are (usually) shorter than grown-ups'. Plan to break your hike into smaller units with something special to do in each part—birds here, lunch there, rock collecting next, photography from the mountaintop, writing messages in the trail registers. Give a kid a short-term achievable project linked to today's hike (such as collecting as many different-shaped leaves as you can from the ground beneath the trees), and you'll probably have a happy, satisfied kid hiker by evening.

Most kids love hiking and camping gear. Get them involved in planning, shopping, packing for, and executing the hike, especially the camping portion. Let them make breakfast. Teach them to set up the tent; then get out of the way. Take pictures and make a family hiking photo album: it's a memory bank for years to come. Put a map on your children's wall at home and mark the trails they have hiked, the peaks they have climbed. A sense of accomplishment is priceless.

Be realistic, too, about what kids can endure on the hiking trail. Their pain (and boredom) thresholds are lower than most adults'. Don't let blisters happen to kids; check their feet at lunchtime. Bring a book to read in case of rain, or a miniature chess set if they're old enough to play. Anticipate your own behavior in an emergency situation. If you panic, the kids will. If you're calm, know where to go for help, and know how to keep dry and warm, most kids will rise to the occasion and come home strengthened by the adventure.

Parking

Do not leave a sign on your car saying where you're going or when you'll return. Try not to leave anything (visible) in your car that might interest burglars. Avoid camping at shelters located very close to easily accessible parking lots. Respect the AT's immediate neighbors by not parking on their private property.

PACKING YOUR PACK

Backpacks and Day Packs

It's not quite a science but it's certainly an art. An incorrectly loaded backpack (badly packed on the inside or poorly fitted or adjusted to your torso and shoulders) can wreck even a sunny day on the world's loveliest trail. Some tips: Fanny packs, worn at hip level, are great for short day hikes as long as you can carry sufficient water, food, clothing, first aid, and map and compass. Less than that and the pack is too small.

Day packs carry proportionately more but without the frame that supports a backpacking pack. For both day packs and true backpacks, similar packing rules apply. Start at the outdoor outfitter. Have a knowledgeable salesperson fit the pack (with realistic dummy weights inside) to your specific torso. Walk around, bend over, squat, and be sure you're comfortable and stable.

At home, make a packing list with items categorized carefully (food, kitchen, first aid, clothes, stove and fuel, etc.). Jettison anything unnecessary. Roll your clothes. Pack one thing inside another. Then use the following scheme for stuffing the pack.

Keep the weight distributed equally on the horizontal plane, but on the vertical, pack lightweight items (sleeping bag) down low and heavy items (food, water, tent) up high. Keep the heavier items close to your body. But be sure to pad any sharp-edged items so as not to poke you or to rip the pack fabric. Use the pack's outside pockets for a water bottle, fuel bottles, and smelly garbage.

Last, buy a rainproof pack cover or make one from a heavy-duty plastic garbage bag. Your clothing and sleeping bag will be glad you did.

Flashlight

Even a day hiker ought to carry a lightweight flashlight, just in case. In winter, early spring, and fall, daylight can disappear quickly, especially if the weather turns bad or you lose time by being temporarily lost. A slim flashlight that's portable in an elastic headband is a good investment.

Check the batteries before leaving home. Bring an extra bulb.

Matches

Even if you do not intend to cook or camp out and have a campfire, bring a supply of waterproof matches or a cigarette lighter. If you're forced to overnight in the woods, a fire may be good company indeed.

Jackknife

A multipurpose pocketknife will do. It needn't have a built-in chain saw or an eyebrow pencil, but a can opener, a Phillips screwdriver, and a tweezers are handy.

Weapons

We strongly discourage hikers from carrying any kind of weapon.

Cellular Phones

People have been hiking safely and contentedly in the woods for several thousand years without the aid or comfort of cellular phones. This is still possible. Many people come to the trail to get away from the electronic web in which we all are increasingly caught up. Here's a way to win friends on the trail: Keep your cell phone, if you bring one, out of sight, beyond earshot, and out of mind for everyone else. Don't use it except for emergencies, and do use it only when you're far away from other hikers. Domino's Pizza does not deliver to most AT shelters anyway. So why even call them?

FINDING YOUR WAY

Map and Compass

Don't go hiking without a map and compass and the skills to use them. In the fog, in the dark, in a storm, even familiar territory can seem like a directionless wilderness. Many hiking clubs offer map and compass (a.k.a. "orienteering") workshops. Map skills are fun to develop and highly useful. Many of the best natural history observations described in this book depend on your ability to locate a spot on the map and to orient yourself once you're there.

At the very least, be sure everyone in your party knows the compass direction of your intended hike, the cars' locations on the map, and the most likely way toward help in an emergency. *Backpacker* has run articles on map and compass skills (check the index on their Web site). The venerable *Boy Scout Handbook* has a good chapter on these skills. Or see Karen Berger's *Hiking & Backpacking: A Complete Guide.*

Being Lost and Getting Found

If you have studied your map before starting the hike, and if you faithfully follow the AT's white blazes or the access trails' blue (or red or yellow) blazes, the chances of getting lost are just about zero. With a map and compass in hand, there's no good excuse for being lost while you're on the AT itself. Your group should have a leader and a backup leader, and both should know the route. Because hikers sometimes get separated on the trail, everyone should know the direction of the hike, the major landmarks to be passed, the estimated timetable, and how to use the sun and the clock to keep themselves oriented.

But mistakes do happen. Inattention and inadequate planning are the enemies. Sometimes nature conspires against us. Fog (or snow) may obscure the blazes or the cairns above treeline. Autumn leaves or a snowfall may obliterate the well-worn trail that otherwise would guide your eyes as clearly as the blazes themselves.

If you are lost, the first thing to do is to decide that you will not panic. You probably have not been off the trail for long. Stay where you are and think. Keep your group together. Study the map and note the last landmark you're sure you passed. Get reoriented with the map and compass, and try to go in a straight line back toward the trail. Do not

wander. Be especially observant of details until you regain the trail.

If all else fails, let gravity and falling water help you out. Except in the deepest wilderness of Maine or the Smoky Mts., at most places along the AT streams flow eventually to brooks, then to rivers, and where there's a river there will soon enough be a house or even a village. If you have to bushwhack to get out of the woods, and if you're really not sure where you are on the map, follow the water downstream. Patience and a plan will get you out.

Common Sense / Sense of Humor

Taking care of yourself successfully in the woods and on the mountains is not rocket science. It starts with preparedness (physical and mental), appropriate equipment, sufficient food and water. It continues with a realistic plan, guided by a map and compass, a guidebook, a weather report, and a watch. It gets better if you and your companions resolve ahead of time to work together as a team, respecting each other's varying needs, strengths, and talents. And it goes best of all if you pack that one priceless essential hiker's tool: a ready sense of humor.

AT LEGEND HAS IT that the 2150-mile footpath from Georgia to Maine is an ancient Native American walkway. Not so. In fact, the AT, as a concept, leapt from the imagination of one federal government civil servant who in 1921 had already recognized that Americans were too citified for their own good and needed more nearby, convenient opportunities for outdoor recreation.

In 1921, Harvard-educated forester and self-styled philosopher Benton MacKaye, of Shirley, Massachusetts, published an article ("An Appalachian Trail, A Project in Regional Planning") in the *Journal of the American Institute of Architects*. His was a revolutionary idea: a linear park, extending from Georgia to Maine. The concept germinated in a hotbed of idealistic left-wing social thinking that called into question many of the assumed values of the capitalist workaday world. Look a little more deeply into MacKaye's thinking and the roots lead directly to the 19th-century romantics and Transcendentalists Thoreau and Emerson. MacKaye had read his John Muir, too.

A whirlwind of self-promoting public relations energy, MacKaye set the ball rolling to develop the AT. Thousands of volunteers and many legislators helped make it a reality. Two other key players were Judge Arthur Perkins of Hartford, Connecticut, who helped found the Appalachian Trail Conference in 1925, and his successor as president of the Conference (1931–1952), Myron Avery, of Maine and Washington, D.C. By 1937, with major assistance from Civilian Conservation Corps workers under President Roosevelt's New Deal Works Progress Administration, the complete trail was essentially in place, though by today's standards much of it was rugged and unblazed.

Thru-hikers are an admirable but increasingly common breed these days. Yet it wasn't until 1948 that anyone walked the entire trail in one season. The first thru-hiker was Earl Shaffer. The first woman to thru-hike in one season was Emma "Grandma" Gatewood, in 1955. By the mid-1990s the National Park Service was estimating that between 3 and 4 million people per year used the trail. In its first 75 years, from MacKaye's brainstorm to today, the AT has gone from a concept about escaping urban crowding to the point where crowding on the trail itself is a big issue.

In 1968, Congress put the AT under the authority of the National Park Service by passing the National Trails System Act. Overall, the story of the AT is a sweet tale of success. Occasionally there has been a sour note when the government's right of eminent domain has been used to take land required to create a 1000-foot-wide corridor of protection for the trail. By 1995 fewer than 44 miles of the trail remained unprotected by the Park Service corridor. In the 1990s, environmental impact concerns (wear and tear, sustainability) and hiker management issues (overuse, low-impact camping and hiking, safety) fill the pages of AT magazines and spark many a late-night campfire conversation. While the educational and environmental protection efforts of the Appalachian Trail Conference, the Appalachian Mountain Club, and all the regional hiking clubs improve yearly, adding strength to an admirable history, the erosion of financial support from Congress in a budget balancing era threatens to undermine many good efforts at a moment when user demands are growing exponentially. It is a time of fulfillment and challenge for all who use and manage the Appalachian Trail.

Note: A more detailed history of the AT can be found in any of the Appalachian Trail Conference's hiking guides. Colorful lore about the earliest days of trailblazing in New England appears in *Forest and Crag: A History of Hiking, Trail Blazing and Adventure in the Northeast Mountains,* by Guy and Laura Waterman. Glenn Scherer's *Vistas and Vision: A History of the New York-New Jersey Trail Conference,* celebrates a 75-year trail-blazing effort in the New York metropolitan area. *An Appalachian Trail Adventure,* a chronicle of the 1995 five-newspaper AT thruhike (in which Don Hopey participated as a writer and photograph-er), presents a vivid image of the AT and trail life. And *The Appalachian Trail Reader,* edited by David Emblidge, contains a diverse collection of writings about the AT.

Appalachian Trail History in Maryland, Pennsylvania, New Jersey, and New York

Benton MacKaye's Appalachian Trail was nothing more than a great dream in 1921. It was the New York-New Jersey Trail Conference, founded in 1920, that boldly put the first miles on the ground. In October 1923, MacKaye joined with other trail enthusiasts to celebrate the opening of the first 6-mile section of the AT at Bear Mt.–Harriman State Parks, New York (see Hike #35). Instrumental in this achievement was NY-NJTC organizer and conservationist and New York newspaper-man Raymond Torrey. Torrey was the first to publish nationally distributed accounts of the new trail and to popularize the AT concept with volunteers. He also almost single-handedly pressed forward with a woodland route stretching from the Delaware River to the Hudson River, complete by 1928. The route north from the Hudson to the Housatonic River in Connecticut (opened in 1930) was blazed by Murray H. Stevens of the New York AMC and a future NY-NJTC chair.

Little work was done on the AT in Pennsylvania and Maryland until retired Connecticut judge Arthur Perkins took over as ATC chair in

1926. He galvanized Pennsylvania volunteers and led many far-flung scouting trips. But it was maritime lawyer Myron Avery who proved instrumental in completing the AT in Pennsylvania and Maryland. Avery organized the Potomac Appalachian Trail Club in 1927 and became ATC chair in 1931. Maryland's trail section was in place by 1932, with Pennsylvania's following in 1933.

The history of the AT since that time parallels that of the American conservation movement. Hundreds of battles have been fought to save these wild lands from development. Sterling Forest, New York (Hike #34), and Tocks Island, New Jersey and Pennsylvania (Hike #27), for example, both located along the AT, represent milestones in the effort to preserve our natural resources. Today, dozens of smaller hiking clubs maintain the AT, working under the umbrella of the NY-NJTC in New York and New Jersey, KTA in Pennsylvania (founded in 1956), and PATC in Pennsylvania and Maryland.

Crampton Gap to Harpers Ferry, WV

Map: PATC Md. # 6

Route: From Crampton Gap to Weverton Cliffs and along the C&O Canal to Goodloe Byron Memorial Footbridge

Recommended direction: N to S

Distance: 10.2 mi. total; 9.8 mi.on AT

Access trail name & length: C&O Canal Towpath, 0.4 mi.

Elevation +/-: 900 to 1100 to 300 ft.

Effort: Moderate

Day hike: Yes

Overnight backpacking hike: No

Duration: 6 hr.

Early exit options: At 1.8 mi., Brownsville Gap Rd.; at 6.7 mi., Weverton Rd.

Natural history features: South Mt.; Weverton Cliffs; Potomac River

Social history features: George Alfred Townsend's Gathland Estate; Crampton Gap Civil War battlefield; Glenn R. Caveney plaque; C&O Canal; Goodloe Byron plaque and footbridge; Harpers Ferry

Trailhead access: *Start:* Take US 340 to MD 67N exit. Go 5.4 mi. and make R on Gapland Rd. Follow for 1.0 mi. to overnight parking area next to Civil War Correspondents' Memorial. *End:* Take US 340 to Keep Tryst Rd. exit. Turn R from Keep Tryst Rd. onto Sandy Hook Rd. (also called Harpers Ferry Rd.). Parking is 0.4 mi. beyond Goodloe Byron Memorial Footbridge.

Camping: Weverton Primitive Camp (no water)

The 9.8-mi. stretch of Appalachian Trail leading from Crampton Gap to Harpers Ferry, West Virginia, is one of the most popular and rewarding AT day hikes in this region, with good reason. It features a secluded forest ridgetop, an exhilarating vista pitching straight down into the Potomac River, and the historic Chesapeake & Ohio (C&O) Canal Towpath. Crossing the Potomac from Maryland into West Virginia, the hiker passes from the Northern states into the Southern, from the Union into the Confederacy, from one culture and climate into another. Hike the trail from north to south and the walking is fairly easy with minimal climbing.

The northern trailhead, in Crampton Gap, is dominated by one of the quirkier structures found along the entire AT: the War Correspondents' Memorial, the product of the whimsical tastes of George Alfred Townsend, a newspaper reporter turned amateur architect who built his estate here. The grand monument, with its gaping arch and tower, stands like a gate gone in search of a castle. Its rather pedestrian inspiration was a blend of two local architectural models: the Hagerstown fire-house and train station. Townsend erected the monument in 1896 in memory of his fellow Civil War journalists, artists, and photographers, and inscribed it with their names.

Heading south, the AT runs in front of the memorial and slightly uphill on a paved driveway. The rest of Townsend's estate, called Gathland, surrounds you. Townsend became famous for his Civil War battlefield dispatches (written under the Biblical pen name "Gath") and for his reporting of Lincoln's assassination. After the war, he grew wealthy as the nation's first nationally known journalist. An 1884 buggy ride through Crampton Gap, the site of heavy Civil War fighting (see "Lee Invades the North" in Hike #2), convinced Townsend to build his home here. Townsend's lodge, Gathland Hall, the ruins of a stone barn, and the tumbledown stone foundation of his library remain today. They offer reminders of the elegant lawn parties, watermelons sweetened with wine, and Victorian entertainments with which Townsend once impressed his summertime guests.

The trail passes a rest room and a soda and juice vending machine. Water is available from a hand pump in season. The AT ascends the paved driveway, passing to the left of a stone wall encircling Townsend's empty mausoleum. The famed reporter came on hard times in later years. He died in 1914 in New York City, and the tomb was never used.

The cast-iron Great Dane that guarded the mausoleum was eventually stolen and the crypt was vandalized. The estate fell into ruin until becoming Gathland State Park in 1958.

The gentle 250-ft. ascent made by the AT over the next 0.7 mi. offers the steepest climbing you'll have to do all day. The trail follows a wide woods road through a thick deciduous forest, and in summer is a lush, leafy, green tunnel, rarely hinting at the 1200-ft. height of South Mt., the ridge crest along which you stroll. Oaks stretch toward the sky, while a variety of ferns grow on the forest floor.

A red granite plaque at 1.4 mi. memorializes Glenn R. Caveney. Set flush to the ground, it can be hidden by snow or leaves, though the AT trail maintainer regularly sweeps it clean. Glenn Caveney and his father once maintained this trail section. When the son died in a car accident, the father established a fund to purchase an acre of land surrounding the plaque. Similar thoughtful memorials have added property to the protected AT corridor from Maine to Georgia.

The AT crosses dirt Brownsville Gap Rd. (1.8 mi.), over which both federal and rebel troops passed during the Civil War. Today, this road, which is impassable by car, can be used to reach MD 67 on the west side of South Mt. There is a steep 1.0-mi. climb down to a picnic area with day parking.

In another 0.1 mi., a clearing for a

buried communications cable provides a narrow view of Pleasant Valley and Elk Ridge to the west. In the 1800s, both Elk Ridge and South Mt. were clear cut, affording sweeping vistas. During the Civil War, Pleasant Valley was converted into an armed Union camp. A firsthand account from Paula Strain's excellent Maryland AT history, *The Blue Hills of Maryland,* describes the view as seen from nearby Maryland Heights:

> At your feet lies Pleasant Valley, a great furrow—two miles across, from edge to edge—plowed through the mountains. It is full of camps, white villages of tents, and black groups of guns.

You see cozy dwellings, with great, well-filled barns, red brick mills, straw-colored fields dotted with shocks of corn and reaching far up into the dark, hill-side woods, green sward fields, mottled with orchards, and a little shining stream (p. 53).

Aside from the absence of feuding armies, the view of the farm valley is little changed today. South Mt. itself is a state park, and has again grown up thick with forest. Bring along a tree identification guide (*The Audubon Society Field Guide to Northern Forests* is recommended), and you'll have a great deal of fun hiking through the green tunnel. Try to differentiate between the deeply fur-

Michael Warren

Harpers Ferry view from Maryland Heights

rowed bark of chestnut oak, the slim vertical gray plates of red oak, and the gray elephant skin of beech trees. Scientists are stumped as to the reasons for the wide range in tree bark colors and textures found in nature. Observe the leaves too. Their shapes, sizes, notchings, lobings, and even the angles at which they hang all contribute to a tree's success in carrying out photosynthesis.

Sadly, the bark of beech trees atop South Mt. has been targeted by graffiti "artists" trying to immortalize themselves and their girlfriends. One huge beech, located at 3.8 mi., has the dates 1892 and 1899 hacked into its trunk. This tree can feel smug, however. It has almost certainly outlived its defacers!

The trail continues following a narrow, level shelf on the western side of the ridge, passing 100 yd. to the right of a wild jumble of boulders. At about 5 mi. into the walk, the ridgetop grows even narrower, as the AT straddles its thinning crest. High winds along this exposed stretch of trail have brought down many large trees, but, thankfully, the volunteers of the Potomac Appalachian Trail Club have cut the way clear.

While walking this crest line one snowy February morning, we scared out four wild turkeys. The large birds rose from their roosts, their wings wide. They spread their triangular tails, offering an iridescent flash of blue feathers, before vanishing in a fog of falling snow. Vast flocks of wild turkeys, a streamlined version of the barnyard variety, once ranged over the East, but were hunted nearly to extinction. They recently have been reintroduced to much of their range, and are a common sight in the Appalachians again. Look for their distinctive three-pronged, pitchfork-shaped tracks.

The trail now begins to descend steadily, as South Mt. drops away toward the Potomac River. At 5.8 mi. the AT turns right, as a blue-blazed side trail leads straight ahead over loose rocks. for 0.1 mi. down to the Weverton Cliffs. This side trip is not to be missed.

The jagged Weverton Cliffs at the southernmost end of South Mt. jut boldly into the sky like the prow of a ship. There is a precipitous drop to the tallest treetops below, then another, larger drop straight down to the Potomac River. The gray-green waters of the river are studded with shrub-covered islands and boulders. The gap at Harpers Ferry is visible to the far right (west): Looking at the surrounding rugged heights, and listening to the steady hum of highway and railroad traffic below, it is easy to see why this mountain pass is so important to east-west travel, and why it was fought over so fiercely during the Civil War.

Set in stone on the cliff is a plaque to Goodloe Byron, a Maryland and U.S. congressman who worked diligently through the 1970s to protect the AT. While the National Trails System Act of 1968 designated the

Thru-Hiking Lab Report

Hiking in the spring is glorious, but there is a substantial risk that you will catch whatever seasonal virus it is that drives people to think they should hike all the way from Georgia to Maine. This insidious disease has a long incubation—so long that you may think you have escaped. However, here are some symptoms that may precede the onset:

- The victims (you or a loved one) start collecting maps and guidebooks.
- They ask everyone they meet about tents, Gore-Tex, and water filters.
- They start introducing themselves by a funny new name.
- They insist on knowing the weight, to the nearest gram, of everything they buy.
- They don't like their 100% cotton underwear and socks anymore.
- They develop an obsessive interest in weather, day length, elevation gains and losses, and how far they can hike in a day.

The most severe form of this syndrome was first described in 1948, but it was rare until the 1960s. Supreme Court Justice William O. Douglas succumbed in 1958. By 1982 there were 1000 cases on record; that number doubled in only 7 years. In the 1990s it became a major epidemic, with thousands coming down with it each year. The virus respects neither age, sex, physical handicap, nor nationality. An 86-year-old got it in 1975, and a 6-year-old got it just 5 years later. Some people get it several times, and many victims write books about their struggle. Several dogs and at least one cat have also fallen prey to it.

More men than women suffer from the disease, but, as with many other conditions, the women are catching up. The causative agent has not been identified; there is some evidence of a tiny parasite that burrows through brain tissue, causing major behavioral changes but minor permanent damage. No remedy has been found; victims harbor the ailment for the rest of their lives and seem to be highly infectious. However, many victims can lead lives that are surprisingly close to normal if they can acknowledge their affliction and get the hiking done, either all at once or in sections. Many self-help books are available, and support groups exist in some communities.

—Doris Gove

AT as America's first National Scenic Trail, the law did little to protect the path. It was Byron who led a congressional fight to fund the AT's full preservation. His 1978 amendment to the Trails Act authorized an appropriation of $90 million to purchase the entire 2100-mi. AT corridor. Sadly, the young congressman died within a year of his victory.

Return to the AT and follow it as it zigzags steeply down over sixteen beautifully engineered switchbacks to the Potomac Valley. To prevent erosion, avoid shortcutting the path.

The trail reaches the base of South Mt., levels out, and exits the woods (6.7 mi.). It immediately crosses Weverton Rd., skirts to the left of the AT parking area (an early exit is possible here), and reenters the woods. The path follows a narrow treadway here, hugging large boulders, as it passes above a steep drop to Israel Creek. It then passes under US 340.

Reaching Keep Tryst Rd. (7.1 mi.), the trail continues straight ahead through a National Park Service gate, crosses the CSX rail line, and arrives at the C&O Canal. To the left are the well-restored Lift Lock No. 31 and a lock tender's house. The AT turns right, following the flat C&O Towpath all the way to Harpers Ferry.

George Washington fathered not only our country, but also the C&O Canal. In the late 1700s, transporting freight by road was thirty times more expensive than moving it by water. Washington saw the wild reaches of the Potomac River as a cheap, flat-water, alternative route west over the Appalachians to the Ohio River Valley. Unfortunately, he died before the private Patowmack Company he founded could begin digging the canal and he could begin making a profit. President John Quincy Adams turned the first shovelful of dirt for the new canal in 1828, a project that eventually would cost private investors $14 million (the equivalent in 19th-century dollars of sending a man to the moon). The C&O, which had to overcome extremely difficult construction challenges, was completed to its terminus in 1850 and ceased operation in 1924. Today the C&O is a national historic park, with its level towpath popular among both hikers and bikers.

The 185-mi. canal begins at tidewater in Maryland's lush, rolling Piedmont, and penetrates to the heart of the Appalachians at Cumberland. The AT section running along the C&O Towpath is a study in contrasts: on one side, the wild, changing moods of the Potomac River; on the other, the luminescent algae of the canal's quiet pools. Above, water-loving sycamores glow like a rain forest canopy. The floodplain hosts pileated woodpeckers, belted kingfishers, and barred owls. Spring arrives earlier here than on the ridgetops. One Easter Sunday we were caught in a snow squall on South Mt., but found newly blossomed Virginia bluebells nodding along the sun-dappled canal.

Within a short distance, Israel Creek passes through a culvert beneath the AT and the C&O Canal. Surrounding this area in the 1800s was the town of Weverton, the money-making dream of Casper W. Wever. He established an industrial center here, hoping that Potomac water-power could be harnessed to rival the industrial clout of New England mill towns. Bad luck and poor business decisions plagued the project. Wever had repeated run-ins with the canal company and overcharged his factory tenants. When Wever died in 1847, others carried on his plans with even less luck. A scheme to put a federally funded national iron foundry here failed, as did a utopian experiment in communal living. In 1916 the last remnant of Wever's dreams went up in smoke. The Savage Distillery burned down, destroying 650 barrels of whiskey and setting Israel Creek afire all the way to the Potomac. *The Appalachian Trail Guide to Maryland and Northern Virginia,* edited by Jean C. Golightly, offers a detailed history of Wever's misadventures and other historical information.

At 7.5 mi. a blue-blazed trail leads 100 yd. left to the Weverton Primitive Camp (no water; do not drink from the Potomac—it is polluted). There are many hiker/biker campsites like this one located at roughly 5-mi. intervals along the C&O, but Potomac River floods frequently shut them down. Call 301-739-4200 to learn campground status.

In another 0.2 mi., the AT passes under Sandy Hook Bridge (US 340). This junction marks a real meeting of the ways. The blue-blazed Loudoun Heights Trail (formerly the AT) leads right, then turns south, crossing the highway bridge over the Potomac and rejoining the AT in 3.2 mi. The AT itself parallels the American Discovery Trail (ADT) along the canal here. This walking path, sponsored by the American Hiking Society, is the nation's newest long-distance trail. It stretches from the Atlantic to the Pacific oceans. The ADT, which includes a giant loop in its midwestern heartland section, is 6357 mi. long.

As the AT closes in on Harpers Ferry, the distance between the Potomac River and the C&O narrows. The towpath tops a high stone flood-wall and looks out over the gray, brooding river as it passes through a rapids and rushes around the bows of ship-shaped stone islands.

At 9.8 mi. this hike officially ends, though you may want to continue following the AT south just a little further by climbing the metal spiral staircase leading up onto the Goodloe Byron Memorial Footbridge. The view from here is spectacular. Trains rush by, heading into and out of Harpers Ferry. Loudon Heights rises up to the south and Maryland Heights to the north. Both were heavily fortified during Civil War struggles to seize control of strategically important Harpers Ferry. Three states merge where the dark green waters of the Shenandoah meet the gray-green waters of the Potomac. You have just left Maryland; Virginia lies to the left across the Shenandoah, and West Virginia begins in Harpers Ferry at the far end of the bridge.

This river gap gouged by the Shenandoah and Potomac, dividing North from South, was acclaimed by Thomas Jefferson in 1782. He wrote elegantly of the meeting place of these two rivers in his *Notes on Virginia*:

In the moment of their junction, they rush together against the mountain, render it asunder and pass off to the sea. The first glance of this scene hurries our senses into the opinion that this earth has been created in time, that the mountains were formed first, that the rivers began to flow afterwards, that in this place particularly . . . they have at last broken over at this spot and have torn the mountain down from its summit to its base. . . . This scene is worth a voyage across the Atlantic.

The stone pillars of two ruined bridges stand in the water, testimony to the terrible floods that regularly push through the gap. Back-to-back floods in 1996 devastated Harpers Ferry, the C&O Canal, and the AT. After the first flood, trail volunteers using hand tools joined with National Park Service employees using heavy machinery to

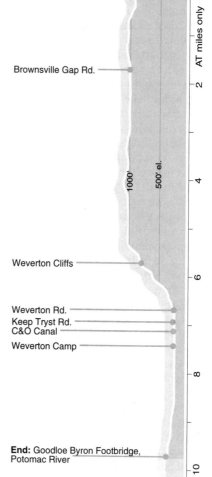

Start: Gapland Rd.

Brownsville Gap Rd.

AT miles only

1000' el.
500' el.

Weverton Cliffs

Weverton Rd.
Keep Tryst Rd.
C&O Canal
Weverton Camp

End: Goodloe Byron Footbridge, Potomac River

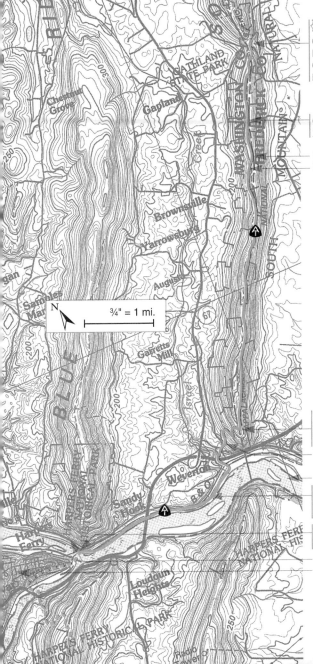

🚶🚶 Crampton Gap,
Gapland Rd. Ⓟ 🚻 🍴
El. 900', Civil War
Correspondents'
Memorial 🏛

Glenn R. Caveney plaque
🏛

Brownsville Gap Rd.
V, cable (buried),El.1000'

Weverton Cliffs, El. 800',
V 🍁 Goodloe Byron
plaque 🏛
Weverton Rd. Ⓟ El. 400'

Potomac River 🍁
Weverton Primitive Camp
⛺ El. 300', C&O Canal
🏛

🚶🚶 Goodloe Byron
Footbridge, El. 300', V
C&O Canal Ⓟ
Harpers Ferry, WV 🏛

¾" = 1 mi.

rebuild the locks and stone walls, which had been thrown about like toy blocks by the deluge. Surprisingly, when the second flood came just months later, much of the stone laid in place by heavy equipment was again thrown aside, while the volunteers' stonework, placed carefully by hand, held.

An entire day can be spent touring the streets of historic Harpers Ferry, West Virginia. The little brick firehouse where abolitionist John Brown made his final stand against federal soldiers in 1859 is only a few hundred yards beyond the end of the Goodloe Byron Memorial Footbridge. The town boasts many museums, a bookstore, and the headquarters of the Appalachian Trail Conference (see Volume 2, *Exploring the Appalachian Trail: Hikes in the Virginias*).

No day or overnight parking is allowed in the lower section of Harpers Ferry, near the rivers. Cars left on National Park Service property here or in the Harpers Ferry train station parking lot will be ticketed and towed. To reach your car, return over the bridge to Maryland, turn left, and walk 0.4 mi. further along the C&O Canal to the parking area.

Miles N	**NORTH**	Elev. (ft./m)	Miles S
	Total: 10.2 mi. with access on C&O Canal Towpath		
9.8	**Start:** Crampton Gap, Gapland Rd. (MD 572), 1.0 mi. W of Burkittsville; overnight parking next to Civil War Correspondents' Memorial Arch and G. Townsend's Gathland estate, rest room, water pump, drinks vending machine; AT follows paved driveway S.	900/274	0.0
8.4	**Glenn R. Caveney Wilderness Memorial.**	1100/335	1.4
8.0	**Brownsville Gap Rd.,** impassable by car, leads R (W) to MD 67; early exit option.	1000/305	1.8
7.9	Buried communication cable and **view.**		1.9
6.0	**Beech tree** scarred by 1892, 1899 graffiti.	1050/320	3.8
4.0	**Weverton Cliffs vista** side trail leads straight ahead 0.1 mi. to view, **Goodloe Byron plaque.**	800/244	5.8
3.9	Steep descent over 16 **switchbacks** built by volunteers.	900/274	5.9
3.1	**Weverton Rd.** (early exit option); AT goes straight ahead, cutting into woods just before overnight parking area.	400/122	6.7
2.9	**US 340 underpass.**	350/106	6.9
2.7	**Keep Tryst Rd.;** AT goes straight ahead through gate, across CSX rail line.		7.1
2.6	**C&O Canal,** Lift Lock No. 31 and lock tender's house to L (E); AT turns R (W) along towpath.		7.2
2.3	**Weverton Primitive Camp.**		7.5
2.1	**Sandy Hook Bridge,** AT passes under bridge; **Loudon Heights Trail** turns R, crosses Potomac on Sandy Hook (US 340) Bridge and rejoins AT 3.2 mi. S in VA.		7.7
1.4	**C&O Canal lock.**		8.4
0.0	**End AT miles:** Goodloe Byron Memorial Footbridge; AT crosses Potomac River into Harpers Ferry, WV.	300/91	9.8
0.4	Access: Walk straight ahead for 0.4 mi. along C&O Canal to day parking.		0.4

SOUTH

HIKE #2
Crampton Gap, Fox Gap, and Turners Gap

Maps: PATC Md. # 6 & 5

Route: From Crampton Gap through Fox Gap and Turners Gap to US 40

Recommended direction: S to N

Distance: 12.3 mi. total; 12.2 mi. on AT

Elevation +/-: 900 to 1772 to 1250 ft.

Effort: Easy

Day hike: Yes

Overnight backpacking hike: Optional

Duration: 8 hr.

Early exit options: At 6.2 mi., Reno Monument Rd.; at 7.2 mi., US Alt. 40; at 9.0 mi., Washington Monument SP

Natural history feature: White Rocks vista on Lambs Knoll

Social history features: South Mt. battlefield sites at Crampton Gap, Fox Gap, and Turner Gap; South Mt. Inn; Dahlgren Chapel; Washington Monument

Trailhead access: *Start:* Take US 340 to MD 67N exit. Go 5.4 mi. and make R on Gapland Rd. Follow for 1.0 mi. to overnight parking area next to War Correspondents Memorial. *End:* Take US 340 to MD 67N to T. Make L on US Alt. 40 and go through Boonsboro, then go R on Mapleville Rd. (MD 66). Turn R on US 40 and go 3.9 mi. to overnight parking area just past I-70.

Camping: Crampton Gap Shelter; Bear Spring Cabin; Rocky Run Shelter; Dahlgren Back Pack Campground

O n a warm, sunny Sunday in 1862 a force of 9000 Rebels used the ramparts of South Mt. as a natural fort from which to stage a delaying action against 30,000 Yankee soldiers. Although they lost the mountain, they won the day, saving Gen. Robert E. Lee's Army of Northern Virginia from almost certain destruction. This AT hike passes through the three mountain gaps over which this bloody battle raged.

The walk crosses easy terrain, and so can be taken as a long day hike (12.2 mi. from Crampton Gap to US 40). However, all of the historical sites are found within the first 9.2 mi.,

allowing for a shorter walk (Crampton Gap to Washington Monument State Park). This AT section also provides an ideal beginner's backpacking trip (7.0 mi. on the first day and 5.2 on the second), with dinner and dessert at the South Mt. Inn serving as a delicious diversion.

Whichever alternative you choose, begin at the parking area just north of the Civil War Correspondents Memorial in Crampton Gap, a Gothic stone arch built in 1896 by George Alfred Townsend, America's first nationally known journalist (see Hike #1). It also marked the southern end of the Rebel line in the Battle of

South Mt. (see "Lee Invades the North"). Before beginning your hike north, take some time to explore, reading the historical markers and enjoying the views into the valleys on either side of the high ridge.

The AT goes through Crampton Gap, passing to the right of the thick stone walls of Townsend's ruined barn, and climbs easily for 700 vertical ft. over the next 3.7 mi. This is a pleasant ridgetop walk along a well-defined path. There are views through the trees east toward Frederick and west into Pleasant Valley.

A blue-blazed trail (0.4 mi.) leads right (0.3 mi.) and steeply downhill to Crampton Gap Shelter. This lean-to has a good eastward view and a privy, but an unreliable spring.

At 3.0 mi. another blue-blazed trail descends steeply for 0.5 mi. to Bear Spring Cabin. This fully furnished hut, operated by the Potomac Appalachian Trail Club, is locked, but available by reservation (703-242-0315).

All along this part of the ridge grows a sun-loving plant called garlic mustard. Its 2-in.-wide, deeply veined, scalloped leaves spread over the forest floor in large colonies. Garlic mustard leaves are edible raw or cooked, but are spicy, so best sampled when picked young and when mixed with other edible greens. The plant is an exotic species, introduced from abroad, and unfortunately forces out many native understory plants. It has become a tasty but irksome Appalachian pest.

White Rocks (3.5 mi.) is a quartzite

Civil War Correspondents Memorial, Crampton Gap, Gathland State Park

cliff and a great spot for lunch or a water break. It faces south along the ridge you just walked. In another 0.2 mi. the trail crests Lambs Knoll with its forest of communications towers. Rumor has it that these innocent towers are more than they seem. Some say that they are part of the National Security Agency (NSA) Critical Intelligence Communications Network, which would flash news of a nuclear attack to the president. Obviously, the closed-lipped NSA (some claim the initials really stand for "No Such Agency") isn't talking.

The AT descends steeply for 800 vertical ft. over the next 2.5 mi. into Fox Gap. It crosses a paved mainte-

Lee Invades the North

The battle of South Mt. was part of a larger autumn 1862 campaign in which Gen. Robert E. Lee boldly divided his Rebel army and invaded the North. While half of Lee's army, under Gen. Stonewall Jackson, surrounded a Union army at Harpers Ferry, the main body, under Gen. Lee and Gen. James Longstreet, penetrated deep into Maryland.

Lee's soldiers captured the city of Frederick, then turned west, crossing South Mt. and descending into Pleasant Valley. Lee left a small rear guard of nine thousand men on South Mt. to protect his divided force. It was these soldiers who met the full brunt of an attack by Union Gen. George McClellan's Army of the Potomac as it arrived from Washington, D.C., on September 14, 1862.

Remarkably, McClellan had learned of Lee's invasion in advance. A Yankee trooper had noticed an envelope in the grass near Frederick. It contained several cigars bundled with a piece of paper on which was outlined the entire Rebel battle plan. The jubilant McClellan waved the secret plans before the eyes of one of his officers and shouted, "Here is a paper with which, if I cannot whip Bobby Lee, I will be willing to go home. If I don't crush Lee now, you may call me whatever you please" (Flato, p. 81). But McClellan, famous for his molasses-slow reaction time, failed to move quickly enough to ambush Lee's far-flung army.

In *The Blue Hills of Maryland,* Paula Strain provides a detailed account of the ensuing Battle of South Mt. Union forces tried to seize Crampton, Fox, and Turners gaps in a three-pronged assault. One Rebel soldier mocked their efforts: "To observe the caution with which the Yankees, with their superior numbers, approached the

---

nance road (4.8 mi.) and meets the blue-blazed Rocky Run Shelter side trail (0.2 mi. long) at 5.3 mi. This fine lean-to was built by the Civilian Conservation Corps (see "With the Boys of the CCC," in Hike #29) in 1940, has a seasonal spring and a privy, and is located within the Maryland Ornithological Society Wildlife Sanctuary.

Back on the AT, there are beautiful views west (5.8 mi.) into Pleasant Valley from a power line clearing. At 6.2 mi. the trail crosses paved Reno Monument Rd. in Fox Gap. An emergency exit may be possible here; there is no parking.

It is worth taking a steep 0.2-mi. detour uphill along the road to view the site of some of the fiercest Civil War fighting on South Mt. Where the road crests, two monuments commemorate the battlefield deaths of Union Maj. Gen. Jesse Reno and Confederate Brig. Gen. Samuel Garland. The battle over this gap raged "in so many directions no one knew which was front," remembered one Confederate soldier (Strain, p. 124).

mountain put one very much in mind of a lion, king of the forest, making exceedingly careful preparation to spring on a plucky little mouse" (p. 94).

The plucky little Rebel mouse bloodied the nose of the federal lion. It took all day for Union troops to capture the gaps. At nightfall, the exhausted Yankee troops rested, failing to follow the retreating Rebs. They also failed to come to the rescue of their eleven thousand Union comrades in Harpers Ferry who surrendered to Confederate Gen. Stonewall Jackson the next day.

The Battle of South Mt. was fought at great cost. One Union soldier recalled the carnage:

"All around lay the Confederate dead . . . as I looked down on the poor, pinched faces, worn with marching and scant fare, my enmity died out. There was no 'secession' in those rigid forms, nor in those fixed eyes staring blankly at the sky. . . . Darkness came rapidly, and it grew very chilly. . . . Drawing our blankets over us, we went to sleep, lying upon our arms in line as we had stood, living Yankee and dead Confederate side by side, and indistinguishable" (Strain, p. 138).

The Confederates' fierce stand at South Mt. gave the main body of Lee's army time to bring its widely separated parts together at Sharpsburg on Antietam Creek. Here the two full armies clashed on September 17, the bloodiest single day of the Civil War. One Rebel said of the battle that "the sun seemed almost to go backwards, and it appeared as if night would never come" (Flato, p. 85). When night did arrive, 23,500 men lay dead or wounded and the two armies had fought to a bloody stalemate. Lee retreated south the next day, but McClellan failed to follow. President Lincoln seized on the Northern "victory" as a chance to issue his Emancipation Proclamation, which freed Confederate slaves.

Lieut. Col. (and future U.S. president) Rutherford B. Hayes was one Yankee wounded in the fray. Leading a charge against a stone wall, he hollered, "Give them hell! Give the sons of bitches hell!" (Strain, p. 122). The Rebels returned his insult with a musket ball in the elbow.

Return to the AT, follow it across Reno Monument Rd,. and continue through an almost pure stand of chestnut oaks. This tree, with its distinctive, deeply furrowed gray bark and its elliptical, wavy-edged leaves is one of the most easily recognizable of oaks. It is a hardy tree, and found on Appalachian ridgetops all through the mid-Atlantic region. Its bark has a high tannin content and was once used for tanning leather before chemical substitutes were invented.

The Dahlgren Back Pack Campground (7.0 mi.) is one of those rare places on the AT where you can tent, take a hot shower, and find a rest room with a real flush toilet. And this Shangri-la offers still more trail magic:

just 0.2 mi. ahead, in the heart of Turners Gap, is the South Mt. Inn. Built sometime between 1750 and 1810, this public house once served as a stagecoach stop on the National Rd. (now US Alt. 40). The inn has also served as a Confederate command post, a private home, and a brothel. Today it is an excellent restaurant. While the evening and Sunday brunch crowd tends toward the well dressed and upscale, hikers in polypropylene and polar fleece are welcomed. One of my fondest backpacking memories was a weekend trip through subfreezing temperatures followed by a soul-satisfying evening meal next to the inn's roaring fireplace, toasting the bitter winds outside with a smooth, locally brewed Blue Ridge ale.

The National Rd. through Turners Gap was cut by British Gen. Braddock's redcoat army in 1755 on its way to a fatal ambush in the French and Indian War. The pass served as a key east-west transportation route until the building of the Potomac River's Chesapeake & Ohio Canal in 1855 (see Hike #1) and the coming of the railroads.

Turners Gap was also the primary focus of the Union advance in the battle of South Mt. Looking east, into the valley, it is possible to imagine the terrible awe and fear with which the outnumbered Confederates must have watched the grand spectacle of the approaching banners of the main body of the Union army. The ensuing battle surged over the rugged, irregu-

Continued on p. 44

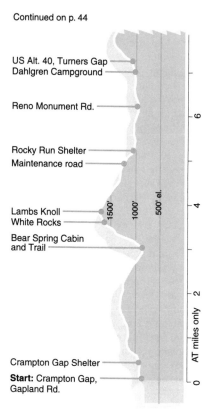

lar terrain of Turners Gap, making orderly fighting nearly impossible. Charges and countercharges surged around trees and slashed through laurel thickets and over boulders.

The little Dahlgren Chapel (7.2 mi.) on US Alt. 40, with its stained glass, stone walls, and belfry, stands in peaceful contrast to the violence that once raged here. It too has a Civil War connection. It was constructed by Madeleine Dahlgren, widow of Adm.

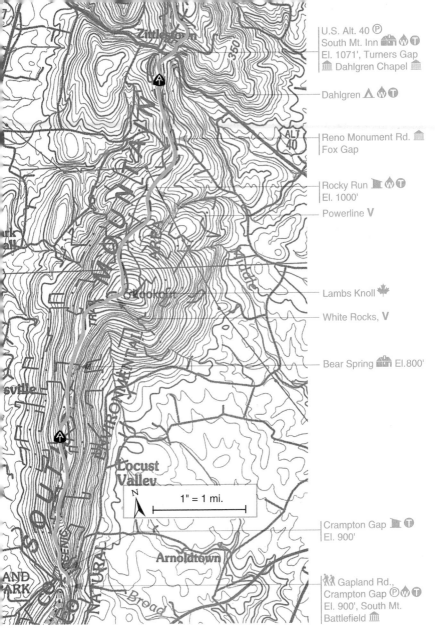

U.S. Alt. 40 Ⓟ
South Mt. Inn 🏨 ⓦ 🅣
El. 1071', Turners Gap
🏛 Dahlgren Chapel 🏛

Dahlgren 🔺 ⓦ 🅣

ALT
40

Reno Monument Rd. 🏛
Fox Gap

Rocky Run 🏕 ⓦ 🅣
El. 1000'

Powerline V

Lambs Knoll 🍁

White Rocks, V

Bear Spring 🏨 El.800'

N
1" = 1 mi.

Crampton Gap 🏕 🅣
El. 900'

🚶 Gapland Rd.,
Crampton Gap Ⓟ ⓦ 🅣
El. 900', South Mt.
Battlefield 🏛

John Dahlgren, inventor of the Dahlgren gun, a deadly naval cannon used by both sides in the War Between the States. Madeleine Dahlgren was a popular novelist, a Washington socialite, and a Christian, opposed to what she considered the unseemliness of women's suffrage. She converted the South Mt. Inn into her own estate in 1875, and constructed the private chapel in 1881. The stone church eventually went to ruin; its family burial vault was vandalized, with bones scattered about in a futile search for hidden treasure. The chapel was restored in the 1960s, and is open on weekends. It is a picturesque and peaceful spot that invites meditation.

A new AT relocation (opening in 1998) eliminates the brief walk along US Alt. 40 and Dahlgren Rd., and instead crosses the highway near the chapel, enters the forest, and follows the ridge into Washington Monument SP. Daytime parking in the upper lot (9.0 mi.) can be used as one end point for this hike.

For those who wish to continue, Washington Monument is reached in another 0.2 mi. This odd stone tower, shaped like an old-fashioned cream bottle, was the first monument constructed in our first president's honor. In 1827, Whig supporters in Boonsboro built the memorial as a show of loyalty to their political party and in opposition to the Democrats under Andrew Jackson. The structure was used as an observation and signal tower by the Union army during the Civil War, and eventually fell into dis-

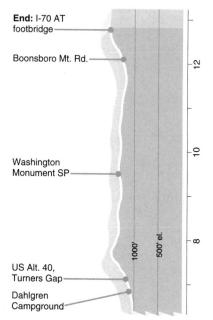

repair. It was mysteriously dynamited during World War I. Some say the explosion was detonated by a German sympathizer; others claim a farmer, tired of his daughters' fraternizing with local boys at the spot, set off the charge (Strain, p. 188). The tower was restored by the Civilian Conservation Corps. Today it is a popular birding lookout.

The AT descends steeply from Washington Monument, reaches a

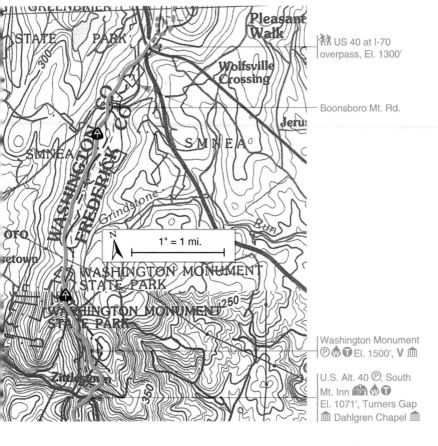

Pleasant
Walk

Wolfsville
Crossing

Jeru

SMNEA

Grindstone

Run

N

1" = 1 mi.

WASHINGTON MONUMENT
STATE PARK

WASHINGTON MONUMENT
STATE PARK
250

oro
etown

Zittli wn

350

US 40 at I-70
overpass, El. 1300'

Boonsboro Mt. Rd.

Washington Monument
Ⓟ Ⓦ Ⓣ El. 1500', V 🏛

U.S. Alt. 40 Ⓟ, South
Mt. Inn 🏨 Ⓦ Ⓣ
El. 1071', Turners Gap
🏛 Dahlgren Chapel 🏛

power line (9.5 mi), climbs briefly, and then passes through a number of old stone walls before crossing Boonsboro Mt. Rd. twice (at 11.4 mi. and 12.1 mi.) and reaching the footbridge over I-70. At the far end of this bridge, a blue-blazed trail leads in 0.1 mi. to an overnight AT parking area on US 40.

Miles N	NORTH	Elev. (ft./m)	Miles S
	Total: 12.3 mi. with access from AT side trail		
0.1	Access: Side trail leads straight ahead to overnight AT parking on US 40.	1250/381	0.1
12.2	**End AT miles:** I-70 AT footbridge, N end, at intersection of I-70 and US 40, 10.0 mi. SE of Hagerstown.		0.0
12.1	AT crosses **Boonsboro Mt. Rd.; I-70 AT footbridge, S end.**		0.1
11.4	AT crosses **Boonsboro Mt. Rd.**	1300/396	0.8
9.5	**Power line.**	1400/427	2.7
9.2	**Washington Monument**; descend steeply.	1500/457	3.0
9.0	**Washington Monument SP**, day parking, water, rest room, museum in summer; ascend steeply; early exit option.	1400/427	3.2
7.2	**US Alt. 40** (early exit option); **Turners Gap; South Mt. Inn; Dahlgren Chapel**; begin steady climb.	1071/326	5.0
7.0	**Dahlgren Back Pack Campground**, tent sites, water, rest room, showers in summer.	1000/305	5.2
6.2	**Reno Monument Rd. (Fox Gap)**, AT goes straight ahead; **Reno Monument** is 0.2 mi to R (E) up rd.; emergency exit option.	900/274	6.0
5.3	**Rocky Run Shelter** side trail leads L (W) for 0.2 mi. to shelter, privy, seasonal spring.		6.9
4.8	Cross paved **maintenance road.**	1300/396	7.4
3.7	**Lambs Knoll summit**, communications towers; AT begins steep 800-ft. descent.	1772/540	8.5
3.5	**White Rocks** view.	1600/488	8.7

Miles N		Elev. (ft./m)	Miles S
3.0	**Bear Spring Cabin Trail** descends steeply to Bear Spring (0.5 mi.) and Bear Spring Cabin (0.7 mi.), available with PATC reservation.	800/244	9.2
0.4	**Crampton Gap Shelter** side trail leads R (E) for 0.3 mi. to shelter, privy, unreliable spring.	900/274	11.8
0.0	**Start:** Crampton Gap, Gapland Rd. (MD 572), 1.0 mi. W of Burkittsville; overnight parking next to **Civil War Correspondents' Memorial** and George Townsend's **Gathland** estate, rest room, water pump, drinks vending machine; AT passes stone barn ruins then climbs out of pass.	900/274	12.2

SOUTH

Pine Knob to Pen Mar County Park

Map: PATC Md. # 5

Route: From US 40 over Pine Knob to Annapolis Rock, Black Rock, Quirauk Mt., High Rock, and Pen Mar County Park

Recommended direction: S to N

Distance: 17.8 mi. total; 17.7 mi.on AT

Elevation +/-: 1250 to 1890 to 1250 ft.

Effort: Easy

Day hike: Optional

Overnight backpacking hike: Yes

Duration: 12 hr.

Early exit options: At 8.3 mi., Wolfsville Rd. (MD 17); at 11.8 mi., Raven Rock Rd. (MD 491)

Natural history features: Annapolis Rock, Black Rock Cliffs, and High Rock vistas; Devils Racecourse boulder field

Social history features: Site of Black Rock Hotel; Pen Mar County Park; Mason-Dixon line

Trailhead access: *Start:* From I-70E, take the Myersville exit. Turn R on Wolfsville Rd. (MD 17), then L on US 40. Overnight parking is located on US 40 at a pull-over spot just before the I-70 overpass. From I-70W take the US 40S exit, cross the I-70 overpass, and park at overnight pull-over spots. *End:* From I-81, take PA 16E. Turn R onto PA 418, and L onto Pen Mar Rd. (PA 2008) to Pen Mar County Park. Day parking for several cars at park gate or overnight in lot inside park.

Camping: Pine Knob Shelter; Pogo Memorial Campsite; Hemlock Hill Shelter; Devils Racecourse Shelter

---

The three fine, west-facing vistas of Annapolis Rock, Black Rock, and High Rock plus a peculiar river of stone called the Devils Racecourse are the highlights of this hike through northern Maryland. This AT section, mostly along the flat-topped South Mt. ridge, makes for a fun, easy 17.7-mi. overnight trip, with camping at Hemlock Hill Shelter (8.2 mi.). The walk can also be neatly divided into two day hikes of 8.3 mi. and 9.4 mi., with the midpoint coming at Wolfsville Rd. (MD 17).

From US 40's hiker parking area,

walk the blue-blazed side trail for 0.1 mi. to its intersection with the AT. Turn right and follow the white blazes north, away from the I-70 footbridge and the deafening road noise. This superhighway replaced the quiet, electric Frederick-Hagerstown interurban trolley, which first penetrated this mountain pass in 1904 and ran until 1938. The trolley not only carried freight and passengers but offered a romantic transportation adventure to farm families who had rarely traveled beyond their small, rural communities.

The trail seems to pass quickly from the 20th century back into the 19th as it crosses under US 40, then takes an old woods road past a farmhouse and overgrown fields. As the path slowly climbs, the traffic sounds fade away and are replaced by birdsong.

At 0.5 mi., a blue-blazed trail leads left for 0.1 mi. to Pine Knob Shelter. This lean-to boasts not only a nearby spring, a privy, and a nifty fold-down dining table, but also, perhaps, its own resident ghost. A thru-hiker named Okeepa claims in a shelter registry entry to have been frightened right out of his polypropylene underwear by the ghost. We witnessed no evidence of the haunting during our visit, though we did experience a refreshing chill as we stepped out of bright sunlight into the shelter's gloom.

The AT continues climbing on the woods road until it crests at Pine Knob (0.9 mi.), where it achieves the top of South Mt. (elev. 1714 ft.). While there is no view here, you may want to keep your eyes open for pink lady's-slipper (also called moccasin-flower because of its shoe shape). Blooming in late May or early June, this showy woodland orchid at one time could be found growing by the hundreds along the AT. However, collectors who picked it and failed in their home garden replanting attempts have diminished its numbers.

The next 7.2 mi. offer a gently undulating ridge walk through a chestnut oak forest. Two views along

Glenn Scherer

Pine Knob Shelter

the way are not to be missed. Annapolis Rock (2.2 mi) is reached by turning left onto a blue-blazed side trail (0.2 mi.). Black Rock (3.2 mi.) is only 40 yd. to the left of the AT, and is reached by several short, unmarked paths.

Both of these spectacular crags include rock slabs, overhanging cliffs, small caves, tumbled boulders, and views that look west across a wide farm valley toward Hagerstown. Four states—Maryland, Pennsylvania, West Virginia, and Virginia—plus the oddly named hamlets of Mousetown, Smoketown, Bagtown, and Jugtown are all visible from the heights. The jagged, exposed quartzite ledges at Annapolis Rock and Black Rock form much of the erosion-resistant bedrock of South Mt.

The view from Black Rock has brought picnickers to the spot for 200 years. In *The Blue Hills of Maryland,* Paula Strain recounts 19th-century

Independence Day festivities that took place near the viewpoint. According to one account of these parties, the Declaration of Independence was read and a fiery oration delivered, followed by "thirteen regular toasts to correspond to the thirteen original states. . . . [More toasts] were proposed and drunk as long as a man was left with sufficient sobriety to guide his glass to his lips" (p. 210). One wonders how these tottering "Sons of Liberty" ever safely guided their wagons down from South Mt. at day's end. Perhaps their wives took the reins.

Just after Black Rock, the trail descends on a woods road to the Pogo Memorial Campsite (3.9 mi.). Located near the site of the Black Rock Hotel, this tenting site, with its spring and privy, was named for Mountain Club of Maryland member Walter "Pogo" Rheinheimer, a sixteen-year-old trail maintainer who drowned in a Potomac River canoeing accident near Harpers Ferry. The hotel, now long gone, was built in 1907 as a summer resort by a successful salesman of tapeworm patent medicine, Jacob Duell Wolfe. It was too remote to attract sufficient customers, and it burned down in the 1920s. Gravel Bagtown Rd. descends left (west) for 0.9 mi. to a trailhead on White Oak Rd. (just off Crystal Falls Rd.).

From the campsite, the trail gradually ascends, again following the ridgeline on woods roads and then

Continued on p. 52

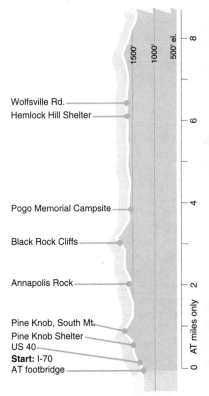

passing over very rocky, ankle-twisting terrain (5.4 mi.) on a narrow footpath. The only good view east along this section (6.1 mi.) is reached by a short rock scramble to the right. This limited vista is best seen when the leaves are off the trees.

Just past this overlook, the AT, thankfully, leaves the rocky treadway behind and again intercepts a smooth woods road, which descends

66

Pleasant Valley

MD 17 (Wolfsville Rd.)
Ⓟ

Hemlock Hill 🏠Ⓦ🚻
El. 150'

Pondsville

153

Jugtown

216

ENVIRONMENTAL

NATIONAL

Creek

Middle

Dry

Run

Wolfsv

Pogo Memorial
Campsite 🔺Ⓦ🚻
El. 1600', site of Black
Rock Hotel

Black Rock,
El. 1800', V🍁

Annapolis Rock,
El. 1600', V🍁

SOUTH

MOUNTAIN

N

⅞" = 1 mi.

Pine Knob 🏠Ⓦ🚻
El. 1300'

Pleasant
Walk

BK

Wolfsville
Crossing

Cataclin

🚶‍♂️ US 40 Ⓟ El. 1250'

steeply to Hemlock Hill Shelter (8.2 mi.). While this lean-to is only 0.1 mi. south of Wolfsville Rd. (MD 17), it is well kept and unlittered. There is a privy, and a good spring is located 0.3 mi. further up the trail at an abandoned house site.

For those doing this walk as an overnight trip, Hemlock Hill Shelter marks the end of your first day out. For those dividing the walk into two day hikes, Wolfsville Rd. (MD 17) has daytime parking for several cars.

A major relocation is planned for the AT in the area of Wolfsville Rd. and Foxville Rd., one of the few sections of the entire AT still located largely on private property. Planners for the National Park Service and Potomac Appalachian Trail Club volunteers are working to complete the purchase of an AT corridor and to relocate the trail into it by 1999 or 2000. Call the PATC for the status of this project.

Currently, the trail crosses Wolfsville Rd. (MD 17), briefly follows a gravel road past houses, climbs along the clearing for a power line and natural gas pipeline with good views west, then descends very steeply (9.2 mi.). Luckily, you are walking downhill; this section of the AT falls more steeply than any other section in Maryland.

At 9.4 mi. the trail crosses a polluted tributary of Grove Creek, then passes beneath and circles to the top of a massive overhanging rock face. This site, with its nearby water source, would have made for a very comfortable Native American hunt-

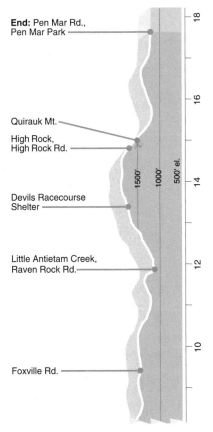

ing camp. Today, the area is occupied by a local rod and gun club.

The AT crosses Foxville Rd. (MD 77) at 9.6 mi., then passes briefly through backyards and past mobile homes and barking dogs. This close brush with civilization may some day be avoided thanks to continuing efforts by government and volunteers to relocate the trail into a forested corridor nearby.

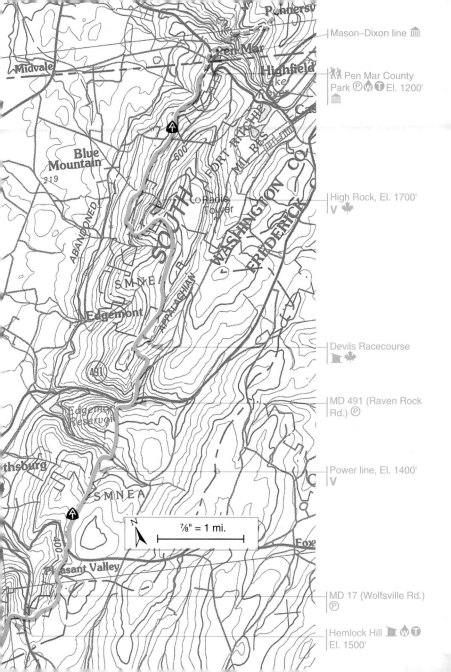

Mason–Dixon line 🏛

Pen Mar County Park Ⓟ ⓦ ⓣ El. 1200'
🏛

High Rock, El. 1700'
V 🍁

Devils Racecourse
🏭 🍁

MD 491 (Raven Rock Rd.) Ⓟ

Power line, El. 1400'
V

MD 17 (Wolfsville Rd.) Ⓟ

Hemlock Hill 🏭 ⓦ ⓣ El. 1500'

For the next few miles, the AT ranges up and down over small hills, passing through overgrown farm fields and over stone walls before finally descending Buzzard Knob into Raven Rock Hollow. Watch your step crossing polluted Little Anti-etam Creek (11.8 mi.). In high water, the lack of a bridge may require the removal of boots for safe fording. The AT climbs up an embankment, crosses MD 491, and continues into the woods.

A long, steady climb takes hikers up onto the back of Quirauk Mt. Once called Mt. Misery, the ridge was given its more euphonious Native American name with the coming of tourists in the late 1800s.

At 12.7 mi. a blue-blazed side trail leads right, descending steeply for 200 vertical ft. over 0.3 mi. to the Devils Racecourse Shelter. Be sure to explore this side trail, even if you aren't planning to stay at the lean-to, which is nestled in a hemlock glen and boasts a privy and a reliable spring.

Continue a few hundred feet downhill past the shelter to reach the Devils Racecourse itself, a riverlike flood of barren boulders that appears to flow along the narrow bottom of this little mountain valley. While glaciers never reached Maryland, the cold weather of the Ice Age did shape the landscape. The heaving action of frost caused the rocks of Devils Racecourse to crack and separate by size, forming the boulder field. A real stream does flow beneath

the rocks, and can be heard at the south end of the racecourse. When rock hopping here in warm weather, watch for the Devil's best buddies, sunbathing snakes.

Return up the blue-blazed trail. The AT then goes right, crossing the relatively flat top of Quirauk Mt. (elev. 1890 ft.) on a woods road. During World War II hikers along this part of the trail might have been startled to see soldiers in full German battle dress approaching them. These were no Nazi paratroopers, but students at America's first school for spies. Nearby Fort Richie was used through-out the war as the Military Intelligence Training Center. The camp included a movie-set-like mock-up of an entire German village, for the practice of raiding techniques, street fighting, and booby trap building. A dark basement labyrinth served as a combat firing range, through which students fought their way with piano wire (for strangling), a knife, a pistol, and one clip of ammunition. They knew they had passed this test if they had three rounds of ammunition left at the end of the exercise with which to shoot effigies of Hitler, Mussolini, and Emperor Hirohito.

The final exam for every cloak-and-dagger class was a 48-hr., 30-mi. bush-whack over the summits of South Mt. At least one group cheated by taking a shortcut along the AT. The Military Intelligence Training Center, or the "Mythical Institute of Total Confusion" as some recruits called it, was closed after V-J Day in 1945.

At 14.4 mi. a blue-blazed side trail goes right for 0.1 mi. to High Rock, once the site of a two-story observation tower. The rock still offers great views west over a checkerboard of farm fields. Unfortunately, unlike Annapolis Rock and Black Rock Cliffs, this vista is reached by a paved road, and can become over-crowded with visitors.

High Rock was once part of Pen Mar County Park, a Gay Nineties amusement center and summertime destination for Washingtonians and citizens of Frederick and other nearby communities (see Hike #4). The blue-blazed trail forms a loop, returning to the AT in another 0.1 mi.

The 440-vertical-ft., 0.5-mi. descent of Quirauk Mt. along the AT would be treacherously steep if not for the fine stone steps and switchbacks installed by volunteers. The trail passes between two giant boulders (15.0 mi.), then levels out. It travels through thick forest and mountain laurel thickets, following a succession of carriage roads and a railroad bed over the next 2.3 mi. into Pen Mar County Park. Pay close attention to blazing here; it is easy to miss the sudden shifts from one carriage road to the next. There are massive stone ruins and a large depression at 16.5 mi., proof of 19th-century habitation on the mountain.

The AT leaves the forest and enters the grassy fields of Pen Mar County Park at 17.3 mi. There are sweeping views west, and every hiker's favorite trail-end destinations: rest rooms, snack bars, and water fountains. These facilities are open May through October. At 17.6 mi. a sign marks the Mason-Dixon line and the border between Maryland and Pennsylvania, and this hike ends at Pen Mar Rd. (17.7 mi.). There is day parking at the Pen Mar County Park gate 0.4 mi. to the right (east), and over-night parking in the lot within the park, to your right off the AT.

Miles N	**NORTH**	Elev. (ft./m)	Miles S
	Total: 17.8 mi. with access on side trail of AT		
17.7	**End: Pen Mar Rd.,** follow to R (E) to Pen Mar County Park day parking at gate, overnight parking in lot inside park.	1250/381	0.0
17.6	**Mason-Dixon line sign.**		0.1
17.3	**Pen Mar County Park:** former amusement park; views, rest rooms, snack bar, water fountains in summer.		0.4
16.5	**Stone ruins.**	1250/381	1.2
15.0	AT passes between two **giant boulders** then levels out.	1200/366	2.7
14.5	Begin steep descent of **Quirauk Mt.**	1700/518	3.2
14.4	**High Rock and High Rock Rd.** loop trail goes R (N) for 0.1 mi. to view and rd. then rejoins AT in another 0.1 mi.		3.3
13.7	Highest point on AT in MD.	1890/576	4.0
12.7	**Devils Racecourse Shelter** side trail descends 200 ft. R (E); reliable spring, privy; (0.3 mi.); **Devils Racecourse** rocky formation 50 yd. below shelter.	1600/488	5.0
11.9	Begin long, steady ascent of **Quirauk Mt.**	1200/366	5.8
11.8	**Little Antietam Creek;** descend to polluted creek; ascend embankment to **Raven Rock Rd. (MD 491) and Ritchie Rd. intersection,** day parking, early exit option.	1100/335	5.9
9.6	**Foxville Rd (MD 77),** no parking.	1500/457	8.1
9.4	**Grove Creek tributary,** polluted; pass beneath overhanging cliff, then circle to its top.	1400/427	8.3
9.2	Steep descent along **power line** (view), then turn R (N) into woods.		8.5

Miles N		Elev. (ft./m)	Miles S
8.9	Reach **power line** and follow to L (W).	1600/488	8.8
8.5	Side trail leads for 100 yd. R (E) to **spring**.	1400/427	9.2
8.3	**Wolfsville Rd.,** day parking and early exit option; AT crosses Wolfsville to nameless gravel road.		9.4
8.2	**Hemlock Hill Shelter,** privy.	1500/457	9.5
7.6	**Begin descending ridge.**	1800/549	10.1
6.1	**View** on L (E).	1800/549	11.6
3.9	**Pogo Memorial Campsite,** tent sites, privy, spring; **Bagtown Rd.** (gravel) descends L (W) for 0.9 mi. to parking on White Oak Rd.	1600/488	13.8
3.2	**Black Rock** unmarked trail leads L (W) for 40 yd. to view.	1800/549	14.5
2.2	**Annapolis Rock** side trail leads L (W) for 0.2 mi. to view.	1600/488	15.5
0.9	**Pine Knob,** South Mt. summit; no view.	1714/522	16.8
0.5	**Pine Knob Shelter** side trail leads L (W) in 0.1 mi. to shelter, privy, and spring; AT continues climbing.	1350/412	17.2
0.1	**US 40 underpass,** begin slow climb.		17.6
0.0	**Start AT miles: I-70 AT footbridge, N end,** at intersection of I-70 and US 40, 10.0 mi. SE of Hagerstown.	1250/381	17.7
0.1	Access: Side trail leads to overnight AT parking (0.1 mi.) on US 40.		0.1

SOUTH

HIKE #4
Pen Mar County Park, MD, to Old Forge Picnic Grounds

Map: KTA Pa. Section 14

Route: From Pen Mar County Park and the Mason-Dixon line through the Michaux State Forest to Little Antietam Creek and Old Forge Picnic Grounds

Recommended direction: S to N

Distance: 7.0 mi.

Elevation +/-: 1200 to 1450 to 1000 ft.

Effort: Easy

Day hike: Yes

Overnight backpacking hike: No

Duration: 3½ hr.

Early exit option: At 2.5 mi., PA 16 (limited parking)

Natural history features: Mt. Dunlop; diverse silviculture of Michaux State Forest

Social history features: Near Civil War

battlefields at Antietam and Gettysburg

Other features: Sunset views at Pen Mar County Park, wading in Little Antietam Creek

Trailhead access: *Start:* Take I-81 N or S to PA 16 (Exit 3), go E 10.0 mi. to Rouzerville, R onto PA 418, and L on Pen Mar Rd. (PA 2008) to Pen Mar County Park where there is overnight parking for a dozen vehicles. *End:* Take I-81 N or S to PA 16; go E 10.0 mi. to Rouzerville and L on Pen Mar Rd. (PA 2007) and 5.0 mi. to Old Forge Picnic Grounds. Overnight parking for a dozen cars in the park lot.

Camping: Deer Lick Shelters; Antietam Shelter and camping area

It is appropriate that the Appalachian Trail passes from Maryland to Pennsylvania through sylvan picnic grounds that were once an amusement park. Just on the southern side of the Mason-Dixon line, in Maryland, the past and present parks at Pen Mar, like the AT itself, were created to offer a getaway from city stress and structure.

After parking in the Pen Mar County Park lot, stroll 100 yd. into the park to the AT along an oak-shaded path, past swings, seesaws, and picnic shelters where amusement park rides thrilled summer pilgrims from Baltimore, Philadelphia, and Washington, D.C., for more than sixty years, beginning in 1878. The parkgoers then came on the Western Maryland Railway, which built the rollercoaster, merry-go-round, and arcades as a refuge from city heat, and to increase waning business. With the advent of the automobile, however, rail travel lost favor and the amusement park closed down, permuting into the quiet groves, playgrounds, picnic shelters, and pavilions you see today.

The AT curls around the park's main pavilion, where dances and band concerts are welcome holdovers from the amusement park days. It passes in front of a second pavilion, perched over a steep hillside where sunset views over a farm-rich valley checkerboarded with crops are spectacular, before rolling gently downhill out of the park on a wide, crushed stone path through tall oaks.

The trail slips around a gate and across Pen Mar Rd., then follows a power line right-of-way. It crosses railroad tracks and enters Pennsylvania through a small but lushly wooded area where, just off the trail, a sign marks the Mason-Dixon line and the official change in pronunciation of the name of this trail.

South of here, at least up through central Virginia, "app-a-LATCH-an" (or "-ian") is the pronunciation of choice for locals and hikers alike. In northern Virginia, and more and more through West Virginia and Maryland, you start hearing it as "app-a-LAY-chan" (or "-ian"). From Pennsylvania on, if you hear a "LACH" instead of a "LAY" you can bet your hiking stick you're talking to a thru-hiker from the South.

Cross Pen Mar Rd. again and follow trail blazes on electric utility poles along the roadbed of an old trolley line that once served Pen Mar County Park. During the summer, the trail here is overgrown but brightened by blue chicory flowers, white Queen Anne's lace, and purple clover. Follow the AT off the utility line to the left, dropping into a wooded stretch. The trail is rocky but the hiking, gently downhill, is easy. A rushing stream, Falls Creek, can be heard through the high canopy of oaks and a younger understory of ash and ferns.

Just 0.5 mi. from the start of the hike, cross the two prongs of Falls Creek on a wooden footbridge that is slippery when wet. Care and good handholds should be taken to avoid having the stream live up to its name. Also note the signs that indicate the stream is polluted and should not be used as a drinking water source.

As you bear right and begin ascending Mt. Dunlop, you will begin to notice more rocks, toe bumpers and knee shockers, beginning to appear underfoot. Still going uphill, cross blacktopped Buena Vista Rd., where the AT turns left along the road for about 50 ft. to a spring near where the trail peels off up the hill to the right. Oaks tower above, maple and sassafras dominate the understory, and chips of white quartz are scattered along the trail. Cross an old logging road just before the summit (elev. 1450 ft.) and another just after.

An easy downhill brings you to Old PA 16 (at 2.2 mi.), and then in just 0.3 mi. more, to PA 16. It is the first road on this hike that announces itself with traffic noise before you see it, and a good early exit option. A jumble of living-room-furniture-sized

Unfriendly Weather

Fact one: It will happen. Rule one: Be prepared. Get the best weather report you can in the twenty-four hours prior to your hike. Use the Weather Channel, NOAA (National Oceanic and Aeronautics Administration) on the weather radio band, or the newspaper. If the report calls for wet, windy, or cold weather, plan for it to be worse in the mountains and woods. If you get soaked in a downpour, keep a sharp lookout for signs of hypothermia (shivering, disorientation, anxiety, weakness). Wet and cold bring it on; fatigue, discouragement, and fear exacerbate it. Group leaders and hiking partners should watch fellow hikers for signs of hypothermia and take preventive steps (shelter, dry clothes, warm liquids, wrap in sleeping bag, reassurance).

Slipping or falling is another real danger in wet weather. Stay together, talk to one another, lend a hand. Keep focused on the slippery path beneath your feet. Many hikers find a walking stick especially helpful in adverse conditions. Keep your backpack load reasonable and properly balanced (see "Packing Your Pack," p. 20).

If a storm approaches (you should be watching the sky for thunderheads or general darkening, and listening to the wind in the trees or distant thunder), take the following steps:

- Get off mountaintops and exposed ledges. Go below treeline. The deep forest is safest (except directly under large standing dead trees).

- If an official campsite is near, try to get there; set up and take shelter. If not, find a level, well-drained place and set up your tent (you should have rehearsed at home so this takes only minutes even in a stiff breeze or fading light). Position the door away from the approaching storm.

- In fog, darkness, or howling wind, confusion is easy. Avoid it by

boulders, many of them green and slippery, must be hopped through to reach the road's wide berm, where there is parking for half a dozen cars. To the right is the town of Blue Ridge Summit (1.8 mi.) and to the left, Waynesboro (5.0 mi.).

There is a picnic table in a pull-off at the trailhead on the south side of the road. The AT shares that amenity with the Bicentennial Tree Trail of Pennsylvania's Michaux State Forest. The 1.0-mi. looping path was built by the Youth Conservation Corps in 1975 through beech, birch, maple, and basswood stands that were saplings during America's colonial period. Such diverse old-growth stands are not found elsewhere in the Michaux. There are also stands of Pennsylvania's state tree, the hemlock, yellow poplar, and various oaks. The side

carrying a compass and a topo map with the trails well marked. Know where you are at all times.

- Once inside your tent, take inventory. Know where dry clothes, food, light, toiletries, and your first-aid kit are. If you have wet feet or hair, dry off the best you can. Keep your sleeping pad and sleeping bag dry.

- Make a plan: What can you eat without cooking over a stove? If your tent has a vestibule, you may be able to use a stove (with a windshield) at its outer perimeter, but never light a stove inside your tent.

- Before dark, decide how you will handle a run to the privy or pit toilet (keep your camp shovel handy, keep toilet paper dry, and keep a self-seal plastic bag handy, too), and how you will hang your food bag outdoors overnight out of the reach of bears (see "Food Storage," p. 16).

After you have made all these commonsense preparations for storm survival, the fun begins. Indulge in a long nap, or sleep a long night through. Write in your journal, taking time for details, even poetry. Read by daylight (did you pack a lightweight paperback?) or briefly by candlelight (in a safe, protective candle holder, never an open flame in a tent) or by flashlight (but conserve batteries). Play word games, sing songs, tell tall tales, re-engineer society, resolve a philosophical dilemma, or just listen to the music of the storm outside, which may be as delicate as a vibraphone or as muscular as the timpani. Imagine the music is nature's performance for you.

You may be in for a long day or night in the tent. Study your trail guide. Reconsider goals. Look for alternative early exit routes. If you are the leader, keep your own counsel and do not spread anger or anxiety. Patience, calm, good humor, and a plan will see you through most any bad weather. Survival, in good form, makes a great story back home.

—David Emblidge

---

trail can be an enjoyable 15-min. walk or an imaginative 200-year amble past trees seen by the state's earliest settlers.

The AT crosses PA 16 and after a couple of hundred yards meets a small, secondary road where it jogs to the left for 100 ft. before plunging back into the woods on the far side. Cross three more old logging roads, then follow the trail along the side of the hill through thick mountain laurel near the former Mackie Run Shelter site. There are still good camping spots here, but, because Mackie Run is polluted, there is no dependable water supply. The forest is very young here with maple saplings dominating. Hiking is flat and easy and the trail is wide, even in midsummer, with no brambles or briars to impede hikers. Cross Mackie Run on Mentzer Gap

Rd., and just after the 3.0-mi. mark, cross Rattlesnake Run Rd.

At 3.4 mi. reach Bailey Spring, dependable even in late summer. A mile or so more brings you to Deer Lick Shelters in a clearing just right of the trail, and another very strong spring. The twin shelters are of the log lean-to type common in Pennsylvania and sleep four apiece. A log home company donated the materials and Pennsylvania Conservation Corps crews built them. There is plenty of flat ground for tenting. Not a bad spot for an early lunch, either.

After the shelters, the trail climbs gently for almost a mile, crossing a wide, grassy pipeline right-of-way, meandering through young oak woods, and crossing yet another dirt road before turning to the right and starting to exhibit some of the rockiness the Keystone State is known for.

Begin descending the side of South Mt., and after some easy walking, listen for the babbling of Little Antietam Creek (6.8 mi.). In spring, when the creek is running high, it is best to follow a blue-blazed trail to the right that goes up to Rattlesnake Run Rd. for the crossing.

At all other times cross the creek on a wooden bridge just downstream from the Antietam Shelter, which is visible from the bridge to the right. The shelter is just a rock toss away from the creek and makes a wonderful stopping point for lunch or to submerge tired feet or whole bodies in the creek pool right in front of the picnic table. Hiker notes

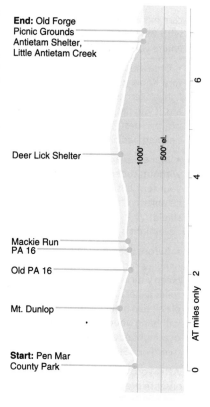

in the shelter register indicate there is a mosquito problem in wet weather. A wide field behind the shelter is available for tent camping.

In less than .3 mi., no more than a fungo away from the shelter, arrive at Old Forge Picnic Grounds and its baseball field, picnic tables, and pavilion. You've gone park to park on the AT, which passes just behind home plate.

Old Forge

MICHAUX

1" = 1 mi.
N

Glen Forney

MOUNTAIN

SCENIC

239

Beartown

Charmian

Monterey

Buena Vista
Springs

Pennersville

Pen Mar

Highfield

FRANKLIN CO
ADAMS CO

NATIONAL

Old Forge Picnic
Grounds Ⓟ Ⓦ Ⓣ
El. 1000'

Antietam ⛺ ⟐ Ⓦ Ⓣ

Little Antietam Creek

Deer Lick ⛺ ⟐ Ⓦ Ⓣ
El. 1450'

Bailey Spring Ⓦ

Mackie Run

PA 16

Old PA 16

Mt. Dunlop ✿

Pen Mar County
Park Ⓟ Ⓦ Ⓣ
El. 1200'

Miles N	NORTH	Elev. (ft./m)	Miles S
7.0	**End:** **Old Forge Picnic Grounds** parking, 5.0 mi. from Rouzerville.	1000/305	0.0
6.8	**Little Antietam Creek; Antietam Shelter,** water, privy.		0.2
4.9	**Pipeline right-of-way.**		2.1
4.5	**Deer Lick Shelters,** spring.	1450/442	2.5
3.4	**Bailey Spring.**		3.6
2.7	**Mackie Run.**		4.3
2.5	**PA 16,** early exit option.		4.5
2.2	**Old PA 16.**		4.8
1.7	**Mt. Dunlop** (estimated mileage).	1450/442	5.3
0.5	**Falls Creek** footbridge.		6.5
0.0	**Start:** **Pen Mar County Park,** on Pen Mar Rd.; overnight parking in lot inside park.	1200/366	7.0

SOUTH

HIKE #5
Old Forge Picnic Grounds to Caledonia State Park

Map: KTA Pa. Section 14

Route: From ascent of South Mt. to Chimney Rocks, over Snowy Mt. and Rocky Mt. to Conococheague Creek and Caledonia SP

Recommended direction: S to N

Distance: 10.5 mi.

Elevation +/-: 1000 to 1940 to 1175 ft.

Effort: Moderate

Day hike: Yes

Overnight backpacking hike: No

Duration: 6 hr.

Early exit option: At 5.5 mi., PA 233 (limited parking)

Natural history feature: Chimney Rocks

Social history features: Remains of old ironworks charcoal staging sites; Waynesboro Reservoir; Snowy Mt. Fire Tower

Other features: Caledonia SP pool, bath houses, picnic pavilions

Trailhead access: *Start:* Take I-81 N or S to PA 16 E (Exit 3), go 10.0 mi. to Rouzerville, L on Antietam Rd. (PA 2007) and 5.0 mi. to Old Forge Picnic Grounds. Parking for a dozen cars in the park lot. *End:* Take I-81 N or S to US 30/Chambersburg exit. Take US 30 E 11.0 mi. to Caledonia SP. Parking in lot near pool.

Camping: Tumbling Run Shelters; Hermitage Cabin; Rocky Mt. Shelters; Caledonia SP (see Hike #6)

This park-to-park ridgetop romp of just 10.5 mi. rates as one of the least dramatic but most delightful day hikes in Pennsylvania. Out of the Antietam Cove area, once the extended Blue Ridge is gained on what is known locally as South Mt., there are several excellent views, an unexpected boggy area, and a good half dozen rock outcroppings to scramble through before a gradual descent into the valley that holds Conococheague Creek and Caledonia SP.

At Old Forge Picnic Grounds, hikers can catch up to the AT by rounding third and heading for home on the ball field, right in front of the parking area. Pass behind the backstop to find a spring house with a frost-free tap, a good place to "water up" before hitting the trail, which runs through some brushy woods along the first-base line.

Out of the park, the trail is parallel to Old Forge Rd. for the first 0.5 mi. before meeting and following it for about 75 yd. Additional parking for a half dozen cars is available along the road on each side of the bridge over Little Antietam Creek, in case the parking lot is full. Once across the

Thaddeus Stevens blacksmith shop, Caledonia State Park

bridge, look for the white AT blaze on the left side of the road and begin a gradual ascent along Tumbling Run that steepens to the ridge.

At 1.0 mi. you will reach the Tumbling Run Shelters area with twin log shelters, a picnic bench, a fire ring, and several tent sites nearby. A blue-blazed trail to the left leads in 0.5 mi. to Hermitage Cabin, which belongs to the PATC. The cabin sleeps twelve but is locked. If you intend to stay there, advance reservations with the club are a must. (See "Address & Telephone" in "Useful Information.")

After passing the shelters, the trail uphill becomes steeper, passing through a medium-aged woods of oak where there is almost no ground cover. As in many of the trail's steeper sections, erosion can be a problem here; don't be surprised if you come upon the PATC trail maintainer build-

ing water dams (also known as water bars). These important antierosion barriers made from rocks, or sometimes tree trunks, are set in the ground at an angle across the trail to intercept water as it runs downhill and channel it off the trail.

If you do see the maintainer, ask to be shown one of the many seemingly incongruous flat areas along this steep section of the trail. The flats are about as big as a one-room house, but without any of the foundation rocks you might expect if mountain cabins once occupied the spots. That's because none ever did.

The flats, now favorite tenting sites, were originally dug out of the mountain a century ago by iron forge workers. They cut trees on the mountain and used mules to drag them to the flats, where the trees were stacked tightly together and burned to create charcoal for the forges along Little Antietam Creek, since charcoal burns slower and hotter than wood. Many thumb-sized chunks of the 100-year-old charcoal, pure carbon, can still be found around the perimeters of the flats.

Two miles after leaving Old Forge Picnic Grounds, hikers will come to the first bonafide vista of the day off the quartzite cliffs at Chimney Rocks, just 100 yd. or so to the right, up a blue-blazed trail, at the highest point on the ridge (1940 ft.). From the weathered and fractured sandstone and quartzite there's a nice view of the Waynesboro Reservoir in the valley more than 600 ft. below and of Green Ridge, which defines the eastern horizon. Evidence that the state's forests are reaching commercial maturity can be seen in the checkerboard logging patterns that drape the distant ridge. Turkey vultures, one of the biggest of the eastern birds, like to ride the updrafts here; you are likely to see one or several. In flight their long wings, which can be 6 ft. across, are held upward in a wide, shallow V—as if for vulture. Chimney Rocks is also where the blue-blazed loop trail to Hermitage Cabin rejoins the AT from the left. The cabin is 1.0 mi. down the side trail.

After leaving Chimney Rocks, the trail is shaded by tall ash, poplar, and oak. It is rockier here, but the hiking is not hard. The trail follows the ridgeline, descending gently through a younger wood that was probably clear-cut twenty or thirty years ago. It

crosses a gas pipeline at 3.0 mi. and passes under a power line at 4.0 mi. Just after the power line there is a blue-blazed trail to the left that leads to the Snowy Mt. Fire Tower in 0.1 mi., where there are fine views of the town of South Mountain.

The AT continues descending, across Snowy Mt. Rd. and through a forest where oaks are giving way to maples and ferns carpet the forest floor. Reach Swamp Rd. at 5.0 mi. and turn left, following the road through a boggy area and around a bend for 0.1 mi. It's easy to miss the trail heading into the woods on the right.

Another 0.4 mi. of hiking that seems longer when the bugs are bad through the swampy woods will bring you to PA 233, a paved road with signs pointing to the town of South Mountain, 1.6 mi. to the right, or east. To the left 2.0 mi. are the village of Mount Alto, Mount Alto State Park, and the Pennsylvania State University Forestry School. An early exit is possible here, with limited parking.

The trail crosses PA 233 and begins its last ascent, an easy 0.5 mi. through mountain laurel, Pennsylvania's state flower. Note too that much of the path is lined at boot tread level with teaberry, easily identified by its red berries and waxy, green, nickel-sized leaves that, when split or crushed, smell like the gum.

Shortly after beginning an easy descent, and as the trees—yellow birch, oak, and pine—get big again, come to a blue-blazed side trail at 7.0 mi. leading 0.2 mi. to the Rocky Mt.

Shelters, unofficially called the Jim Thorpe Shelters after the famous Native American football, baseball, and track athlete of the 1930s from nearby Carlisle. A spring is to the south on the west side of an old road.

From here on in to Caledonia SP the trail is more challenging, following the rocky eastern edge of the ridge through a series of sometimes lengthy rock jumbles that require some leaping and handholds. Some of the stacked outcroppings show off big boulders with bands of white quartz running through them like the broken lines in the center of a highway.

From some of the rocks there are good views of the South Mt. Restoration Center, a sanitarium, and Snowy Mt. But reserve most of your attention for the trail. Its white blazes can get lost against the light-colored quartzite and get you lost as well.

The trail flattens out and turns sandy before crossing the last clearing for a gas pipeline and dropping toward the sound of traffic on US 30 at 10.1 mi. Cross the busy road after checking for cars and enter Caledonia SP. The trail is wide and flat as it follows along Conococheague Creek, where brook, brown, and rainbow trout abound. Cross the creek on a footbridge and follow the AT through picnic pavilion areas to the large public parking lot near the pool, park office, and picnic groves at 10.5 mi. A little preplanning will allow you to cool your heels in the creek while dinner sizzles over a charcoal grill.

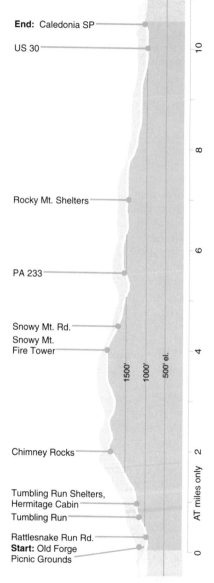

Greenwood

Creek

Caledonia Park

Brownsville

Caledonia SP Ⓟ △ 🐾
Ⓣ El. 1175'

US 30

Mountain

Creek

A

Rocky

Mountain

Rocky Mt. △ ■ 🐾Ⓣ

Mountain

Knob S

PA 233

468

SOUTH MOUNTAIN
RESTORATION CEN

South Mountain

Snowy Mt. Rd.

TO STATE PARK

Snowy Mt. Fire Tower

Tarburner
Spring

N
$\frac{13}{16}$" = 1 mi.

A

STATE

Chimney Rocks,
El. 1940', V

Tumbling Run △ ■
🐾Ⓣ

Rattlesnake Run Rd.

Old Forge Picnic
Grounds Ⓟ🐾Ⓣ

CHAUX

Old Forge

El. 1000'

Miles N	NORTH	Elev. (ft./m)	Miles S
10.5	**End:** Caledonia SP pool parking lot, on US 30.	1175/358	0.0
10.1	**US 30.**		0.4
7.0	**Rocky Mt. Shelters** side trail, spring, privy, campsites.		3.5
5.5	Cross **PA 233,** early exit option.		5.0
4.5	Cross **Snowy Mt. Rd.**		6.0
4.0	**Snowy Mt. Fire Tower** side trail.		6.5
3.0	**Pipeline** crossing.		7.5
2.0	**Chimney Rocks** and view of **Waynesboro Reservoir.**	1940/591	8.5
1.0	**Tumbling Run Shelters,** spring, privy; side trail (0.5 mi.) to **Hermitage Cabin.**		9.5
0.7	**Tumbling Run.**		9.8
0.2	**Rattlesnake Run Rd.**		10.3
0.0	**Start:** Old Forge Picnic Grounds parking, 5.0 mi. from Rouzerville.	1000/305	10.5

SOUTH

Caledonia State Park and Big Pine Flat Ridge

Map: KTA Pa. Section 13

Route: From Caledonia SP over Big Pine Flat Ridge to Arendtsville-Shippensburg Rd.

Recommended direction: S to N

Distance: 11.2 mi. total; 10.9 mi. on AT

Access trail name & length: Old AT, 0.3 mi.

Elevation +/-: 900 to 2000 to 1850 ft.

Effort: Moderate

Day hike: Yes

Overnight backpacking hike: Optional

Duration: 6¼ hr.

Early exit options: At 3.7 mi., Ridge Rd.; at 6.8 mi., Means Hollow Rd.

Natural history features: Caledonia State Park; Chinquapin Hill; Big Pine Flat Ridge; Conococheague Creek; Michaux State Forest

Social history features: Thaddeus Stevens's Iron Furnace and Blacksmith's Shop

Other features: Caledonia SP pool; Big Flat Fire Tower

Trailhead access: *Start:* Take I-81 N or S to US 30/Chambersburg exit. Take US 30 E 11.0 mi. to Caledonia SP, on L at intersection of US 30 and PA 233. Access trail to AT is directly across US 30 from hiker parking area near Caledonia Park Cottage No. 1, where there is room for 20 cars. Register at park office if leaving vehicle overnight. *End:* Take PA 233 N from Caledonia SP for 7.0 mi.; go L onto Arendtsville-Shippensburg Rd. and go 2.5 mi. to a pull-off on R. Parking for 6 cars at signed AT trailhead. (For alternate route see Hike #7.)

Camping: Caledonia SP; Quarry Gap Shelters; Milesburn Cabin (PATC, reservations required); Birch Run Shelters

aledonia was the name given to ancient Scotland by invading Romans, but hikers don't need to be Bravehearts to enjoy the first leg of the AT's ridge top route between Caledonia and Pine Grove Furnace state parks. The hike up to and along Big Pine Flat Ridge is through as pretty a section of Penn's woods as you'll find. It starts in Caledonia SP, named not for Scotland but for Caledonia County, Vermont, home-town of Thaddeus Stevens, an attorney who moved to the area in the 1820s and made his mark as an abolitionist, statesman, and father of the Pennsylvania public school system. Stevens financed the iron industry in the area and got to name the settlement. That's also why his name appears on the reconstructed iron furnace and blacksmith's shop in the park, even though he never shod a horse. Originally built in 1830, the smithy and ironworks were destroyed in 1863 by Confederate troops under the command of Gen. J. A. Early. They were restored in 1927 by the Pennsylvania Alpine Club and are worth a visit.

The smithy is directly across US 30 from the park's designated hikers' parking lot. The hike begins in front of the blacksmith's shop on a flat, gravel park path that was once a part of the AT and now connects to it. The path goes between the park swimming pool and a field that was used as an open-air hospital for soldiers wounded in the battle of Gettysburg, just 15 mi. to the east. On the right is a footbridge to picnic tables and park pavilions. The blue-blazed Midland Trail to one of the park's two campgrounds crosses here, and a drinking fountain at the edge of the field offers a last chance to fill up water bottles for the hike. There are a total of 185 tent and trailer campsites available, and the campgrounds provide flush toilets, hot showers, and a sanitary dump station.

As the path enters a wooded area, just 0.3 mi. from the parking lot, it joins the AT and immediately crosses Conococheague Creek on a wide wooden footbridge. The creek's tumbling runs and gentle, slow pools are home to many trout, and fly casters can often be seen trying to tempt them to strike a hook adorned with feather or fur. The AT winds through groves of tall hemlock, tulip-poplar, and oak and between popular picnic pavilions that are always in use during the summer. There is also a rest room along the trail here. The wooded area beyond the last of the pavilions is an excellent place to sight deer any time of the day.

Across a grassy park road, the AT begins ascending, steeply at times, between Orebank Hill on the left and Chinquapin Hill (elev. 1522 ft.) on the right. The trail climbs past a park campground on welcome wooden steps built into the hillside, until these give way to a series of switchbacks through an older forest of hemlock and oak. The trees get younger as the trail tops the hill (1.4 mi.) where there are mountain laurel and blueberry bushes lining the way, and the blue-blazed Caledonia SP Three Valley Trail, just 0.7 mi. long, joins the AT from the left.

The AT passes along a snow fence and a line of young white pines near the site of a former rifle range at 1.6 mi., where it is joined from the left by the blue-blazed Locust Gap Trail, a 4.8-mi. route from Greenwood Rd. to Milesburn Rd. The AT flattens here on a wide, old logging road before bearing off the road to the left and through several boggy areas where the footing is often soupy.

Ascending, pass the former Locked Antlers Camp site and still-active spring at 1.8 mi., and cross Hosack Run, a tumbling mountain brook on the right. The trail is gated here to control off-road vehicle access to the Quarry Gap shelters at 2.2 mi. The two new, four-person shelters are in a pleasant clearing surrounded by tall

Hiking with a Hand Lens

Some of the best views on the AT require no blue sky: the hairy underside of a lousewort leaf, the downy silencer of a discarded owl feather, the bloodsucking gear of a mosquito.

I always carry a 10X hand lens in my pack. It weighs less than my compass and has a string so that I can hang it around my neck. Most nature centers and college bookstores sell them.

Make sure you get one that magnifies at least ten times. Plastic 3X or 5X lenses don't help much, though they are easier for small children to use. A glass lens that slides into a protective case will last the longest. You can also buy 16X lenses that require more light and a bit of practice, or compact field microscopes with about 30X magnification and their own light source.

To use a 10X hand lens, place the lens close to your eye, almost touching your eyebrow, and bring, say, the owl feather closer and closer until it's in focus — usually within a few inches. If you want to look at flowers or mosses, get down to their level; don't pick them just to get a good look at them.

Look at everything. For example, whether a flower is new to you or you're reacquainting yourself with a familiar one, look at its stamens and pistil. Look at each plant part to find out why botanists need so many words for "hairy."

Hand lenses are cheaper and lighter than binoculars, and you will get views you never knew were there.

—Doris Gove

oaks, with a spring in front and privy behind. The trail crosses a small, unnamed tributary on rocks that could be submerged in a rainy spring and passes several primitive campsites before continuing the ascent of the ridge through impressive thickets of mountain laurel. At 2.9 mi. Hosack Run Trail splits off on the right. It joins the Locust Gap Trail in 1.1 mi., which loops west back to the AT or east to Milesburn Rd.

At 3.6 mi. the AT tops the ridge and turns right onto Ridge Rd. for 0.1 mi. to Sandy Sod, at the potentially confusing junction of Stillhouse Rd.,

Ridge Rd., and a gated forest road. This is one of the few spots in Pennsylvania where the trail is poorly marked. The trail follows Ridge Rd., which bears to the right, across the intersection and then *immediately* branches off into the woods on the left. The trail into the woods is poorly marked, and obscured, in season, by leafy brush and trees. A tip: ignore the gated road to the left, and stop if you begin going downhill on the road. That means you walked through the intersection and are on Stillhouse Rd. The key is to take the soft right turn on Ridge, not the hard right on Stillhouse. This is a possible early exit option with parking along the berm of the roads.

The AT follows the top of Big Pine Flat Ridge, gently descending through medium tall ash and oak. Much of the hiking here is under such a canopy. There are beautiful views of checkerboard farmlands in the valley to the left. The trail crosses a power line and two grassy logging roads before crossing Middle Ridge Rd. at the 6.3-mi. mark. If the season has stripped trees of their foliage, hikers can get a peek at the Big Flat Fire Tower, about 5 mi. ahead on the trail. Just 0.1 mile further, the blue-blazed Rhododendron Trail peels off of the AT on the left. The 1.8-mile loop rejoins the AT less than half a mile to the north. Soon, the AT meets and runs parallel to Middle Ridge Rd. for several hundred yards before joining it for 50 yd. The trail crosses to the left side of the road and starts downhill. At 6.8 mi. the trail arrives at the intersection of Canada Hollow Rd., Means Hollow Rd., and Ridge Rd. This is a much more clearly marked road juncture than the previous one. Means Hollow Rd. is an early exit option to PA 997. There is parking for a half dozen cars.

After the Rhododendron Trail rejoins the AT from the left, the trail begins a steep descent through tall, shady oaks to the locked Milesburn Cabin of the PATC at 7.2 mi. Reservations must be obtained in advance from the club. There is a privy behind the cabin, and a blue-blazed trail to

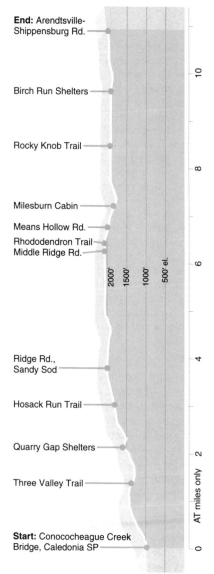

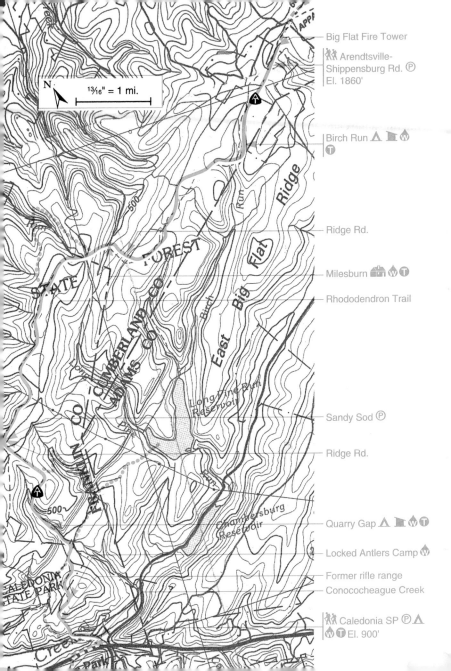

Big Flat Fire Tower

Arendtsville-
Shippensburg Rd. Ⓟ
El. 1860'

Birch Run △ ▰ Ⓦ
Ⓣ

Ridge Rd.

Milesburn ⌂ Ⓦ Ⓣ

Rhododendron Trail

Sandy Sod Ⓟ

Ridge Rd.

Quarry Gap △ ▰ ♠ Ⓣ

Locked Antlers Camp Ⓦ

Former rifle range

Conococheague Creek

Caledonia SP Ⓟ △
Ⓦ Ⓣ El. 900'

the left leads downstream and across Milesburn Rd. 0.2 mi. to a spring. The small stream is picturesque, and pools right in front of the cabin. This is a nice spot to break for lunch on the front porch or around a nearby fire ring if the cabin is unoccupied. If someone is staying at the cabin, follow the AT across the stream and Milesburn Rd. and begin ascending through a pretty, mixed forest of young hemlocks and older oaks for about a quarter mile to several flat, primitive camping areas that are also perfect for lunching.

After the camping flats, the trail ascends steeply. Numerous log water dams serve as steps. At 7.5 mi., cross Ridge Rd. again and pass under a power line. In the next mile there are some primitive but pretty campsites under large hemlocks. At 8.5 mi., the Rocky Knob Trail crosses the AT, which gradually descends through pretty, medium-aged stands of oak and ash. If need be, this is a good place to make up time lost to a long lunch.

The trail crosses a power line right-of-way at 9.0 mi., and the old road-bed of Fegley Rd., which is no longer used. There are some primitive camp-sites here. At 9.7 mi. the trail splits a rolling, grassy clearing occupied by the twin Birch Run Shelters. A privy is behind the shelters on a path that runs between them. The strongly flowing spring is in front, to the left of the trail. The water is very good and worth stopping for, even though there is only 1.0 mi. left to hike. There are also some excellent tenting spots in the area. The AT continues through the clearing and crosses Birch Run in a boggy area where there are plenty of ferns and many downed mossy trees.

At 10.9 mi., the trail crosses Arendtsville-Shippensburg Rd. to a wide field and the parking pull-off. A good way to end this hike is with a side trip to the Big Flat Fire Tower. To reach the tower, turn right off the trail onto Arendtsville-Shippensburg Rd., walk 0.3 mi., and make a left onto Ridge Rd. Pass the radio tower and come to the fire tower on the left. There are fine views of valley farms and the treed ridges of the Michaux State Forest from the top.

Miles N	NORTH	Elev. (ft./m)	Miles S
	Total: 11.2 mi. with access on park trail		
10.9	**End:** Arendtsville-Shippensburg Rd., parking along road at trailhead, 2.5 mi. from PA 233.	1850/564	0.0
9.7	**Birch Run Shelters,** spring, privy.		1.2
9.0	**Power line** crossing.		1.9
8.5	Cross **Rocky Knob Trail.**		2.4
7.2	**Milesburn Cabin,** trail to **spring.**		3.7
6.8	**Means Hollow Rd.,** early exit option.		4.1
6.4	**Rhododendron Trail** loop, first intersection.	2000/610	4.5
6.3	**Middle Ridge Rd.,** AT parallels, joins, then crosses road and heads downhill.		4.6
3.7	**Sandy Sod,** confusing intersection; early exit option.		7.2
3.6	AT begins following **Ridge Rd.** for 0.1 mi.		7.3
2.9	**Hosack Run Trail** splits off on R.		8.0
2.2	**Quarry Gap Shelters.**	1575/480	8.7
1.8	Former **Locked Antlers Camp,** active spring.		9.1
1.6	Former **rifle range.**		9.3
1.4	**Three Valley Trail** joins AT.		9.5
0.0	**Start AT miles:** Conococheague Creek Bridge.	900/274	10.9
0.3	Access: **Old AT** from overnight hiker parking in Caledonia SP, on US 30.		0.3

SOUTH

HIKE #7
South Mt. Ridge to Pine Grove Furnace State Park

Map: KTA Pa. Section 13

Route: From Big Flat along South Mt. Ridge to Pine Grove Furnace SP

Recommended direction: S to N

Distance: 8.4 mi.

Elevation +/-: 1850 to 900 ft.

Effort: Easy

Day hike: Yes

Overnight backpacking hike: No

Duration: 5 hr.

Early exit option: At 3.9 mi., Woodrow Rd.

Natural history features: Tumbling Run Game Preserve; Sunset Rocks overlook

Social history features: Camp Michaux prisoner of war camp; Ironmaster's Mansion Underground Railroad stop

Trailhead access: *Start:* Take PA Turnpike (I-76) to Carlisle exit (16), then PA 34S to I-81S, go 10.0 mi. to PA 233S, then 20.0 mi. to Arendtsville-Shippensburg Rd., turn R. Pull-off on R in 2.5 mi. Parking for 6 cars at signed AT trailhead. (For alternate route see Hike #6.) *End:* From I-81, take PA 233S to Pine Grove Furnace SP. (For alternate route see Hike #8.) Parking for AT hikers is available in the lot on Quarry Rd., next to the old iron furnace, a pavilion, and rest rooms. Register at park office if parking overnight.

Camping: Anna Michener Memorial Cabin of the PATC (reservations required); Toms Run shelters; numerous primitive campsites

This section of the AT is steeped in history. Hessian troops in the 1700s, escaped slaves in the 1800s, and Nazi submarine commanders earlier in this century all passed this way. Today it is a pleasant day hike, starting atop the plateaulike ridge of South Mt. in an open, grassy field dotted with young pines and wildflowers in summer. By the time the mostly downhill ramble ends, hikers will have gleaned rare peeks at historical curiosities from two wars and what was literally, if clandestinely, the nation's first civil rights movement.

From the well-signed trailhead and a good staging area in a grove of young pines, the AT meanders through the grassy roadside field for approximately 0.3 mi. before breaking into the woods through a stand of young elms. The trail soon crosses two prongs of a small stream on rocks. It descends easily through some rocky sections before entering a boggy area on wooden planks set on the spongy black dirt. At 1.1 mi., the AT crosses the former Dead Woman Hollow Rd., now closed but still a popular route with snowmobilers. There are good views of Mt. Holly and Long Mt. here, and on a long, gentle descent of more than 0.5 mi., during which the AT joins a gated, one-lane road of crushed shale. At 1.9 mi. a blue-blazed trail to the right leads 0.2 mi. to the locked Anna Michener Memorial Cabin. Reservations must be obtained from the PATC in advance. The AT itself leaves the crushed stone roadway a short way past the side trail, bearing to the left and descending into a young forest of ash and maple—prime deer habitat. Each time we've hiked here, we've seen several.

At 2.6 mi. cross a gated entrance road to the private Tumbling Run Game Preserve. No camping or fires are permitted along this section of the AT, which runs poker straight and gradually downhill through young, dense woods along the boundary of the preserve. A gentle uphill stretch of trail brings hikers into older oaks and tulip-poplars before crossing Woodrow Rd. at 3.9 mi., where there are fine vistas of farms and forest to the left, and limited parking for an early exit from the hike southeast to PA 233. Just after the road crossing there are good primitive campsites to the right of the trail. If you choose to camp here, expect company from locals who park up on the road and tote coolers and elaborate camping paraphernalia down to the sites.

The trail continues downhill through a series of switchbacks with sometimes tricky footing. It is best to pay attention to your next step and not

Jack-in-the-pulpit

look around, and the gurgle of a tumbling stream off the trail to the left fills the senses well enough. Its music crescendos until the trail meets and crosses this unnamed tributary of Toms Run on stepping stones.

At 4.9 mi., the blue-blazed Sunset Rocks Trail peels off to the right. The 2.4-mi. loop ascends Little Rocky Ridge and some large quartzite boulders striped with white quartz bands. It then runs parallel to the AT along the fence line of Camp Michaux—the former Revolutionary War work farm, former Civilian Conservation Corps camp, former Presbyterian Church camp, and former World War II prisoner of war camp. (See "What's a Nazi Submarine Commander doing on the AT?".)

Like the state forest that surrounds the camp and through which the trail passes, the camp was named for André Michaux, a famous French botanist who explored the region in the late 18th century at the behest of King Louis XVI, with an eye to gathering plants for the royal gardens. During his eleven years in America, Michaux traveled extensively in the Appalachians, discovering and naming many plants.

At 5.0 mi., cross the many prongs of Toms Run on a wooden footbridge and reach the two new Toms Run shelters on the right. A picnic table is in front, with spring and privy to the rear and left of the trail. The forest is wide open here, with little brush under the tall, leathery-leaved chestnut oaks. The area around the shelters can be boggy on occasion, leading to mosquito problems. The trail out of the shelter area, along an old logging road, is usually wet from a multitude of seeps, which produce some standing water hazards and boot-sucking mud that should be skirted if possible.

At 6.0 mi., turn right onto Michaux Rd., also called High Mt. Rd. Follow the dirt and gravel road downhill for 0.2 mi. In the summer, impenetrable wild grapevines and brush hide the campsite, which served as a work camp for Hessians captured during the Revolutionary War and a prisoner-of-war camp for Germans and Japanese during World War II. A hand-carved stone plaque commemorating the wartime use is located several hundred yards to the right down a gated road into the camp area. The AT turns left off Michaux Rd. and passes two large pines near an old stone wall—the only thing still standing from a barn built by the Hessian prisoners, who were often loaned to locals to help with farm work. The AT joins an unnamed mountain road and follows it under some impressively old oaks and American beech, many 100 ft. tall. The trail leaves the road to the right, down a short, steep, erosion-rutted hill to Toms Run. There is a 50-yd., unblazed side trail to the right that leads to Half Way Spring.

The AT at 7.0 mi. passes the former Pine Grove Furnace Cabin of the PATC on the left, now a park ranger residence. Behind the cabin is the blue-blazed Wildcat Rocks Trail, which leads 2.1 mi. to Ridge Rd. and the white quartz-veined quartzite outcropping for which the trail was named. After the blue-blazed Sunset Rocks Trail loop rejoins from the right at 7.2 mi., the AT crosses a footbridge, and turns through a pretty, mixed stand of young hemlock and older oak and beech. There are plenty of primitive campsites here, and ample opportunities to soak tired feet in the creek. The trail meanders across a small, unnamed tributary and past old charcoal flats that provided fuel for the Pine Grove iron furnace, which began operating in 1764 and continued producing cast-iron products such as ten-plate stoves, fireplace backs, iron kettles

What's a Nazi Submarine Commander Doing on the AT?

One of the best-kept secrets of World War II was that there were Nazi submarine commanders living in the hills of Pennsylvania along the AT. They were joined by German tank commanders from Rommel's Afrika Korps, the inventor of the German buzz bomb, and even a few officers from the Japanese Imperial Army.

It is still not widely known that they were all held as the unwilling guests of the U.S. Army at Camp Michaux, a prisoner-of-war stockade that housed up to 1500 from 1942 until the end of the war in 1945. The camp, on the AT two miles west of Pine Grove Furnace State Park, was a perfect place to keep the highest-ranking war prisoners. It was close to the Carlisle Army Post and just two hours from Washington, D.C. Most importantly, it was isolated and could be kept a secret. Hikers passing the camp today will vouch for that. Heavy underbrush, wild grapevines, and tall trees all combine to screen the former prison camp from curious hikers passing on Michaux Road. Because it was kept a secret, very little information is available about its operation.

In 1972 the camp became part of the Michaux State Forest and all the old buildings were removed. Still, there are signs for those willing to look. The high watchtower that once overlooked the prison is gone, but the base of the tower remains. And German words and names are etched into concrete bridges and steps constructed by the war prisoners throughout the camp.

Strangely, the Nazi prisoners were not the first Germans forced to labor there. Almost 200 years earlier the area was known as the Bunker Hill Farm, and was used as a prisoner work site during the Revolutionary War. After the Battle of Trenton in 1776, in which Gen. George Washington defeated British and Hessian troops near the present capital of New Jersey, Hessian prisoners were taken to the Carlisle Army Post. From there they were issued to various farms as workers. An enormous stone barn that once stood where the AT turns off Michaux Road was probably built by the Hessian prisoners. The one stone wall of the barn still standing, and easily visible from the trail, closely resembles the old Hessian-built guardhouse at the Carlisle Army Post. Now, use of the former prison camp grounds is shared by the United Presbyterian Church and the United Church of Christ.

and military supplies for more than 100 years.

The trail joins an old woods road at 7.7 mi. It passes several privately owned cottages on the left that border Pine Grove Furnace SP on the way to PA 233, a paved and lined blacktop at 8.2 mi. The trail turns left and follows PA 233 for about 100 yd. before branching off to the right on a park road that passes in front of the Ironmaster's Mansion. This large stone and brick building with an end-to-end front porch sits on a rise to the left of the trail. Now operated by the American Youth Hostel, the mansion, which dates to colonial times, was once a stop on the Underground Railroad for fleeing slaves. Ask the hostel manager to show you the false floor in a first-floor closet and the space below where the slaves hid when marshals came calling. The mansion is a good place to overnight after day hikes in the area. Phone 717-486-7575 for information.

Next to the mansion is the park store, which, in addition to having a good assortment of eats and treats, is where hikers going end to end on the AT can join the Half-Gallon Club. Membership is open to all who have developed enough of an appetite during their hike from Georgia or Maine to eat a half gallon of Hershey's ice cream in one sitting. Dues are usually a headache or a stomachache (and the price of the ice cream), but the hungriest hikers do get to keep the nifty wooden spoon they've used to scoop their way through the frozen

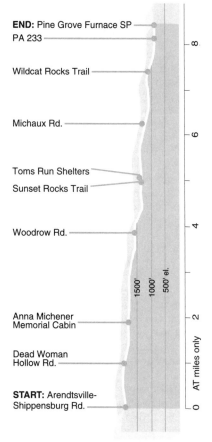

treat. Day-trippers might want to limit themselves to a cone, which they can lick as they follow the trail into the park and in front of the old iron furnace. The parking lot for hikers' cars is on the left, just beyond the furnace, and close enough that if you ordered a double scoop at the store you'll still be working on your cone when you arrive at your car.

Pine Grove
Furnace SP ⚠ Ⓟ🅆🆃
El. 900'

Ironmaster's
Mansion 🏛
PA 233

Half Way Spring 🅦

Camp Michaux 🏛

Toms Run ⚠ ◼🅦🆃

Woodrow Rd.

Anna Michener
Memorial Cabin 🏠

Tumbling Run Game
Preserve

Dead Woman
Hollow Rd.

Arendtsville-
Shippensburg Rd. Ⓟ
El. 1850'

SOUTH MOUNTAIN STATE

SCENIC

Little
Rocky Ridge

Mountain

Hill

400

NATIONAL

Big

TUMBLING RUN
GAME PRESERVE

APPALACHIAN

600

Mountain 400

233

233

Creek

Mountain

N

15/16" = 1 mi.

Ridge

Miles N	NORTH	Elev. (ft./m)	Miles S
8.4	**End:** Pine Grove Furnace SP on PA 233, hiker parking lot.	900/274	0.0
8.3	**Pine Grove Furnace SP** store, home of Half-Gallon Club; **Ironmaster's Mansion.**		0.1
8.2	**PA 233;** AT joins for 100 yd. then branches R.		0.2
7.3	**Brook** crossing.		1.1
7.0	**Wildcat Rocks Trail.**		1.3
6.8	**Half Way Spring.**		1.6
6.3	**Old stone barn foundation.**		2.1
6.2	**Camp Michaux.**		2.2
6.0	**Michaux Rd. (High Mt. Rd.).**		2.4
5.0	**Toms Run Shelters,** spring, and privy.		3.4
4.9	**Sunset Rocks Trail.**		3.5
3.9	**Woodrow Rd.,** early exit option and view.		4.5
2.6	**Tumbling Run Game Preserve.**		5.8
1.9	**Anna Michener Memorial Cabin** side trail.		6.5
1.1	**Dead Woman Hollow Rd** (closed).		7.3
0.0	**Start:** Arendtsville-Shippensburg Rd., parking along the road, 2.5 mi. from PA 233.	1850/579	8.4

SOUTH

Pine Grove Furnace State Park to Sheet Iron Rd.

Map: KTA Pa. Sections 11 & 12

Route: From Pine Grove Furnace SP along Mountain Creek, up Piney Mt., across Tagg Run, up Trents Hill, to PA 94 and Sheet Iron Rd.

Recommended direction: S to N

Distance: 11.0 mi.

Elevation +/-: 900 to 1450 to 625 to 800 ft.

Effort: Moderate

Day hike: Yes

Overnight backpacking hike: No

Duration: 6 hr.

Early exit option: At 6.4 mi., blue-blazed trail to Hunters Run Rd.; at 8.9 mi., PA 34

Natural history feature: Pole Steeple overlook

Social history features: Pine Grove iron furnace; Fuller Lake; Ironmaster's Mansion (see Hike #7)

Other features: AT midpoint, Green Mt. General Store

Trailhead access: *Start:* Take PA Turnpike (I-76) to Carlisle exit (16), then PA 34S 10.0 mi. Turn R on Hunters Run Rd., go 7.0 mi. to Pine Grove Furnace SP. (For alternate route see Hike #7.) Parking for AT hikers is available in the lot on Quarry Rd., next to the old iron furnace, a pavilion, and rest rooms. Register at park office if parking overnight. *End:* From I-76 take Carlisle exit to PA 34; go S 1.5 mi. through Mt. Holly Springs to PA 94 on L at Y; go 1.0 mi. to signed AT trailhead. There is parking for 3 or 4 cars along the road, or continue 0.1 mi. and turn L onto Sheet Iron Rd. Parking for 6 cars in pull-off at AT trailhead in 0.1 mi.

Camping: Pine Grove Furnace SP campground; Mt. Creek Campground (0.7 mi. off AT); Tagg Run Shelters

O n the hump of Piney Mt., hikers will pass the AT's nominal midpoint. It is marked with a sign and draped with the hopes of all the end-to-enders who started the hike of 2150-plus mi. in Georgia or Maine. The 8-ft.-tall sign was fashioned out of Pennsylvania poplar and erected in 1987 by Chuck Wood (trail name: Woodchuck) of Norristown, who thru-hiked in 1985. Day-trippers

won't feel either the exhilaration or the foot-weary fatigue of hikers who reach the milepost after hitting the trail every day for three months. But even hikers who have pulled on their boots less than 2 mi. down the mountain in Pine Grove Furnace SP can feel the energy and see the aura around the marker.

"It's where we start counting the miles backwards," said 1995 thru-hiker

David Heinstadt, known on the trail as Red Fox. Because of trail relocations that have changed the length of the trail, the marker has become more symbolic and less accurate over the years. There has been semi-serious talk of putting the signpost on wheels and moving it each year to reflect actual mileage, but for most of those with more than 1000 mile under their boots, it's close enough where it is. The signpost's thru-hiker register has entertaining and illuminating entries, such as one by Ramblin' Man, who in September 1996 left the cheery message: "Hooray, halfway! Hope it just keeps getting better for everyone." Or the one by Flash, who wrote in hopeful script, "I hear the second half is easier than the first."

To start this hike, pick up the AT in Pine Grove Furnace SP on Quarry Rd., next to the remains of the old iron furnace, built in 1764 and placed on the National Register of Historic Places in 1977. Firearms used in the Revolutionary War and the Civil War were made from iron produced by the furnace and fashioned at nearby Laurel Forge.

Just out of the hikers' parking lot, turn left onto Quarry Rd. and follow it for 50 ft. before branching left again onto a wide footpath of crushed stone that follows the old railroad line on the left side of Mountain Creek. The rail line once connected the furnace to iron strip mines along the base of Piney Mt. This is an easy, flat path under a canopy of tall white pine and oak. About 0.4 mi. along,

the AT passes a rest room and water fountain, and then a concession stand, open in summer for swimmers at Fuller Lake.

The lake was created when groundwater filled the main iron ore pit for the Pine Grove furnace shortly after the Civil War. If you take a dip, take care. The hole left from 100 years of mining is 90 ft. deep, and the lake's emerald green water is extremely cold. Pay attention to the depth markers extending out from the sandy beach. They indicate rapid drop-offs.

The AT crosses Mountain Creek via a footbridge (0.6 mi.) and turns immediately left onto another footbridge over the outflow at the east end of the lake. Sunfish feed hungrily in the shallow corner near the outflow and provide good sport for hikers who have packed their fly rods. For approximately the next mile, the trail runs on the old railroad bed through a boggy area between Mountain Creek and the base of Piney Mt. Tall elm, oak, and hemlock shade the trail, and there are many places along the creek to picnic, wade, or fish for stocked brown, brook, and rainbow trout.

The AT leaves the creek and the park at a yellow gate (1.3 mi.) that bars vehicle access to the rail bed from a paved road that ends at the gate. The trail goes around the gate and turns right, ascending, sometimes steeply, old Petersburg Rd., which is no longer used by vehicles and quickly deteriorates to the point

They Called Him Crazy

Like ghost sightings, Earl Shaffer's fleeting appearances on the AT cause excitement. They are noted in trail registers over the 45 miles from Pine Grove Furnace to Duncannon, and talked about whenever hikers meet in shelters or on the trail in those segments. "Hey, we saw Earl yesterday" is as common a greeting on the trail as "They were hitting yesterday" is among fishermen on the trout streams the trail crosses. Both comments spark hope for being in the right place at the right time. Both often leave that hope unfulfilled.

In 1948, Shaffer became the first person to hike the eleven-year-old trail from Georgia to Maine. In 1965, he became the first to complete hikes in both directions, strolling from Maine to Georgia in 99 days. He is to the AT what Babe Ruth is to baseball: a man who changed the game. Now in his late seventies, Shaffer lives near the trail, on a small farm in York Springs that he shares with goats and cats. Though something of a recluse, he still frequently day-hikes on the trail and usually enjoys encountering hikers who know his name.

He says his trail name is "Crazy One," and jokes that the second man to thru-hike the trail was "crazy too."

In the years after his first thru-hike —which kindled widespread public interest in the AT—Shaffer joined trail pioneers Benton MacKaye (who first proposed the trail in 1921) and Myron H. Avery, founding president of the Potomac Appalachian Trail Club, on frequent trips to Washington to lobby for trail protection. His journal of the first thru-hike, *Walking with Spring,* though out of print, remains a trail classic.

In the years after his thru-hikes, Shaffer helped relocate many segments of the trail off the roads that he walked to fields and forested areas. He knows the trail well and freely imparts hiking wisdom. He favors a pith helmet for hiking because "it's cool, it's a hard hat to protect you from tree branches, and it sheds rain and shields you from the sun." He also advises, "Be careful late. After a full day of hiking, when you're tired, that's when accidents happen."

Even in short, chance meetings with Shaffer on the trail or at the Green Mountain General Store, it is evident he has used his chosen solitude and simple lifestyle wisely. He is well spoken on a variety of subjects from gardening to politics to beekeeping to religion. He is a poet and a composer, and although he's shy about it, friends say he plays a mean guitar.

at which it couldn't be. Stay alert for deer and red fox, which are often seen along the trail here, especially at dusk near a small, open field.

The AT climbs the mountain for more than a mile, and about a third of the way up—approximately 1.8 mi. from the start of the hike—is the trail's midpoint marker. The joke at the halfway point is that "it's all downhill from here." It may look that way for hikers traveling north to south, but for northbounders that notion is dispelled with their first step, as the AT continues to ascend through a tunnel of mountain laurel, the Pennsylvania state flower, which blooms through June at various elevations.

At 2.7 mi. the trail crosses Old Forge Rd. A blue-blazed side trail to the left leads 0.5 mi. to Pole Steeple, a famous, rugged thrust of quartzite cliffs that affords views of Fuller and Laurel lakes in the park. The sheer cliffs, which angle up toward the valley, are riddled with the remains of worm tube fossils and bear the patterns of the dark tubes, which are the size and shape of soda straws. The Steeple, as it is known, is a favorite of climbers but may stress those with vertigo. Parents are advised to supervise children closely.

About 100 yd. after the Pole Steeple left turn, the AT itself dips to the left through quartzite and sandstone outcroppings. The going is rocky, and hikers must skip from one big green chunk of sandstone to the next under tall oaks. In wet weather the rocks can be slippery, especially on the hill-side traverses up to the Piney Mt. summit of 1450 ft. at 3.8 mi. Pick your way through this half mile and take your time. This is not an area where you should try to make up minutes lost to a late start or a long bathroom break. There are also some old charcoal flats (see Hike #5) from the iron furnace days. Fire rings mark a more recent use by campers. At 4.0 mi., an old trail enters from the right. In the summer, this section is notable for ferns, mountain laurel, and blueberry bushes; in the fall, for the sound of acorns raining from the tall oaks.

After gently descending for about a mile under an oak canopy, the AT turns right at 5.0 mi. and starts uphill where a blue-blazed trail comes in from the left. The woods are enchanting here, with lots of mountain laurel, sassafras, and leafy chestnut. In the fall, be on the lookout for tree toads the size of a quarter that are not always fast enough to hop out of the way of boots.

Cross Limekiln Rd. at 6.1 mi. To the right it leads 2.5 mi. to the village of Goodyear. To the left 0.9 mi. is Hunters Run Rd. At 6.4 mi. a blue-blazed trail leads downhill 0.7 mi. to the Mountain Creek Campground, accessible by vehicle from Hunters Run Rd. This is a good early exit option. The privately owned campground offers cabins, tent sites, showers, a laundromat, and a store where hikers can buy pizza, subs, sandwiches, drinks, and ice cream. It is open all year.

On the AT, continue a gentle descent to Tagg Run. Pass a blue-blazed trail at 7.4 mi. to a spring 0.2 mi. on the left, and some primitive campsites on the right shortly thereafter. At 7.5 mi., a blue-blazed trail to the right, just before the wooden footbridge over Tagg Run, leads 0.2 mi. to the Tagg Run shelters with a privy and another spring 100 ft. beyond. The two shelters are each able to sleep five hikers. This is a good spot for a lunch stop. But do not drink from the creek, which appears pristine but is polluted upstream by agricultural runoff and feces from wading livestock.

Cross the bridge over Tagg Run and hike through an area where maple and white pine are older. Sassafras, with its silky, mitten-shaped leaves, abounds. The roots are good for brewing tea, and the leaves can be crushed and put up under your hat or rubbed on your face and neck to keep bugs away. Native Americans used this repellent — plus, it smells better than deet.

Cross blacktopped Hunters Run Rd. at 7.9 mi. and after a short walk downhill, turn right onto an abandoned railroad bed that splits a swampy area and is shaded by tall white pine. In hot weather, the sassafras will come in handy here. The rail bed parallels an active rail line no more than 30 yd. to the right where a freight train will occasionally make an incongruous appearance through the arching pines. The trail emerges from the boggy woods flush with the active rail line and behind a warehouse. Welcome to civ-

ilization and the low point of this hike at 625 ft. Walk along the active tracks for 100 yd., and at 8.9 mi., cross over the active tracks and through a field to PA 34, and early exit option.

If you're ready for food, drink, or a slice of Americana, this is the place for a short detour. Turn right off the trail, which crosses the blacktopped road and turns left, and walk 0.2 mi. along PA 34 to the Green Mt. General Store. There's a big front porch with a bench and rocking chairs, and a picnic table for hikers on the shaded lawn out front. Walk through the store's vintage wood-frame screen door and you'll swear you've traveled back in time fifty years. There are old tinted postcards, outdated calendars, and colorized photographs on the walls. Also memorable are the sandwiches, soups, and old-fashioned milkshakes. A hiker register just inside the door is a record replete with hikers' reverent sightings of Earl Shaffer, who in 1948 was the first person to hike the AT end to end, and now lives nearby (see "They Called Him Crazy").

If local flavor or a great chocolate milkshake doesn't interest you, skip the side trip and follow the AT across PA 34 and to the left over a short highway bridge from which trout can usually be seen in the tiny stream below. Turn right onto the signed Appalachian Trail Rd. Within 50 ft. the AT disappears into the woods on the left for the winding ascent up Trents Hill. At 9.7 mi. and the top of the hill, bear left through an area thick with sassafras and blueberry bushes and begin the mile-long descent to PA 94 at 10.7 mi. There is parking for three or four cars along this paved road. To the left 2.5 mi. is the village of Mt. Holly Springs. Follow the AT across PA 94 and through a young oak woods to Sheet Iron Rd. at 11.0 mi., where wide turnouts at the trailhead offer space for up to half a dozen cars.

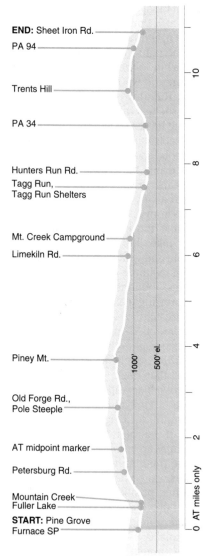

Sheet Iron Rd. ℗
El. 800'

PA 94

Trents Hill

Green Mt. General Store

PA 34

Hunters Run Rd.

Tagg Run ▲ ◣ ◍ ⊤

Mountain Creek ℗ ▲ ◍ ⊤

Piney Mt. summit,
El. 1450'

Pole Steeple, V ❧

AT midpoint marker

Mountain Creek

Fuller Lake iron furnace
🏛

Ironmaster's Mansion 🏛

Pine Grove Furnace
SP ℗ ▲ ◍ ⊤ El. 900'

N

¹³⁄₁₆" = 1 mi.

Miles N		NORTH	Elev. (ft./m)	Miles S
11.0	**End:** Sheet Iron Rd., parking at trailhead, 2.1 mi. from Mt. Holly Springs.		800/244	0.0
10.7	Cross **PA 94.**			0.3
9.0	Begin ascent of **Trents Hill.**			2.0
8.9	Cross **PA 34,** an early exit option; leads in 0.2 mi. to **Green Mt. General Store.**		625/191	2.1
8.8	Cross **railroad tracks.**			2.2
7.9	**Hunters Run Rd.**			3.1
7.5	**Tagg Run; Tagg Run shelters,** privy, and spring.			3.5
6.4	Trail (0.7 mi.) to **Mt. Creek Campground** and early exit option.			4.6
6.1	Cross **Limekiln Rd.**			4.9
5.0	**Turn R;** blue-blazed trail on L.			5.7
4.0	**Old trail** enters AT.			7.0
3.8	**Piney Mt.** summit.		1450/442	9.2
2.7	**Old Forge Rd.;** side trail (0.5 mi) to **Pole Steeple** overlook.			8.3
1.8	**AT midpoint marker.**			9.2
1.3	Begin ascent along old **Petersburg Rd.**			9.7
0.6	**Mountain Creek** footbridge.			10.4
0.5	**Fuller Lake.**			10.5
0.0	**Start:** Pine Grove Furnace SP on PA 233; park in hikers' overnight parking lot.		900/274	11.0

SOUTH

Center Point Knob and Boiling Springs

Map: KTA Pa. Sections 11 & 12

Route: From Sheet Iron Rd. to Rocky Ridge, Whiskey Spring, Little Rocky Ridge, and Center Point Knob, across Yellow Breeches Creek to Boiling Springs at PA 174

Recommended direction: S to N

Distance: 8.3 mi.

Elevation +/-: 800 to 1150 to 1210 to 450 ft.

Effort: Easy

Day hike: Yes

Overnight backpacking hike: No

Duration: 5 hr.

Early exit option: At 2.5 mi., Whiskey Spring Rd.

Natural history features: Rocky Ridge; Whiskey Spring; northern terminus of Blue Ridge Mts.; Campbell Spring; Yellow Breeches Creek; Boiling Springs

Social history features: Onetime mid-point of the AT at Center Point Knob; Children's Lake; Carlisle Iron Works

Other features: Boiling Springs pool; ATC Regional Headquarters in Boiling Springs

Trailhead access: *Start:* Take PA Turnpike (I-76) E or W to Carlisle exit (16) onto PA 34S. Go through Mt. Holly Springs and 1.5 mi. to L at Y onto PA 94, and 1.0 mi. to where AT crosses, then 0.1 mi. to L on Sheet Iron Rd., 0.1 mi. to AT trailhead. Parking in pull-off for 6 cars. *End:* From Carlisle exit on I-70 take PA 34S 5.0 mi. to L onto PA 174 into Boiling Springs (3.0 mi.). Parking near iron furnace at S end of Children's Lake.

Camping: Alec Kennedy Shelter

This rollercoaster hike rides up and down the northern end of the Blue Ridge Mts., which the AT has been following since Georgia, then smooths out with some field hiking through the agrarian Cumberland Valley. The contrast from woodlands to rocky outcroppings to lowlands gives hikers ample opportunity to experience a great variety of geology on a relatively short and easy hike. An added bonus is the dictionary-definition-quaint town of Boiling Springs, punctuating the end of this hike like some scaled-down, Victorian-era Oz.

The AT crosses busy, blacktopped PA 94 2.5 mi. south of Mt. Holly Springs. There is parking for two or three cars along the road at the trailhead, but it's better to drive another 100 yd. down the hill, turn left onto Sheet Iron Rd., and park in a pull-off area where the trail crosses. After the crossing, which is direct, the AT parallels the road for 200 yd. before bearing right into a spindly woods of oak, ash, and maple. The hiking here is flat and easy, with few rocks to grab at hikers' boots.

At 0.5 mi., the trail crosses a wooden footbridge over a small, unnamed brook. The trail near the brook is usually wet and muddy. Wooden planks track it through this boggy area where the earth is loamy black and bugs can be bad in spring and summer. There are some crab apple trees mixed with hemlocks before a second creek crossing at 0.8 mi. Look closely and you can usually find small trout trying to blend in with the gravelly creek bed around the footbridge. To fish for these you will have to approach on your belly, as any shadow causes them to dart into hiding.

The trail passes through a stand of white pines and an understory of sassafras before crossing Old Town Rd. at 1.2 mi. There are many blueberry bushes here and the trailside brush briefly lives up to its name. Long pants or gaiters come in handy through this area. The trail soon starts its ascent of Rocky Ridge, which lies on a geologic fault line, through a series of switchbacks. The hump's namesake sandstone is actually a help, with the rocks serving as a natural staircase up the incline, which tops out at 1150 ft., 1.6 mi. into the hike. There is a view of valley farms, and there are nice spots to have a late brunch or early lunch.

The AT follows the descending ridge east for almost a mile, passing through a maze of massive sandstone and quartzite jumbles in slots so narrow that hikers toting big backpacks sometimes must pass through sideways, although day hikers with rucksacks should not have much trouble. The boulders are so massive they weather by exfoliation or scaling. The result is an area of rounded boulders rather than the blocky formations more typical of the quartzite seen on other parts of the AT in Pennsylvania. Pay close attention to the trail blazes on trees and rocks. Handholds are recommended for some of the scrambles over the green, lichen-mottled rocks, which make for interesting, if not speedy, hiking. There are no good views directly from the trail in this section, but 50 yd. to the left are rocky cliffs overlooking valley farms and the town of Mt. Holly Springs that offer many vantage points.

At the east end of the ridge, the AT begins a gentle descent to Whiskey Spring Rd. through a tall oak forest. In the fall this section can be treacherous because of thousands of brown and yellow acorns the size of shooting marbles littering the trail. At 2.5 mi., the trail drops onto Whiskey Spring Rd., an early exit option with parking along the road near the spring. The strong, piped spring has two outlets, the first directly across the road. The AT follows the road to the left for 30 yd. where the spring again emerges next to wooden steps that the AT follows up and off the road. There is parking for four or five cars along the gravel road at several pull-offs near the spring. If you spend any time here, you're sure to see some local folks stop to fill up water jugs. Just up the stairs, approximately 50 yd. off the road, there are some big rocks, downed trees, and a campfire ring on level ground—a primo lunch stop. The Mason-Dixon Trail System crosses here on a blue-blazed route.

The AT ascends sometimes steeply about 350 vertical ft. to Little Rocky Ridge through spindly oak, maple, and cherry trees that prevent hikers from seeing deep into the woods. There are more rock outcroppings at the top of the ridge (elev. 1210 ft.), at 3.2 mi. From there, descend through mostly oak woods on a trail littered with splintered white quartzite. At 3.8 mi. the trail crosses a pipeline clearing that looks like a narrow road and then easily ascends Murphy Hill, also known as Cabin Hill.

Along this section, notice a good number of small American chestnut trees, their 7-in., leathery, canoe-shaped leaves sad reminders of the stately, 100-ft.-tall trees that dominated the mid-Atlantic forests until after the beginning of this century. A fungal blight, introduced into America in 1904 when Chinese chestnut trees were imported for the Bronx Zoo arboretum, killed 99 percent of the chestnuts in the East by 1950. The 10-to-15-ft.-tall trees beside the trail have sprouted from the still-living roots of those trees, but the blight continues and almost always kills the young trees in five to seven years.

From the top of Murphy Hill, the trail descends on a narrow, steep, hill-

Carlisle Iron Furnace

side route that eventually flattens, moving through tulip-poplars and fields of forest ferns before reaching flat, well-used campsites near Little Dogwood Run at 4.7 mi. Cross the small stream on rocks and immediately cross an orange-blazed trail that leads right 1.7 mi. to Boy Scout Camp Tuckahoe. The trail begins ascending Colon Hill, and about 100 yd. up passes a blue-blazed trail to the right that leads 0.2 mi. to the Alec Kennedy Shelter. A privy is in front of the shelter and a good spring is just down the hill. At the top of Colon Hill there are several flat, primitive campsites just before an easy descent.

The AT crosses an old woods road at 5.7 mi. and ascends, sometimes steeply, 0.1 mi. to the blue-blazed White Rocks Ridge Trail on the right. This trail follows the ridge for a hard-hiking mile, before dropping onto Kuhn Rd. in 1.3 mi. Along the ridge it scrambles and slips through quartzite outcroppings that outline South Mt. and mark the end of the Blue Ridge Mts. Geologists estimate the quartzite here is 550 million years old. The mountains themselves formed shortly thereafter when the west coast of South America played a little continental bump-and-run with North America's east coast. Those were the days.

The AT ascends steeply for another 100 yd. to Center Point Knob (5.8 mi.), the original midpoint of the Georgia-to-Maine route. Although a monument noting that historic milepost disappeared long ago, it is not hard to find great views of valley farms. The descent from the Knob is easy, but pay attention when blazes mark a left turn. It is easy to miss, especially when thinking about how pretty the young oak and mulberry forest is here. The trail descends for about 0.5 mi. before it flattens out near Campbell Spring (6.3 mi.) and the site of the former Campbell Spring Shelter. The shelter is gone, but the spring is still usable. The trail passes a number of large holes here, all that is left of iron mines that fed the furnace at Boiling Springs.

At 6.7 mi., the trail breaks out of the trees into a farm field and turns left, along the treeline. Follow the white-blazed, 6-ft.-tall posts that skirt the hay and corn fields. There are barns and silos in the distance and a road along which a handful of houses comprise the rural sprawl of

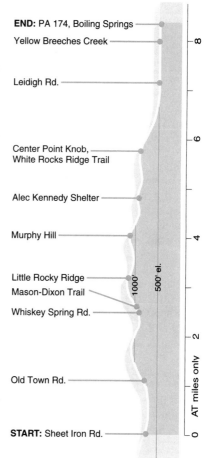

END: PA 174, Boiling Springs

Yellow Breeches Creek

Leidigh Rd.

Center Point Knob,
White Rocks Ridge Trail

Alec Kennedy Shelter

Murphy Hill

Little Rocky Ridge

Mason-Dixon Trail

Whiskey Spring Rd.

Old Town Rd.

START: Sheet Iron Rd.

1000'

500' el.

AT miles only

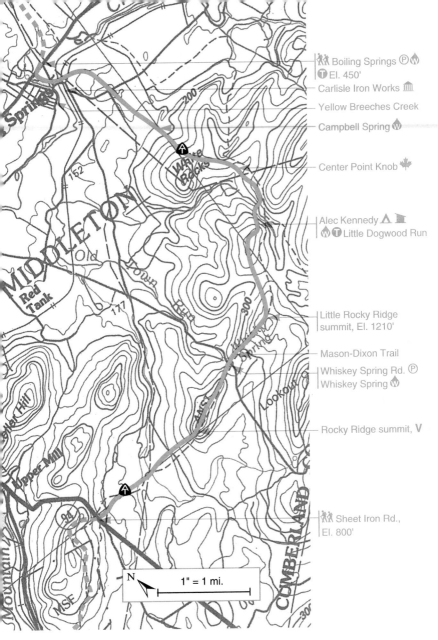

Boiling Springs Ⓟ Ⓦ
Ⓣ El. 450'
Carlisle Iron Works 🏛
Yellow Breeches Creek
Campbell Spring Ⓦ

Center Point Knob 🍁

Alec Kennedy ▲ 🏚
Ⓦ Ⓣ Little Dogwood Run

Little Rocky Ridge
summit, El. 1210'

Mason-Dixon Trail
Whiskey Spring Rd. Ⓟ
Whiskey Spring Ⓦ

Rocky Ridge summit, V

Sheet Iron Rd.,
El. 800'

N   1" = 1 mi.

Boiling Springs. After 0.5 mi. of field hiking, the AT crosses asphalted Leidigh Rd. onto a dirt road, which it follows for 100 yd. before turning left into a field and paralleling the paved road.

This is flat hiking, but it can be treacherous when thick grass covers lumpy, ankle-turning terrain. It can also be very hot in sunny summer weather. Your hat (you do have one) will provide the only shade for 1.5 mi. In spring the rye grass tastes sweet; in summer, the corn grows tall. In the fall, the ears are old and bursting and there are areas where the stalks have been crushed by resting deer. Near the end of the field hiking, the trail passes through big, tumbling raspberry bushes that bear ripe fruit in mid-June. There is an overnight campsite for thru-hikers only, 0.1 mi. to the right, near an old, abandoned farmhouse that is visible from the trail. The Appalachian Trail Conference and the Cumberland Valley Appalachian Trail Management Association provide a portable privy at the campsite from Memorial Day through Labor Day.

At the end of the last field, the AT passes around a yellow gate, and turns right across active railroad tracks and onto a paved road. Follow the road across Yellow Breeches Creek, named for the pants worn by Revolutionary War soldiers, at 8.0 mi. on a one-lane stone arch bridge. The creek is one of the most famous trout streams in Pennsylvania and among the top twenty in the United States.

At the end of the bridge, the township park and pool are on the left side of the road and the trail turns sharply right, dipping off the road and through 100 yd. of trees before crossing a wood footbridge over another arm of the creek. From the footbridge, next to a parking area for twenty cars and the restored Boiling Springs iron furnace, many of the 20-in. trout that make the creek so famous can be viewed in the shallow water. Watch as the ever-present, ever-frustrated fly casters make perfect casts over usually disinterested trout that have seen all their feather and fur offerings before.

The AT goes through the parking lot and passes picturesque Children's Lake (8.2 mi.), in the middle of the town of Boiling Springs. Ducks and Canada geese abound, noisily cruising the lake and its shore. It follows the crushed stone path along the east shore under arching sycamores to the Appalachian Trail Conference Mid-Atlantic Regional Field Office, located in a small, white, wood-frame building on PA 174. There is parking for a few cars in front of the ATC office, but a better place is in the lot next to the iron furnace at Children's Lake.

The trail was rerouted off roads and through the farm fields and Boiling Springs in 1990 (see Hike #10). The town, which has quickly become a hikers' favorite, was founded as an iron industry settlement in the 18th century, only to become a tourist village in the 19th century when the

Boiling Springs Village, Children's Lake

ironworks closed. It has many old Victorian, gingerbread-bedecked homes and is on the National Register of Historic Places. The Boiling Springs Tavern, across PA 174 from the ATC office, is a fine place to stop and replenish fluids lost during the hike. A path next to the tavern parking lot and along a creek feeding the lake leads 200 yd. to the impressive springs after which the town was named. Like other springs in the area, Boiling Springs flows out of the porous limestone that underlies the valley. These have a flow of 24,000 gallons a day and are among the largest in the state. Locals know the hamlet as "Bubbletown," and the high school teams are called "The Bubblers." Take the walk and you'll know why.

Miles N	**NORTH**	Elev. (ft./m)	Miles S
8.3	**End:** ATC Regional Headquarters, parking lot at Carlisle Iron Works in Boiling Springs.	450/137	0.0
8.2	**Children's Lake** in Boiling Springs.		0.1
8.0	**Yellow Breeches Creek.**		0.3
7.2	Cross **Leidigh Rd.**		1.0
6.7	Enter **farm fields.**		1.6
6.3	**Campbell Spring.**		2.0
5.8	**Center Point Knob; White Rocks Ridge Trail.**		2.5
5.7	Cross **woods road.**		2.6
4.8	**Alec Kennedy Shelter,** spring, privy.		3.5
4.7	**Little Dogwood Run.**		3.6
3.8	Cross **pipeline clearing.**		4.5
3.2	**Little Rocky Ridge** summit.	1210/369	5.1
2.6	**Mason-Dixon Trail.**		5.7
2.5	**Whiskey Spring Rd.,** early exit option; **Whiskey Spring.**		5.8
1.6	**Rocky Ridge** summit.	1150/351	6.7
1.2	Cross **Old Town Rd.**		7.1
0.5	Cross brook on **footbridge.**		7.8
0.0	**Start:** Sheet Iron Rd., parking at trailhead, 2.1 mi. from Mt. Holly Springs.	800/244	8.3

SOUTH

Boiling Springs to Scott Farm Trail Work Center

Maps: KTA Pa. Sections 9 & 10

Route: From Boiling Springs through the Cumberland Valley to the Scott Farm Trail Work Center on Bernhisel Rd.

Recommended direction: S to N

Distance: 11.3 mi.

Elevation +/-: 450 to 460 to 425 ft.

Effort: Easy

Day hike: Yes

Overnight backpacking hike: No

Duration: 5½ hr.

Early exit options: More than half a dozen paved roads cross the AT in this section. Parking is available at 3.0 mi. on the N side of PA 74 (York Rd.) next to an old barn foundation.

Natural history features: Follows ironstone ridge that is lowest on the AT; Boiling Springs; Conodoguinet Creek

Social history features: Carlisle Iron Works; town of Boiling Springs on the National Register of Historic Places

Other features: ATC Regional Headquarters in Boiling Springs

Trailhead access: *Start:* Take PA Tpk. (I-76) to Carlisle exit (16) and take PA 34S 5.0 mi. Turn L onto PA 174; go E 3.0 mi. to Boiling Springs. Limited parking in front of ATC Regional Headquarters (register with staff before leaving car) next to Children's Lake, at the PA Fish Commission lot next to the Carlisle Iron Works ruins, or along village streets. *End:* Take I-81 to Wertzville Rd. exit, turn L on PA 114 (New Willow Mill Rd.), go N 0.5 mile, turn L on PA 944. Go W for 3.0 mi., through Donnelleytown, then L onto Bernhisel Rd. for 1.0 mi. to Scott Farm Trail Work Center on R, just before the Bernhisel Bridge. There is parking for a dozen cars in front of the white barn, but make sure to get permission from the caretaker before leaving your vehicle for the day. He can occasionally arrange shuttles to Boiling Springs.

Camping: None allowed, no shelters

N orth of picturesque Boiling Springs, the AT traverses the Cumberland Valley in what can only be described as a beautiful English country walk — along hedgerows, stone walls, and farm fields — with a decidedly American attitude. That is not to say that this easy, 11.3-mi. stroll along and through fields of wheat, corn, and clover, does not hold considerable charm. But the long lowland glide, only recently relocated from blacktop to barn-dotted countryside, is already suffering the intrusions of sprawling subdivisions full of $250,000 houses and vistas spoiled by truck terminals. It is an unhappy and inefficient use of this once uniformly pastoral setting atop some of the world's finest agricultural soils. While hiking along fields and through thickets, there is an unmistakable feeling of being on the edge of something that is just out of sight but not quite out of mind.

Step onto the trail in the village locals call "Bubbletown" (see Hike #9 for details) at the Appalachian Trail Conference Regional Headquarters, located in a low, wood-frame building next to the Children's Lake. There is an outdoor water spigot at the headquarters, and inside a variety of maps and books as well as information on trail conditions. About 20 mi. of the AT was rerouted through Boiling Springs and the Cumberland Valley between 1984 and 1993. The section through Boiling Springs was finished in 1990.

Karen Lutz, the ATC's regional director since 1981, remembers those years of trying to move the trail off a grid of roads and into farm fields as controversial and exciting times. "People were livid. Farmers thought they would lose their farms. We did a huge environmental assessment, and one proposal even included installing 16 miles of sidewalks along the roads," she said. "But we wanted to get the trail off the roads, and in the end we selected a ridge route, the lowest on the AT, that took us into contact with eighty-six landowners."

Property rights and easements were painstakingly acquired to create a section of rural, pastoral hiking unique on the AT. "Unfortunately it isn't that [pastoral] anymore," Lutz said. "It has become instead a greenway through an urban sprawl of housing developments and truck stops. Where once there was opposition to the relocation from realtors, they now advertise properties as adjacent to the AT. At least the route itself is protected in perpetuity."

From the front of the ATC headquarters building the trail turns right onto PA 174N, following the left berm for 0.3 mi. and passing an historical marker for the Carlisle Iron Works, founded in 1762 by John Rigby. Ruins of the old iron furnace still stand 200 yd. down a road to the right, along Yellow Breeches Creek, a flow internationally famous for its large, though finicky, brown trout population (see Hike #9).

The AT leaves the road, turning left into and through a grassy farm field. Here and elsewhere in the valley during the spring and summer and well into fall, you may pick up an unwelcome hitchhiker — the deer tick, a carrier of Lyme disease, which can be fatal if untreated (see "Tick Talk").

In the field, the low, 75-ft.-wide ridge of diabase (basalt) that the AT follows across the valley is visible poking occasionally through the soil. The ridge is harder and less susceptible to erosion than the sedimentary rock (shale, sandstone, limestone, and quartzite) around it, which have weathered away to varying degrees. Follow the white blazes on 6-ft.-tall treated wood posts along the field, then through a young, spindly woods

Tick Talk

Ticks can be as small as the head of a pin, don't weigh a thing, and usually don't cause pain when they bite, but they are the last things you'll want to pick up and carry on the trail.

From spring through fall, ticks are a problem along the AT, especially in Pennsylvania's Cumberland Valley where they will hitch a ride with unsuspecting hikers brushing through thickets and fields of tall grasses. There are two kinds: the wood tick and the deer tick. Both will suck blood.

The wood tick is about twice as large as the deer tick and is dark brown or black with white marks near the head. It can get really ugly — expanding to 300 times its original size when engorged with blood — but isn't as dangerous as its smaller cousin.

The deer tick disproves the old adage that good things come in small packages. The pinhead-sized deer tick is orange-brown with a black spot near the head. It can carry Lyme disease, a bacterial infection that can cause serious problems involving the heart, joints, or nervous system. The disease has been known in the United States since 1975, when an outbreak was diagnosed near Lyme, Connecticut, giving the disease its name.

Because of variable symptoms or even a lack of symptoms the disease is often misdiagnosed. The symptoms may include some or all of the following: a ring-shaped rash, appearing around the bite within four to twenty days, fever, chills, headache, stiffness in joints, weakness, and fatigue. Sometimes there are no symptoms. If detected early, the disease usually responds to antibiotic treatment.

Because of the difficulty of diagnosing the disease, care should be taken to avoid coming into contact with ticks. Precautions include wearing a hat, long-sleeved shirt, and long pants. Tuck pant legs into socks and apply repellents containing permethrin to clothing. If possible, wear light-colored clothing so the dark ticks are more visible. If the weather is too hot for long pants and sleeves, gaiters are helpful to protect legs. When walking keep to the center of the trail and avoid dense or high grass. A hiking stick is helpful to push brush and grass from the path.

Regular "tick checks" should be a part of a hiker's daily and nightly routine. If dogs are along, they should be brushed after hiking. They can pick up hundreds of ticks during a day in the woods and pass them along to you.

If you do pick up any ticks, remove them by grasping the skin with tweezers directly below where the tick is attached. Pull up and straight out, removing the tick and a small bit of skin. Try not to squeeze the tick's body. Wash the bite with soap and water, and apply antiseptic.

of ash, oak, and cherry before turning out along another field and then through a gap in an old stone wall, similar to those found in England and New England.

At 3.0 mi., the AT crosses PA 74 (York Rd.), a good early exit option with parking. Within 200 yd. the trail climbs the first of several stiles—ladders or stairways that allow hikers to get over electrified fences around farm fields. For the next mile the trail moves over stiles, through fields, and along treelines. At 4.0 mi., just before the trail crosses Lisburn Rd., there is a young stand of white-barked paper birches, a species not widely seen in Pennsylvania. At 4.5 mi., the AT crosses Byers Rd., and follows another stone wall. Keep an ear out for mooing cows, whinnying horses, and farm tractors, and an eye out for deer, waving their white tails as they retreat into stands of young oak.

After cresting a rise, the trail crosses PA 641 (Trindle Rd.) at 5.2 mi. In this section, the similarities and contrasts with English country walks are striking. The route passes through rolling fields and along thickets; then, suddenly, housing developments pop out of fields like mushrooms after a spring rain. Sometimes the homes are separated from the trail by rows and rows of corn, sometimes only by bushy breakers of blackberries and honeysuckle at the end of long backyards containing children's swing sets.

At 6.2 mi. the trail crosses a wooden-plank bridge over an un-

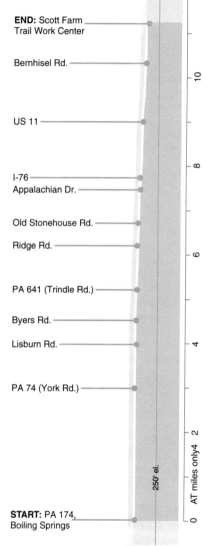

END: Scott Farm Trail Work Center

Bernhisel Rd.

US 11

I-76
Appalachian Dr.

Old Stonehouse Rd.

Ridge Rd.

PA 641 (Trindle Rd.)

Byers Rd.

Lisburn Rd.

PA 74 (York Rd.)

250' el.

AT miles only4

START: PA 174, Boiling Springs

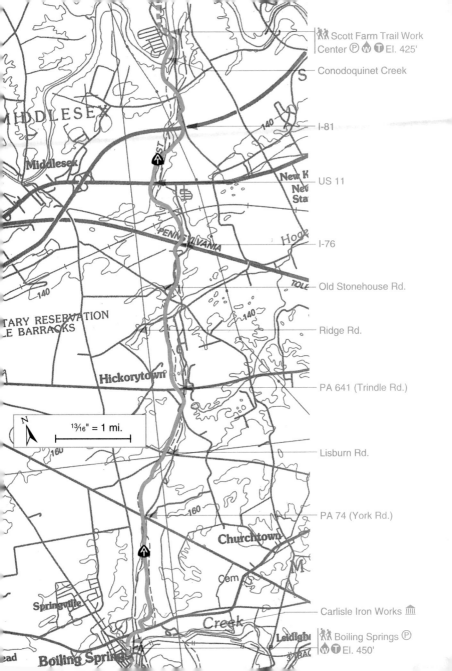

Scott Farm Trail Work Center Ⓟ Ⓦ Ⓣ El. 425'

Conodoquinet Creek

I-81

US 11

I-76

Old Stonehouse Rd.

Ridge Rd.

PA 641 (Trindle Rd.)

Lisburn Rd.

PA 74 (York Rd.)

Carlisle Iron Works 🏛

Boiling Springs Ⓟ Ⓦ Ⓣ El. 450'

MIDDLESEX

Middlesex

PENNSYLVANIA

New K

Ne
Sta

Hoo

TOLE

MILITARY RESERVATION
LE BARRACKS

Hickorytown

¹³⁄₁₆" = 1 mi.

N

Churchtown

Cem

Springville

Creek

Leidigh

Boiling Spring

ead

M

named stream, and then Ridge Rd. at 6.3 mi. before skirting a wetlands area containing enough open water to attract ducks throughout the year. There are good spots to stop for lunch and the waterfowl appreciate bread crusts from sandwiches. The trail crosses Old Stonehouse Rd. at 6.8 mi., climbs over another stile and through a field next to a black iron-fenced rural graveyard shaded by old, arching black walnut trees. The trail crosses Appalachian Dr. at 7.5 mi. and a short while later hikers will begin to hear the buzz of steel-belted highway sounds from the Pennsylvania Tpk., which the trail crosses on a highway overpass at 7.8 mi. The trail soon turns left off the road and along the edge of a field, but the pastoral feeling is diminished by the traffic sounds and the sight of dozens of orange tractor-trailers at a terminal visible just beyond a narrow treeline. The trail crosses a railroad track at 8.0 mi., where there are plenty of raspberries and blackberries in June and orange daylilies in July.

After passing through a young woods dominated by spindly black cherry and across another old rock wall, the AT crosses US 11 (9.0 mi.)

on a footbridge opened in 1990. At 9.8 mi., the trail meets Bernhisel Rd., turns left, and follows the road over I-81 before it dips to the right, crosses the road (10.1 mi.), and enters a farm field, where it runs parallel to the road but 100 yd. below it. In summer sun this stretch can be brutally hot. A hat is recommended, not only for the heat but to shade your eyes as they sweep over a bucolic quilt of fields and farm buildings stretching to the eastern horizon.

The trail recrosses Bernhisel Rd. (10.4 mi.) and, with the help of several stiles, dips down through a succession of well-worn and muddy pastures to the east bank of Conodoguinet Creek. After crossing an unnamed tributary on a wooden footbridge, the trail goes through a wetland on elevated wood planks set on railroad ties. It emerges from the woods onto Bernhisel Rd., turns left and crosses the creek on Bernhisel Bridge (11.3 mi.), on which a wooden sidewalk was built in 1997 for hikers' use. The ATC's Scott Farm Trail Work Center is on the left side of the road on the west end of the bridge.

Miles N	**NORTH**	Elev. (ft./m)	Miles S
11.3	**End:** Scott Farm Trail Work Center at Bernhisel Bridge, parking with caretaker's permission.	425/130	0.0
10.1	Join **Bernhisel Rd.**		1.2
9.0	Cross **US 11** on footbridge.		2.3
8.0	Cross **railroad track.**		3.3
7.8	**PA Tpk. (I-76).**		3.5
7.5	Cross **Appalachian Dr.**		3.8
6.8	Cross **Old Stonehouse Rd.**		4.5
6.3	Cross **Ridge Rd.**		5.0
6.2	Stream crossing on **footbridge.**		5.1
5.2	Cross **PA 641 (Trindle Rd.).**		6.1
4.5	Cross **Byers Rd.**		6.8
4.0	Cross **Lisburn Rd.**		7.3
3.0	Cross **PA 74 (York Rd.),** early exit option.		8.3
0.3	Enter **farm fields.**		11.0
0.0	**Start:** ATC Regional Headquarters, Boiling Springs; parking lot at Carlisle Iron Works.	450/137	11.3

SOUTH

HIKE #11
Cove Mt. to Duncannon

Map: KTA Pa. Sections 9 & 10
Route: From PA 850 over Cove Mt. to Duncannon
Recommended direction: S to N
Distance: 8.7 mi.
Elevation +/-: 650 to 1200 to 300 ft.
Effort: Moderate
Day hike: Yes
Overnight backpacking hike: No
Duration: 5 hr.
Early exit option: At 2.4 mi., unnamed blue-blazed trail
Natural history features: Hawk Rock; Sherman Creek; Little Juniata Creek

Social history features: Thelma Marks Memorial Shelter; Duncannon
Other features: The real start of PA's rocks
Trailhead access: *Start:* Take PA Turnpike (I-76) E or W to Carlisle exit (16), then PA 34S to I-81N to US 11/15N (Exit 21). Go 3.0 mi. to PA 850W, then 10.0 mi. to gravel parking lot on S side (L) of rd. where AT crosses. Room for 10 cars. *End:* Follow US 11/15 along Susquehanna River to Duncannon. Parking in town along the streets.
Camping: Thelma Marks Memorial Shelter; state Game Lands on Cove Mt.

Cove Mt. is where Rocksylvania really begins. It is where hikers start to complain about seeing the Key*stone* State three feet at a time. Because of the rocks, they have to focus on their two feet and where their next footfall will land. At the end of 8.7 mi., the town of Duncannon, despite its faded charm, is a sight for sore feet.

At first, the only rocks hikers see at the beginning of this mountain traverse selected and blazed by Earl Shaffer himself in 1956 are those in the gravel of the new parking lot along PA 850. The Mountain Club of Maryland built and maintains the lot, along with a bulletin board that displays maps and gives emergency

phone numbers and hiker information. From the parking lot, hikers troop through a farm field along PA 850 for 25 yd. to the trail and cross the blacktop road directly into another farm field. The trail is marked on posts in the field and more or less follows the treeline on gently rolling terrain down to a small, wood-plank bridge over a brook and wetlands.

The AT enters a brushy woods at 0.3 mi. The trail then ascends easily up a ravine dominated by some mature oaks and along a small stream. At 0.6 mi., the trail turns right onto a mountain road and opens up. At 0.9 mi., the trail meets and turns left onto another old woods road that is even wider. The hiking is easy in this section, along a mostly dirt path lined with mosses and through a young black cherry forest, as the trail traverses the foot of Cove Mt. before beginning the ascent to the ridge.

The trail crosses a small stream on a bridge of flat-faced logs at 1.3 mi. Approach the crossing cautiously and, if recent rains haven't clouded the flow, you are likely to see some native brook trout under the bridge and in some of the stream's deeper holes. The ascent of Cove Mt. begins soon after the stream crossing and northbound hikers get their first preview of coming distractions—the infamous rocks of Pennsylvania. Sharp, mobile, canted at odd angles, the sandstone and quartzite will continue for the next 90 mi. For thru-hikers that is reason for depression, if not despair. For day hikers, the rocks present a manageable challenge. You'll tip off which you are by how hard you laugh at the old AT joke about how the "ridgerunners" come out every spring with files to sharpen the rocks.

At 2.4 mi., the trail tops the mountain (elev. 1200 ft.) and crosses a pipeline clearing with excellent views of the Susquehanna River to the right, and of farmland and forest off rocks to the left. There is a blue-blazed trail to the left leading to a state Game Commission parking lot in about 1 mi. on a mountain road to Pine Hill Rd. and Dellville. The AT, bearing left, crosses the pipeline. Just before entering the woods, the trail passes some comfortable rocks that

Downy woodpecker

are a good bet for a water break or an early lunch.

When the trail enters the mature oak forest, the hiking is flat, if not easy. Every footfall is a rocky one. Despite the barking dogs in your boots, this is a very quiet hike, away from the roads that hug the river. At 3.9 mi., an unmaintained, blue-blazed trail to the left leads steeply down to a Duncannon Water Co. service road. The AT bears right and ascends to the top of the ridge, where hiking is easier, through a young cherry, white pine, and oak forest.

At 4.9 mi., the trail reaches the Thelma Marks Memorial Shelter, 500 ft. down a blue-blazed trail to the right. The privy is 30 yd. behind the shelter. The spring is 130 yd. further down the mountain, also following the blue blazes. The shelter is one of a half dozen that Shaffer, in 1948 the first man to hike the AT end to end, built or helped to build in the years after his hike. It is also the shelter where thru-hikers Geoff Hood and Molly LaRue were murdered in 1990 by a homeless wanderer who was not a hiker. A lot of hikers seem to stop by the shelter out of curiosity or to pay their respects. Some continue down to the spring for water. Judging by the shelter register, fewer spend the night, even though the hike back up the mountain to the trail is a huffer. There are memorial trees planted for Hood and LaRue near where the shelter trail meets the AT.

Back on the AT, the hiking along the ridge is good, even if the footing is bad along a low band of light-colored sandstone that was deformed by mountain-building pressures from the southeast some 240 million years ago. Hikers should take care not to confuse the irregularly shaped, white Pennsylvania Game Commission boundary markers on trees along the ridge with the AT blazes, which are smaller and rectangular.

The trail passes through a hemlock thicket on the ridge, where there are several nice camping spots, then drops off the ridge through several switchbacks to reach Hawk Rock at 6.7 mi. There are excellent views to the north from several jutting ledges; you can see Sherman Creek, Little Juniata Creek, the Susquehanna River, and the town of Duncannon. Hawks occasionally visit this sandstone outcropping in the fall, but the

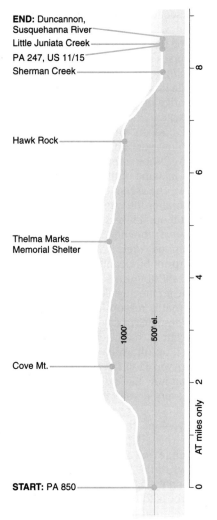

END: Duncannon, Susquehanna River
Little Juniata Creek
PA 247, US 11/15
Sherman Creek

Hawk Rock

Thelma Marks Memorial Shelter

Cove Mt.

START: PA 850

1000'
500' el.

AT miles only

🚶 Duncannon Ⓟ 💧 🚻
El. 300'

PA 274 and US 11/15
Sherman Creek 🍁

Hawk Rock 🍁

Thelma Marks Memorial
⛺ 🏚 💧 🚻

Service road

Cove Mt., El. 1200' 🍁

N ↙   1" = 1 mi.

🚶 PA 850, El. 650'

more habitual users of the updrafts here are turkey vultures.

Enjoy the birds and the distant sights. For the remaining 2.0 mi., hikers with good survival skills will confine their gaze to the location of their next footfall during a steep descent of the mountain. For a short distance, the rocks are arranged in crude steps by a benevolent mountain god and strong, creative trail maintainers. But some of the steps are shaky, while others require big stretches down and can be awkward with a heavy pack. This is not a section in which to try to make up time. Go slow, especially through a rock slide area at 7.0 mi.

At 7.5 mi., after following an old mountain road downhill, the trail branches to the right and begins a short and treacherous ascent over the rocky nose of Cove Mt. The traffic noise from roads along the Susquehanna rises to meet the trail as it rejoins the old mountain road and skirts the backyards of businesses and residences along Sherman Creek in Duncannon.

The AT drops out of the woods, making a sharp left onto Susquehanna Ave., and after passing several residences, crosses Sherman Creek on a bridge. The trail follows that blacktop road to the junction of PA 274, turning right and passing under US 11/15. The AT crosses Little Juniata Creek at 8.6 mi., continuing on North Market St. into the center of Duncannon—once known as "The Jewel of the Susquehanna." Now more of a diamond in the rough, the town is a bit frayed. But its people are friendly and hospitable to hikers. A must-stop for hikers needing to cut trail dust quickly is the bar in the Doyle Hotel, on North Market. The Doyle was built circa 1900 by the Anheuser-Busch Co. and has been a favorite stop for thru-hikers and day hikers since the rocks started poking at their feet.

Miles N	NORTH	Elev. (ft./m)	Miles S
8.7	**End:** US 11/15 at Duncannon, parking in town.	300/91	0.0
8.6	Cross **Little Juniata Creek.**		0.1
8.5	Intersection of **Susquehanna Ave. and PA 274;** underpass of **US 11/15.**		0.2
8.2	Cross **Sherman Creek.**	300/91	0.5
8.0	Reach **paved road.**		0.7
7.5	**Bear R** and ascend.		1.2
7.0	Cross **rock slide.**		1.7
6.7	**Hawk Rock.**		2.0
4.9	**Thelma Marks Memorial Shelter,** privy, spring.		3.8
3.9	Blue-blazed **trail** down to Duncannon Water Co. service road.		4.8
2.4	**Cove Mt.;** blue-blazed trail to early exit option.	1200/366	6.3
1.3	Cross **stream.**		7.4
0.9	**Turn L** onto wider woods road.		7.8
0.6	**Turn R** onto woods road.		8.1
0.3	Enter **woods.**		8.4
0.0	**Start:** PA 850, parking lot at trailhead, 7.5 mi. W of Marysville.	650/198	8.7

SOUTH

Clarks Ferry Bridge to Peters Mt. Ridge

Map: KTA Pa. Sections 7 & 8

Route: From Clarks Ferry Bridge up and along Peters Mt. to PA 225

Recommended direction: S to N

Distance: 7.3 mi.

Elevation +/-: 350 to 1394 to 1200 ft.

Effort: Moderate

Day hike: Yes

Overnight backpacking hike: No

Duration: 5 hr.

Early exit option: None

Natural history features: Peters Mt.; views of the Susquehanna and Juniata rivers

Social history features: Berkeheimer Farm; Rockville Railroad Bridge

Trailhead access: *Start:* Take I-81 N or S to Exit 23; go N on US 22/322, following E side of Susquehanna River to Clarks Ferry Bridge at Duncannon. Just before crossing bridge, follow PA 147 off ramp to R for 300 yd.; parking for a dozen cars along the river. Or cross bridge and make immediate L into Duncannon for limited on-street parking. *End:* 1.0 mi. S of E end of Clarks Ferry Bridge on US 22/322, take PA 325 8.0 mi. to PA 225N (L at T); go up mountain to overnight parking lot for 15 cars on R at crest.

Camping: Clarks Ferry Shelter

A lthough the AT climbs 750 vertical ft. up the stern visage of Peters Mt. and follows its rocky spine for much of this 7.3-mi. hike, it is the long, wide Susquehanna River that dominates. At 444 mi., the Susquehanna is the longest river crossed by the AT (the Connecticut River is second at 411 mi.), and the shallow beauty evidenced in its riffles and jutting rocks has helped it resist the abuses of industry and barges that make so many eastern rivers sluggish, dirty, and old before their time.

Start on the Clarks Ferry Bridge over the Susquehanna. The traffic noise is loud and unrelenting, but the view downriver from the bridge's pedestrian walkway is worth it. The bridge is named for Daniel Clark, who in 1785 operated a ferry service here, the earliest means across the river for nonswimmers. The Clark family continued to operate the ferry until 1828, when the state replaced it with a dam and a highway toll bridge. The structure supported a towpath, which transported canal boats across the river as part of the state's once-extensive canal system. By 1915, the canal system was largely abandoned, and in 1924 the Clarks Ferry Bridge Co. replaced the original structure with another bridge. The present bridge was built in the 1980s.

From the parking area near the east end of the bridge, the AT, which is well signed, crosses PA 147 and active railroad tracks before ducking behind a stone wall and starting to climb Peters Mt. on the first of a series of switchbacks through a mostly oak woods.

In just 0.3 mi. the AT reaches a bench, or level area, and the first of several viewpoints along the ascent, which was designed by Karen Lutz, the ATC regional director, to take full advantage of the wide valley and river vistas. The vantage offers views of the Juniata River joining the Susquehanna and of the rooftops of Duncannon. The AT follows along the bench past an old stone foundation for a mule barn that was part of the Berkeheimer Farm, which burned between 1910 and 1920. The trail goes through a gap in an old stone wall, bears left up the mountain and reaches an old woods road that it follows to the end of the mountain, where to the south there is another good vista of the Susquehanna and another tributary, Sherman Creek. Two switchbacks past the viewpoint there is a signed spring to the left of the trail.

The AT continues climbing on switchbacks through large outcroppings of pink and green sandstone and quartzite. Each provides fine views to the north and south of the Susquehanna, which wraps around both sides of the mountain. The steep hike up is aided in several areas by stairways of rock, arranged by a benevolent nature and York Hiking Club volunteers. By the time the ridgetop is gained at 1.5 mi., the traffic sounds of US 22/322 have mostly faded, although occasionally a six-

White-tailed deer

teen-wheeler coming across the bridge can still be heard.

The trail follows the ridge through woods and over rock outcroppings, and at 2.3 mi. crosses a clearing created by a former power line that provides good views of the river on both sides. At 3.0 mi., a blue-blazed trail leads straight ahead along the ridge to the old Clarks Ferry Shelter, and the AT leaves the crest, settling into a bench on the south face of the mountain that is filled with thickets of mountain laurel. The state flower of Pennsylvania has beautiful white blooms in May and early June. At 3.3 mi., a blue-blazed trail to the right leads 100 yd. down to the new Clarks Ferry Shelter, built in 1987. A composting privy built in 1996 is nearby. A spring is another 200 yd. down the hill from the shelter.

After the shelter, the trail regains the ridge and passes some very nice views of the Susquehanna and its valley to the left. It winds over large rocks before crossing under a power line that provides very good views of the Juniata and Susquehanna rivers to the north, and valley farms and the Rockville Railroad Bridge to the south. The Rockville Bridge, built in 1902, is the longest stone arch railroad bridge in the world, and carries Conrail's mainline tracks across the Susquehanna River.

The trail leaves the power line clearing, where rattlesnakes and copperheads are common in the summer, and follows a brushy old woods road bounded by lots of poison ivy. The

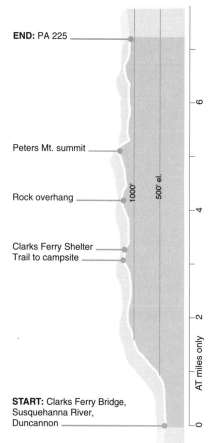

hiking is easy, but gaiters or long pants will help prevent itches. At 4.2 mi., after the trail has left the overgrown road, there is a rock overhang that could be used as an emergency shelter during a thunderstorm. When the trail gains the ridge, the Susquehanna is visible on both sides. Footing on

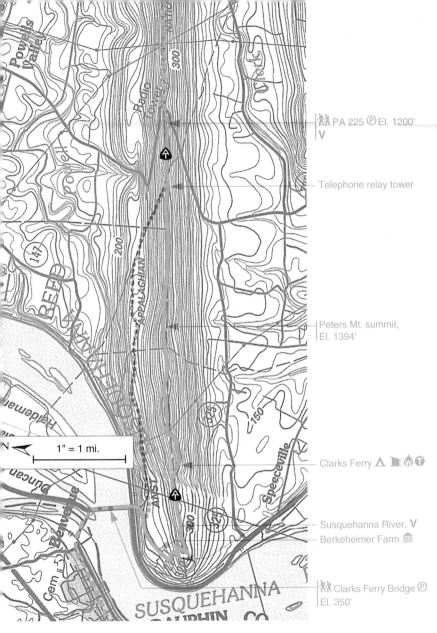

1" = 1 mi.

PA 225 Ⓟ El. 1200'
V

Telephone relay tower

Peters Mt. summit,
El. 1394'

Clarks Ferry

Susquehanna River, V
Berkeheimer Farm

Clarks Ferry Bridge Ⓟ
El. 350'

the green sandstone outcroppings can be slippery when wet and ankle turning in good weather. A hiking stick helps.

At 4.5 mi., the trail crosses a pipeline clearing with good views south to Dauphin Gap, the Rockville Bridge again, and the city of Harrisburg. At 5.2 mi., a Bailey Geodetic Survey marker, located to right of the trail, shows an elevation of 1394 ft., the highest spot on the ridge. The AT, after crossing another pipeline clearing at 6.4 mi., passes to the left of a Bell Telephone Co. relay tower (6.5 mi.) before reentering the woods and continuing along the ridge. An alternate way to PA 225 is along the dirt road leading downhill to the right. The AT continues along the ridge to the 6.7-mi. mark, where it meets the relay tower access road and turns left, following it for about a quarter mile. The trail turns left, off the access road, at 7.0 mi., and follows the ridge again. At 7.3 mi. the AT descends to PA 225 and a dangerous crossing on a curve near the crest of the ridge. After negotiating the crossing, follow the berm for 100 ft. to a gravel road leading to the right and uphill to the trailhead parking area. From the gravel there is a nice view to the north of the valley's checkerboard farms, the town of Halifax, and the wide, looping Susquehanna.

Miles N	NORTH	Elev. (ft./m)	Miles S
7.3	**End:** PA 225, parking at trailhead at crest of Peters Mt., approx. 9 mi. NE of Clarks Ferry.	1200/366	0.0
6.7	Microwave tower **access road.**		0.6
6.5	Telephone relay **tower.**		0.8
6.4	**Pipeline** crossing.		0.9
5.2	**Peters Mt.** summit.	1394/423	2.1
4.5	**Pipeline** crossing.		2.8
4.2	**Rock overhang** (possible shelter).		3.1
3.8	**Power line** crossing.		3.5
3.3	**Clarks Ferry Shelter,** spring.		4.0
3.0	**Blue-blazed trail** to campsite.		4.2
2.3	Cross former **power line** clearing.		5.0
1.5	**Peters Mt.** ridge.	1000/305	5.3
1.2	**Berkeheimer Farm** ruins.		6.1
0.7	Cross **railroad tracks.**		6.6
0.0	**Start:** Clarks Ferry Bridge, Duncannon, parking at either end of bridge.	350/107	7.3

SOUTH

Peters Mt. Ridge to Clark Creek

Maps: ATC Pa. Sections 7 & 8

Route: From PA 225 along the Peters Mt. ridge, past Shikellimy Rocks to PA 325

Recommended direction: S to N

Distance: 9.6 mi.

Elevation +/-: 1200 to 1360 to 575 ft.

Effort: Easy

Day hike: Yes

Overnight backpacking hike: No

Duration: 5 hr.

Early exit option: At 3.8 mi., Victoria Trail

Natural history features: Table Rock; Shikellimy Rocks; Peters Mt.

Other feature: Climbing fumitory (a mountain vine)

Trailhead access: *Start:* Take I-81N or S to Exit 23; go N on US 22/322, following the E side of the Susquehanna River, 10.0 mi. to PA 225 N, follow up mountain to crest. Make R on dirt rd. 50 yd. to parking lot for 15 cars. *End:* From Exit 23 on I-81, take US 22/322N 10.0 mi. to PA 225. Follow 225 to R onto PA ; go 10.1 mi. to where AT crosses. Parking for 20 cars in PA Game Commission lot on R side of road next to Clark Creek.

Camping: Peters Mt. Shelter

Views of the wide, blue Susquehanna River from Shikellimy Rocks and Table Rock are the expected highlights on this rocky, if fairly level, ridgetop walk, but don't be surprised if your most memorable sight turns out to be a Pennsylvania black bear. Peters Mt. is prime bruin habitat — unpopulated, remote, roadless. Plus, when bears run amuck in nearby Harrisburg or its sprawling suburbs, they are often trapped or tranquilized and relocated to the mountain's state Game Lands, creating a kind of minimum security penal colony.

This section of the AT gets lots of local visitors on summer and fall weekends, and it is not unusual to find the parking lot off PA 225 nearly full. The trail passes along the east side of the lot and continues on a wide, straight, gentle ascent under a mostly oak canopy along the ridge. In just 0.2 mile the trail passes a radio tower owned by the Pennsylvania Fish Commission, and at 0.7 mi. it crosses under a power line. There are good views of the valley farms from the power line cut. The Zeager Overlook, at 1.6 mi., is the next spot for a long-distance view. This is the site of a former shelter, removed in 1994, and, in the rocks below the overlook, home to a good collection of copperheads. Watch your step.

Still along the sharp-rocked ridge, at 1.9 mi. the trail climbs over Fumitory Rocks, named after a climbing vine that, while common on many mountain ledges from Canada to Georgia, is found nowhere else on the AT. Also known as mountain fringe or Allegheny vine, fumitory can grow to 12 ft. long. Hike this section of the trail in early July and you will likely see this member of the poppy family in bloom.

Just a few steps down the trail bring you to Table Rock (2.1 mi.), located about 20 yd. from the trail on the right. Table Rock, a prime destination for local hikers who just want to do a 4.2-mi. loop from the parking lot, provides excellent views of the Susquehanna River and its valley, stretching toward Harrisburg, the state capital. This is a nice spot for a midmorning break or an early lunch. A few more steps on the trail takes hikers past a yellow-blazed side trail leading 1.5 mi. to Camp Hebron, a church camp.

At 3.1 mi., the trail reaches the Peters Mt. Shelter, one of the AT's modern, two-story "Hiker Hiltons" with room for twenty sleeping bags. There is also a new composting privy about 150 ft. behind the shelter. The old shelter, which remains in place nearby, was once named after Earl Shaffer, the first man to hike the AT end to end (see "They Called Him Crazy" in Hike #8). During that 1948 hike, Shaffer penned the trail classic *Walking with Spring*, a book about his 124-day trip that contains a poem about the beauty and solitude he found on this section of the trail in Pennsylvania.

Shaffer, who helped with several trail relocations in the area and lives outside of Mt. Holly Springs, asked that his name be taken off the old shelter when a wood-plank floor was added. The earth floor was good enough, he maintained, for a back-country hiker. There is little doubt what he thinks about the new shelter. But the spring would get Shaffer's Spartan seal of approval—though usually reliable, it is located 0.3 mi. down a steep, rocky trail. A

Michael Warren

Blazing the trail with reflective white paint

1987 thru-hiker commented in the shelter register that "the reason the spring is so cold is it's in Canada." It's not quite that far, but day hikers are advised that it is probably easier just to tote an extra jug of water from home. Another attraction at the shelter is a family of black snakes that resides in the "cellar." Hikers tell stories about one 8-ft-long snake that likes to slither up nearby trees, wrapping itself around the trunks "barber pole" style as it climbs in search of birds' eggs.

North of the shelter, the AT continues along the ridge through a young oak forest with a sometimes thick understory of mitten-leafed sassafras bushes. At 3.8 mi., the trail crosses the Victoria Trail. The blue-blazed trail to the right, this hike's early exit option, meets PA 325 in 1.5 mi. To the left it peels down the ridge into the Powell Creek valley, and in 4.0 mi. arrives at the village of Enterline. The AT continues along the ridge, and at 5.7 mi. a blue-blazed side trail to the right leads 30 yd. to an unnamed viewpoint. While hiking this section be alert for bear sightings, especially early in the morning. It was here, in 1995, that we saw a burly black bruin amble across the trail not 20 yd. ahead as we hiked shortly after dawn. He looked back just once before crashing loudly through sassafras and oak saplings, making his own path down off the ridge.

With prospects of a bear sighting

Continued on p. 124

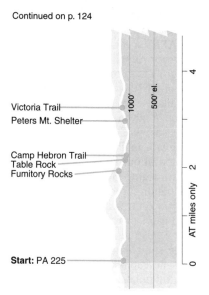

grabbing for hikers' attention, it would be easy to focus on distant shadows in the woods along the trail. That would be an injury-causing mistake. In several areas along this ridge, the rocks get sharp and nasty. It is easy to turn an ankle, especially when rocks that appear to be stable are not.

The trail climbs on to Shikellimy Rocks at 6.4 mi., where there are fine views again of the Susquehanna River valley to the south. At 7.1 mi., the AT passes the blue-blazed Shikellimy Trail, which leads right 1.0 mi. to PA 325 and, across the road, Camp Shikellimy, a YMCA summer camp. The AT, still following

Victoria Trail

Peters Mt. △ ◢ ⓜ ⓣ

Camp Hebron Trail

Table Rock, **V**

Fumitory Rocks, **V**

Zeager Overlook, **V**

Radio tower

🚶 PA 225 Ⓟ
El. 1200', **V**

N

1" = 1 mi.

the ridge, briefly drops through a shallow gap at 7.4 mi., before ascending again to its highest point at 1360 ft.

The trail turns sharply right off the ridge at 8.3 mi., and it's all downhill for the final mile-plus. Hikers will pass a spring about halfway down, on a blue-blazed side trail 100 yd. to the right. At 9.6 mi., the trail crosses PA 325 directly into the state Game Commission parking lot. It's located next to Clark Creek, a fine, almost always clear, mountain trout stream, a good place to wet a line or tired, rock-weary feet.

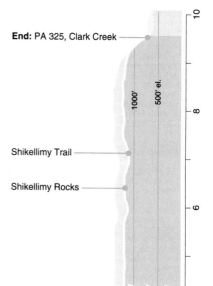

End: PA 325, Clark Creek

1000'

500' el.

Shikellimy Trail

Shikellimy Rocks

10

8

6

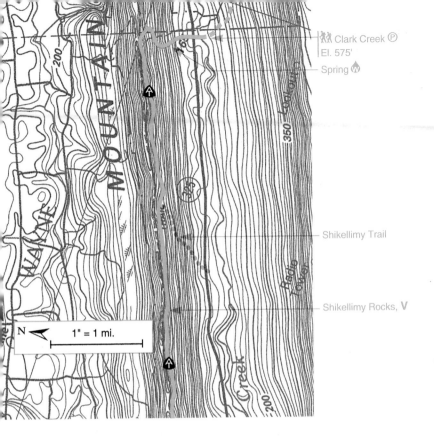

Clark Creek Ⓟ
El. 575'

Spring ⓦ

Shikellimy Trail

Shikellimy Rocks, **V**

N◀ 1" = 1 mi.

Miles N	NORTH	Elev. (ft./m)	Miles S
9.6	**End:** Clark Creek at PA 325, parking at trailhead, 17.0 mi. E of Duncannon.	575/175	0.0
9.2	Spring.		0.4
8.3	Trail leaves ridge.	1360/415	1.3
7.1	Shikellimy Trail.		2.5
6.4	Shikellimy Rocks.		3.2
5.7	Blue-blazed trail to view (R).		3.9
3.8	Victoria Trail, early exit option.		5.8
3.1	Peters Mt. Shelter, spring.		6.5
2.2	Camp Hebron Trail.		7.4
2.1	Table Rock.		7.5
1.9	Fumitory Rocks.		7.7
1.6	Zeager Overlook.		8.0
0.7	Power line crossing.		8.9
0.2	PA Fish Commission radio tower.		9.4
0.0	**Start:** PA 225, parking lot at trailhead at crest of Peters Mt., approx. 8 mi. NE of Clarks Ferry.	1200/366	9.6

SOUTH

Clark Creek to Swatara Gap

Map: KTA Pa. Sections 7 & 8 (color map © 1996 shows this section of trail)

Route: Clark Creek to Rausch Gap to Swatara Gap

Recommended direction: S to N

Distance: 15.9 mi.

Elevation +/-: 575 to 1560 to 450 ft.

Effort: Moderate

Day hike: Optional

Overnight backpacking hike: Yes

Duration: 2 days or 9 hr.

Early exit option: At 8.7 mi., Sand Spring Trail

Natural history features: Clark Creek; St. Anthony Wilderness; Stony Mt.; Second Mt.

Social history features: Yellow Springs Village; Rausch Gap

Other feature: Horseshoe Trail intersection

Trailhead access: *Start:* Take I-81 N or S to Exit 23, go N on US 22/322 10.0 mi. to PA 225N, and 1.0 mi. to PA 325N, then 10.1 mi. to PA Game Commission parking lot for 20 vehicles on E (R) side of road. *End:* Take I-81 to Exit 30, then PA 72W 2.5 mi. to L onto PA 443. Parking lot for a dozen vehicles is on L, 100 yd. from turn.

Camping: Rausch Gap Shelter; camping permitted in the state Game Lands

---

This is a walk on the wilderness side. That does not mean that man's hand is not visible along the almost 16 mi. of trail beginning at PA 325, only that for the most part it has fallen gently and long ago. For much of the route up and over Stony Mt. and Second Mt., this section of the AT follows a long-abandoned stagecoach road through the St. Anthony Wilderness, where human presence is limited to hikers, hunters, and history's echoes.

The wilderness, so named on a 1770 map made for Thomas and Richard Penn, is the largest roadless tract of land in southeastern Pennsylvania (one in the Allegheny National Forest in the northeast part of the state is bigger). Wilderness visitors will see several abandoned coal mines that operated more than 100 years ago and were served by a branch of the Reading Railroad. And the trail passes Yellow Springs Village and Rausch Gap, two ghost towns that flourished as mining settlements around 1850. Now owned and managed by the Pennsylvania Game Commission, the wilderness has no permanent human inhabitants. Even overnight camping is banned for 14 mi. along the trail. It is allowed only at the Rausch Gap Shelter and the several obvious campsites nearby.

Pick up the AT on the eastern edge of a Game Commission parking lot. The lot is next to Clark Creek, a state-designated Scenic River. The pine-and-hemlock-shaded creek is almost always clear and cold, even when other streams in the area run summer-warm and milky with storm runoff. There is a healthy and wary trout population that appreciates those attributes. The trail crosses the creek on a wide earthen bridge and follows a logging access road for 0.3 mi. before turning left onto an old fire tower road for the 3.0 mi. ascent of Stony Mt.

Along the rocky road, the trail ascends easily up the mountain through a mostly oak, hemlock, and black cherry woods that quickly screens out traffic sounds from the road. Sofa-sized boulders of sandstone and quartzite conglomerate, green with lichen, litter the mountainside. The trail has its rock ottomans. They make it difficult, along with the steepness, to get a good hiking rhythm going. There are several seeps coming out of the hillside and the trail can turn into a watercourse in wet weather. At 1.3 mi. there is an iron-orange, bubbling acid drainage flowing from a long-abandoned deep mine to the right of the trail.

At 3.2 mi., the yellow-blazed Horseshoe Trail branches off to the right. On a stone at the juncture there is a plaque honoring Cyrus C. Sturgis Jr., "linguist, translator, editor, trail companion par excellence." The Horseshoe Trail goes downhill 1.5 mi. to

Continued on p. 130

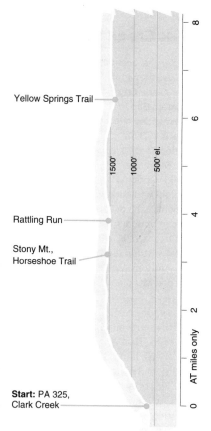

the old railroad bed of the Susquehanna & Schuylkill Railroad, and then to Valley Forge, a total of 137 mi.

At 3.3 mi. the AT reaches the summit of Stony Mt., actually a wide, flat ridgetop. There are plenty of rocks, and the concrete pylons of the old fire tower, on which to take a break

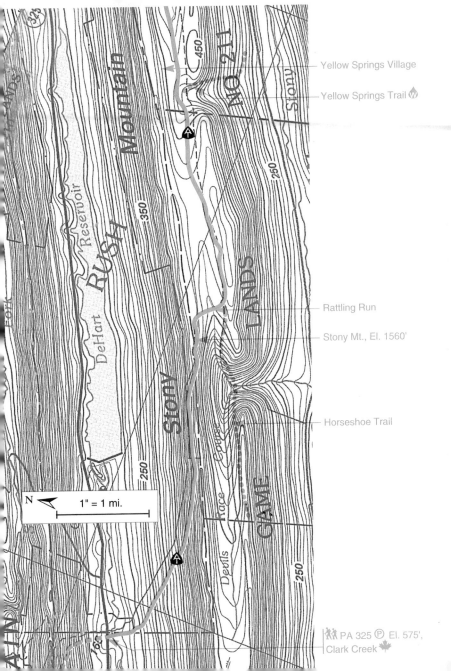

Yellow Springs Village

Yellow Springs Trail 🔥

Rattling Run

Stony Mt., El. 1560'

Horseshoe Trail

N ◄ 1" = 1 mi.

🚶🚶 PA 325 Ⓟ El. 575',
Clark Creek 🍁

or an early lunch under spreading hemlocks. There are good views of wooded valleys off either side of the ridge.

After reaching the summit on the old fire tower road, the AT follows a narrower path, descending briefly through the oak and hemlock woods, and then hopping onto a wide and gently declining ridge known as Sharp Mt. At 3.9 mi., the trail crosses small Rattling Run, and at 4.0 mi. turns left onto the old stagecoach road from Dauphin to Pottsville used in the 1800s. It rides the stage route along the ridge for the next 7.0 mi.

The trail dips into a narrow ravine at 6.4 mi., and intersects the cross-ridge Yellow Springs Trail, a blue-blazed trail that goes right to the old Susquehanna & Schuylkill rail bed in 0.8 mi., and left 0.4 mi. to a vantage point known as Stone Tower. Hikers can see here the remains of an old inclined plane—picture a slow, ground-hugging rollercoaster climbing up and down the hill—used in the 1880s to transport coal and sightseeing travelers from the railroad and a valley resort at Cold Springs Station, to the ridge and over it to the tower. The AT follows a creek bed uphill out of the ravine, passing through the remains of Yellow Springs Village, an abandoned coal mining community. The Yellow Springs Trail leads left 0.4 mi. to the tower, an old mine entrance, and a loading ramp for the inclined plane, then loops back to the AT.

The AT follows the ridge to a junc-

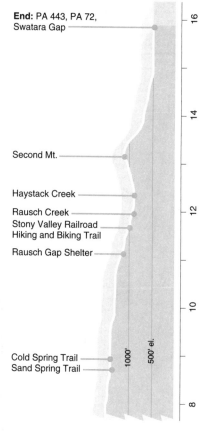

End: PA 443, PA 72, Swatara Gap

Second Mt.

Haystack Creek

Rausch Creek

Stony Valley Railroad Hiking and Biking Trail

Rausch Gap Shelter

Cold Spring Trail

Sand Spring Trail

1000'

500' el.

16

14

12

10

8

tion with the blue-blazed Sand Spring Trail at 8.7 mi. The Sand Spring Trail, an early exit option, leads left 1.6 mi. to the valley and PA 325. At 8.9 mi., the AT meets the Cold Spring Trail, coming in from the right, which goes downhill 0.9 mi. to a state Game Commission parking lot and rough administrative road near the army base at Fort Indiantown Gap.

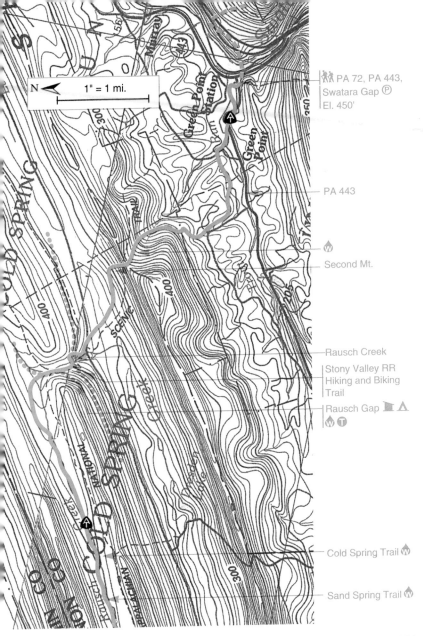

N 1" = 1 mi.

Mill

Green Point Station

Green Point

COLD SPRING

SCENIC TRAIL

Creek

Creek

OLD SPRING

APPALACHIAN

COLD SPRING TRAIL NATIONAL

NOR CO

PA 72, PA 443,
Swatara Gap Ⓟ
El. 450'

PA 443

Second Mt.

Rausch Creek

Stony Valley RR
Hiking and Biking
Trail

Rausch Gap

Cold Spring Trail

Sand Spring Trail

At 11.0 mi., the trail turns right, leaving the old stagecoach road and passing coal waste piles and a large, open-cut strip mine on the right, with Rausch Creek on the left. A blue-blazed trail to the right at 11.2 mi. leads 0.3 mi. to the Rausch Gap Shelter, built in 1972. There is a piped spring next to the shelter. A privy is 100 yd. from the shelter, along the access trail. This is the only area where camping is permitted along the trail, and the area shows signs of overuse by weekend campers who have easy access from a nearby forest road. Still, good campsites can be found, especially along the creek to the right of the trail. The creek is polluted with acid mine drainage, but a treatment system funnels creek water through a bed of limestone to add alkalinity.

At 11.8 mi., the AT turns left onto a Game Commission administrative road that was once the roadbed of the Susquehanna & Schuylkill Railroad, which ceased operations in the 1940s. The old rail bed now also serves as the route for the Stony Valley Railroad Hiking and Biking Trail, which goes east 3.7 mi. to Gold Mine Rd. and a Game Commission parking lot. The AT follows the old rail bed only to the Rausch Creek crossing on an old stone arch railroad bridge at 12.0 mi. Immediately after crossing the bridge, the trail turns right onto a woods road. An old train turntable pit is 50 yd. ahead to the right of the road. On the left is the site of the old Rausch Gap train sta-

tion. The trail then passes through the ruins of old Rausch Gap Village. Wandering through the old coal mining settlement, hikers can see building foundations, hand-dug wells, a cemetery, and other remains of a community that flourished in the 1850s. It was large enough at one point to support a Catholic mission. Headstones in the cemetery all belong to members of the John Proud family and date from 1853.

At 12.3 mi., the trail bears right where the road forks and crosses Haystack Creek on a wooden footbridge before beginning an 0.8-mi. ascent of Second Mt. At 13.2 mi. the trail reaches the crest of Second Mt. A planned trail relocation begins here; it may or may not be completed by 1998 (although the KTA Pa. Sections 7 & 8 map shows the relocation on a dotted line as "pending"). The relocation has been marked in the woods. Check with the Keystone Trails Association or the ATC to find out if it is open.

Until the relocation is finished, the AT descends into Swatara Gap following a wide, rutted, and rocky mountain road through a young, mostly oak forest. The trail leaves the Game Lands and enters private property at 13.9 mi., emerging from the woods onto a well-used dirt country road. Summer cottages are left and right. A road leads straight ahead 200 yd. to the Bleu Blaze Hostel for thru-hikers only. (The Bleu Blaze was closed to hikers for the summer 1997 season, but scheduled to reopen in

Swatara Creek iron bridge (see Hike #15)

1998.) The AT turns right onto a paved road, which turns to gravel for 200 yd. and then, after a left turn, back to macadam at 14.4 mi. After a half mile on Tomstown Ridge Road, turn left (14.9 mi.) onto PA 443, and pass the Green Point grocery, which has a spotty business history and may be closed. When open it offers a nice break for hikers coming off the mountain. After a half mile on PA 443 the trail turns right into the small hikers' parking lot near PA 72.

When the relocation is done, the trail will go straight off Second Mt. (instead of turning right) and descend from 1250 ft. to 600 ft. over the next 2.0 mi. The relocation keeps the trail in the state Game Lands for a greater distance before traversing a swathe of National Park Service land that links to Swatara State Park, which is under development. The trail will then cross Greenpoint School Rd. at the park border and PA 443. The AT will parallel the blacktop road for 0.3 mi. before recrossing it twice more, the second time into the same gravel parking lot used by hikers now.

Miles N	NORTH	Elev. (ft./m)	Miles S
15.9	**End:** Swatara Gap at PA 443, parking at trailhead, 100 yd. from intersection with PA 72.	450/137	0.0
14.9	PA 443.		1.0
13.9	Turn R onto paved road.		2.0
13.6	Spring.		2.3
13.2	Second Mt. summit; begin descent to Swatara Gap.		2.7
12.4	Haystack Creek.		3.5
12.3	Bear R at fort.		3.6
12.1	Rausch Gap Village ruins.		3.8
12.0	Rausch Creek, stone arch railroad bridge.		3.9
11.8	Stony Valley Railroad Hiking and Biking Trail.		4.1
11.2	Trail to R (0.3 mi.) to Rausch Gap Shelter, spring.		4.7
8.9	Cold Spring Trail.		7.0
8.7	Sand Spring Trail, early exit option.		7.2
6.6	Yellow Springs Village ruins.		9.3
6.4	Yellow Springs Trail.		9.5
4.0	Turn L onto old road; follow for 7.0 mi.		11.9
3.9	Rattling Run.		12.0
3.3	Stony Mt. summit.	1560/475	12.6
3.2	Horseshoe Trail intersection.		12.7
0.0	**Start:** Clark Creek at PA 325, parking at trailhead, 17.0 mi. E of Duncannon.	575/175	15.9

SOUTH

Swatara Gap and Blue Mt. Ridge

Map: KTA Pa. Section 6

Route: From Swatara Gap up Blue Mt. to PA 645

Recommended direction: S to N

Distance: 11.1 mi.

Elevation +/-: 450 to 1460 to 1250 ft.

Effort: Moderate

Day hike: Yes

Overnight backpacking hike: No

Duration: 6 hr.

Early exit option: At 4.3 mi., Monroe Valley Trail

Natural history feature: Blue Mt.

Social history features: Waterville Bridge

Trailhead access: *Start:* Take I-81 N or S to Exit 30, then PA 72W 2.5 mi. to L onto PA 443 (see KTA map, Sections 7 & 8). Parking lot for a dozen vehicles is on L, 100 yd. from turn. *End:* Take PA 443N 8.0 mi. to PA 645S at Pine Grove; 3.0 mi. to AT trailhead on W side of road. Parking for 6 cars.

Camping: William Penn Shelter; Blue Mt. Campsite

Swatara Gap, where Pennsylvania has had plans to build a park over an old coal strip mine for twenty-eight years, is finally getting graded and planted and roaded and signed. It's nature but it's too new, like landscaping without shade or character in a just-built suburban subdivision. Except for the bridge.

In the graceful style of another century, the Waterville Bridge carries the AT over Swatara Creek on curving, pale green, wrought-iron trusses and under ornate, pointed spires. Built by the Berlin Iron Bridge Co., of East Berlin, Conn., in 1890, the bridge spanned Little Pine Creek at the town of Waterville until 1986, when increased traffic heading for Little Pine State Park and Pine Creek Gorge, known as "the Grand Canyon of Pennsylvania," required its replacement. It was scheduled for demolition, but the state's environmental agency intervened, moving it 75 mi. south to Swatara. It is a fine example of the lenticular-truss (lens-shaped) bridge, and is listed on the National Register of Historic Places. Its use as an AT footbridge spans more than Swatara Creek, appropriately carrying the trail from some of the youngest rocks it crosses in Pennsylvania (300 million years old on Stony Mt. and in Rausch Creek Valley to the south) to some of the oldest (over 430 million years old on Blue Mt. to the north).

This hike, which starts the AT on a 110-mi. ridgetop route north to the Delaware Water Gap on the New Jersey border with minimal interuptions, begins a mile west of the bridge in the trail parking lot on PA 443. The trail leaves the lot around a metal gate at the far end of the parking lot and runs along a creek and the edge of a grassy field. The sounds of spring peepers are often drowned out by Army helicopters on training maneuvers from the Fort Indiantown Gap Military Reservation, 4.0 mi. to the east.

The trail skirts the field for 0.4 mi. before turning right and entering the woods. It gently ascends through scraggly oak and a sprinkling of maturing white pines and hemlock, never straying far enough from PA 72 to completely lose the traffic noise as it crosses a spur of Blue Mt. cut off from the main rock mass by Swatara Creek. After winding through several free-flowing seeps and a couple of rhododendron thickets and some rocky terrain, the trail dips to the left and begins descending toward PA 72, crossing the blacktop directly opposite the historic Waterville Bridge at 1.0 mi.

The wood-plank pedestrian and bicycle bridge carries the AT over tumbling Swatara Creek. The trail turns sharply left on a paved bike trail, separated by a steel guardrail from a macadam park road that runs along the east side of the creek. The bike path feeds onto the road after 50 yd. and the AT doubles back to the right along the road and creek. At 1.2 mi., it turns sharply left, off the road and up a hill under the north end of the I-81 bridges. On the south end of those bridges, across the creek, Ordovician shale that is more than 430 million years old and contains starfish fossils from an ancient sea has been found.

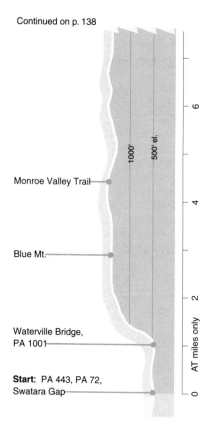

Continued on p. 138

Monroe Valley Trail

1000' 500' el.

Blue Mt.

Waterville Bridge, PA 1001

Start: PA 443, PA 72, Swatara Gap

AT miles only

At the top of the hill the AT turns left again, keeping to the right of a fence in the woods where there is a spring.

At 1.4 mi. the trail turns right, away from the fence along I-81, and at 1.6 mi. crosses a woods road and begins the 1000-ft. ascent of Blue Mt. At 2.0 mi. the trail turns right onto a woods road, and at 2.2 mi. crosses an old charcoal hearth, where shards of charcoal can still be found.

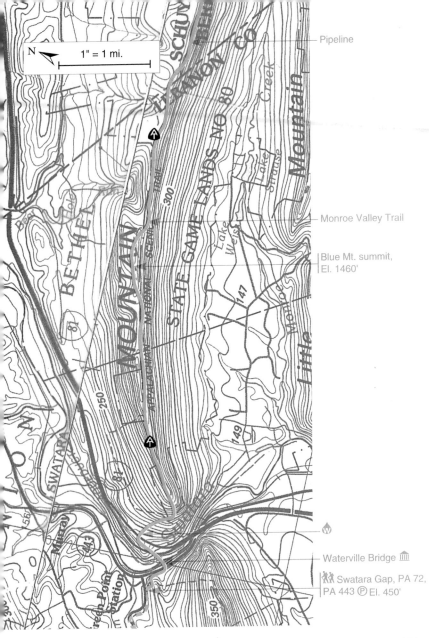

N 1" = 1 mi.

Pipeline

Monroe Valley Trail

Blue Mt. summit,
El. 1460'

Waterville Bridge

Swatara Gap, PA 72,
PA 443 Ⓟ El. 450'

The trail, at 2.3 mi., reaches the crest of Blue Mt. and the oak-wooded ridge of 410-to-430-million-year-old Silurian sandstone. Take care not to confuse the larger, irregularly shaped, white Game Lands boundary markers with the white AT blazes, which are rectangular. At 4.3 mi., a blue-blazed trail to the right that is an early exit option leads to the Monroe Valley in 1.2 mi. The AT continues along the ridge, passing several good views of farmland and forest to the right. At 5.7 mi. the trail crosses an overgrown, abandoned power line clearing, turning left and then right. At 6.5 mi. the trail turns right onto a path, and at 6.9 mi. goes right onto an old woods road used by stagecoaches in the early 1840s, and now bordered by oak and sassafras. At 7.1 mi. the trail crosses an underground oil pipeline. To the right 200 yd. is a 4-ft.-tall concrete marker on the intersection of Berks, Lebanon, and Schuylkill counties.

The trail reaches the Blue Mt. Campsite at 8.7 mi. A blue-blazed trail to the right (southeast) leads 0.1 mi. to the William Penn thru-hiker shelter, built in 1993. It's one of the AT's "Hiker Hiltons," with a second-story loft sleeping area and windows. The campsite, on the left (northwest) side of the AT, is on a blue-blazed trail that leads to a spring in 200 yd., and has a permanent place in thru-hiker lore because of an unusual

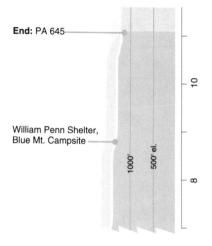

End: PA 645

William Penn Shelter,
Blue Mt. Campsite

theft that occurred in 1985. "Indiana John," a thru-hiker, had everything but the sleeping bag and underwear he was sleeping in stolen one night. Wrapped in his bag, he hiked the 2.5 mi. to PA 645; then, embarrassed, hitched into the town of Pine Grove. When residents heard of his plight they pitched in to help. Suitably reequipped with boots, pack, stove, clothes, and food, he went on to finish his thru-hike.

After the shelter the AT continues along the rocky ridge road, descending gently but steadily and passing through a clearing at 9.5 mi. It reaches PA 645 at 11.1 mi. The parking area is to the left, on the west side of the road.

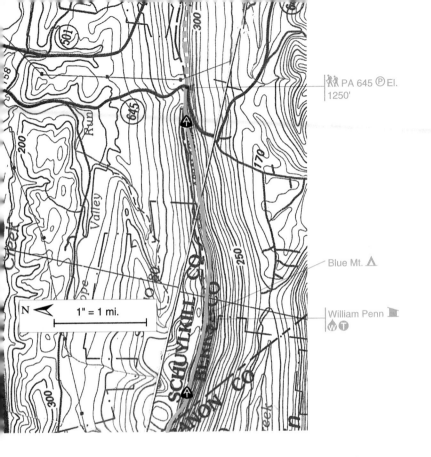

ЖЖ PA 645 Ⓟ El.
1250'

N ◀ 1" = 1 mi.

Blue Mt. ▲

William Penn 🏠
Ⓦ Ⓣ

Miles N	NORTH	Elev. (ft./m)	Miles S
11.1	**End:** **PA 645,** parking at trailhead, 5.0 mi. from Exit 2 on I-78.	1250/381	0.0
9.5	Clearing.		1.6
8.7	To R, 0.1 mi. trail to **William Penn Shelter; Blue Mt. Campsite** on L on AT.		2.4
7.1	Cross **pipeline.**		4.0
5.7	Cross **abandoned power line** clearing.		5.4
4.3	**Monroe Valley Trail;** early exit option.		6.8
2.3	**Blue Mt.** crest.	1460/445	8.8
1.6	Cross woods road and **begin ascent** of Blue Mt.		9.5
1.2	**Spring.**		9.9
1.0	**Waterville Bridge; PA 1001.**		10.1
0.4	**Turn R** into woods.		10.7
0.0	**Start:** **Swatara Gap at PA 443,** parking at trailhead, 100 yd. from intersection with PA 72.	450/137	11.1

SOUTH

HIKE #16
Along Blue Mt. Ridge

Map: KTA Pa. Section 6

Route: Along Blue Mt. ridge from PA 645 to Pilger Ruh, PA 501, and PA 183

Recommended direction: S to N

Distance: 10.4 mi.total; 10.1 mi. on AT

Access road name & length: PA 183, 0.3 mi.

Elevation +/-: 1250 to 1565 to 1375 ft.

Effort: Moderate

Day hike: Yes

Overnight backpacking hike: No

Duration: 5 to 6 hr.

Early exit option: At 2.1 mi., PA 501

Natural history feature: Round Head

Social history features: Pilger Ruh; Fort Dietrich Snyder

Other feature: Shower Steps

Trailhead access: *Start:* Take I-78 E or W to Exit 2, then PA 645N 5.0 mi. Parking for 6 cars on W side of road at trail crossing. *End:* Take I-78 E or W to Exit 7, then PA 183N 2.0 mi. to PA Game Commission parking lot S of ridge on E side of road. Parking for 12 cars 0.3 mi. from trailhead at ridge crest.

Camping: 501 Shelter; Pilger Ruh Campsite; Hertlein Campsite

O n this 10-mi. rock hop along the Blue Mt. ridge, history-minded hikers walk a path blazed by Native Americans, interpreters, missionaries, and soldiers. The focal point is Pilger Ruh (Pilgrim's Rest) spring. Located on a route from Philadelphia to the Native American capital of Shamokin (now Sunbury) on the Susquehanna River north of Harrisburg, the spring was a must stop for travelers over the Appalachian ridges. It was visited by Chief Shikellimy of the Iroquois Federation; the Moravian missionary Count Zinzendorff, who settled Bethlehem, Pennsylvania, in 1740; and Conrad Weiser, an interpreter who grew up among the Mohawks, learned their language and customs,

and became a trusted and influential intermediary between several Iroquois chiefs and descendants of William Penn.

This hike starts at the parking lot on PA 645 at the AT trailhead. The trail crosses the cross-ridge black-

Henry Lafleur

Monarch butterfly

topped road directly and ascends gradually through a mostly oak woods along the north side of the rocky ridge before crossing to the south side and a view from Fisher Lookout at 1.4 mi. There's another view at 1.8 mi. from the Kimmel Lookout, named for Dick Kimmel, a trail worker for more than forty years. On warm, sunny days, take care to check for rattlesnakes at both of these rocky lookouts before sitting down to admire the views.

At 2.1 mi. the trail directly crosses paved PA 501, where there is parking along the road, making an early exit possible. Immediately after the crossing, a blue-blazed trail leads left 0.1 mi. to the 501 Shelter, which is open free to thru-hikers. The former potter's workshop, an enclosed building with bunks, table, chairs, skylight, outside privy, and solar shower, is maintained by the Blue Mt. Eagle Climbing Club. Water is available from the adjacent house, where caretakers George and Joan Shollenberger reside, and sodas and ice cream are available for a donation. Heed the posted warnings: their dog *does* bite.

The trail meanders through a rocky, wooded stretch, reaching Pilger Ruh at 2.4 mi. The colonial-era watering hole is located a short distance down a blue-blazed trail to the right. Camping is permitted at several flat clearings just to the left of the junction of the side trail and the AT.

Past Pilger Ruh, the AT ascends gradually, skirting a steep-sided valley known as the Kessel (kettle), before

Continued on p. 144

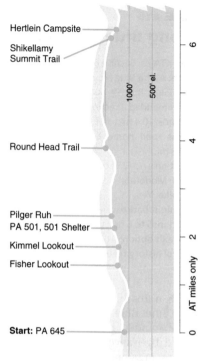

reaching a blue-blazed side trail at 3.9 mi., leading right to Round Head, a vantage point notable for its valley views and large boulder field, known to geologists as a talus slope. This slope—and others like it along the trail in Pennsylvania at Little Gap, Blue Rocks, River of Rocks, and Devil's Potato Patch—was formed when ice built up in cracks of hard rock and broke it into blocks that crept slowly downhill over geologic time. Such slopes are found along

N ⬅ ⅞" = 1 mi.

Hertlein Campsite ⛺
🔥

Shikellamy Summit
Trail **V**

Round Head/Shower
Steps, **V**

Pilger Ruh 🚰 🏛

PA 501

501 🏠 🚰 ⊕

Kimmel Lookout, **V**

Fisher Lookout, **V**

🥾🥾 PA 645 Ⓟ
El. 1250'

the AT from Georgia to Maine but are particularly notable on this quartzite ridge.

The 1.5-mi. loop trail to Round Head follows Showers Steps, a path of 500 rough stone steps built by Lloyd Showers, an early trail worker. There is a spring at the foot of the steps, and Round Head is a great lunch stop. The side trail circles back to the AT, passing the Shanaman Marker, which commemorates the efforts of another early trail worker, William F. Shanaman, who was mayor of Reading, Pennsylvania.

The AT follows the descending ridgeline to a blue-blazed trail to the right at 6.2 mi., leading 0.4 mi. to the Shikellamy Summit, another fine lookout. Continuing to descend, at 6.3 mi. the trail crosses a small brook and arrives at a spring and the Hertlein Campsite. There are plenty of flat areas for tenting to the left of the trail, and a nearby pond at Shuberts Gap offers an opportunity for a bracing swim for hikers bold enough to brave the spring-fed icy water. Below the dam is private property.

The trail climbs out of the gap and crosses an oil pipeline in a clearing at 7.1 mi. At 9.7 mi. it reaches Shuberts Summit and an abandoned cross-mountain road. The AT turns right for 100 yd., then left onto a woods road. A marker here commemorates the site of Fort Dietrich Snyder. A blue-blazed side trail leads 0.2 mi. to a piped spring located in the woods to the left of the road.

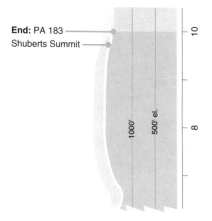

If Pilger Ruh is the focal point for this walk, Fort Dietrich Snyder is the exclamation point. In 1756, Col. Benjamin Franklin supervised construction of the fort, a lookout post for Fort Northkill and one of a chain of forts erected along the Blue Mt. ridge to protect frontier settlers from Delaware (Lenape) and Iroquois attacks in the 1750s. Known collectively as "Franklin's Forts" and extending from Easton to Mercersburg, the forts were built at 20-mi. intervals generally paralleling the route of the AT, but usually off the ridges on the mountainsides to afford better protection to farms and settlements. Blockhouses were built every 5 mi. in between to provide temporary shelter for families until militia from the forts could be dispatched. The forts, completed in 1756, did not end the raids, nor the French and Indian War (1754–1763), but gave settlers living

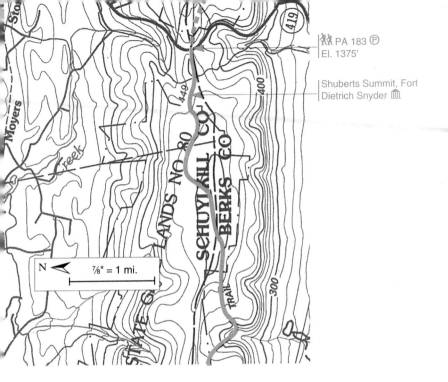

〽 PA 183 Ⓟ
El. 1375'

Shuberts Summit, Fort
Dietrich Snyder 🏛

N ◄ ⁷⁄₈" = 1 mi.

on what was then the colonial frontier some sense of security.

From the site of the fort it's a long historical march, but just a short walk, to the four lanes of PA 183 at 10.1 mi. Watch out for the traffic along the broad curve of blacktop on the way to the Game Commission parking lot located 0.3 mi. down the mountain to the south.

Miles N	NORTH	Elev. (ft./m)	Miles S
	Total: 10.4 mi. with access from parking lot		
0.3	Access: **PA Game Commission** lot on PA 183 2.0 mi. from Exit 7 on I-78.		0.3
10.1	**End AT miles:** PA 183.	1375/419	0.0
9.7	**Shuberts Summit,** Fort Dietrich Snyder marker.		0.4
7.1	Cross **pipeline.**		3.0
6.3	**Hertlein Campsite,** spring.		3.8
6.2	**Shikellamy Summit Trail.**		3.9
3.9	**Round Head Trail.**	1565/477	6.2
2.4	**Pilger Ruh** spring and campsites.		7.7
2.1	**PA 501,** early exit option; trail to **501 Shelter.**		8.0
1.8	**Kimmel Lookout.**		8.3
1.4	**Fisher Lookout.**		8.7
0.0	**Start:** PA 645, parking at trailhead, 5.0 mi. from Exit 2 on I-78.	1250/381	10.1

SOUTH

Blue Mt. Ridge to Port Clinton

Map: KTA Pa. Section 5

Route: From PA 183 along Blue Mt. ridge to Port Clinton

Recommended direction: S to N

Distance: 15.3 mi. total; 15.0 mi. on AT

Access road name & length: PA 183, 0.3 mi.

Elevation +/-: 1375 to 1600 to 400 ft.

Effort: Moderate day hike, easy overnight

Day hike: Yes

Overnight backpacking hike: Optional

Duration: 8 hr.

Early exit options: At 5.3 mi., Sand Spring Trail; at 11.6 mi., Marshalls Path

Natural history feature: Auburn Lookout

Social history feature: Port Clinton, "Buzzard Capital of the Northeast"

Other feature: The real start of PA's rocks

Trailhead access: *Start:* Take I-78 E or W to Exit 7, then PA 183N 2.0 mi. to PA Game Commission parking lot on E side of road. Parking for 12 cars 0.3 mi. from trailhead. *End:* Follow I-78 E or W to Exit 9, an PA 61N 2.0 mi. to Port Clinton. Turn L on Broad St., cross bridge over the Schuylkill River, and turn L after crossing railroad tracks. Hikers' parking in lot for 20 cars along the tracks. Parking also available in Port Clinton on Penn St., near the Historical Association Museum, and a 10-car lot 0.2 mi. S of Port Clinton along PA 61. Robert Breon (610-562-7342), who lives next to The Peanut Shop in town, can arrange shuttles to PA 183 or into nearby Hamburg where there are 2 camp stores, restaurants, and hotels.

Camping: Permitted in state Game Lands; Eagles Nest Shelter; town pavilion in Port Clinton

Thru-hikers know Pennsylvania by the name Rocksylvania. Before too long, day-trippers on this 15.0-mi. hike along the Blue Mt. ridge discover why. Truth be told, there are some early stretches of this walk through a maturing oak forest where a footstep will land on soil instead of sharp rock. Enjoy them. By hike's end they will be distant, obscure memories. Mostly there are the rocks: gray-green, often jagged, quartzite shards, ranging in size from pork chops to pumpkins to Plymouths. Hikers will find them generally unsorted by size, and occasionally unsecured.

Find the AT trailhead 0.3 mi. north of the Pennsylvania Game Commission parking lot on the east side of PA 183, which at the top of the ridge has been widened to four lanes to allow cars to pass trucks crawling up and down the steep ridge. The trailhead, well marked, ascends from the shoulder of the road following an old state Game Lands road long unused by vehicles. Immediately on the left, 15 yd. off the trail, is the Rentschler marker. It commemorates the work of Dr. H. F. Rentschler, who in 1926 led work parties that marked and cut the original AT between the Lehigh and Susquehanna rivers.

The rocks on which they did their fine work were in place for some time before that. The sandstone and quartzite were created 400 million years ago from glacial deposits of sand, and turned on edge approximately 150 million years later when Africa played a little continental bump and run with North America. Just 2 million years ago, a series of freeze/thaw cycles began cracking the folded quartzite into the big angular blocks, slabs, and wedges hikers hop along on the Blue Mt. ridge.

On this hike the rocks start out small, but sharp, as the trail follows the old road through a young oak, ash, and beech forest that is a haven for birds. It is not uncommon for hikers to flush quail and ruffed grouse, the Pennsylvania state bird, from their trailside hideouts. The noisy whup-whup-whup of frantic wing beats is the signal of a grouse or two in full retreat.

The trail leaves the old timbering road at 0.4 mi., and at 0.6 mi. crosses another grassy Game Commission road leading to the parking area 0.2 mi. to the right. That road is an alternate way onto the AT for hikers who don't want to step along PA 183's berm to the trailhead. The hik-

Continued on p. 150

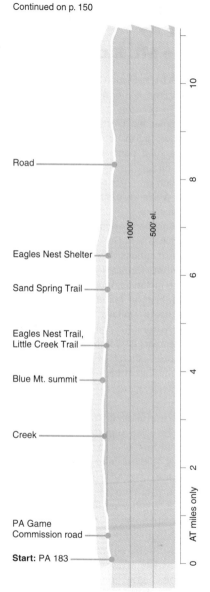

WEISER STATE FOREST

BLUE MOUNTAIN STATE

Northkill

Eagles Nest ▲ 🏕 Ⓦ
Ⓣ

← Sand Spring Trail Ⓦ

Eagles Nest/Little
Creek trails

Blue Mt. summit,
El. 1600'

Birch

Black Swatara Spring
Ⓦ

N ◄ ⅞" = 1 mi.

🥾🥾 PA 183 Ⓟ
El. 1375'

419

ing here is typical Pennsylvania ridge-top, with low horizons obscured by trees on both sides of the trail, which runs poker straight, if rockier after crossing the grassy road. A gradual ascent is made difficult by the sharp, oddly angled rocks, which make for slow going.

Mountain laurel and blueberry bushes grow along the trail, which descends gently before meeting a blue-blazed side trail at 1.4 mi. leading right 200 yd. to Black Swatara Spring. There are some camping sites near the intersection. Immediately after the side trail to the spring, the AT, on a gentle descent, passes through thickets of mountain laurel and rhododendron. At 2.5 mi., after going through some muddy seeps, the trail crosses a small, unnamed stream on tree roots and rocks. Some downed logs make this a nice place for a first break.

Over the stream, the trail turns slightly uphill, through a young oak forest with a mountain laurel under-story. Teaberry is everywhere along the trail, which parallels an old mountain road. At 4.2 mi., the trail crosses the grassy Game Lands road and meets the Eagles Nest Trail on the right and the Little Creek Trail on the left. Each is less than a mile long. The AT for the next mile is noticeably rockier, with plenty of ankle turners and toe biters. At 5.3 mi., after a rolling quarter mile downhill, the AT meets the Sand Spring Trail. Hikers can follow its blue blazes to a fine, walled spring 200 yd. to the right,

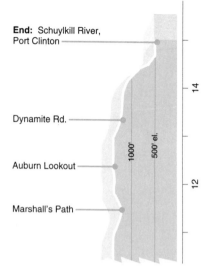

End: Schuylkill River, Port Clinton

Dynamite Rd.

Auburn Lookout

Marshall's Path

1000'

500' el.

14

12

and in 2.0 mi., a parking area that can be used for an early exit option to Northkill Rd.. The orange-blazed Tom Lowe Trail starts in the parking area and makes a nice 4.0-mi. loop with the Sand Spring Trail, joining it back at the spring.

At 5.9 mi. the AT crosses a Game Commission administrative road, and at 6.1 mi. crosses from state Game Lands into the Weiser State Forest, and meets the blue-blazed side trail that leads 0.3 mi. to the Eagles Nest Shelter. This is your destination for the night if you are making two days out of this hike. If this is a one-day ramble, plan on lunch at the shelter. The rocky 6.2 mi. can start your feet barking and this is a good spot to rest the dogs, either by dangling them in the

N ◄ ⅞" = 1 mi.

icy creek or by getting off of them overnight. The shelter is the common three-sided log variety, if a little larger than most and with three small Plexiglas windows cut into the back wall. The water source is the strongly flowing spring creek crossed on a bridge on the way to the shelter. A composting privy is located 50 yd. past the shelter, and there are plenty of flat spots for tent camping in front of the shelter.

Back on the AT the trail follows a rocky course through thickets of mountain laurel. This is another section of ridgetop trail where hikers complain about seeing Pennsylvania three feet at a time (see Hike #11). Eventually, about a mile out of the shelter, the trail is flat and there are interesting views over the Weiser State Forest lands just off the trail to the left. At about 7 mile, the trail begins a gradual descent and the rocks go into remission for a mile, affording some of the easiest hiking on this section. In summer, the trail here is lined with high grass, making gaiters or long pants advisable for tick protection.

At 8.1 mi., the trail meets a cross-ridge road that leads to a Game Lands parking lot 1.6 mi. to the right, with the town of Shartlesville another 2.0 mi. further. The AT crosses that road and follows a wide, old logging path for just 200 yd. before turning right and dipping down off the ridge on a much narrower path. Watch the blazes here. The tendency is to enjoy the wide open, relatively rock-free logging path and miss the right turn. After that turn, the AT descends steadily through young cherry and oak growth. There are several spring seeps in this stretch that can provide a water source in wet weather.

At 8.5 mi. the trail bears left onto the old AT, still descending, but becomes rockier. At 9.0 mi. the trail turns sharply right and becomes sharply more rocky as it begins a steep ascent back to the ridge. Just when thigh and calf muscles are starting to argue about who is burning worse, the rock scramble turns into a rough, rock-slab staircase that, although just as steep, makes the final leg of the ascent seem much easier. At 9.4 mi., beyond the top of the ridge, the AT crosses a wide Game

Commission road. Although it seems impossible by this point in the hike, the trail gets noticeably more rocky, and begins to lay claim to a hiker's soul or soles, or both. Clay Crowder, a thru-hiker in 1995, ripped up a pair of heavy-duty $250 boots on a boulder field south of Port Clinton, and later wrote in a shelter register, "I hope there are more rocks ahead to push me to the edge of sanity."

At 10.2 mi. pass the Phillips Canyon Spring Trail leading to the left and steeply downhill for 135 yd. to a variable spring. At 11.4 mi., the trail crosses a Game Lands road diagonally and reenters the mostly oak and cherry woods through a mountain laurel thicket. At 11.6 mi. it meets Marshall's Path, a well-worn blue-blazed trail to the right that leads to Bellmans Gap and a paved mountain road at the foot of the mountain in 1.0 mi.

The trail reaches almost-always windy Auburn Lookout at 12.5 mi. It offers a 180-degree view of Weiser State Forest, the small town of Stony Creek, and the headwaters of the Schuylkill River. Usually, one or more turkey vultures will be floating on the wind, wing feathers outstretched like bony fingers, giving credence to Port Clinton's un–Chamber of Commerce–like appellation of "Buzzard Capital of the Northeast." From the lookout to Port Clinton the trail steeply descends 1000 ft. in 2.0 mi.

Just 0.1 mi. past the lookout, the trail comes to a wide Game Lands road, follows it without crossing for

45 yd., and reenters the woods to begin a torturous rock scramble for 0.2 mi. before coming to the Game Lands road again, at 12.8 mi., this time crossing it. At 13.4 mi. the trail crosses Dynamite Road, actually a blue-blazed trail leading 0.3 mi. to the right to Mountain Rd. at the foot of the mountain. The AT turns sharply left here, over sharp, small rocks to a pipeline cut at 13.5 mi., which the trail crosses directly. At 13.9 mi. the trail crosses another pipeline, with a view of the valley to the right. It begins a steeper descent along several switchbacks, then feeds onto an old rail bed from which the track has been removed. It follows the black-cindered rail bed to the left for 50 yd., before turning right to descend steeply on a set of old stone steps to the active tracks of the Blue Mt. and Reading Railroad line—known as "The Road of Anthracite."

Along the Schuylkill River, the restored old-time steam engines and passenger cars are a tourist attraction at a refurbished station along the river next to a large parking lot. The AT crosses three tracks and turns left into the train station parking lot. It follows a blacktop walkway leading across a bridge over the Schuylkill River. There is hikers' parking on the east side of the bridge, north of the tracks. The trail crosses a second bridge and turns right into town. A block away, on PA 61, the Port Clinton Hotel serves the biggest cheeseburgers and cheapest draft beer on the trail in Pennsylvania.

Miles N	NORTH	Elev. (ft./m)	Miles S
	Total: 15.3 mi. with access from parking lot		
15.0	**End:** **Port Clinton,** parking at trailhead along railroad tracks near Schuylkill River.	400/122	0.0
14.7	Cross abandoned **railroad bed.**		0.3
13.5	Cross **pipeline.**		1.5
13.4	**Cross Dynamite Rd;** begin descent to Port Clinton.		1.6
12.5	**Auburn Lookout.**		2.5
11.6	**Marshall's Path,** early exit option.		3.4
10.2	**Phillips Canyon Spring Trail.**		4.8
8.1	**Road crossing.**		6.9
6.2	Trail to **Eagles Nest Shelter,** spring, privy (0.3 mi).		8.8
6.1	Enter **Weiser State Forest.**		8.9
5.3	**Sand Spring Trail,** early exit option.		9.7
4.2	**Eagles Nest and Little Creek trails.**		10.8
3.7	**Blue Mt.** summit.	1600/488	11.3
2.5	Cross unnamed **creek.**		12.5
1.4	**Black Swatara Spring.**		13.6
0.6	**Cross PA Game Commission road,** alternate 0.2-mi. route to and from parking lot (R)		14.4
0.0	**Start AT miles:** **PA 183; Rentschler Marker.**	1375/419	15.0
0.3	Access: **PA Game Commission** parking lot on PA 183 2.0 mi. from US 78.		0.3

SOUTH

Port Clinton to Pine Swamp Rd.

Map: KTA Pa. Section 4

Route: From Port Clinton to Hamburg Reservoir to The Pinnacle to Pine Swamp Rd.

Recommended direction: S to N

Distance: 15.1 mi. total; 14.9 mi. on AT

Access trail name & length: Blue-blazed trail, 0.2 mi.

Elevation +/-: 400 to 1635 to 500 ft.

Effort: Strenuous

Day hike: Yes

Overnight backpacking hike: Optional

Duration: 9 hr.

Early exit option: At 6.0 mi., gravel road at Hamburg Reservoir

Natural history features: Pulpit Rock; Blue Rocks; The Pinnacle

Social history feature: Windsor Furnace

Other features: Hamburg Reservoir; Astronomical Park of the Lehigh Valley Amateur Astronomical Society

Trailhead access: *Start:* Take I-78 E or W to Exit 9, and PA 61N 2.0 mi. to Port Clinton. Parking across bridge over the Schuylkill River along N side of railroad tracks for 20 cars. There is also a 10-car lot S of Port Clinton along PA 61. To arrange shuttles see Hike #17. *End:* Take I-78 E or W to Exit 11, then PA 143N 3.0 mi. to L onto paved, unnumbered road to Eckville. Turn L in Eckville onto unpaved Pine Swamp Rd. A PA Game Commission parking lot is 0.5 mi. S of Eckville, on the R side of the road, 0.2 mi. from the AT.

Camping: YWCA Blue Mt. Camp; Hamburg Reservoir campsites; Windsor Furnace Shelter and campsites

---

Somewhere on the steep 900-ft. climb out of Port Clinton up the rocky face of Blue Mt., hikers can be excused for idly wondering if the turkey vultures floating overhead on outstretched wings are there solely for the updrafts swirling off the mountain. Port Clinton is known as the "Buzzard Capital of the Northeast," and the favorable flying winds allow it to come by the title honestly. But the carrion-eating birds seem to sense that the hump up the mountain ridge is a tough survival test for hikers and a rigorous way to begin this 14.9-mi. trek.

Out of the parking lot along the tracks of the Blue Mt. and Reading Railroad line, hikers pick up the AT on the railroad bridge over the Schuylkill River. Cross the river, turn right on Broad St., and then right again at 0.2 mi., on Penn St. The trail follows residential Penn St. to its end and then continues through tall brush, raspberry cane, and oak and maple woods along the Schuylkill River. At 0.7 mi., the trail bears left and crosses under PA 61, and then crosses a local macadam road and begins ascending Blue Mt. up rocky, steep switchbacks. Time rest stops to coincide with the fine views of the Schuylkill River and the Hamburg Reservoir from various spots along the climb. If you're lucky, the switchbacks peter out before your legs do.

The AT finally gains the ridge at 1.5 mi. on a rock outcropping. It descends to the left before again cresting the ridge and following it, crossing a telephone line clearing at 2.5 mi. The trail bears right at 3.2 mi. and begins a fairly steep descent from the ridge, reaching the Pocohontas Spring at 3.3 mi. A blue-blazed trail to the right leads 1.0 mi. to the YWCA Blue Mt. Camp. Due to its distance from the AT, this should be considered a camping option of last resort. Although the trail is rocky in this area, it pays to stop every now and then and look around—the prudent sequence—at the carpet of ferns stretching out under a canopy of maturing maple, oak, and hickory.

The trail ascends from the spring, bearing left at 3.7 mi., at a fork in the mountain road it has been following under a canopy of oak and ash. The trail passes an unnamed spring at 4.6 mi. that is often dry, then begins a steep descent of almost 400 ft., reaching the Hamburg Reservoir at 6.0 mi. To the south (right), a gravel road leads 0.4 mi. to a parking area that creates an early exit option. To the north, follow the road past the remains of Windsor Furnace, a brick-lined pig-iron works. An old engine lies rusting in the weeds. The furnace produced iron that was made into stoves and renderings of Christ's Last Supper. Glassy black slag from the round furnace lies along the trail. And artificially flattened spots where wood was partially burned to make charcoal for the furnace can be found for miles along the AT in both directions.

The Hamburg Reservoir also lies to the north of the trail. The land in this area is owned by the Hamburg Water Authority, which does not permit swimming in either the reservoir or Furnace Creek, the stream flowing into and out of the reservoir. Fires and camping are also prohibited except at a designated campsites that can be reached via a blue-blazed trail that leads 500 yd. to the right, past several water authority buildings and a grove of hemlocks. Drinking water is available from the small creek but should be filtered. A privy is just beyond the campsites. For hikers who intend to leisurely take in the sights at Pulpit Rock and The Pinnacle, and therefore need to break this hike into two days, this is a good overnight camping spot.

The AT follows the gravel road across Furnace Creek (6.1 mi.) and bears to the left. At 6.2 mi. it turns right where a blue-blazed trail to the left leads 500 ft. to the Windsor Furnace Shelter. There is a privy behind the shelter, the water source is Furnace Creek, and there is limited camping around the shelter. This

Day hikers at The Pinnacle

camping area may also be used by hikers doing the Port Clinton–Pine Swamp Rd. section in two days.

From the shelter and campsite, the AT climbs more than 1000 ft. up Blue Mt., at first gently, but then more steeply. The trail reaches and passes around the Astronomical Park of the Lehigh Valley Amateur Astronomical Society (8.1 mi.), a ridgetop property that offers starry-bright views on clear nights. At 8.2 mi., the AT scales Pulpit Rock (elev. 1582 ft.), which offers outstanding views not only of checkerboard farmland, but also of Blue Rocks, a 40,000-year-old river of massive sandstone and quartzite boulders more than a city block wide and a mile long. The rock river gets its name from the quartzite and other minerals in the rocks that produce a

bluish tinge on moonlit nights and sometimes in the early morning sunlight. There is also an excellent view of The Pinnacle to the left.

The trail continues past a radio tower at 8.3 mi. and a quartzite rock outcrop at 8.4 mi., with more good views to the south of farmland and blue-hazed ridges. At 8.6 mi. the trail crosses a rock field that offers views of farms and fields to the north, and at 8.7 mi. passes through a cleft or notch in a large jumble of rocks. At 9.9 mi., a yellow-blazed trail to the south (right) leads steeply down for 1.3 mi. to Blue Rocks. The privately owned Blue Rocks Campground, which sells hiking and camping supplies, is located another 0.2 mi. down that trail, and is an alternate place to camp.

The AT reaches a blue-blazed trail at 10.3 mi. that leads 80 yd. south (right) to The Pinnacle (1635 ft.), a jutting ridge end that provides spectacular views of Pennsylvania farmlands and low Appalachian ridges. Many hikers say this quartzite outcrop offers the best views along the AT in Pennsylvania. Near the end of The Pinnacle, some large rocks are tilted out from the mountain. One crack in these rocks extends down 30 ft. and is covered with rock in the middle but open at the ends, where fossilized burrows can be seen in the quartzite. There are at least two such caves below the Pinnacle rocks that are worth exploring if you can get the permission of the copperheads that live there.

From The Pinnacle, the AT turns sharply west or left, but stays mainly on the rocky ridge. At 10.6 mi. the trail passes through a flat charcoal hearth, and at 11.0 mi. it enters a clearing where hikers will want to stay right. At 11.3 mi. the trail bears right where an old woods road goes to the left.

The trail is wide and generally flat, but rocky, in this section. An old woods road leads to the left at 12.0 mi., descending to the headwaters of Furnace Creek, which flows into the Hamburg Reservoir. At 12.3 mi., the trail reaches Gold Spring, a reliable spring located 30 yd. off the trail to the left. Because the spring is part of the reservoir watershed, no camping or fires are permitted. The AT ascends gently after passing the

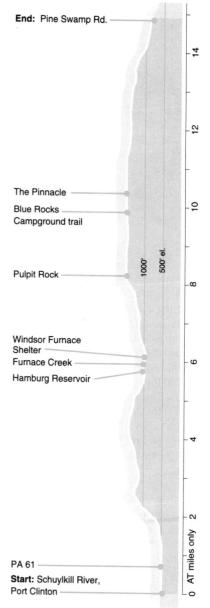

End: Pine Swamp Rd.

The Pinnacle

Blue Rocks
Campground trail

Pulpit Rock

1000'   500' el.

Windsor Furnace Shelter

Furnace Creek

Hamburg Reservoir

PA 61

Start: Schuylkill River, Port Clinton

AT miles only

XX Pine Swamp Rd.
Ⓟ El. 500'

The Pinnacle, V

Blue Rocks
▲ Ⓦ Ⓣ

Pulpit Rock, V

Gold Spring Ⓦ

Panther Spring Ⓦ

Windsor Furnace
▲ ▬ Ⓦ Ⓣ

Windsor Furnace 🏛
Hamburg Reservoir

Ⓟ

Ⓦ

Pocohontas Spring
▲ Ⓦ

N ◣   ⁷⁄₈" = 1 mi.

PA 61

XX Port Clinton Ⓟ Ⓦ
Ⓣ El. 400'

spring, turning right at 12.9 mi. and ascending more steeply.

The trail reaches the ridge crest at 13.2 mi. and turns left, beginning a long, sometimes steep, descent toward Eckville through an oak woods interspersed with isolated hemlock stands. Take care not to confuse the AT blazes with white state Game Commission boundary markers in this area. At 13.5 mi. the trail bears right where a grassy woods road joins from the left and descends steeply to Panther Spring at 13.9 mi. The AT now follows the old Windsor Furnace Rd. through state Game Lands for a mile through thick oak and hemlock woods where there are lots of seeps that sometimes produce muddy footing. At 14.9 mi., the AT bears left off the road and a blue-blazed trail that follows the old AT route leads right 0.2 mi. to the Game Commission parking lot.

Miles N	NORTH	Elev. (ft./m)	Miles S
	Total: 15.1 mi. with access to parking lot		
0.2	Access: **Pine Swamp Rd.** PA Game Commission parking lot, 0.5 mi. S of Eckville.		0.2
14.9	**End AT miles:** Approaching **Hawk Mt.**; AT bears L; take blue-blazed trail to R.	500/152	0.0
13.9	**Panther Spring**; join old **Windsor Furnace Rd.**		1.0
13.2	**Turn L** and begin descent to Eckville.		1.7
12.3	**Gold Spring.**		2.6
10.3	**The Pinnacle.**	1635/498	4.6
9.9	**Blue Rocks Campground** trail (R 1.3 mi.).		5.0
8.2	**Pulpit Rock.**	1582/482	6.7
6.2	**Windsor Furnace Shelter,** creek, privy; begin climb up Blue Mt.		8.7
6.1	**Furnace Creek.**		8.8
6.0	**Hamburg Reservoir; Windsor Furnace;** camping; early exit option.		8.9
4.6	Unnamed **spring.**		10.3
3.3	**Pocohontas Spring.**		11.6
3.2	**Bear R** and begin steep descent.		11.7
2.5	**Cross telephone line clearing.**		12.4
1.5	Reach top of **Blue Mt.** ridge.		13.4
0.7	Cross under **PA 61;** begin steep ascent.		14.2
0.0	**Start: Port Clinton,** parking at trailhead along railroad tracks near Schuylkill River.	400/122	14.9

SOUTH

Hawk Mt. to PA 309

Map: KTA Pa. Section 4

Route: From Hawk Mt. over Blue Mt. ridge to Dan's Pulpit and PA 309

Recommended direction: S to N

Distance: 13.5 mi. total; 13.3 mi. on AT

Access trail name & length: Blue-blazed trail, 0.2 mi.

Elevation +/-: 500 to 1600 to 1350 ft.

Effort: Moderate

Day hike: Yes

Overnight backpacking hike: Optional

Duration: 7½ hr.

Early exit option: At 11.3 mi., Jacksonville-Snyders Rd.

Natural history features: Hawk Mt.; Hawk Mt. Sanctuary

Social history features: Dan's Pulpit; Tri-County Corner

Trailhead access: *Start:* Take I-78 E or W to Exit 11, then PA 143N 3.0 mi. to L onto paved, unnumbered road to Eckville. A PA Game Commission parking lot is 0.5 mi. S of Eckville on Pine Swamp Rd., on the W (R) side of road, 0.2 mi. from the AT. *End:* Take I-78 N or S or NE Extension PA Tpk. (PA 9) to PA 309N near Allentown, go 23.0 mi. to PA Game Commission parking lot for 12 vehicles at top of Blue Mt. ridge, just past AT trailhead sign on E side of road.

Camping: Eckville Shelter; Allentown Shelter

Hawks and rocks. Hikers have plenty of opportunities to look up for one and down for the other on this 13.3-mi. stroll up and along the Blue Mt. ridge. The AT skirts the side of Hawk Mt., once a popular raptor hunting area but since 1934 an internationally recognized sanctuary for the study of more than fourteen species of hawks, falcons, and eagles. The birds use the mountain's strong updrafts to carry them south for the winter. More than 80,000 people visit annually. More than 30,000 birds come too, most between mid-August and mid-December.

This rocky-all-the-way hike begins at the state Game Commission parking lot on Pine Swamp Rd. A blue-blazed side trail leads out of the west end of the lot and 0.2 mi. uphill through a young woods of oak and hemlock, with an understory of mountain laurel, to the AT. Turn right and follow the generally descending trail on a series of old logging roads, all of them fairly rocky. Take care to distinguish the rectangular white AT blazes from the boundary markers for the Game Lands, which are also white but are more irregularly shaped. At 0.5 mi., the trail makes a sharp left uphill and then continues on a logging road, and

Tail Winds

This is the mountain where birds of a feather float aloft on warm updrafts together. Hawk Mountain is famous for its winds, called thermals, and famous too for its magnetic draw on naturalists and birders from around the world. Some have called it the "Crossroads of Naturalists." *Silent Spring* author Rachel Carson, ecologist Roger Tory Peterson, and wildlife artist Robert Bateman are just a few of the many renowned observers of nature who have walked the sanctuary's trails since 1934.

That was the year conservationist Rosalie Edge of New York City heard about how hundreds of gunners had slaughtered hawks, eagles, and falcons as they soared along the Kittatinny Ridge and passed by what is now the North Lookout, 2 miles west of the AT. Edge purchased 1400 acres of mountaintop land at a cost of $2.50 an acre and hired a warden to protect the site, thus establishing the world's first refuge for birds of prey.

The sanctuary had 1250 visitors in 1935, the first year it was open. "A Sunday afternoon in late September rolled around, and to our amazement a steady stream of visitors rolled up the road, many of them to see what it was all about," the sanctuary's first curator, Maurice Broun, recalled during an interview several years later.

Now, located as it is within an easy day's drive for 40 million people, it attracts 75,000 a year. Most come to see the fall migrations, but the sanctuary offers scenic views of the mountains that are year-round attractions. On some lookouts, accessible by footpaths, a 70-mile horizon-to-horizon view is possible.

A science-based conservation organization, Hawk Mountain Sanctuary is an internationally recognized birding site. Its various programs work to protect birds of prey and the mountain's central Appalachian habitat through environmental education, ecological research, and public policy analysis.

But the birds continue to be the draw, just as they were before Edge bought the mountain. In early September the American bald eagle soars over, followed in mid-September by the great broad-winged hawks. Broad-winged hawks, sometimes 100 or more at a time, can be seen above the lookouts, spiraling at various altitudes in circular formations called "kettles." October brings the largest variety of hawks, plus the southern migration of waterfowl, which can be viewed against autumn's colorful backdrop. Visitors in late November can often see golden eagles, especially if the wind is blowing strongly from the northwest.

The 1973 book *Feathers in the Wind,* coauthored by former curators Jim Brett and Alex Nagy, was the first natural history of the sanctuary; it is out of print now. For more information about the sanctuary, see Brett's later book, *The Mountain and the Migration.*

at 0.6 mi. at a crossroads in the woods, it turns right.

The trail reaches the blacktopped Hawk Mt. Rd. at 0.8 mi. The Hawk Mt. Sanctuary (610-756-6961) is 1.2 mi. to the left, up the mountain. Admission is charged. There is no camping permitted in the sanctuary. To the right, Hawk Mt. Rd. descends 0.2 mi. to the Eckville Shelter, on the right (west) side of the road. The shelter is the white building behind the house of the Blue Mt. Eagle Climbing Club caretaker, who is in residence year-round. The shelter has bunks, a stove, water from a tap on the back porch, and a picnic table. Candy bars, sodas, and Coleman fuel by the ounce are for sale. There are tent camping pads and a picnic table in the mowed field across the road.

The AT crosses Hawk Mt. Rd. directly and begins a squiggly route along the side of the mountain through the oaks and hemlocks. At 1.1 mi. it turns left onto an old logging road. There are rhododendron thickets under the high oak canopy. At 1.3 mi., the trail turns left off the road, and then sharply right, crossing a bridge and wood-plank walkway over a creek and a swamp. After the swamp, the trail turns right and then left. After making another left at 1.4 mi. it begins ascending the mountain. At 1.8 mi. the trail crosses a gully on a log bridge, then turns left at 1.9 mi.

The trail in this ascent is very rocky and gullied, and as it climbs to the Blue Mt. ridge it crosses several fields of large, loose quartzite blocks or

Continued on p. 166

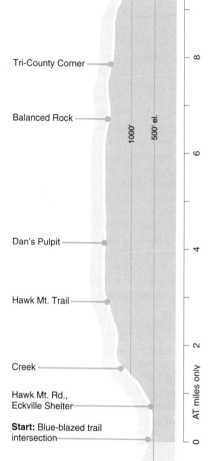

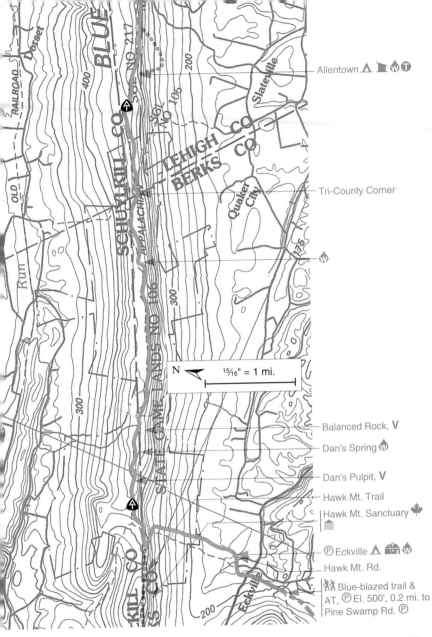

Allentown △ ⊩ ⓦ ⓣ

Tri-County Corner

ⓦ

N ◀ ¹⁵⁄₁₆" = 1 mi.

Balanced Rock, **V**

Dan's Spring ⓦ

Dan's Pulpit, **V**

Hawk Mt. Trail

Hawk Mt. Sanctuary 🍁
🏛

ⓟ Eckville △ 🏚 ⓦ

Hawk Mt. Rd.

🥾 Blue-blazed trail &
AT, ⓟ El. 500', 0.2 mi. to
Pine Swamp Rd. ⓟ

talus. These talus sections alternate with less rocky sections. At 2.5 mi., the trail turns left onto an abandoned cross-mountain road and continues climbing to the oak-and-maple–topped ridge. At 2.9 mi., the AT reaches a blue-blazed trail on the left that leads 2.0 mi. to the northern lookout of the Hawk Mt. Sanctuary. The AT continues up to and along the rocky ridge, leaving the old mountain road at 3.6 mi. and continuing along the ridge on a narrower foot trail.

At 4.2 mi. the trail arrives at Dan's Pulpit (elev. 1600 ft.), a rocky, broken, bedrock ledge sloping to the north. The overlook is named for Danny Hoch, a hiker who often conducted Sunday services on the rocks. From the upper edge there are excellent views south, across the rolling fields and woods around Eckville to The Pinnacle. The view north is of rolling lowland fields, and, in the distance, ridges cut through by the Schuylkill River.

The AT continues ascending along the ridge. At 5.3 mi. it meets a blue-blazed trail on the right that leads downhill 0.75 mi. to a spring and 1.9 mi. to a mountain road in the valley. The ridge begins a gentle decline, taking the trail with it. At 6.1 mi. a blue-blazed trail to the right leads downhill 90 yd. to Dan's Spring, which is sometimes dry. The AT passes Balanced Rock, another outcropping of broken quartzite, to the right of the trail at 6.7 mi. There are views toward The Pinnacle to the south.

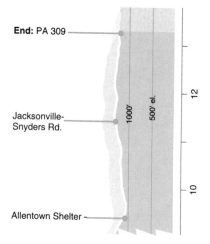

The trail stays on the ridge, continuing a gradual decline to Old Dresher Rd., an unused cross-mountain road, at 7.9 mi. The AT turns right and continues descending through oaks and hemlocks. To the left, a blue-blazed trail leads a short distance to the top of a rock pile known as Tri-County Corner, where there are excellent views and a marker indicating the convergence of Berks, Lehigh, and Schuylkill counties. Tri-County Corner is also the site of the first Appalachian Trail blazing in Pennsylvania, done in 1926 by a Blue Mt. Eagle Climbing Club crew.

The trail turns left into the woods at 8.0 mi., and continues a very rocky descent. A blue-blazed trail straight ahead feeds onto Old Dresher Road and leads 1.8 mi. to the valley to the

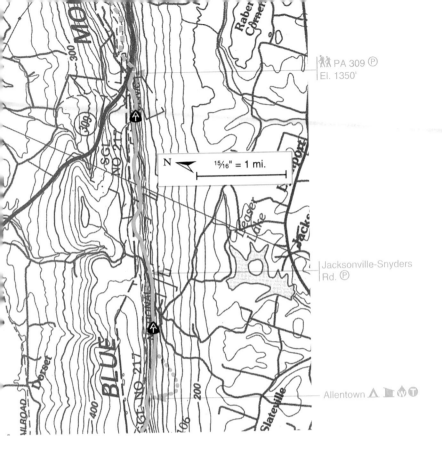

south and an unnumbered country road. The AT continues along the ridge, reaching a woods road through tall oaks, ash, and maple at 9.1 mi. and turning right. At 9.3 mi., a blue-blazed trail to the right leads 30 yd. to the Allentown Shelter, with room for six and a privy. The blue blazes lead 300 yd. to a spring, and the side trail then reconnects to the AT. The spring may not flow in dry seasons, but a lower spring, 0.5 mi. down the mountain on a yellow-blazed trail, is never dry.

The AT ascends gradually with the ridge after the shelter, crossing the Jacksonville-Snyders Rd., a gravel road passable by motor vehicles, at 11.3 mi. This is an early exit option, and there is parking for a handful of vehicles along the road to the right of the trail crossing. The trail continues along the ridge, then turns left and descends at 11.6 mi. In 80 yd. the trail reaches an old woods road and turns right uphill. On the often rocky trail, the ascent is gradual to the Blue Mt. summit (elev. 1350 ft.) on PA 309 at 13.5 mi. The Blue Mt. B & B, which opened in 1997, and a restaurant that serves deli-style meals are here. A water spigot is available outside. The trail turns right along the highway for 0.1 mi. before crossing to the state Game Commission parking lot.

Miles N	**NORTH**	Elev. (ft./m)	Miles S
	Total: 13.5 mi. with access from parking lot		
13.3	**End:** **PA 309,** atop Blue Mt. ridge; parking in PA Game Commission lot (50 yd.)	1350/411	0.0
11.3	**Jacksonville-Snyders Rd.,** early exit option.		2.0
9.3	**Allentown Shelter,** spring, privy.		4.0
7.9	**Tri-County Corner.**		5.4
6.7	**Balanced Rock.**		6.6
6.1	**Dan's Spring** side trail.		7.2
5.3	**Blue-blazed trail** to R leads to spring (0.75 mi.); **AT** **descends** along ridge.		8.0
4.2	**Dan's Pulpit.**	1600/488	9.1
2.9	**Hawk Mt. Trail.**		10.4
1.8	**Log bridge** over gully.		11.5
1.3	Cross unnamed **creek.**		12.0
0.8	**Hawk Mt. Rd.; Eckville Shelter,** spring.		12.5
0.0	**Start AT miles:** Approaching **Hawk Mt.,** intersection of blue-blazed side trail and AT; turn R.	500/152	13.3
0.2	Access: **Pine Swamp Rd.** PA Game Commission parking lot, 0.5 mi. S of Eckville; take blue-blazed trail from W end of lot.		0.2

SOUTH

The Cliffs and Bear Rocks

Map: KTA Pa. Section 3

Route: From PA 309 to the Cliffs (Knife Edge), Bear Rocks, and Bake Oven Knob

Recommended direction: S to N

Distance: 4.9 mi.

Elevation +/-: 1350 to 1520 to 1400 ft.

Effort: Moderate

Day hike: Yes

Overnight backpacking hike: No

Duration: 3 hr.

Early exit option: None

Natural history features: The Cliffs; Bear Rocks

Trailhead access: *Start:* Take I-78 N or S, or NE Extension PA Tpk. (PA 9) to PA 309N near Allentown, go 23.0 mi. to PA Game Commission parking lot for a dozen vehicles at top of Blue Mt. ridge and trailhead. *End:* Take PA 309 to Lehigh Furnace Rd. (2.0 mi. S of Blue Mt. ridge), go 2.0 mi. to Bake Oven Knob Rd., a cross-mountain gravel road, and 2.0 mi. to PA Game Commission parking lot.

Camping: New Tripoli Campsite

This short hike, just under 5 mi. along the rocky Blue Mt. ridge, is long on breathtaking scenery. It is also treacherous enough because of generally rocky footing and a narrow stretch along jutting, knife edge blades of quartzite, known as The Cliffs, to warrant a warning: This hike is not for those with vertigo or without good boots.

The fearless and well-shod can join the AT on the east side of PA 309, just south of the top of the ridge, from the Pennsylvania Game Commission gravel parking lot. There is a 20-yd., blue-blazed trail straight out of the parking lot entrance connecting to the AT, or hikers can walk the 50-yd. gravel road down to PA 309 and turn left and then left again to the trailhead. The trail follows an old rutted mountain road from PA 309, through mountain laurel thickets to where the parking lot trail enters on the left. The AT turns immediately into the spindly oak and ash woods to the right, then turns quickly left through more thickets of mountain laurel.

The trail emerges from the woods at 0.2 mi., and feeds right onto an old mountain road with sharp, jutting rocks passable only by four-wheel-drive vehicles. The trail follows the road on the south side of the ridge under a canopy of oak and ash, and the occasional, remarkable, white paper birch, relatively rare in Pennsylvania. Mountain laurel is scattered throughout the understory, along with a number of campsites. The trail, still following the road, turns rockier as it begins a gradual ascent to the ridge at 0.9 mi. There are good agrarian views off the trail to the right.

At 1.8 mi., the AT, still on the ridge road, reaches a clearing at a power line crossing where again there are good farm views off both sides of the ridge. A blue-blazed trail to the left just beyond the power line leads down to the base of the valley in 0.2 mi., and then to the New Tripoli Campsite with multiple tenting sites and a spring. After the power line crossing, the mountain road peters out, the trail turns narrower, and the footing considerably more rocky, with blazes more often than not painted on quartzite and sandstone rocks instead of trees. It was on this section, in the summer of 1995, that thru-hiker Woodrow "Beorn" Murphy stumbled on a rock classification system that owes nothing to geology. According to Beorn, there are "vampire rocks" that want a hiker's blood, and "hip" rocks that just want a little skin. There are also "jumping rocks" that grab hikers' boots when they think they are in the clear.

As treacherous as the rocks along this section can be, they are nothing compared to those of The Cliffs, or Knife Edge, at 2.6 mi. The trail balances on the knife-edge blades of quartzite for 200 yd. The large, dark-stained slabs show slick, smooth sides with parallel streaks and areas polished from sliding against one another as they move along a fault. This is an area where extreme care is

David Emblidge

Timber rattlesnake

necessary for a safe traverse. Following the trail blazes requires some dexterity and a few handholds. A slip or stumble could result in a dangerous fall onto more rocks. A large pack can make the passage more difficult than it may seem at first, and the always-blowing wind doesn't help. As you screw up courage for the next steps, notice the fine views of checkerboard Pennsylvania farm fields stretching southeast toward the towns of Neffs, Germansville, and Pleasant Corners. Above the scenery buzzards and often hawks ride the updrafts.

The trail lurches from one notable rock outcropping to another, coming to Bear Rocks at 3.5 mi., located just 50 yd. off the trail to the left. To get to the top of the very large and very irregular stack of quartzite requires a 10-min. scramble with handholds up and over boulders ranging in size from refrigerators to tractor trailers. The many vantage points on the top offer a 360-degree panorama of the valleys on both sides of the ridge. This is a popular hangout for local teens on the weekends, and a good spot to watch hawks and vultures glide and ride the wind almost any time. Don't be discouraged by the crowds. There are enough rocks for hikers to find their own and the views are spectacular. This is a don't-miss side trip.

After passing Bear Rocks (also referred to on some maps and guides as Baers Rocks) the trail widens and becomes less rocky, though not rockless, through a spindly oak and white pine woods. It bears right on a grassy road at 4.5 mi. There are plenty of well-established campsites along both sides of the trail. Although the road is rough, there are some signs of recent vehicle use. The campsites, located about a mile from the Bake Oven Knob parking lot, get heavy use by local hikers out for a weekend. Be careful not to confuse the irregularly shaped, white Pennsylvania Game Lands boundary paint on trees along the roadway with the rectangular AT blazes. At 4.9 mi. the trail passes a 3-ft.-tall concrete obelisk just off the trail on the left, marking where Carbon, Lehigh, and Schuylkill counties meet, then skirts the Game Commission parking lot on Bake Oven Knob Rd.

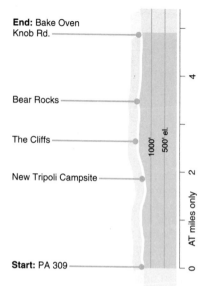

N 1" = 1 mi.

🚶🚶 Bake Oven Knob
Rd. Ⓟ El. 1400'

Bear Rocks, **V**

The Cliffs, **V**

New Tripoli Campsite
⛺ 🔥

Power line, **V**

🚶🚶 PA 309 Ⓟ
El. 1350'

CARBON CO.
SCHUYLKILL CO.
LEHIGH CO.

MOUNTAIN

300

400

200

300

309

Millers

Raberts Corner

Miles N	NORTH	Elev. (ft./m)	Miles S
4.9	**End:** **Bake Oven Knob Rd.,** parking in PA Game Commission lot at trailhead, 2.0 mi. from Lehigh Furnace Rd.	1400/427	0.0
4.5	**Bear R** onto grassy road.		0.4
3.5	**Bear Rocks.**	1520/463	1.4
2.6	**The Cliffs** (Knife Edge).		2.3
1.9	**New Tripoli Campsite** trail.		3.0
1.8	**Power line clearing.**		3.1
0.2	**Bear R** onto rocky mountain road.		4.7
0.0	**Start:** Game Commission parking lot, 50 yd. from **PA 309** atop Blue Mt. ridge.	1350/411	4.9

SOUTH

HIKE #21
Bake Oven Knob to Lehigh Gap

Map: KTA Pa. Section 3

Route: From Bake Oven Knob to Lehigh Furnace, Devil's Pulpit, and Lehigh Gap

Recommended direction: S to N

Distance: 9.5 mi.

Elevation +/-: 1400 to 1560 to 400 ft.

Effort: Moderate

Day hike: Yes

Overnight backpacking hike: No

Duration: 5 hr.

Early exit options: At 1.0 mi., Bake Oven Knob Shelter Trail; at 4.4 mi., Ashfield Rd.

Natural history feature: Bake Oven Knob

Social history features: Lehigh Furnace; Lehigh Gap Superfund site

Trailhead access: Start: Take I-78 N or S or NE Extension PA Tpk. (PA 9) to PA 309N near Allentown; go 21.0 mi. to R on Lehigh Furnace Rd. (2.0 mi. S of Blue Mt. summit), 2.0 mi. to L on Bake Oven Knob Rd., a cross-mountain gravel road that in 2.0 mi. leads to PA Game Commission parking lots for 100 vehicles. End: Take I-476 N or S to Exit 34 at US 209; go S for 2.0 mi. to PA 248E and 5.0 mi. to PA 873 bridge over Lehigh River at Weiders Crossing. There is parking for 6 cars on each end of the bridge and for 20 vehicles on an old rail bed above PA 248, E of the traffic signal at PA 145.

Camping: Bake Oven Knob Shelter, George W. Outerbridge Shelter

---

This hike from Bake Oven Knob to Lehigh Gap is one of the more scenic in the state, although the scenery varies considerably—from hawks floating on mountain updrafts to the stark and stunted landscape caused by a century of zinc mining and smelting at Lehigh Gap.

At the top of the Blue Mt. ridge, where Bake Oven Knob Rd. intersects the AT, the trail passes through Pennsylvania Game Commission parking lots and onto a rocky mountain road impassable by any vehicle this side of a military Humvee. Sandstone and quartzite rocks are the obstacles, and the trail climbs through piles of them. In 0.4 mi. it reaches the Bake Oven Knob summit at 1560 ft. The knob, with views off cliffs to the north and south, is an internationally recognized vantage point for viewing fall hawk migrations. The southern view, reached after scrambling over 50 yd. of boulders to the right of the trail, is the better of the two. Also at the summit hikers can inspect the concrete foundation remains of an old tower that served as an airplane beacon. The trail leading off the knob and through a rock slide on the north side of the mountain presents some of the most

Bake Oven Knob

challenging hiking on the AT in Pennsylvania. Hikers must traverse large boulders and slabs canted at odd angles. Some require daring, broad leaps — especially daring with anything more than a day pack on one's back. Trail markings can also be hard to follow on the light-colored quartzite and sandstone. Take care here. This is a test.

Although it seems that the rocks will go on forever, they gradually peter out and all but disappear as the trail reaches the Bake Oven Knob shelter at 1.0 mi. There are several flat areas for tent camping past the shelter, 20 yd. to the right. A blue-blazed trail in front of the shelter leads quickly to a spring, sometimes dry, and a second spring 200 yd. farther down the hill. The side trail continues

0.7 mi. to Bake Oven Knob Rd., and an additional 1.1 mi. to a paved valley road connecting to PA 309 and PA 873. Unlike at almost all other shelters for long-distance hikers in Pennsylvania, there is no privy at this location. Take care to dispose of human waste properly by burying it.

After the shelter, the trail stays on top of the ridge, on a narrow path through spindly young oak. There is a fine view from an outcrop at 2.9 mi. over forested land on the north side of the ridge. This is an excellent spot for a break or early lunch. The trail continues, still on rocks, into an area where the oaks are more mature. It then crosses a very rocky crest to the north side of the mountain at 3.5 mi., before dipping down the north side and under a transmission line. At 4.4 mi. the trail turns right on Ashville Rd., a cross-mountain road, at Lehigh Furnace. The trail follows the road to the top of the ridge. It passes a gated woods road on the left, and then, in 20 yd., turns left off the road and into the woods. The trail here is rutted and rocky as it ascends at first gently and then more steeply to a state Game Commission boundary at 4.7 mi.

The trail turns right, ascending along the poker-straight hunting lands border for 0.7 mi. through the young oak and ash woods before turning left, away from the Game Lands' boundary and its irregularly shaped white blazes. The AT crosses an abandoned telephone line at 5.4 mi., and vegetation dramatically changes to the desolate, windswept landscape dotted with stunted pines, oak, and brushy ground cover that dominates the wide crest of Blue Mt. into the Lehigh Gap. Blueberry bushes abound, their fruit ripening in June. The trail is alternately grassy and rocky on the flat ridge top.

At 5.7 mi., a very rocky bypass follows blue blazes to the right over an unmaintained trail to a large rock outcrop with wonderful views to the south and the town of Slatedale. The bypass loops back to the AT in 0.7 mi. At 6.9 mi., the AT passes over the Northeast Extension of the Pennsylvania Tpk., which goes through a tunnel 675 ft. below.

At 7.1 mi., the blue-blazed North Trail branches to the left of the AT. The North Trail follows the northern crest of Blue Mt. for 2.4 mi. before rejoining the AT and is the more scenic of the two routes. The hiking is uneven as the grassy trail clings to the side of the ridge. It is not a wholly unpleasant respite from the rocks. The North Trail is more exposed to winter storms, but is recommended at all other times as the preferred path, with fine views of Palmerton and the Lehigh River valley all along the route, as well as several magnificent campsites. At 2.0 mi. along the North Trail another blue-blazed trail leads down to the left 0.4 mi. to Devil's Pulpit. There are good views from the Pulpit of the Lehigh Gap and Lehigh River, and of the mountainside across the river largely denuded by emissions from a century of zinc mining and smelting in Palmerton. Trees that remain are gray and dwarfed. The federal government shut down the zinc furnaces in 1980 and put the area on the federal Superfund cleanup list in 1982. The acidic soil is slowly being revegetated through the application of Ecoloam, a mixture of municipal waste sludge, fly ash, lime, fertilizer, and seeds. Pines, tall grasses, and blueberry bushes are starting to take hold, although big swathes of mountain on the opposite side of the valley still look like coppery-colored moonscapes. The North Trail rejoins the AT at 8.7 mi. and, 0.1 mi. later, passes in front of the George W. Outerbridge Shelter, which has a privy below and a piped spring 150 yd. farther along the trail.

After passing the spring, the trail turns rockier and steeply descends to a meadow, passing under power lines at 9.2 mi., where there are good views of the river and bridge. The trail zigzags through a sloping, barren field down to PA 873, at 9.5 mi., where it passes through a gravel parking lot before crossing the road and then the bridge over the Lehigh River.

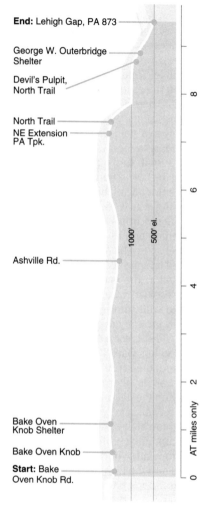

End: Lehigh Gap, PA 873

George W. Outerbridge Shelter

Devil's Pulpit, North Trail

North Trail

NE Extension PA Tpk.

Ashville Rd.

1000'

500' el.

Bake Oven Knob Shelter

Bake Oven Knob

Start: Bake Oven Knob Rd.

AT miles only

8

6

4

2

0

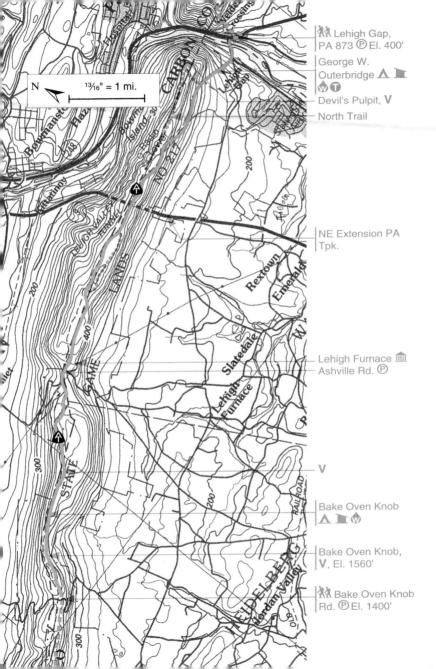

N 13⁄16" = 1 mi.

Lehigh Gap, PA 873 ℗ El. 400'

George W. Outerbridge ▲ 🏕 ⊛ ☕

Devil's Pulpit, **V**

North Trail

NE Extension PA Tpk.

Lehigh Furnace 🏛
Ashville Rd. ℗

V

Bake Oven Knob ▲ 🏕 ⊛

Bake Oven Knob, **V**, El. 1560'

Bake Oven Knob Rd. ℗ El. 1400'

Miles N	NORTH	Elev. (ft./m)	Miles S
9.5	**End:** In Lehigh Gap at PA 873 bridge, parking at trailhead.	400/122	0.0
8.8	**George W. Outerbridge Shelter,** spring, privy.		0.3
8.7	**North Trail** northern terminus; 0.8 mi. to **Devil's Pulpit.**		0.5
7.1	**North Trail** southern terminus (L), recommended route.		2.4
6.9	NE Extension PA Tpk. **tunnel** under AT.		2.6
5.7	Blue-blazed trail to **scenic view.**		3.8
4.4	**Ashville Rd,** early exit option.		5.1
2.9	**Scenic view.**		6.6
1.0	**Bake Oven Knob Shelter,** spring, early exit option.		8.5
0.4	**Bake Oven Knob** summit.	1560/475	9.1
0.0	**Start:** Bake Oven Knob Rd., parking at trailhead in PA Game Commission lot, 2.0 mi. from Lehigh Furnace Rd.	1400/427	9.5

SOUTH

Lehigh Gap to Smith Gap Rd.

Map: KTA Pa. Section 2

Route: From Lehigh Gap over Blue Mt. ridge to Smith Gap Rd.

Recommended direction: S to N

Distance: 12.6 mi.

Elevation +/-: 400 to 1420 to 1580 to 1560 ft.

Effort: Strenuous

Day hike: Yes

Overnight backpacking hike: No

Duration: 7½ hr.

Early exit option: At 5.1 mi., Little Gap Rd. (PA 4001)

Natural history feature: Little Gap

Other feature: EPA Superfund site

Trailhead access: *Start:* Take I-476 N or S to Exit 34 at US 209; go S for 2.0 mi. to PA 248E and 5.0 mi. to PA 873 bridge over Lehigh River at Weiders Crossing. There is parking for 6 cars on each end of the bridge and for 20 vehicles on an old rail bed above PA 248, E of the traffic signal at PA 145. *End:* From AT trailhead at Lehigh Gap, take PA 248E 2.0 mi. to PA 946E; go 10.0 mi. to Klecknersville, turn L onto cross-mountain Smith Gap Rd. connecting Point Phillip to Kunkletown and 3.0 mi. to AT crossing. Pavement changes to gravel 0.7 mi. before trailhead at crest of ridge. (For an alternate route see Hike #23.) There is parking for 6 to 10 cars along the road here, but cars have been vandalized overnight. There is parking for 20 vehicles at a PA Game Commission lot 0.3 mi. S of the trailhead.

Camping: Trail is through state Game Lands most of the way, where camping is permitted.

This 12.6-mi. hike begins with a steep 1000-ft. climb through a polluted, barren Superfund cleanup site. It's not as bad as it sounds. In fact, many hikers find the scramble out of Lehigh Gap, up a pockmarked Blue Mt. face shaved clean of vegetation by a century of unregulated emissions from zinc mining and smelting industries, an interesting change of pace. While most of the AT in Pennsylvania is a woods-lined walk under a leafy canopy, this section, coming out of the spectacular gorge cut by the Lehigh River through Blue Mt. (see Hike #21), could easily pass for the Dakota Badlands or gold mining country west of Denver, Colorado. Or the moon.

Start at the PA 873 bridge over the Lehigh River at Weiders Crossing. Cross to the east side and turn right along PA 248. At 0.4 mi., cross the highway at the traffic light at PA 145. Turn left along the highway for 150 ft., then right up an embankment and cross an abandoned railroad bed where there is alternative parking for hiker vehicles.

The trail ascends to the right, gradually at first, and then much more steeply, requiring hikers to use handholds to scramble up ledges and boulders in some places. Low on the climb there is evidence of direct glacial action—the first northbound hikers will see in Pennsylvania. Although there is nothing to show that glacial ice covered the top of Blue Mt., a few long, rounded ledges paralleling the mountain show signs that extremely erosive moving ice containing abrasive sand and grit did flow along the valley on the south side of the mountain. The rounded ledges contrast sharply with the blocky, angular quartzite on the upper half of the climb and with those along the trail to the south where the glaciers did not have an impact.

The trail reaches the shoulder of the ridge, where there are fine, wide views of Palmerton, the former zinc smelter, and the meandering Lehigh River. The U.S. Environmental Protection Agency closed the Palmerton zinc furnaces in 1980 when they could not meet clean air standards, and declared the area a Superfund site in 1982. On the other, southern, side of Lehigh Gap, vegetation is slowly returning, but on the northeast side's coppery-colored moonscape, regreening remains mostly a good thought.

The trail crosses a rock slide as the grade becomes easier, and at 1.0 mi. the AT turns right at a sign for the

Continued on p. 184

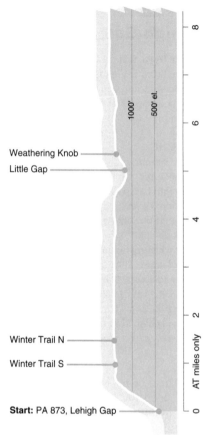

blue-blazed Winter Trail, which rejoins the AT at 1.5 mi. The AT, still very rocky, bears right at 1.3 mi., and at 1.8 mi. reaches a dirt road that it follows through an open, barren area on top of the wide, flat ridge. This area can be brutally sunny and hot in summer, and it is recom-

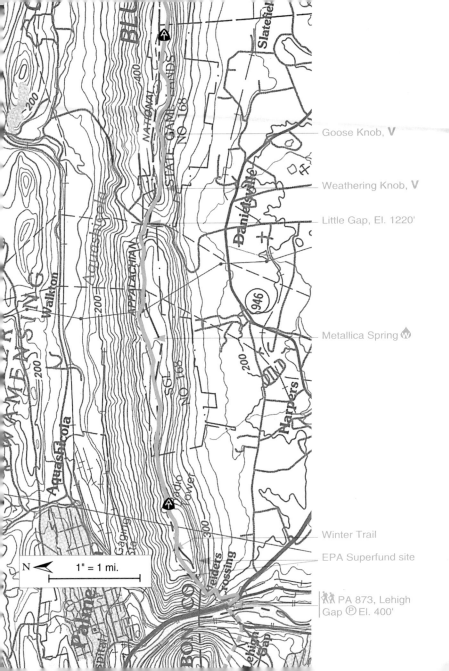

Goose Knob, **V**

Weathering Knob, **V**

Little Gap, El. 1220'

Metallica Spring

Winter Trail

EPA Superfund site

PA 873, Lehigh
Gap Ⓟ El. 400'

N 1" = 1 mi.

mended that hikers pack extra water. A spring at 4.0 mi., located 200 ft. down a blue-blazed trial to the left of the AT, has been dubbed "Metallica Spring." While reliable, it carries an EPA pollution warning.

Just past the spring, the trail crosses under high-tension electric lines. A rise to the right of the trail offers good views toward Slatington to the south. There is a clearing through scrub oaks and brush for a pipeline crossing at 4.3 mi. and the trail begins its descent into Little Gap. It crosses paved Little Gap Rd. (PA 4001), a cross-mountain road, at 5.1 mi. There is parking along the road and this is a good early exit option. The town of Danielsville is 1.5 mi. to the right.

After the road crossing, the trail passes through a boggy area, then climbs out of the gap on a steep talus slope; hikers must sometimes use handholds to scale the large quartzite blocks. The trail reaches Weathering Knob at 5.4 mi. There are good views of the Aquashicola Creek valley and Chestnut Ridge to the north and northwest. The trail turns right at 5.7 mi., and turns right again at 5.9 mi. onto an old mountain road. The trail climbs to Goose Knob at 6.1 mi., which offers good views of farmland to the south and southwest.

Following the knob, the trail enters a medium-aged oak woods, leaving the mountain road at 6.4 mi., and turning right at 7.2 mi. The trail continues on a mostly flat ridgetop route, crossing a power line at 9.0 mi.,

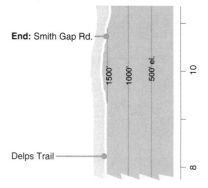

before climbing gently to reach the blue-blazed Delps Trail at 10.0 mi., which goes right 1.1 mi. to a mountain road. A spring is located 0.4 mi. down this side trail, but is reliable only in spring and late fall. A sign at the AT-Delps intersection usually gives water status for the spring. There are two springs located 1.3 mi. down Delps trail that are usually reliable.

From the Delps Trail intersection, the AT traverses familiar Pennsylvania terrain — wooded, canopied, rocky, and along the top of a ridge — down to Smith Gap Rd. at 12.6 mi. There have been numerous bear sightings in the area around the trailhead over the last several years. John Stempa, a trail maintainer in the area (see Hike #23) is happy to roll an up-

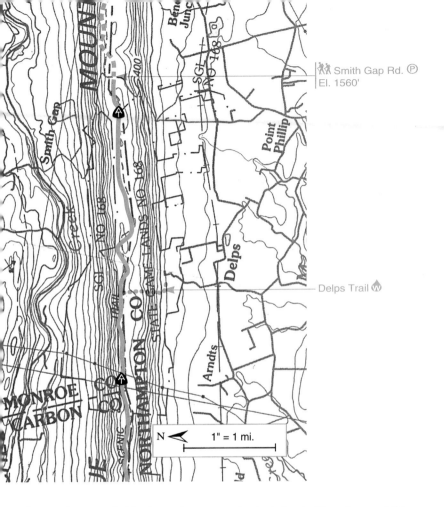

Delps Trail 🐾

1" = 1 mi.

close-and-personal videotape of one papa bear who paid a visit to Stempa's "Blue Mountain Dome" home, just down the mountain. Although bears are not uncommon along this section of trail, Stempa warns that the greater danger may be from vandals who target vehicles parked at the trailhead overnight. The state Game Commission lot, 0.3 mi. south of the trailhead, down the steep, unpaved Smith Gap Rd. may be a better bet.

Miles N	NORTH	Elev. (ft./m)	Miles S
12.6	**End:** Smith Gap Rd., parking at trailhead, 3.0 mi. from Klecknersville.	1560/475	0.0
10.0	**Delps Trail** to spring.	1580/482	2.6
9.0	**Power line.**		3.6
6.1	**Goose Knob.**		6.5
5.4	**Weathering Knob.**		7.2
5.1	**Little Gap;** cross Little Gap Rd. (PA 4001), early exit option.		7.5
4.3	**Pipeline.**		8.3
4.0	**Metallica Spring.**		8.6
1.5	**Winter Trail** loop rejoins the AT.		11.1
1.0	**Winter Trail** loop southern terminus; AT turns R.	1420/433	11.6
0.0	**Start:** In Lehigh Gap at PA 873 bridge, parking at trailhead.	400/122	12.6

SOUTH

Smith Gap Rd. to Wind Gap

Maps: ATC Pa. Section 2

Route: From Smith Gap Rd. to Lookout Rocks to Wind Gap

Recommended direction: S to N

Distance: 8.0 mi.

Elevation +/-: 1560 to 1420 to 960 ft.

Effort: Easy

Day hike: Yes

Overnight backpacking hike: No

Duration: 5 hr.

Early exit option: At 3.4 mi., Katellen Trail

Natural history features: Hahn's Lookout; Lookout Rocks; Wind Gap

Trailhead access: *Start:* Take I-78 N or S (becomes US 22 N of Allentown) to PA 512E to Bath, then PA 946/987N to Klecknersville, and L onto cross-mountain Smith Gap Rd. (connecting Point Phillip to Kunkletown) for 3.0 mi. Pavement changes to gravel 0.7 mi. before trailhead at crest of ridge, where there is parking for 6 to 10 vehicles along the road. Vandalism of vehicles parked overnight has been reported. Parking also for 20 vehicles at a state Game Commission lot 0.3 mi. S of the trailhead. *End:* Take PA 512E to Wind Gap; turn L onto Saylorsburg-Wind Gap Rd. (For an alternate route see Hike #24.) Parking area for 10 vehicles at trailhead on R or E side of road.

Camping: Leroy A. Smith Shelter; camping permitted in state Game Lands

H ikers who spend any time at all gearing up for this 8.0-mi. ridgetop walk at the AT's Smith Gap Rd. trailhead are likely to meet John Stempa, a.k.a. The Mechanical Man. The gregarious trail maintainer and hiker always seems to be in the area, and ready with reports on local trail conditions (good since horses and off-road vehicles were barred from this section of the trail), recent bear sightings (numerous), and vehicle vandalism (it happens, but not as much as it once did). He is also free with invitations to the Blue Mountain Dome, the home he shares with Linda "Crayon Lady" Gellock, his wife and trail partner. At their home, 1.0 mi. north of the trailhead, hikers can get water from an outdoor spigot or review scrapbooks of AT news clippings. Thru-hikers can even use an outdoor shower.

The AT crosses Smith Gap Rd. directly, passing an informational kiosk maintained by Stempa and entering a young woods with a typical oak and maple canopy and mountain laurel understory. It descends gently from Smith Gap Rd., turning right onto a woods road at 0.2 mi. before reaching the actual gap.

The trail ascends out of the gap and again attains the broad, rocky, wooded ridge top. Red quartzite appears in places, but the gray, cross-bedded (or pebbled) conglomerate quartzite is more common. Is it *ever* common. The sharp, uneven, and highly mobile rocks along this section of the trail make it tough on tender-footed thru-hikers and weekend tenderfoots.

At 1.3 mi. the trail bears right, making a flat crossing to the southeast side of the ridge. There are white state Game Lands boundary markers spray-painted on trees in this area that can be confusing to hikers. Generally they are larger and have a more irregular shape than the AT blazes, which are well defined and rectangular. Care should be taken to properly identify the trail route.

After a gentle decline and steeper ascent, the trail reaches the blue-blazed Katellen Trail on the right (south) at 3.4 mi. The Katellen Trail crosses a field, goes into the woods, and bears right on an old woods road that leads to the Leroy A. Smith Shelter in 0.1 mi. There is a new solar composting privy at the shelter and springs at 0.2 mi., 0.4 mi., and 0.5 mi. down the side trail, which leads to a vehicular road at 0.9 mi. The first and second springs are sometimes dry, but the third is usually flowing, though it requires a long walk. Water here has failed potability tests in the past, but the new privy should help. Treatment is still recommended. Watch out for

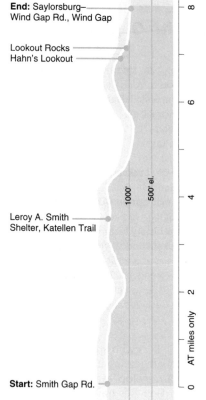

bears, which have been frequently spotted in the area.

Just past the shelter, at 3.6 mi., the AT crosses a power line clearing that offers fine views to the north of Chicola Lake and Aquashicola Creek. The trail continues to follow the north side of the ridge, crossing an underground pipeline clearing at 5.3 mi. and beginning the 500-ft., almost-

Saylorsburg–Wind Gap Rd., Ⓟ El. 960'
Lookout Rocks, **V**
Hahn's Lookout, **V**

Pipeline, **V**

Power line, **V**
Katellen Trail
Leroy A. Smith ▲ 🛏
🔥 ☕

Smith Gap Rd. Ⓟ
El. 1560'

3-mi. descent into Wind Gap. At 7.0 mi., the trail reaches Hahn's Lookout, with southern views to Wind Gap village and, in the distance, South Mt.

The trail takes to the south side of the ridge after Hahn's Lookout, reaching Lookout Rocks at 7.2 mi. The rocks afford fine northern views of the Chestnut Ridge and Aquashicola Creek in the foreground and the Pocono Mts. in the distance. The trail begins descending toward Wind Gap more steeply, on a very rocky route, crossing a power line at 7.7 mi.

Wind Gap's geological origin is noteworthy and a bit controversial. The best evidence now shows that a stream once flowed south across the mountain in a water gap, like those of the Schuylkill and Lehigh rivers. Long ago, another stream captured the headwaters of the Wind Gap stream, leaving the gap high and dry. The land slowly rose over time and the former stream valley was reduced to a notch in the ridge.

The trail reaches Wind Gap at Saylorsburg-Wind Gap Rd. at 7.9 mi. A series of newly constructed switchbacks and steps made from cut railroad ties lead to the roadway. The trail passes underneath PA 33, and at 8.0 mi. crosses to a parking area on the east side of the road at the marked AT trailhead.

Miles N		NORTH	Elev. (ft./m)	Miles S
8.0	**End:** **Saylorsburg-Wind Gap Rd.** in Wind Gap; parking lot at trailhead.		960/293	0.0
7.9	Pass under **PA 33.**			0.1
7.7	**Power line.**			0.3
7.2	**Lookout Rocks.**		1420/433	0.8
7.0	**Hahn's Lookout.**			1.0
5.3	**Pipeline.**			2.7
3.6	**Power line,** views.			4.4
3.4	**Katellen Trail** R to **Leroy A. Smith Shelter,** springs, early exit option.			4.6
0.2	**Turn R** onto woods road.			7.8
0.0	**Start:** **Smith Gap Rd.,** parking at trailhead, 3.0 mi. from Klecknersville.		1560/475	8.0

SOUTH

Wind Gap to Fox Gap

Map: KTA Pa. Section 1

Route: From Wind Gap over Little Offset to Wolf Rocks to Fox Gap

Recommended direction: S to N

Distance: 8.1 mi.

Elevation +/-: 960 to 1575 to 1220 ft.

Effort: Moderate

Day hike: Yes

Overnight backpacking hike: No

Duration: 5 hr.

Early exit option: None

Natural history feature: Wolf Rocks

Trailhead access: *Start:* Take I-80 E or W to PA 33, go S 5.0 mi. to Wind Gap exit and S onto Saylorsburg-Wind Gap Rd. Parking for 10 vehicles is at trailhead on E side of road at the exit. *End:* Take I-80 E or W to Stroudsburg exit. Go S on PA 191 for 4.0 mi. to Fox Gap. Parking for 6 vehicles on W side of road at trailhead.

Camping: Permitted in state Game Lands

Rocksylvania saves some of the toughest hiking for last. This 8.1-mi. toe stubber proves it, with many closely, if erratically, spaced rocks that make it more of a job than an adventure. The unfunny joke among the hiking set is that the trail maintainers use files to sharpen the quartzite shards each spring. One thru-hiker from Michigan, encountered during a rest stop on the way up the ascent from Fox Gap during the summer of 1997, commented that he wasn't too keen on the trail through Pennsylvania because of all the rocks, but couldn't offer a good opinion on the rest of the state because he never was able to look up long enough to see it. This section of trail skips from Blue Mt. to Kittatinny Mt. with barely a dip or a change in the rocky footing. The best parts of this hike are the stops, at outcrops that offer scenic views over forested valleys.

The AT climbs steeply out of the parking lot on Saylorsburg-Wind Gap Rd. in Wind Gap, up a rocky hillside through small, spindly oaks. Traffic sounds from PA 33, a nearby four-lane highway, can be heard distinctly for the entire 0.6-mi. ascent, adding insult to the physical injury. Rocks litter the trail like hungry piranhas, biting the boots of unwary hikers. At the top of the ridge, the trail meanders under a canopy of scrawny oaks and elms, through rocks too small to sit on, thus depriving the hiker of any benefit from their presence. They are sized instead to be obstacles, and perform that role quite well.

At 1.9 mi. the trail crosses the private road of the Blue Mt. Water Co.

There are good forested views to the north, and the road to the left reaches the Nazareth Reservoir in 1.3 mi. The AT continues along the rocky ridge top, eventually crossing from Blue Mt. to Kittatinny Mt. at a fold in the rock bed. The divide between them is so broad and flat that most hikers don't even notice they're stepping from one mountain to the other. The name Kittatinny derives from the Delaware (Lenape) Indians' name for the mountain, "Kekachtanin," meaning "endless mountain." The rock fold created the Big Offset and Little Offset ridges. Loose rocks are common and small quartz crystals and molds of seashells can sometimes be found by hikers. At 5.3 mi., a blue-blazed trail to the right leads down 0.3 mi. to a spring that is not always reliable.

The trail reaches Wolf Rocks at 6.5 mi., where there are good views to Fox Gap, the Delaware Water Gap, and all the way into New Jersey. The rocks themselves are tall, broken ledges of very smooth quartzite. Unlike most other rock beds in Pennsylvania's Appalachians, which are angled to the northwest, the Wolf Rocks outcrop dips toward the southeast. At the rocks and along the trail to the north there is evidence of glacial scouring—grit, gravel, and even sand.

The trail turns left from Wolf Rocks and drops off their north side under a canopy of oak and through an understory of mountain laurel. At 6.8

David Emblidge

Checking the Trail Register

mi., the trail meets an old roadway that comes up from Cherry Valley to the left. The trail turns right on the mountain road, passes under a power line, and begins a gradual, 300-ft. descent into Fox Gap. At 7.4 mi., the trail turns left, leaving one woods road and following another. An old telephone cable clearing at 7.9 mi., which is slowly being reclaimed by trees, still offers mostly unobscured views of Stroudsburg to the north. The trail is wide, shaded by tall oaks, and surprisingly less rocky as it descends to the parking lot for six vehicles at the trailhead on PA 191 in Fox Gap.

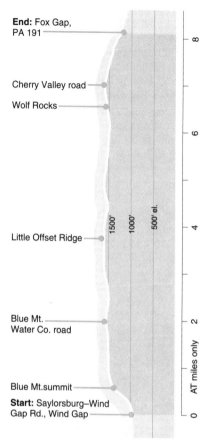

End: Fox Gap, PA 191

Cherry Valley road

Wolf Rocks

Little Offset Ridge

Blue Mt. Water Co. road

Blue Mt. summit

Start: Saylorsburg–Wind Gap Rd., Wind Gap

1500' 1000' 500' el.

8

6

4

2

0

AT miles only

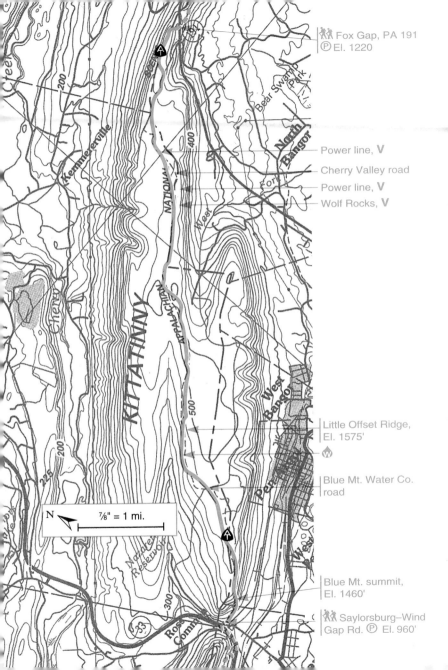

🚶 Fox Gap, PA 191
Ⓟ El. 1220

Power line, **V**

Cherry Valley road

Power line, **V**

Wolf Rocks, **V**

Little Offset Ridge,
El. 1575'

Ⓦ

Blue Mt. Water Co.
road

N ↘ ⊢—— 7/8" = 1 mi. ——⊣

Blue Mt. summit,
El. 1460'

🚶 Saylorsburg–Wind
Gap Rd. Ⓟ El. 960'

Miles N	NORTH	Elev. (ft./m)	Miles S
8.1	**End:** PA 191 at Fox Gap, parking at trailhead, 4.0 mi. to I-80.	1220/372	0.0
7.9	Old **telephone cable clearing**.		0.2
6.9	**Power line**.		1.2
6.8	**Cherry Valley** road.		1.3
6.5	**Wolf Rocks**.		1.6
5.3	Trail to **spring** (0.3 mi.).		2.8
3.7	**Little Offset** ridge.	1575/480	4.4
1.9	**Blue Mt. Water Co.** road.		6.2
0.6	**Blue Mt.** ridge summit.	1460/445	7.5
0.0	**Start:** **Saylorsburg-Wind Gap Rd.,** parking at trailhead in lot.	960/293	8.1

SOUTH

Fox Gap to Delaware Water Gap

Map: KTA Pa. Section 1

Route: From Fox Gap to Mt. Minsi to Delaware Water Gap

Recommended direction: S to N

Distance: 7.0 mi.

Elevation +/-: 1220 to 1480 to 300 ft.

Effort: Easy

Day hike: Yes

Overnight backpacking hike: No

Duration: 4 hr.

Early exit option: None

Natural history features: Fox Gap; Mt. Minsi; Lake Lenape; Delaware Water Gap

Other feature: Profile of Chief Tammany on mountain across from Winona Cliff

Trailhead access: *Start:* Take I-80 E or W to Stroudsburg exit and PA 191S for 4.0 mi. to Fox Gap. Parking for 6 vehicles on W side of road at trailhead. *End:* Take I-80 E or W to Delaware Water Gap village, then PA 611S to Broad St. Turn L at traffic signal onto Main St., R onto Mt. Rd., L onto Lake Rd. Parking for 20 vehicles in Lake Lenape lot on R side of Lake Rd. at trailhead.

Camping: Kirkridge Shelter

The footing on this 7.2-mi. section of Kittatinny Mt. is sharp and jagged and rough, like much of the rest of the AT through northern Pennsylvania. But how can you not like a hike that passes Lunch Rocks, the most hospitably named chunk of quartzite on the ridge? It gives hikers something to look forward to for at least half the day. Lunch Rocks overlook does not appear on hiking maps of the area, but it is listed as a destination on the informational kiosk erected by the Wilmington Trail Club, 0.2 mi. from the parking area along PA 191 in Fox Gap, the lowest point (1220 ft.) on the trail's traverse of the Kittatinny ridge. The trail crosses the cross-mountain blacktop directly from the parking area and descends gently through a young-to-middle-aged woods of maple and oak to the kiosk, which also provides information about Pennsylvania's hunting seasons, emergency phone numbers, and water filtration advice (just do it). It should also be noted that water can be scarce along this trail section, especially in late summer or during dry spells, so it's best to tote a good supply even though this hike is relatively short.

At 0.6 mi. the trail reaches the Kirkridge Shelter, located 200 ft. up a blue-blazed trail to the left. A composting privy is 75 ft. to the right of the shelter. Water is available from an outside spigot provided by the owners of Kirkridge Retreat, a religious meeting hall. The spigot is located 200 ft. behind and to the left of the shelter. If stopping for water, make sure the faucet is turned off. The trail leaves the shelter and ascends, crossing a gravel road leading to the retreat building and a radio tower and then crossing to the north side of the ridge, where it moves through a young woods of ash, oak, and poplar with an understory of mountain laurel. The trail in this section is littered with thousands of small, sharp rocks jutting from the path at angles aggravating to ankles and toes. The trail reaches Lunch Rocks at 1.4 mi. on the right, with ample room to spread a picnic or take a break on the smooth quartzite ledges and enjoy fine valley views to the south.

Following the ridge on its rocky way down to Totts Gap, the trail crosses two power lines at 2.3 mi., and reaches the gap after a descent of 200 ft., at 2.5 mi. The AT bears right into the woods, passing two communications towers. At 2.8 mi., the trail turns left, and then right, onto a gravel road. It follows the climbing road for almost 2 mi., reaching the wooded summit of Mt. Minsi (elev. 1480 ft.) at 4.6 mi. From the summit the trail begins its more than 1100-ft. descent on a series of switchbacks that offer excellent views of the Delaware Water Gap. Take care to follow the trail. The broad ridge, where big clusters of blue forget-me-nots bloom in May in the sunshine dapples, is crisscrossed with side trails to viewpoints. It is easy to lose track of

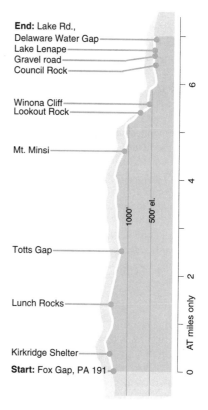

End: Lake Rd., Delaware Water Gap
Lake Lenape
Gravel road
Council Rock

Winona Cliff
Lookout Rock

Mt. Minsi

Totts Gap

Lunch Rocks

Kirkridge Shelter
Start: Fox Gap, PA 191

the white blazes, which are often painted on the rocks. Note too that some of the rocks in this section are not quartzite, but younger red slates and sandstone.

At 5.5 mi. reach Lookout Rock. On a clear day, there are exceptional views to the east and north stretching for 20 mi. or more over the Delaware River and multiple ridges into a surprisingly green, forested New Jersey. The trail hugs the side of the mountain, descending gently

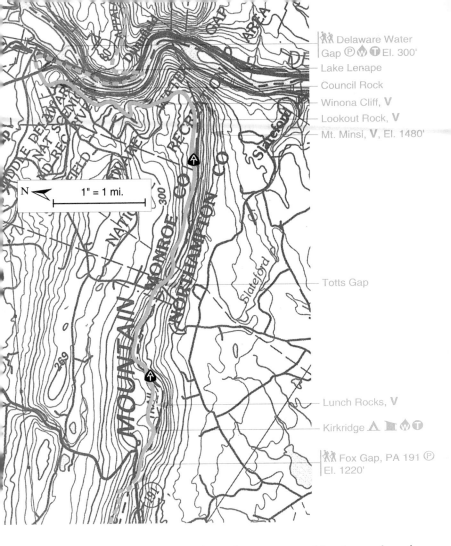

Delaware Water Gap ℗ 🏕 🚾 El. 300'
Lake Lenape
Council Rock
Winona Cliff, **V**
Lookout Rock, **V**
Mt. Minsi, **V**, El. 1480'

N ◄ 1" = 1 mi.

Totts Gap

Lunch Rocks, **V**

Kirkridge ▲ 🛏 🏕 🚾

Fox Gap, PA 191 ℗ El. 1220'

below Lookout Rock through woods made dark and refreshingly cool by tall hemlock and waxy-leaved rhododendron that bloom throughout June and into July. The trail crosses a small brook at 5.6 mi., where water tumbles down a broad rock face slick with green algae, then returns to the edge of the escarpment along the river. At 5.7 mi., the view from Winona Cliff is of Mt. Tammany, across the Delaware River.

Native American lore has it that the bare, canted rock beds of the mountain that dip to the north show the profile of Delaware (Lenape) Chief Tammany. After Winona Cliff, the wide and well-worn trail drops through more hemlock and rhododendron and crosses big, blocky rocks that make rough steps. Traffic noise from I-80 along the Delaware River begins to intrude.

At Council Rock, an open area under a grove of older hemlocks (6.3 mi.), the trail bears to the left, climbing through several primitive camping areas to a gravel service road at 6.5 mi. The trail turns right onto the road and descends gently, passing tranquil Lake Lenape on the left at 6.9 mi. Hundreds of lily pads dot the surface of the lake, and around its edges blue and green herons often fish.

The trail goes around a metal gate that bars vehicular traffic from the mountain road, and in less than 100 yd. passes to the right of the lake parking lot.

Kick off the hiking boots and slip into the charming tourist village of Delaware Water Gap, which fills the flatlands on the Pennsylvania side of the Delaware River between Mt. Minsi and Mt. Tammany. The mountains— actually two parts of Kittatinny Mt.— were separated by the Delaware River, which cut across the northeast-southwest ridge by taking advantage of weakened, broken beds of otherwise very hard and resistant rock. The ridges rose as the river continued to erode the center, leaving the high ridges of Minsi and Tammany.

In between, the village has flourished as a tourist stop with more charm than tackiness. The Deer Head Inn, at the corner of Mountain Rd. and Main St., is a regional center for jazz and fine dining.

Also on Main St. is the Presbyterian Church of the Mountain, which operates a year-round hostel, for thru-hikers only, in its basement. Across from the church is the Trail's End Cafe, offering meat dishes and vegetarian fare in a relaxed bistro atmosphere.

Around the corner on Broad St. is the Water Gap Diner, offering filling hiker fare (great milkshakes) and next door, the Gap Fruitstand and Bakery, home of the best doughnuts in the world.

The Water Gap Trolley is a 1-hr. ride that visits the scenic and historic points of interest in the Gap.

Miles N	NORTH	Elev. (ft./m)	Miles S
7.0	**End:** Delaware Water Gap, parking at trailhead in lot on Lake Rd.	300/91	0.0
6.9	**Lake Lenape.**		0.1
6.5	**Gravel road.**		0.5
6.3	**Council Rock.**		0.6
5.7	**Winona Cliff;** profile in rock of Chief Tammany.		1.2
5.6	Cross **brook.**		1.3
5.5	**Lookout Rock.**	1000/305	1.4
4.6	**Mt. Minsi** summit; begin descent on switchback.	1480/451	2.3
2.5	**Totts Gap.**		4.4
2.3	**Power lines.**		4.6
1.4	**Lunch Rocks.**		5.5
0.6	**Kirkridge Shelter,** water spigot, privy.		6.3
0.0	**Start:** PA 191 at Fox Gap, parking at trailhead in lot, 4.0 mi. to I-80.	1220/372	6.9

SOUTH

Sunfish Pond and Mt. Mohican

Maps: ATC N.Y. & N.J. Map 6; NY-NJTC Kittatinny Trails S Map 15

Route: From Dunnfield Creek Natural Area to Sunfish Pond, Mt. Mohican, and Camp Rd.

Recommended direction: S to N

Distance: 8.8 mi.

Elevation +/-: 350 to 1500 to 1100 ft.

Effort: Strenuous

Day hike: Yes

Overnight backpacking hike: Optional

Duration: 6 hr.

Early exit options: At 1.5 mi., Beulahland Trail and Holly Springs Trail; at 3.1 mi., Douglas Trail; at 4.1 mi., Garvey Springs Trail

Natural history features: Dunnfield Hollow hemlock ravine; Sunfish Pond (glacial lake); Mt. Mohican vistas

Social history features: Yards Creek Reservoir; Herb Hiller plaque

Trailhead access: *Start:* Take I-80 W to Exit 1 in NJ. Turn L at stop sign and in 0.4 mi. come to Delaware Water Gap National Recreation Area Kittatinny Information Center. Turn L through the I-80 underpass, L again on far side of underpass, and immediately R into Dunnfield Creek Natural Area parking lot (overnight). *End:* Take I-80 E or W to NJ 94N for 8.0 mi. to Jacksonburg. Turn L onto Mohican Rd. and follow for 3.5 mi. (bearing R at the forks). Turn L on Gaisler Rd. and go 0.5 mi. Turn R onto Camp Rd. (dirt) for 0.8 mi. Daytime parking for 3 or 4 cars just beyond trail around bend.

Camping: Sunfish Pond Backpacker site; Delaware Water Gap National Recreation Area (tent camping 75 ft. off trail or at least 0.5 mi. off roads); AMC Mohican Outdoor Center (call 908-362-5670 for information)

S unfish Pond is one of the most popular hiking destinations in New Jersey, with good reason. The rocky shores of this crystal clear glacial lake are postcard perfect. Get an early start for this hike, or go on a weekday or in winter. You will miss the crowds and improve your chances of spotting the plentiful but shy wildlife.

Before starting out, stop at the Delaware Water Gap National Recreation Area Information Center at Kittatinny Point. Its rangers and books on local flora, fauna, history, and geology will enrich your hike. Behind the visitor center is a spectacular view of the Water Gap. The river flows by in a graceful curve, while the towering heights of Pennsylvania's Mt. Minsi and New Jersey's Mt. Tammany rise 1200 ft. above. Exposed rock strata display millions of years of geological history. The gorge was not, as people imagine, created by the stream forcing its way through the mountain wall from north to south. The currently accepted theory states that an aggressive mountain stream on the south side of the ridge found a weakness in the erosion-resistant stone and cut downward, opening the gap (a process geologists call "headward migration").

The AT follows the paved road in front of the information center. Skip this road walk by driving your car along the "trail." Make a right out of the information center parking lot, then a quick left through the I-80 underpass, a left at the far side of the underpass, and an immediate right into the Dunnfield Creek Natural Area parking lot, where you can leave your car overnight. The AT goes into the woods at the end of the lot. A pump provides water.

Within seconds of exiting the parking area, the trail leaves the bright, hurried human world behind. Highway noise is replaced by the comforting sound of a rushing mountain stream as the AT crosses Dunnfield Creek on a rustic wooden bridge. It is easy to imagine the small 19th-century river village of Dunnfield that once stood just behind you, where I-80 traffic now roars by.

The trail climbs gently through a green grotto of ferns, rhododendron, and towering hemlock trees. It parallels the creek, which pitches over waterfalls and rushes down flumes into pools and potholes where native brown trout swim. Layered ledges of

red shale and sandstone, sculpted by fast-moving water, are hung with ferns and moss. Stay on the trail to avoid trampling fragile vegetation.

Sadly, the ravine's hemlock trees are dying. Their bony limbs shed needles and open the glen to the sky a little more each year. This is the destructive work of the hemlock woolly adelgid, an Asian insect that caught a ride into the United States on imported ornamental trees about fifty years ago. Though biological controls (other imported bugs that eat the adelgid) are being tested, there is little money for research, and soon the Eastern hemlock may disappear entirely from our forests.

The AT follows Dunnfield Creek for 0.4 mi., then forks left, ascending on a woods road atop a massive stone retaining wall built by volunteers and the Mid-Atlantic Appalachian Trail Conference work crew in 1993. Such work prevents erosion. The green-blazed Dunnfield Creek Trail continues along the stream to the site of a 19th-century sawmill, and is a 3.5-mi. alternate route to Sunfish Pond. The blue-blazed Mt. Tammany Trail also starts at this point, crossing the creek to your right and climbing in 3.1 mi. to cliffs with stunning Water Gap vistas.

Within a few hundred yards, the trail leaves the cool, dark ravine behind and enters a sunny hardwood forest. The steep, worn road that the AT follows upward for the next 3.3 mi. to Sunfish Pond probably began life as a Native American trail, turned logging road, turned carriage

Sunfish Pond

road. By 1930, Model A Fords were clattering up the path. The AT passes several other trails as it climbs. The yellow-blazed Beulahland Trail meets the AT 1.5 mi. into the hike. This old wagon road goes left, and in 1.3 mi. reaches the Fairview parking area on Old Mine Rd. along the Delaware River. At the same point on the AT, the Holly Springs Trail goes right and connects in 0.4 mi. with the Dunnfield Creek Trail (which returns to the Dunnfield Creek Natural Area parking lot in 1.2 mi.). The spring goes dry in summer.

In 1995, the trail here was used as a firebreak, the line at which a wildfire sweeping up and out of Dunnfield Hollow was controlled. The flame-scarred trees to the right of the AT, from just beyond the Holly Springs Trail almost to the pond, are in fairly good shape, though the understory has been fully burned away and the ground blackened. Look for signs of the forest's recovery.

The AT soon becomes a sunken road, eroded 4 ft. below ground level in some places. Major stone water bars and rock steps built by volunteers curb further erosion. One beneficial effect of all this disturbance has been to uncover artifacts. We once saw an archeologist friend pick up a 2000-year-old arrowhead along this section of the path.

Smooth rock beds along the ascending route look like pavement, and invite drowsy black racers and Eastern hog-nosed snakes to sunbathe. Watch your step. The nonpoisonous hog-nosed snake, or puff adder, is one of nature's great bluffers. When aggravated, the snake inflates and flares out its neck vertebrae into a cobralike hood. It slithers toward its attacker, hissing wildly. If this line of defense fails, the snake rolls over and plays dead. Pick it up and place it upright, and the critter again rolls onto its back. In this game, the puff adder is determined to convince you that the *only* dead snake possible is a snake on its back! We recommend against picking up any snakes, however. Rattlers also live in these woods.

At 3.1 mi. into your hike, the AT intersects the Douglas Trail, which descends to the left for 1.7 mi. to a hiker parking area next to the Worthington State Forest headquarters on Old Mine Rd. along the Delaware River. Trail namesake Supreme Court Justice William O. Douglas hiked here in a 1960s crusade to save Sunfish Pond. New Jersey public utilities planned to bury the pond under a giant artificial reservoir. Public protest led to state protection of the land.

A backpacker campsite is also located here. Thanks to careless campers who over the years left food scattered about, this area has become one of the best spots to observe black bear in New Jersey. If you camp here, don't leave a candy-bar-scented bear invitation in your pack or tent. Hang food from a rope using the bear poles installed for that purpose. In summer, an AT "ridgerunner" tents here, educating hikers about the trail. Water can be

retrieved and purified from Sunfish Pond 0.6 mi. ahead. There is a privy. This site receives heavy use in summer. Campers, get there early!

After a steady 1050-vertical-ft. and 3.7-mi. climb, the AT pulls up in front of Sunfish Pond. Its boulder-lined shore, abrupt cliffs, and surrounding hardwood forest remind many hikers of New England, with good reason. This is the southernmost glacial lake on the AT. About 15,000 years ago the Wisconsin glacier scooped a basin in the bedrock to form this mountaintop pond.

In 1992, we saw beaver playing here. They have moved on since, but tree-cutting evidence is visible where the AT makes its way among boulders along the left (west) shore of the lake. Watch where you put your feet. This is a favored spot of dozing rattlesnakes. The little five-lined skink, a native New Jersey lizard, also catches the rays here. You'll probably find the sun-warmed stones appealing, too. With most of your climbing done for the day, stop for lunch. But resist the urge to dive in; rangers ticket illegal swimmers.

The AT crosses the pond's outlet at 4.0 mi. A cascade tumbles away into the woods and down to meet the Delaware River. In a few hundred feet the blue-blazed Garvey Springs Trail comes in from the left. This pretty 1.2-mi. trail descends to the Douglas Trail parking area next to Worthington State Forest headquarters along Old Mine Rd. beside the Delaware River. For those who can't arrange a car shuttle, the north end of Sunfish Pond makes a good out-and-back turnaround point, resulting in an 8.0-mi. hike.

The AT leaves the pond behind and passes through hardwoods and past swampy depressions, a reminder of the glacier that scraped over this broad highland. At 6.0 mi., you cross an open power line, offering views on both sides of the ridge. In another 0.2 mi., the trail crests Mt. Mohican (also called Raccoon Ridge). This bare rock summit, with 360-degree views, is the Herb Hiller overlook, named for the NY-NJTC volunteer who, in the 1970s, led the effort to place the entire AT in New Jersey on protected land. Look for the plaque placed in Herb's honor.

The Hiller vista looks north to where the spine of the Kittatinny Ridge splits into several ridges, east to the Yards Creek Reservoir, and west over Pennsylvania's Pocono High-lands and down to the Delaware River. The cultivated fields of the val-ley bordering the river were home to Native Americans for 12,000 years. Dutch settlers arriving in the 1600s found Lenape longhouses, thriving fields of squash and corn, plus dugout canoes plying the waterway. This always-breezy vista is a favorite gliding zone for hawks and turkey vultures, and a perfect stopping point for a snack or water break. (You can tell a turkey vulture from a hawk by the irregular back-and-forth wobble of the vulture's wings, as compared to the hawk's smoother flight. The soar-

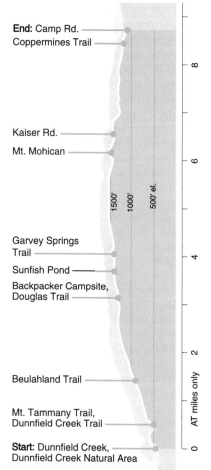

ing vulture also folds its wings into a shallow "V" shape, while hawks glide with wings held flat.)

Just beyond the vista, the trail enters the Delaware Water Gap National Recreation Area (see "A Pox Called Tocks" in Hike #27). At 6.6 mi.

N

¾" = 1 mi.

THE
TIONAL
RIVER
Tocino
Island
Labar
GAP
WATER
GAP
MONROE CO.
WARREN CO.
PENNSYLVANIA
NEW JERSEY
PAHAQUARRY
300
Kittatinny Mountain
400
Coppermine
BLAIRSTOWN
Yards
Kaiser R.
275
DELAWARE
Depue
WORTHINGTON STATE FOREST
Sunfish
Pond
200
Mount Vernon
0
Subsa
V
Hemlock
Glen
400
Landing
Style
Station
Mount
Pleasant
Ha.

Shawnee
Landing
Shoe
200
PAHAQUARRY
WORTHINGTON
300
Haines
GAP
AREA

🚶🚶 Yards Creek and
Camp Rd. Ⓟ Ⓦ
El. 1100', AMC Mohican
Center

— Coppermines Trail

— Kaiser Rd.

Mt. Mohican, El. 1500',
V 🍁 Herb Hiller plaque

— Power line V

— Garvey Springs Trail

— Sunfish Pond Ⓦ 🍁

— Backpacker ▲ Ⓣ
— Douglas Trail, El. 1300'

— Dunnfield Creek Trail

Holly Springs Trail to Ⓦ
0.2 mi.

— Beulahland Trail
— Blue Dot Trail

— Mt. Tammany, El. 1549'

— Red Dot Trail

🚶🚶 Ⓟ Dunnfield Creek
Natural Area Ⓦ El. 350'

the AT briefly follows Kaiser Rd., named for a local landowner. The windswept ridge walk that follows is less traveled than the Sunfish Pond area, and offers several great views east over New Jersey farmland. Camping is legal inside the National Recreation Area (stay at least 75 ft. off the trail and 0.5 mi. from roads). Wildlife abounds. A friend doing a solo backpack trip here once heard an urgent scurrying sound rushing his tent. Looking out, he spotted a red fox barreling straight toward him. The fox suddenly thought better of its bold move, turned, and dashed back into the woods. Surprisingly, this agile animal is a European immigrant, brought to New Jersey after 1760 by wealthy English landowners who missed fox hunting.

The trail descends through mountain laurel at 8.5 mi., and soon reaches the Coppermines Trail (8.7 mi.). This 2.0-mi.-long trail is one of the area's most lovely, descending to the Delaware River through a hemlock ravine, past waterfalls and the openings to several copper mines. These mines, dug in 1904, yielded little profit for unwary investors (only two copper bars were ever smelted), though the operation did line unscrupulous promoters' pockets.

At 8.8 mi., the AT crosses Yards Creek on a newly built bridge, arriving at Camp Rd. and hike's end. Parking for a few cars is found uphill and around the bend from the trail. The Appalachian Mountain Club's Mohican Outdoor Center is about 0.4 mi. up the road from this AT crossing. The AMC is hoping to open a day-hiker parking area by late 1998. Call 908-362-5670 for parking information or for AMC Mohican camping reservations. Overnight tent sites and cabin space are available to the public at reasonable rates.

Miles N	**NORTH**	Elev. (ft./m)	Miles S
8.8	**End:** **Yards Creek,** water; **Camp Rd.** day parking; AMC Mohican Outdoor Center 0.4 mi. to L (N).	1100/335	0.0
8.7	**Coppermines Trail** to Coppermines Trail parking area on Old Mine Rd. (2.0 mi.).		0.1
6.6	**Kaiser Rd.** to Coppermines parking area on Old Mine Rd. (2.0 mi.).	1400/427	2.2
6.2	**Mt. Mohican (Raccoon Ridge);** Herb Hiller plaque.	1500/457	2.6
6.0	**Power line;** view.		2.8
4.1	**Garvey Springs Trail** to Douglas Trail parking area on Old Mine Rd. (1.2 mi.), early exit option; unreliable water.	1400/427	4.7
3.7	**Sunfish Pond,** water.		5.1
3.1	**Backpacker Campsite,** privy, no water; **Douglas Trail** to Douglas Trail parking area on Old Mine Rd. (1.7 mi.), early exit option.	1300/396	5.7
1.5	Early exit options: **Holly Springs Trail** to water (0.2 mi.) and Dunnfield Creek Trail (0.4 mi.); **Beulahland Trail** to Fairview parking area on Old Mine Rd. (1.3 mi.).	900/274	7.3
0.4	**Mt. Tammany Trail** R (E) to Mt. Tammany summit (3.1 mi.); **Dunnfield Creek Trail** straight ahead to Sunfish Pond (3.5 mi.); AT forks to L.	500/152	8.4
0.0	**Start:** **Dunnfield Creek Natural Area,** 0.4 mi. from I-80 Exit 1, overnight parking, water pump; AT enters woods, crosses Dunnfield Creek on bridge, then follows creek.	350/106	8.8

SOUTH

Catfish Mt. to Flatbrookville Rd.

Maps: ATC N.Y. & N.J. Map 6; NY-NJTC Kittatinny Trails S Map 16

Route: From Camp Rd. to Catfish Mt. and along Kittatinny Ridge to Flatbrookville Rd.

Recommended direction: S to N

Distance: 7.1 mi.

Elevation +/-: 1100 to 1565 to 1370 ft.

Effort: Easy

Day hike: Yes

Overnight backpacking hike: Optional

Duration: 4½ hr.

Early exit option: At 3.3 mi., Millbrook-Blairstown Rd.

Natural history features: Kittatinny Ridge ledges; Black's Pond beaver activity; Rattlesnake Swamp

Social history features: Catfish Fire Tower; B-17 plane crash site; view of Tocks Island Dam site

Trailhead access: *Start:* Take I-80 E or W to NJ 94N for 8.0 mi. to Jacksonburg. Turn L onto Mohican Rd. and follow for 3.5 mi. (bearing R at the forks). Turn L on Gaisler Rd. and go 0.5 mi. Turn R onto Camp Rd. (dirt) for 0.8 mi. Daytime parking for 3 or 4 cars just beyond trail around bend. *End:* Take I-80 E or W to NJ 94N. Turn L onto Millbrook-Blairstown Rd. (County Rte. 602); go over and down W side of Kittatinny Ridge to R at Millbrook Village onto Old Mine Rd. and R on Flatbrookville Rd. (Blue Mt. Rd./County Rte. 624). Follow to dead end at barricade. Overnight AT parking on L for 10 cars.

Camping: AMC Mohican Outdoor Center (call 908-362-5670 for information); entire hike is within Delaware Water Gap National Recreation Area (tent camping 75 ft. off trail or at least 0.5 mi. off roads)

The Kittatinny Ridge stretches northeast from the Delaware Water Gap for 43 mi. to High Point, New Jersey, and is topped the entire way by the Appalachian Trail. When you look down from this precipitous 1400-ft. rampart you quickly understand why it hindered the east-west movement of Native Americans and colonizing Europeans, and why the Lenape tribe named it Kittatinny, meaning "endless mountain."

This 7.1-mi. skyline hike runs along a section of the ridge locally known as Catfish Mt.

Drive up dirt Camp Rd. for about 0.8 mi. until you see the AT blazes on your left. Park around the next bend, where there is a pull-off spot for several cars (day parking only). The Appalachian Mountain Club's Mohican Outdoor Center is 0.4 mi. up the road from the trail, and hopes to open a day-hiker parking lot by late

1998. The center offers reasonably priced tenting and cabin rentals to hikers. Call 908-362-5670 for camping reservations and information about the facilities for cross-country skiing, ice climbing, hiking, canoeing, and other group activities and workshops.

Walk back down Camp Rd. and turn left onto the AT, going north into the woods (away from Yards Creek). The trail begins a stiff, 0.5-mi., 350-ft. climb, the most strenuous of the day, then levels off atop Kittatinny Ridge's Catfish Mt.

The ridgetop ecosystem at 1450 ft. is very different from the diverse deciduous forest of the valley floor far below. Only hardy plants, growing in dry, rocky, acidic soils and able to withstand violent winter storms, live on the exposed ridge. Chestnut oaks dominate (look for this tree's deeply furrowed bark and large, elliptical leaves with rounded teeth). The loose forest canopy opens the ridge to the sky, and allows it to support a tangled understory of scrub oak, blueberries, and mountain laurel. One of the hardiest inhabitants of the Kittatinny Ridge, the pitch pine, is also found here. These trees grow where no others can, often hanging precariously from ledges. Shaped by brutal winter winds, the pines take on stark but beautiful forms. There's a fine pitch pine specimen with an AT blaze on it just before the trail reaches the ridge crest.

A high rock ledge (1.2 mi.) looks east over New Jersey farmland. Sway-backed red cedars, bent by violent

David Emblidge

A Pox Called Tocks

When the Appalachian Trail opened along the Kittatinny Ridge in the late 1920s, its central section crossed large tracts of private property and was unprotected. Over the decades, vacation homes sprouted on the skyline like mushrooms, spoiling the wildness of the country. Similar unrestricted development threatened the pastoral farm villages of the Upper Delaware Valley far below. Then in 1962 the Federal government announced a plan to dam the Delaware River just north of the Water Gap, flooding 12,300 acres of forest and farmland with a 37-mi.-long lake. The proposed Tocks Island Dam would have destroyed 12,000 years of human prehistory, 300 years of colonial U.S. history, 2500 homes, more than 100 farms, and a vast habitat for black bear, migrating eagles, and spawning Delaware River shad. The Army Corps of Engineers went quickly to work buying or condemning land for the reservoir and driving people from their homes. Some evicted families had settled here over 200 years before and bade tearful farewells to their homesteads. This being the 1960s, the vacant properties quickly attracted groups of hippie squatters. The Zion Lutheran Church, built in 1851, became the Church of Ecology, and marijuana bloomed in its cemetery. Cloud Farm raised its own livestock and became a self-sufficient "back-to-the-earth" commune.

Soon a holy war was raging as former property owners, hippies, and environmental groups united to de-

---

winter winds, lean into the ridgetop. In another 0.1 mi. the orange-blazed Rattlesnake Swamp Trail comes in from the left. It forms a loop with the AT, descending west into a small, sheltered pocket valley, then reconnecting with the AT. The swamp is a haven to animals. A friend recently saw a mother bear with three cubs in this marsh and heard the howl of a lone coyote echoing off the hills. Fiddlehead ferns make a flashy appearance here every spring. The AT/Rattlesnake Swamp Trail combination (begun at Millbrook-Blairstown Rd.) is a terrific 4.5-mi. wildlife loop

hike, perfect for families with young children.

At 2.3 mi. the AT reaches Catfish Fire Tower, elevation 1565 ft. This 50-ft. tower was built in 1922 and is a lookout for New Jersey Forest Fire Service crewmen, who watch for wisps of smoke in dry times. It is unoccupied most of the year. The tower has a 360-degree view but is closed to the public.

The trail descends, following and leaving the gravel fire tower access road several times. Pay attention to the white blazes. This area supports a stand of mature rhododendron,

feat the proposed dam. Interior Secretary Stewart Udall called the furor over Tocks Island "a turning point in our nation's outlook toward its resources." At this defining moment, people realized that an untouched watershed could be more valuable than a dam. Protest reached a fevered pitch: lawsuits, rallies, and bulldozer sabotage challenged the project. Meanwhile, armed Federal marshals made a predawn raid on the hippie squatters, driving them out. Homes and farms were then bulldozed under.

As late as 1971, Congressman James Wright of Texas defended Tocks by reminding the House that the Book of Genesis called upon man to subdue the Earth. In the end, though, it was Tocks itself that was subdued. Massive cost overruns, Army Corps mismanagement, and public outrage turned government against its own project. The dam plan was scrapped in 1975, leaving behind a 70,000-acre public park.

Today the Delaware Water Gap National Recreation Area protects the Appalachian Trail and surrounding landscape. Nancy Shukatis, a local leader in the fight to stop the dam, says of the struggle, "The Upper Delaware survived largely due to the energy of those who once lived here; people who loved this land and lost it. Some still make forlorn visits to what were once their homes, to find only a foundation or a lilac bush they planted. I think it enriches your experience here to remember that someone sacrificed quite a lot so this wonderful park could be" (Scherer, "The Making of a Park," p. 38).

which blooms in late spring. The orange-blazed Rattlesnake Swamp Trail reconnects with the fire road at 2.9 mi.

There is overnight parking at the paved Millbrook-Blairstown Rd. (3.3 mi.). The trail crosses the road, then skirts the edge of Black's Pond at 3.7 mi. In 1995, the National Park Service fought a losing battle to stop beavers from flooding the AT here. Drainage pipes, called "beaver foolers," were installed to empty the pond. The beavers, however, weren't fooled; they just plugged up the pipes. In late 1996, the Park Service finally surrendered and AT volunteers put in bog bridging to keep hikers' feet dry. This is a great spot for lunch. Be patient and quiet; you may see the animals at work and play.

The trail makes a 250-ft. ascent back up to the Kittatinny Ridge crest. A power line clearing offers great views east and west (4.0 mi.). In a short distance, a natural vista looks east over Sand Pond and Boy Scout Camp No-Be-Bo-Sco (not a Native American name, but the abbreviation for North Bergen Boy Scout Council). In 1980 this sleepy little camp was host to ghoulish goings-on: the filming of *Friday the 13th,* the first in a seemingly endless series of slasher movies in which boy meets girl, boy gets girl, psychotic killer hacks boy and girl into stew meat.

A few hundred yards past the vista, a grisly real-life tragedy took place when a World War II B-17 Flying Fortress met its fiery end on the AT. The 49,000-lb. bomber, with its 103-ft. wingspan, crashed during a February 1944 whiteout. It sheared off treetops for a quarter of a mile, exploded, and burned, killing the crew of twelve. The Army used the AT to carry out the plane's wreckage. Days later, Boy Scouts at Camp No-Be-Bo-Sco held a memorial service for the dead airmen. Nature healed itself and no sign of the disaster is left on the tranquil landscape. Ron Dupont, an historian who documented the crash, suggests a simple memorial cairn be placed at the spot.

At 5.5 mi. the AT comes out onto a crumbling asphalt road that passes thirty-one former cottage sites in the next 1.6 mi. Hikers in the early 1960s complained about this housing development on the mountain crest. But it was the proposed Tocks Island Dam project that finally reduced the cottages to rubble. The Army Corps of Engineers bought up the properties and leveled the houses when they created the Delaware Water Gap National Recreation Area around 1970 (see "A Pox Called Tocks"). Nature is reclaiming the land, hiding the lots, driveways, stone garden walls, and trash, blending ornamen-

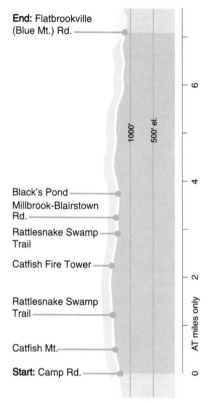

tal trees and shrubs with natural growth. Trail maintainers call this the "birch walk" because of the gray birch saplings lining the way. Sunlight on the white trunks and luminescent leaves is magical. The AT reaches paved Flatbrookville Rd. (Blue Mt. Rd.) at 7.1 mi., completing the hike. There is cold water at a pump (purify before drinking) and overnight parking.

Flatbrookville Rd.
(Blue Mt. Rd.) Ⓟ 🚻
El. 1370'

Power line, **V**

Black's Pond 🍁
Millbrook-Blairstown
Rd. Ⓟ

Catfish Fire Tower,
El. 1565', **V** 🏛

Rattlesnake Swamp
Trail

V

Catfish Mt., El. 1450'

🚶 Camp Rd. Ⓟ AMC
Mohican Center ⛺ 🏠
🚻 🚰 El. 1100'

Miles N	NORTH	Elev. (ft./m)	Miles S
7.1	**End:** Flatbrookville Rd. (Blue Mt. Rd./County Rte. 624); water pump.	1370/418	0.0
5.5	Crumbling asphalt road and **former summer homes site**; views.	1500/457	1.6
4.0	Top of 250-ft. ascent to **power line**; views.	1493/455	3.1
3.7	**Black's Pond,** beaver activity.	1200/366	3.4
3.3	**Millbrook-Blairstown Rd.,** overnight parking, early exit option.		3.8
2.9	Northern terminus **Rattlesnake Swamp Trail,** forms loop with AT (2.5 mi.).	1450/442	4.2
2.3	**Catfish Fire Tower.**	1565/477	4.8
1.3	Southern terminus **Rattlesnake Swamp Trail,** forms loop with AT (2.5 mi.).	1500/457	5.8
1.2	**Rock ledge**; view.	1500/457	5.9
0.5	**Catfish Mt.** at top of 350-ft. ascent.	1450/442	6.6
0.0	**Start:** Camp Rd. day parking; AMC Mohican Outdoor Center 0.4 mi. to L (N).	1100/335	7.1

SOUTH

Rattlesnake and Bird Mts.

Maps: ATC N.Y. & N.J. Maps 6 & 5; NY-NJTC Kittatinny Trails Maps 16 & 17

Route: Along Kittatinny Ridge from Flatbrookville Rd., over Rattlesnake Mt. and Bird Mt. to US 206 at Culvers Lake

Recommended direction: S to N

Distance: 11.0 mi.

Elevation +/-: 1370 to 1550 to 900 ft.

Effort: Strenuous

Day hike: Yes

Overnight backpacking hike: Optional

Duration: 7½ hr.

Early exit options: At 3.0 mi., Buttermilk Falls Trail; at 7.1 mi., Brink Rd.

Natural history features: Crater Lake; many vistas over the Upper Delaware Valley; Rattlesnake Mt. and Bird Mt. raptor viewing

Social history features: Harding Lake Rock Shelter; ruins of Blue Mt. Lakes and Skyline Acre resort developments

Trailhead access: *Start:* Take I-80 E or W to NJ 94N. Turn L onto Millbrook-Blairstown Rd. (County Rte. 602); go over and down W side of Kittatinny Ridge to R at Millbrook Village onto Old Mine Rd. and R on Flatbrookville Rd. (Blue Mt. Rd./ County Rte. 624). Follow to dead end at barricade. Overnight AT parking on L. *End:* Take US 206 N or S to Culvers Gap. Turn onto County Rte. 636 (Upper N Shore Rd.) for 0.2 mi., and at Y go L. Turn immediately L into AT parking lot. Permit from Stokes State Forest office required for overnight parking.

Camping: Delaware Water Gap National Recreation Area (tent camping 75 ft. off trail or at least 0.5 mi. off roads); Brink Shelter

This strenuous 11.0-mi. day hike tops the most remote and wild section of the 43-mi.-long Kittatinny Ridge. While this is a ridge walk with few climbs, much of the trail goes through rocky, ankle-wrenching terrain. Rattlesnake Mt. and Bird Mt. are heaven on earth for migrating raptors and birders. Allow plenty of time to hike, watch the wildlife, and soak up the scenery.

Start at the dead end of paved Flatbrookville Rd. (County Rte. 624). Surveyed in 1824, this road once crossed all the way over the Kittatinny Ridge, but is now barricaded to the east. It is the only paved road you will see until you reach US 206 at hike's end. Follow the AT north from the road.

For the first mile the trail passes through dense mountain laurel thickets and beneath young red oak and birch trees. There are also groves of healthy hemlocks. They have yet to be attacked by the woolly adelgid insect, a bug introduced from Asia that is destroying all Eastern hemlocks. A sign warns hikers that there is no camping for the next 3.5 mi. (an attempt by the National Park Service to curb overuse in this beautiful area).

Just past the 1.0-mi. mark, the trail descends around a smooth rock slab and comes upon an unmarked trail to the left, leading down to Long Pine Pond, site of Boy Scout Camp Ken-Etiwa-Pec. Opened in the 1930s, now abandoned, this is just one of many scout camps once found in the Kittatinnies. The camps inspired Norman Rockwell's *Boys' Life* imagery: here children awoke to bugles at dawn, canoed, swam, hiked, earned merit badges, and camped out under the stars. This age of innocence ended abruptly in the 1960s, when most camps were bought out and bulldozed by the U.S. government to make way for the (eventually canceled) Tocks Island Dam (see "A Pox Called Tocks" in Hike #27).

A rock-strewn depression with a grass-filled pond at its heart is worth exploring at 1.4 mi., to your right. A little farther on, an illegal campsite is slowly being taken over by sweet fern. This knee-high plant is not truly a fern. Rub its fernlike leaves with your fingers, sniff, and you'll see how this plant's refreshing, sweet-smelling scent inspired its name.

As the trail ascends a very steep rock ledge at 1.6 mi., look for a large overhang in the cliff face to your left. This is the Harding Lake Rock Shelter. Projectile points (arrowheads

and spearheads) found here in 1941 prove this to have been a Native American hunting camp circa 3000 B.C. The shelter was enlarged and enclosed with poles and thatch laid across its open mouth.

At the top of the cliff, a sawed-off telephone pole indicates more recent human habitation. Just ahead are the ruins of Skyline Acres and Blue Mt. Lakes, two vacation home developments. In the 1950s the Kittatinny Ridge fell victim to the postwar housing boom, and this 5000-acre forest tract was slated to become "the largest recreational lake community in New Jersey." Swamps were turned into lakes, miles of road were cut, and cottage sites laid out. The Appalachian Trail (here since the 1920s) went from a remote woodland path to a gravel road lined with summer homes. The Tocks Island Dam Project put an end to the development, as the Federal government bought out the developers, demolished the cottages, and let the land return to forest.

Just beyond the cliff top (1.8 mi.) is a vista looking west out over a low ridge that hides the Delaware River from view. A blue-blazed trail to the right uses cement blocks and other summer cottage refuse as stairs to aid in the steep descent to Crater Lake. Be careful, for this is not a maintained path. Beside the lake are gnawed logs and stumps, telltale evidence of past beaver activity.

The trail takes a break from its rocky course to follow the ex-development's gravel roads for the next 1.4 mi., making a few turns. Keep one eye on the white blazes. The orange-blazed Hemlock Pond Trail intersects the AT at 2.5 mi. This trail makes a steep 0.25-mi. descent to a pretty pond cradled in a hollow between two ridges. The AT continues on, passing beneath a canopy of young gray birch. Climb a steep, sloping rock slab to the right for views west to Pennsylvania's Pocono Highlands.

New Jersey's highest waterfall can be reached from the Buttermilk Falls trailhead (3.0 mi.). This trail descends very steeply for 1.9 mi. to the falls, a small daytime parking area, and a paved road that leads left to County Rte. 615 in the Delaware River Valley. The falls are at their most impressive in high water. During dry times, they turn into a pretty but thin liquid ribbon. If you can arrange a car shuttle, a 4.9-mi. hike from Flatbrookville Rd. to Buttermilk Falls makes a relatively easy and interesting day hike.

In another 0.2 mi. the AT turns left, leaving the gravel road. It eventually descends into a dark hemlock hollow (4.5 mi.), an ideal camping area with a spring bubbling up from underground. Remember that you're within the Delaware Water Gap National Recreation Area and must be at least 75 ft. off the trail before pitching a tent. Be sure to purify the spring water.

The trail makes a steep 0.3-mi. climb out of the hollow to the bare summit of Rattlesnake Mt., a good spot for lunch. This windswept bald has sweeping vistas to the west and north over the Upper Delaware Valley, and limited views east and south back toward Crater Lake. For those unable to arrange a two-car shuttle hike, the top of Rattlesnake Mt. (4.8 mi.) makes a good turnaround spot, resulting in a 9.6-mi. out-and-back hike.

The mountain is an ideal viewing platform for birders watching raptors glide up and down the Atlantic flyway on their annual migrations in April and September (the fall migration is the more spectacular of the two, with greater numbers of birds concentrated along this ridge). Nearly 17,000 hawks, ospreys, eagles, falcons, kestrels, and merlins were counted over the Kittatinny Ridge in one recent year. The birds ride the updrafts coming off the ridge, conserving energy for their long migrations north and south. A raptor banding station is seasonally located atop Rattlesnake Mt.

While looking up to the skies, be sure to also look down at your feet. This mountain is called Rattlesnake Mt. with good reason. On our last hike there, we found a baby rattler curled in a rock crevice, its head poised to strike. Our shadows sent it slithering for cover. These remote Kittatinny peaks are a last refuge for this much-feared snake. Early settlers waged all-out war on the animal. They sought out wintering dens, loaded them with black powder charges, and blew the snakes to perdition. If you encounter a rattler, give it the respect it deserves; after all, it does live here full-time and you are only a guest. Take a few pictures and yield right of way to this state endangered species.

The AT descends briefly, then ascends Bird Mt, another scrub-oak-covered lookout and prime birding spot (5.7 mi.). The white steeple of Walpack Church is visible far below to the west. Shortly, the trail leaves the Delaware Water Gap National Recreation Area and enters Stokes State Forest.

A third, unnamed, vantage point is reached at 6.3 mi.; it looks north along the thin spine of the Kittatinny Ridge. Many hikers find it hard to believe that the surrounding country is in New Jersey at all. There's not an oil refinery in sight! Green hills sweep to the horizon.

From here, descend through ferns and birches to dirt Brink Rd. (7.1 mi.). The road is not passable by car to the east, but can be driven from the west to within 0.2 mi. of the AT (day parking only). From the parking area, Brink Rd. descends to County Rte. 615 and the little town of Walpack. The road is open only from March 31 to December 31 each year. Brink Shelter and a dependable spring (purify) are 900 ft. to the left of the AT along Brink Rd. No fires are allowed at shelters in New Jersey. This small shelter was once a popular party place, but recent policing has made it into a more inviting camp spot.

Continued on p. 222

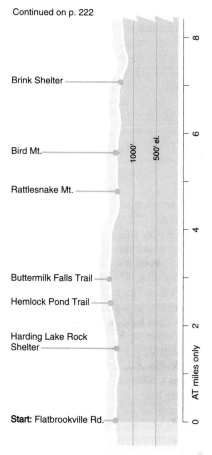

A short climb takes the trail back up to the ridge crest, where the hiker is surrounded by Eastern white pines and silence. The AT is less rocky now and sees little elevation change until the steep descent into Culvers Gap. The ridge is very narrow, only 300 ft. wide in places. Here we once met "Boomer," Kevin Galizio, a south-

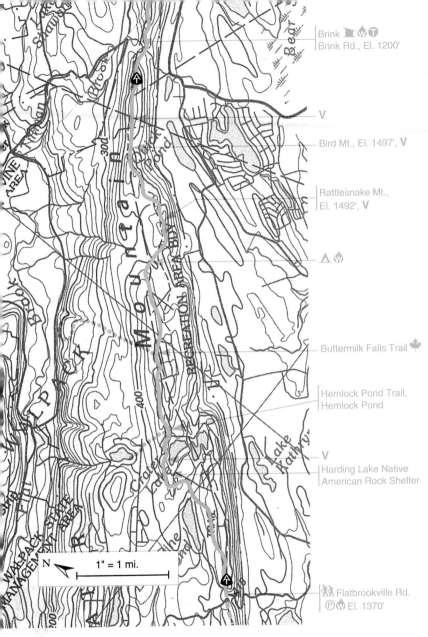

Brink 🏚 Ⓦ Ⓣ
Brink Rd., El. 1200'

V

Bird Mt., El. 1497', V

Rattlesnake Mt.,
El. 1492', V

⛺ Ⓦ

Buttermilk Falls Trail 🍁

Hemlock Pond Trail,
Hemlock Pond

V
Harding Lake Native
American Rock Shelter

🏃 Flatbrookville Rd.
Ⓟ Ⓦ El. 1370'

N
1" = 1 mi.

bound thru-hiker carrying an intricately carved ash wood walking staff. He told us how he and several other thru-hikers had found the mystery staffs left by the Appalachian Stick Man in Massachusetts. "The stick was just sittin' there, in the middle of the trail, waitin' for me with a little ribbon and note on it," explained Boomer. The note read:

> When you're hiking and your
>   feet get sore,
> sit down on your duff and hike
>   no more.
> While you're sitting there feel-
>   ing lonesome and blue
> there's something you can do.
> Get off your duff and hike away.
> Be thankful you can hike
>   another day
> (with my lucky stick of course).
> — C. L. LeClair, Sarasota, Florida

A thru-hiker who met LeClair described him as an elderly man who thru-hiked the AT in 1978. Now LeClair carves his sticks, goes out on day hikes, and leaves them behind. At least four ash wood sticks that we know of made their way to Georgia. "They're great for cutting the cobwebs," said Boomer.

At 8.3 mi. an unmarked trail leads right a few feet to a vista that looks east from a sheer cliff out over Lake

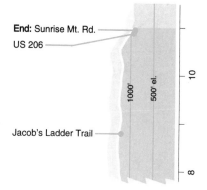

Owassa. At 8.7 mi. the blue-gray-blazed Jacob's Ladder Trail cuts off to the left, descending west to Coss Rd. in about 0.5 mi. At 9.4 mi. the AT comes out of the forest into a large, rocky, steeply sloped clearing with a spectacular view north over Culvers Lake.

The path then makes a very rapid, 475-ft. descent over loose rock, reaching US 206 at 10.8 mi. A thru-hiker mecca, the Worthington Bakery, is just to your left up the road. An end-of-hike pastry stop is a must. Afterwards, cross the highway and follow a level stretch of trail through a pine tree plantation. You will arrive at the Culvers Lake AT parking lot in 0.2 mi.

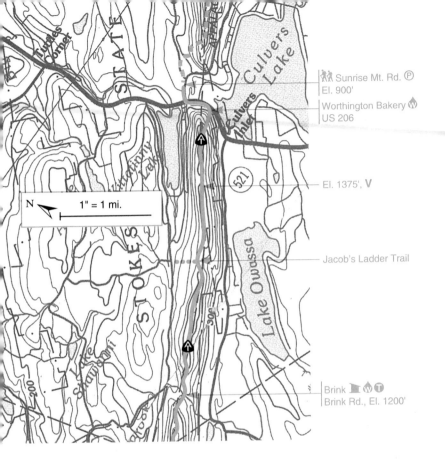

🥾 Sunrise Mt. Rd. ℗
El. 900'

Worthington Bakery 🆆
US 206

El. 1375', **V**

Jacob's Ladder Trail

Brink 🖼🆆🆃
Brink Rd., El. 1200'

N

1" = 1 mi.

Miles N	NORTH	Elev. (ft./m)	Miles S
11.0	**End:** **AT hiker parking area (Sunrise Mt. Rd.)**, overnight parking; 0.2 mi. E of Culvers Gap.	900/274	0.0
10.8	**US 206;** Worthington Bakery.	900/274	0.2
9.4	Open **ledges** above Culvers Lake (view), begin steep, 475-ft. descent.	1375/419	1.6
8.7	**Jacob's Ladder Trail** to Coss Rd. (0.3 mi.).	1250/381	2.3
8.3	Unnamed trail leads R (E) to view.	1350/412	2.7
7.1	**Brink Shelter;** Brink Rd. leads 900 ft. L (W) to shelter and spring, 0.2 mi. to parking, early exit option.	1200/366	3.9
6.3	Unnamed **view.**	1400/427	4.7
5.7	**Bird Mt.,** view.	1497/456	5.3
4.8	**Rattlesnake Mt.,** view.	1492/455	6.2
4.5	Unnamed hemlock hollow and **spring** (primitive camping).	1300/396	6.5
3.0	**Buttermilk Falls Trail** to Buttermilk Falls (1.9 mi.), parking, early exit option.	1550/472	8.0
2.5	**Hemlock Pond Trail** to Hemlock Pond (0.25 mi.).	1450/442	8.5
1.8	Unnamed trail goes R (E) to **Crater Lake view** (150 ft.).		9.2
1.6	**Harding Lake Rock Shelter;** Native American campsite.		9.4
1.1	Unmarked trail L (W) to **Long Pine Pond.**		9.9
0.0	**Start:** Flatbrookville Rd. (County Rte. 624), water pump.	1370/418	11.0

SOUTH

HIKE #29
Sunrise Mt. and High Point

Maps: ATC N.Y. & N.J. Map 5; NY-NJTC Kittatinny Trails N Maps 17 & 18

Route: From US 206 to Sunrise Mt., Deckertown Turnpike, High Point, and County Rte. 519

Recommended direction: S to N

Distance: 17.0 mi.

Elevation +/-: 900 to 1700 to 1100 ft.

Effort: Strenuous

Day hike: Optional, using Deckertown Tpk. as Start or End (US 206 to Deckertown Tpk., 8.7 mi./ Deckertown Tpk. to County Rte. 519, 8.3 mi.)

Overnight backpacking hike: Yes

Duration: 25½ hours

Early exit options: At 5.3 mi., Sunrise Mt. Rd.; at 8.7 mi., Deckertown Tpk.

Natural history features: N Kittatinny Ridge walk with views over Wallkill River valley and Delaware River; High Point, 1803 ft., highest point in NJ

Social history features: Normanook (Culver) Fire Tower, Sunrise Mt. Pavil-

ion, and AT shelters, built by the Civilian Conservation Corps; High Point Monument

Trailhead access: *Start:* Take US 206 N or S to Culvers Gap. Turn N onto County Rte. 636 (Upper N Shore Rd.) for 0.2 mi., and at Y go L. Turn immediately L into AT parking lot. Permit from Stokes State Forest office required to park here overnight. *Midpoint:* From N edge of town of Sussex, go N 0.5 mi. on NJ 23, then L on Deckertown Tpk. (County Rte. 647). Follow about 9 mi. to Stokes State Forest boundary. Continue 0.6 mi. to top of Kittatinny Ridge. Daytime parking lot and water pump are on L. *End:* Take NJ 23 N or S to County Rte. 519N. Go 3.0 mi. to AT pull-off on L. Room for 4 or 5 cars (daytime parking only).

Camping: Gren Anderson, Mashipacong, Rutherford, and High Point lean-tos

T he northern Kittatinny Ridge rises in an uninterrupted rampart, climbing to 1803 ft. at High Point, the greatest elevation above sea level in New Jersey. This rugged AT ridge walk is punctuated by craggy ledges, far-reaching vistas, plus the Normanook Fire Tower, Sunrise Mt. Pavilion, and High Point Monument, man-made features that ascend above the natural landscape.

This 17.0-mi. AT section can be explored in a two-day backpacking trip from US 206 to Mashipacong Shelter (8.5 mi. on the first day), and from Mashipacong Shelter to County Rte. 519 (8.5 mi. on the second day). Or it can be covered in two day hikes (8.7 mi. and 8.3 mi. each), using the daytime AT parking lot on Deckertown Tpk. as the dividing line between the two walks. While there is not a great deal of altitude change on the walk, the terrain is rocky and uneven, making the footing tricky and the hiking more tiring.

The AT exits the northwest corner of the Culvers Gap AT parking lot. Follow the white blazes to the right, through a pine plantation that protects Kittatinny Lake (a municipal drinking water source). In 0.2 mi. you will reach Sunrise Mt. Rd. The trail briefly follows the road left, then goes right into the woods. This Stokes State Forest byway was built in the 1930s by the Civilian Conservation Corps, and is the first of many CCC projects that you will walk over, eat inside, sleep at, or otherwise enjoy on this hike (see "With the Boys of the CCC"). A gate closes off Sunrise Mt. Rd. at dusk.

The well-worn trail climbs steeply, switchbacking up for 400 strenuous vertical ft., before finally leveling out atop a breathtaking vista at 0.7 mi. The view looks east over Culvers Lake and south along the spine of the Kittatinny Ridge as it twists its wild way to the Delaware Water Gap. This vantage point was frivolously named "Mt. Whiffenpoof" by 19th-century summer visitors to Culvers Lake. The resort community by the lake was born circa 1850 and boomed by 1870 when railroad service to nearby Branchville began. Huge hotels, including the 400-room Culvermere Lodge, lined the lake shore and steamboat taxis puffed their way from door to door. On Sunday evenings boaters lit candles and lanterns and

sailed to the lake's center for a religious service conducted from a barge-turned-church. A preacher, organist, and choir inspired their waterborne congregation with open-air sermons and hymns. Culvers Lake is still a vacationers' playground, though cottages and speedboats have replaced the great hotels and steamboats.

It is easy to be overwhelmed by the grand view (one of the best in the state) while ignoring the microcosm beneath your feet. Lichens, mosses, grasses, and sedges battle for a foothold on this bald perch. They tenaciously build up soils in rocky clefts, only to have their hard labor swept away by screaming winter winds and torrential summer rain. As you walk north, away from the exposed vista, the pioneering lichens and mosses have done a more thorough job in building up deeper soils, allowing chestnut oaks to fill in around the trail.

The trail continues along the widening Kittatinny Ridge backbone, offering more good views to the east, south, and west until it reaches the Normanook, or Culver, Fire Tower (1.7 mi.). A wooden tower stood here until 1934, when CCC workers lugged this 47-ft. steel tower piece by piece up the mountain on their backs. The fire tower survived a near crash by three low-flying Army bombers in 1941, and a 130-acre brush fire in 1994. Though it offers an unobstructed 360-degree view, it is officially closed to the public. I remember my excitement as a small

With the Boys of the CCC

In 1933, at the height of the Great Depression, when many of Europe's unemployed young men were choosing fascism and militarism, American youth pinned their hopes on a vast peacetime army: the Civilian Conservation Corps. Instead of taking up arms for the state, these young volunteers mobilized by taking up picks and shovels. The work was hard, the pay only a dollar a day, but thousands enlisted just for "three squares" and a roof (often made of canvas) over their heads.

When President Franklin D. Roosevelt proposed the corps as part of his New Deal, few could imagine the positive, lasting impact it would have on America's natural landscape. Between 1933 and 1942 the formerly unemployed young men of the corps left home to build hundreds of miles of U.S. park roads, trails and trail shelters, bridges, dams, lakes, buildings, fire towers, and picnic grounds. They also planted forests, fought fires, surveyed boundaries, cleared vistas, landscaped, and dug wells and sewer lines.

The CCC's work was launched from makeshift camps throughout the nation. Camp Kuser at High Point State Park was typical. The young men lived a rough but vital life there, rising early each day and setting off to accomplish ambitious conservation-related building projects around the park. CCC projects are characterized by their rustic style, which some call "parkitecture." The corps worked in native materials, harvesting local trees and quarrying local stone for their constructs. Their timber and log, stone and masonry buildings were carefully scaled and proportioned to blend in with, not overcome, the natural landscape. It was a labor-intensive, time-consuming style that demanded great skill, enthusiasm, and attention to detail.

Today, in every state up and down the AT, you will see evidence of the boys of the CCC. It is very likely that the road you use to drive to the trailhead, the picnic grove you eat at, or the lean-to that you sleep in is the product of the CCC. In fact, it was a six-man corps crew who built the final 2-mi. missing link in the 2100-mi. AT, completed on August 14, 1937, at Sugarloaf Mt., Maine. World War II brought a sudden end to this highly successful public works project as its young men gave up their shovels for M-1 rifles.

boy when a ranger invited me up inside and I watched him call in a faint puff of distant smoke to firefighters. Insurance liability laws prevent such friendly scenes today.

In a short distance, the green-blazed Tower Trail steeply descends left for 0.4 mi., down to Sunrise Mt. Rd. In another mile, the blue-blazed Stony Brook Trail descends left 0.3 mi. to the Gren Anderson Shelter. This log shelter was built in 1958 by

Sunrise view of the New Jersey Highlands from Kittatinny Ridge

the Green Mountain Club. It features a privy and a reliable spring (purify). Continue north past several shallow depressions gouged into the ridgetop by the Wisconsin glacier 15,000 years ago. These form temporary ponds and swamps and are home to peeper frogs in wet spring weather. It's easy to hear their exuberant song as a celebration of winter's end.

At 4.2 mi. into your hike, the yellow-blazed Tinsley Trail cuts left for 0.2 mi., to connect with Sunrise Mt. Rd. The AT now begins a steady, easy ascent of Sunrise Mt. (elev. 1653 ft.) through chestnut oak. At the summit (5.1 mi.), the AT emerges onto an open ledge with views east over the rustic barns and farm fields of the Wallkill River Valley.

Just 50 yd. past this ledge the trail arrives at the Sunrise Mt. Pavilion. This rough-hewn stone structure is typical of the rustic "parkitecture" style created by the CCC in its public works construction, a style that can be found up and down the AT. It was built in 1937 and, with its sweeping views east and west over forest and farms, is a good spot for lunch, though you may have to share a picnic table with sightseers who have driven to the top via Sunrise Mt. Rd. Just 0.2 mi. north of the pavilion, the AT passes through the Sunrise Mt. Rd. parking area, where there are rest rooms. For those unable to arrange a shuttle hike, the pavilion is a good turnaround point, creating an out-and-back hike of 10.2 mi.

The trail reenters the woods, crosses dirt Crigger Rd. (6.0 mi.), then continues for the next 2.5 mi. through what some AT hikers refer to as "a long green tunnel." This is an unspectacular but very pleasant hike through a mixed oak forest, with no major vistas or landmarks along the way. While you are unlikely to see many animals in this dense forest, you can readily spot signs of their presence. Look for acorns and hickory nuts that display the teeth marks of squirrels, mice, and other foraging mammals and birds. Also look for frayed, broken twigs on maple leaf viburnum, a favorite food of browsing deer. White-tailed deer have incisors only on their bottom jaw, so must tear at plants, rather than neatly nipping off twigs as rabbits can with their double incisors.

The trail makes minor descents and ascents on this gentle woods walk, passes without a sign from Stokes State Forest into High Point State Park, then arrives at the Mashipacong Shelter (8.5 mi.), another gift from the CCC. There is a privy here, and a water pump (purify) is 0.2 mi. up the trail at the Deckertown Tpk. AT daytime parking area. If you are spending the night, be sure to store all of your food in the large metal "bear box." Mooching bears are regular Mashipacong visitors. If you are day hiking, this is a good place to rest your feet before walking 0.2 mi. further to your car.

From Deckertown Tpk. (another CCC improvement project), the AT cruises through a relatively level chestnut oak forest. There are no stiff climbs or tricky descents, and the gentle terrain along this stretch invites you to get into the hiker's "hum," or steady forward stride.

The thriving plant community in this particular area has been carefully analyzed by scientists studying New Jersey biodiversity. Chestnut oaks are the dominant tree species here, making up 55 percent of the forest. Most have been growing for about 95 years, and are 9 to 14 inches in diameter. Red oak is the second most common tree, with black oak, white oak, and black birch completing the mix. The understory tree layer is primarily made up of red maple, downy juneberry, and sprouts of American chestnut and pignut and shagbark hickory. In some spots, black huckleberry and lowbush blueberry cover the ground, while in others mountain laurel is dominant. You will be walking through similar chestnut oak forest for the rest of the hike.

The AT reaches the red-blazed Iris Trail for the first time at 9.4 mi. The two trails combine to form a rough figure eight, with the Iris crossing the AT twice more, once at 10.7 mi. and again at 13.8 mi. The AT/Iris Trail combination is a favorite circuit day hike. While the AT hugs the ridge, the Iris descends into a thickly forested valley. It follows a shady woods road, parallels the shore of Lake Rutherford, and reconnects with the AT just short of the NJ 23 AT parking lot.

After the second crossing of the Iris Trail, the AT passes a vista and the blue-blazed Rutherford Shelter Trail. Don't make the descent to the lean-to unless you plan to stay or use the privy or really need to obtain water at the spring. The descent is straight down and the area around the shelter can be muddy.

Back on the AT, a series of vistas, each better than the last, opens first to the east, then to the west. The views east look into a pocket mountain valley that holds glacially formed Lake Rutherford, site of prehistoric Native American camps. Views west look over Sawmill Lake (an artificial lake built by the CCC in 1934), and to the heights of Pennsylvania's Pocono Plateau. Check out the boulders and rock shelves at these overlooks. They are composed of extremely erosion-resistant Shawangunk conglomerate and form the backbone of the Kittatinny Ridge. Fifteen hundred feet thick and 440 million years old, this Silurian sandstone is made of small white pebbles embedded in a smooth gray matrix. The mix began as a sandy river delta, which was then compressed and folded skyward, withstanding water, wind, and repeated glacial cutting.

The trail reaches a last viewpoint west at 13.0 mi., and in a short distance the Blue Dot Trail descends 0.5 mi. to the Sawmill Lake Campground, a High Point State Park campground. There is tent camping here, but advance reservations and a per-

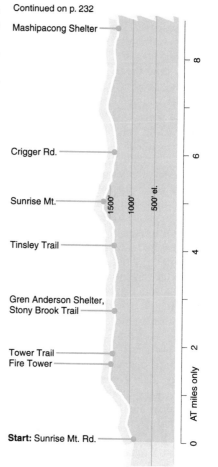

Continued on p. 232

Mashipacong Shelter

Crigger Rd.

Sunrise Mt.

Tinsley Trail

Gren Anderson Shelter, Stony Brook Trail

Tower Trail
Fire Tower

Start: Sunrise Mt. Rd.

1500' 1000' 500' el.

8

6

4

2

AT miles only

0

mit are needed and are sometimes difficult to get during the peak summer season. The yellow-blazed Mashipacong Trail comes in from the left (13.8 mi.), the Iris Trail comes in from the right again, and the trail passes the High Point AT parking lot

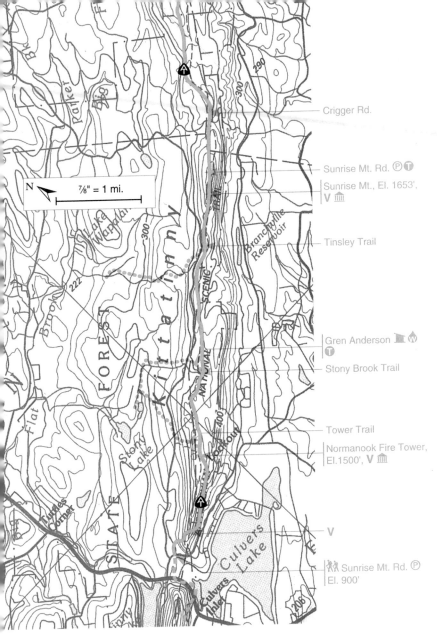

N ⅞" = 1 mi.

Crigger Rd.

Sunrise Mt. Rd. Ⓟ 🚹

Sunrise Mt., El. 1653',
V 🏛

Tinsley Trail

Gren Anderson 🏠 Ⓦ
🚹

Stony Brook Trail

Tower Trail

Normanook Fire Tower,
El.1500', V 🏛

V

🚻 Sunrise Mt. Rd. Ⓟ
El. 900'

(overnight), before reaching the park headquarters. By now you will be able to recognize the building style: those CCC boys again. Originally planned as a teahouse and restaurant, it now houses a small museum, with a dusty 3-D model of the mountains you've crossed, Native American artifacts, and natural history exhibits. Water and rest rooms are courtesy of the CCC.

High Point SP has the honor of being New Jersey's first major park, mostly because no one really wanted this mountain land. The ridge's Shawangunk conglomerate was resistant to far more than just the weather; it also prevented settlement. Native American and colonial settlers hunted the steep slopes but didn't stay. Later the hills were scalped of trees for lumber, firewood, and charcoal. In 1890 the High Point Inn, with room for 200 guests, was built and its owners began promoting "the beauty of the scenery, the healthfulness of its climate, and the abundant opportunities which it affords to devotees of the rod and gun." But the hotel folded in just nineteen years. Mountain ownership passed to the Kuser family, who remodeled the inn as a mansion and created a vast estate with carriage roads and trails. In 1923 the Kusers generously donated the entire tract to the people of New Jersey. The Olmsteds (designers of New York City's Central Park) and the CCC reshaped the land, making it inviting to thousands of visitors. Not everyone loved the park concept. One local paper called the nature preserve "a waste and a stamping ground for wild and destructive animals." Today you are likely to see coyote tracks playfully crisscrossing the trail, or even bear tracks.

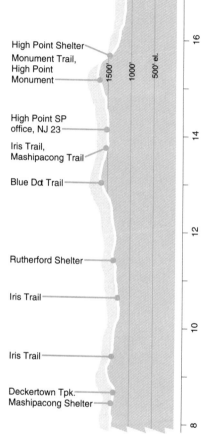

End: County Rte. 519

High Point Shelter
Monument Trail,
High Point
Monument

1500'
1000'
500' el.

16

High Point SP
office, NJ 23

14

Iris Trail,
Mashipacong Trail

Blue Dot Trail

12

Rutherford Shelter

Iris Trail

10

Iris Trail

Deckertown Tpk.
Mashipacong Shelter

8

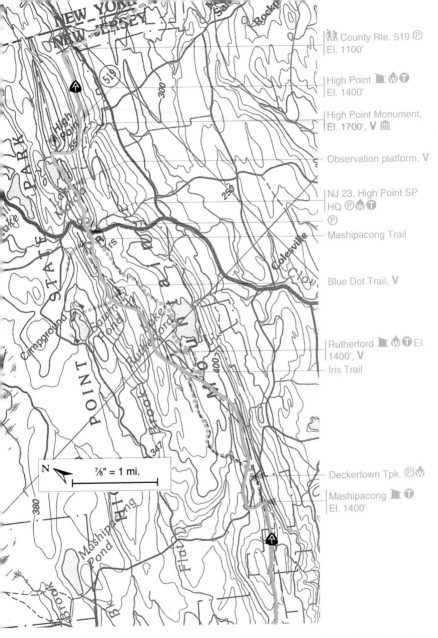

County Rte. 519 Ⓟ
El. 1100'

High Point 🏚️ⓌⓉ
El. 1400'

High Point Monument,
El. 1700', V 🏛️

Observation platform, V

NJ 23, High Point SP
HQ ⓅⓌⓉ

Ⓟ

Mashipacong Trail

Blue Dot Trail, V

Rutherford 🏚️ⓌⓉ El.
1400', V

Iris Trail

Deckertown Tpk. ⓅⓌ

Mashipacong 🏚️Ⓣ
El. 1400'

N   ⅞" = 1 mi.

From the headquarters, the AT crosses NJ 23, reenters the chestnut oak forest, and soon comes to a clearing where a ski jump was located in the 1930s. The park was promoted as "the Switzerland of New Jersey" until the 1960s, when the downhill slopes were abandoned. Recently, a privately run cross-country ski area, with beautifully groomed trails, has made the park popular in winter. You can call 973-875-4800 for High Point SP information.

At 14.8 mi. the trail reaches a north-facing vista and the most surprising sight on the AT in New Jersey. In the distance stands High Point Monument, a trim pinnacle of stone resembling the Washington Monument. It rises 220 ft. above the state's highest peak of 1803 ft. There are AT states with higher mountaintops, but none graced by such a monument. This veterans' memorial was another donation of the Kuser family.

There is a second view of the monument, from a raised wooden observation platform on the AT (15.0 mi.). Then, 0.2 mi. farther on, the red-and-green-blazed Monument Trail leads left to the monument itself. This side trip is highly recommended. The Monument Trail climbs steeply for 0.3 mi. to the base of the obelisk. Faced with cream-colored New Hampshire granite and hit with spotlights at night, the monument dominates the ridge top. Views stretch from the ramparts of the Catskill Mts. to the Delaware Water Gap, from the curves and bends of the Delaware River to the rolling farm country of the Wallkill River Valley and beyond to the Wawayanda escarpment. From this single spot you can see almost all of the terrain crossed by New Jersey's 73-mi. AT section. Only one thing ruins the view, and that's the summer tourists arriving by the bus- and carload. Hike in winter and you will have the place to yourself. From the Monument Trail, the AT quickly descends over rocky terrain and through chestnut oak forest, leaving the Kittatinny Ridge. A blue-blazed side trail (15.7 mi.) goes right to the High Point Shelter (you guessed it, another CCC project!). This is a truly choice camping spot, with a hemlock grove and bubbling stream facing your door, a privy, and a metal "bear box" for storing food.

As you continue to descend, crossing several farmers' stone walls, look for bundles of old, rusted wire fencing. This is all that remains of the Kuser estate's elk and reindeer park. The state of New Jersey kept the elk here into the 1930s. The animals earned their keep by working as "Santa's reindeer" every Christmas at the Bamberger's department store in Newark.

The trail descends on switchbacks, through woods, over crumbling outcrops of deep gray Martinsburg shale (also called Hudson River slate), and arrives at County Rte. 519 at 17.0 mi., ending the hike.

Miles N	NORTH	Elev. (ft./m)	Miles S
17.0	**End:** County Rte. 519 day parking, 2.9 mi. N of High Point SP headquarters at NJ 23.	1100/335	0.0
15.7	**High Point Shelter,** side trail leads R (E) to shelter, stream, and privy (0.1 mi.).	1400/427	1.3
15.2	**Monument Trail,** climbs steeply to High Point Monument (0.3 mi.).	1650/503	1.8
15.0	**Wooden observation platform,** view.		2.0
14.8	**High Point Monument,** view.	1700/518	2.2
14.1	**High Point SP Headquarters, NJ 23,** information, rest rooms, water, nature museum.		2.9
14.0	Unmarked trail leads R to AT overnight **parking.**		3.0
13.8	Northern intersection with **Iris Trail;** intersection with **Mashipacong Trail.**	1500/457	3.2
13.0	**Blue Dot Trail** to Sawmill Lake campground, High Point SP permit required (0.5 mi.); view.	1600/488	4.0
11.5	**Dutch Shoe Rock,** view; **Rutherford Shelter,** side trail leads R (E) to shelter, privy, and spring (0.4 mi.).	1400/427	5.5
10.7	Second intersection with **Iris Trail.**	1300/396	6.3
9.4	Southern intersection with **Iris Trail,** forms figure-eight loop with AT.	1350/412	7.6
8.7	**Deckertown Tpk.,** overnight parking, water pump, early exit option.	1300/396	8.3
8.5	**Mashipacong Shelter,** privy.	1400/427	8.5
6.0	**Crigger Rd.,** no parking.	1420/433	11.0

(continued on next page)

Miles N		Elev. (ft./m)	Miles S
5.3	**Sunrise Mt. Rd.** parking area, day use parking, rest room, early exit option.	1600/488	11.7
5.1	**Sunrise Mt.,** summit, view, stone picnic pavilion.	1653/504	11.9
4.2	**Tinsley Trail** to Sunrise Mt. Rd. (0.2 mi.).		12.8
2.8	**Stony Brook Trail** to Gren Anderson Shelter, privy, and spring (0.3 mi.).	1300/396	14.2
1.8	**Tower Trail** to Sunrise Mt. Rd. (0.4 mi.).		15.6
1.7	**Normanook (Culver) Fire Tower.**	1500/457	15.7
0.7	View of **Culvers Lake.**	1300/396	16.3
0.2	**Sunrise Mt. Rd.,** AT briefly follows road, then turns R (E) and begins 400-ft. strenuous climb.		16.8
0.0	**Start:** AT hiker parking area (Sunrise Mt. Rd.), overnight parking; 0.2 mi. E of Culvers Gap.	900/274	17.0

SOUTH

The Great Valley of the Appalachians

Maps: ATC N.Y. & N.J. Maps 5 & 4

Route: From County Rte. 519 through the Great Valley of the Appalachians to Oil City Rd. and Wallkill River National Wildlife Refuge

Recommended direction: S to N

Distance: 9.0 mi. total; 8.7 mi. on AT

Access trail name & length: Oil City Rd. (State Line Rd.), 0.3 mi.

Elevation +/-: 1100 to 400 ft.

Effort: Easy

Day hike: Yes

Overnight backpacking hike: No

Duration: 5½ hr.

Early exit options: At 0.8 mi., Courtwright Rd.; at 2.0 mi., Ferguson Rd.; at 2.6 mi., Gemmer Rd.; at 3.6 mi., Goodrich Rd.; at 4.1 mi., Goldsmith Rd.; at 4.5 mi., Goldsmith Lane; at 4.9 mi., Unionville Rd.; at 5.2 mi., Quarry Rd.; at 5.9 mi., Lott Rd.; at 6.9 mi., NJ 284; and at 7.4 mi., Lower Rd.

Natural history features: Great Valley of the Appalachians; Wolf Pit Hill; Vernie Swamp; Wallkill River

Social history features: Many 19th-century farms and stone walls; site of the first major oil pipeline in America

Trailhead access: *Start:* Take NJ 23 N or S to County Rte. 519N. Go 3.0 mi. to AT pull-off on L. Room for 4 or 5 cars (daytime parking only). *End:* Take NJ 23 N or S to County Rte. 519N for 1.5 mi. Make R onto Mt. Salem Rd. Follow 4.0 mi. to T, turning L onto Unionville Rd. Follow for 1.6 mi. into Unionville, turning R on NJ 284. Follow for 0.5 mi. and turn L onto Oil City Rd. (State Line Rd.). Follow for 1.4 mi. over the Wallkill River Bridge. In another 0.6 mi. look for parking lot of Wallkill River National Wildlife Refuge. Room for 6 cars (daytime parking only).

Camping: None

The rocky heights of the Appalachian Mts. are shadowed along almost their entire length by an equally prominent though less dramatic physical feature. The Great Valley of the Appalachians is a vast, fertile lowland, stretching uninterrupted from Alabama to southern New York. Once the continental shelf, the Great Valley now divides the older, more jumbled mountains of New England from the younger, parallel ridges of the central and southern Appalachians.

The AT crosses the Great Valley just twice: in the Cumberland Valley of Pennsylvania and in the Wallkill River Valley of New Jersey and New York. In New Jersey, it offers much easier hiking than do the rugged ridges of the Kittatinny Range to the west or the New Jersey Highlands to the east.

Beaver lodge

This 8.7-mi. hike parallels the New York–New Jersey border and is a walk through farm fields, over small slate hills with sweeping vistas, and across wetlands—the perfect pastoral terrain for seniors, small children, or first-time hikers.

This gentle lowland landscape has welcomed human beings for 12,000 years. Here the walker can find evidence of Native American campsites and prehistoric rock quarries where glasslike chert was dug out to be shaped into stone tools. The AT also passes through farms and along country roads evoking colonial and early American rural life; it goes near the remains of mills, quarries, rail lines, and pipelines used during the nation's first industrial age.

The walk begins at the base of the Kittatinny Ridge. The AT crosses County Rte. 519 and heads out across open fields. At twilight, you're likely to catch a glimpse of deer gathered at treeline, standing in stillness and warily eyeing your every move. A close approach sends them fleeing, with their white tails flashing. These beautiful animals were once hunted nearly out of existence in New Jersey. Luckily, a small number were preserved in the private estates of the Rutherford and Worthington families. From this small nucleus, starting in about 1900, their population was replenished. Today there are an estimated thirty-five deer per acre in the Great Valley, all descended from those few captives.

White-tailed deer deserve watching. They have developed prodigious skills in eluding predators: wolves prior to the 19th century and humans thereafter. They can hit speeds of up to 36 mph in open country and can bound over a 7-ft. fence from a standing start. A most exciting discovery for hikers is to come upon spotted fawns in springtime. Adult females hide their multiple young in sheltered places, beside fallen logs or in underbrush, and nurse them by making the rounds every three or four hours. Quiet hikers may startle the small animals from their hiding places, sending them scurrying for deeper cover. While walkers sometimes fail to see deer, they can't miss their ever-present signs: heart-shaped tracks, browsed oak and hemlock twigs, grassy deer beds, tree scrapes (where the animals have fed on cherry, striped maple, shadbush, and other edible barks), and, in autumn, antler rubs.

For the first 6.9 mi. of this hike the AT makes a steady descent, interrupted briefly by a few easy climbs. The trail passes through cultivated and overgrown fields and pastures, goes near picturesque barns and farmhouses, skirts small ponds, climbs over stone walls in open woods, crosses little streams on AT bridges, and traverses marshy spots on plank puncheons.

The entire area blossoms in late spring with a dizzying display of wildflowers. In wetland areas, the ground is blanketed with the mottled leaves and bell-shaped yellow flowers of the trout-lily. Drier ground is sprinkled with common purple violets and a scattering of rarer yellow violets. Low clumps of intensely white bloodroot also bloom. The red juice taken from the underground stem of this plant was once used by Native Americans as dye for blankets,

baskets, and face painting and also served as insect repellent. A parade of Great Valley wildflowers progresses through spring and summer until, by early autumn, yellow goldenrod, purple loosestrife, bull thistle, ironweed, wild bergamot, red clover, black-eyed Susans, and scattered clusters of nodding wood asters predominate. Each of these flowers is its own micro-ecosystem and rewards watching. The common bull thistle, for example, supports a multitude of life: tree-hopper insects anchor their tubular mouths beneath the thistle's green skin and languidly sip plant juices. Snails crawl on the foliage, while humingbirds, bees, and butterflies hover above or land atop the thistle's tight crown of pink flowers to collect nectar. Praying mantises, assassin bugs, and crab spiders feast on less wary members of the thriving insect community.

The two most exceptional spots on this walk come at a high point atop Wolf Pit Hill (3.9 mi.), and at one of its lowest points, in Vernie Swamp (4.2 mi.). The summit of Wolf Pit Hill (elev. 700 ft.) is crowned by open pasture and a twisted old apple tree right out of *The Wizard of Oz*. A 180-degree vista looks west toward the Kittatinny Ridge, which is topped by the stone obelisk of High Point Monument (see Hike #29). The hill was named for a deep trap dug by locals to cash in on the $25 bounty for wolf scalps (a princely sum in 1825).

During the 1880s, William Elston, a Wolf Pit Hill farmer, waged a different kind of war on a different kind of "varmint." Elston was rather proud of his well-kept farm's neatly stacked stone fences, and became outraged when chubby woodchucks persistently undermined the walls for their burrows. The farmer claimed to have used no gun—only his hunting dogs —to track down and annihilate 365 of the animals over a four-year period. Luckily, one look at the tumbledown condition of the stone walls of today tells you that Elston may have won a few battles, but ultimately he lost the war.

Vernie Swamp (4.2 mi.) is a memorial to yet a third kind of war: the battle against the beavers. In the early 1990s AT hikers were shocked to find this beautiful little swamp's boardwalk afloat in several feet of water. Trail maintainers hunted downstream for the source of the blockage and found it: a brand-new beaver dam. Repeated attempts by New Jersey state park officials failed to drive the animals from their new lodge. Finally, in 1996 and 1997, the Mid-Atlantic AT crew and local volunteers surrendered, adjusting to the animals' presence. The volunteers spent several weekends slogging through knee-deep muck and dealing with a freak April nor'easter that dumped 24 in. of snow to build a massive walkway above the swollen waters. Today the beavers are happy and hikers' feet stay dry—we hope.

A succession of quiet country roads with small pull-over spots provide opportunities for shorter day

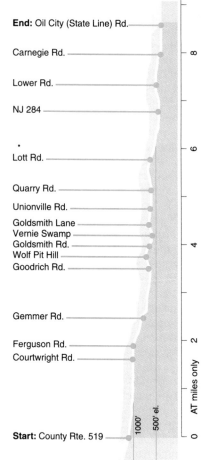

End: Oil City (State Line) Rd.

Carnegie Rd.

Lower Rd.

NJ 284

Lott Rd.

Quarry Rd.

Unionville Rd.

Goldsmith Lane
Vernie Swamp
Goldsmith Rd.
Wolf Pit Hill
Goodrich Rd.

Gemmer Rd.

Ferguson Rd.
Courtwright Rd.

Start: County Rte. 519

1000' el.
500' el.

AT miles only

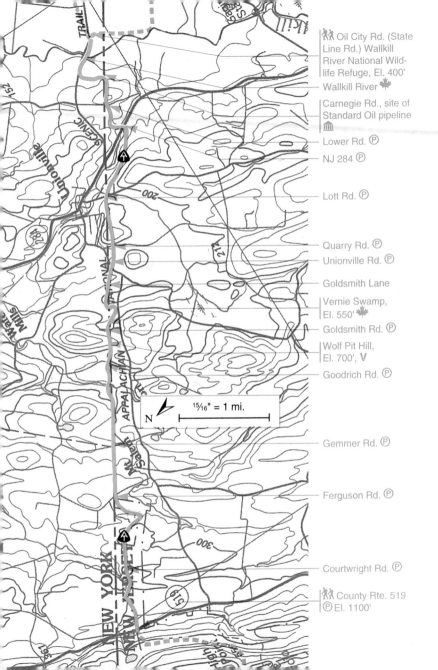

Oil City Rd. (State Line Rd.) Wallkill River National Wildlife Refuge, El. 400'

Wallkill River

Carnegie Rd., site of Standard Oil pipeline

Lower Rd. Ⓟ

NJ 284 Ⓟ

Lott Rd. Ⓟ

Quarry Rd. Ⓟ
Unionville Rd. Ⓟ

Goldsmith Lane

Vernie Swamp, El. 550'

Goldsmith Rd. Ⓟ

Wolf Pit Hill, El. 700', V

Goodrich Rd. Ⓟ

15/16" = 1 mi.

N

Gemmer Rd. Ⓟ

Ferguson Rd. Ⓟ

Courtwright Rd. Ⓟ

County Rte. 519
Ⓟ El. 1100'

NEW YORK
NEW JERSEY

SCENIC

Unionville

APPALACHIAN NATIONAL SCENIC TRAIL

hikes on this trail section. The AT crosses Courtwright Rd. (0.8 mi.), Ferguson Rd. (2.0 mi.), Gemmer Rd. (2.6 mi.), Goodrich Rd. (3.6 mi.), Goldsmith Rd. (4.1 mi.), Goldsmith Lane (4.5 mi.; no parking permitted here), Unionville Rd. (4.9 mi.), Quarry Rd. (5.2 mi.), Lott Rd. (5.9 mi.), and NJ 284 (6.9 mi.). While most of these byways are named for local 19th-century farmers, two have wider, if nearly forgotten, significance. Goldsmith Rd. and Goldsmith Lane are named for a family that in the 1860s bred one of the greatest racehorses of all time. Goldsmith Maid was as famous in her day as Secretariat was in ours, and was one of the most high-winning trotters in history.

As the trail heads east across the Great Valley, the character of the old stone walls abruptly changes. The neat, slablike stacks of Martinsburg shale that make up the rock walls on Wolf Pit Hill and near Vernie Swamp are replaced by the irregularly shaped, melon-size limestone of the Wallkill River Valley. The entire valley makes fine farm country, due to the rich deposits of glacial till left behind by the Wisconsin glacier 15,000 years ago.

At 7.4 mi. the AT crosses paved Lower Rd., and at 8.0 mi. exits the woods onto paved Carnegie Rd., which almost immediately passes the red brick buildings of what is today known as Carnegie Industries (a small wire-coating factory). In the 1800s this plant was the smoke-belching pumping station for America's first cross-country crude oil pipeline. John D. Rockefeller's Standard Oil (today's Exxon) easily gained right-of-way for this pipeline from naive farmers. Little did the locals realize that they would be the victims of America's first oil spills. A hundred years before the Exxon *Valdez* accident in Prince William Sound, Alaska, the pressurized pipeline through the Great Valley repeatedly burst, sending crude oil spurting as much as 60 ft. into the air, damaging crops, killing livestock and fish, and polluting wells and springs. As New Jersey historian Ron Dupont writes in *Hiking with History*, "The farmers soon found that getting Standard Oil to pay for their damage and losses from these spills was like getting blood from a proverbial stone." In 1914, two 30,000-gal. oil tanks blew up at this site, sending a plume of oily smoke into the air that could be seen from the top of the newly constructed Woolworth Building in Manhattan. Fortunately, the pipeline is no more; the land has healed and largely returned to forest.

The AT follows Carnegie Rd. to the left, then intersects with Oil City Rd. (8.2 mi.), also called State Line Rd. The trail turns right onto Oil City Rd. and crosses the Wallkill River (8.4 mi.).

The Wallkill River is unusual among New Jersey's waterways in that it drains not into the Delaware River or the Atlantic Ocean, but flows from south to north into the Hudson River. The Wallkill also offers some of the finest flat water canoeing in the region and was a major thoroughfare for

Native Americans. Just to the south, at Bassett's Bridge, there is a Native American village site and there are large limestone cliffs with veins of black chert, which made excellent cutting tools and spear and arrow heads.

The Wallkill winds its way through the heart of the Drowned Lands, a part of the Great Valley that was annually inundated by river floods, making it largely unsuitable for farming and settlement. Large-scale drainage projects solved this problem in the late 1800s (see Hike #31).

On the opposite side of the Wallkill, the hike continues along Oil City Rd. for 0.3 mi., to where the AT turns right, passing through a gate into the Wallkill River National Wildlife Refuge (the only national refuge on the AT). Leave the trail, walking straight ahead (east) on Oil City Rd. for 0.3 mi. to a parking area on the right (south) side of the road. A sweeping view west out across open terrain to Pochuck Mt. marks the end of this walk across most of the Great Valley.

Miles N	NORTH	Elev. (ft./m)	Miles S
	Total: 9.0 mi. with access on Oil City Rd. (State Line Rd.)		
0.3	**Access:** Go straight on Oil City Rd. to parking lot on S side of road.		0.3
8.7	**End AT miles:** Oil City Rd. (State Line Rd.)	400/122	0.0
8.4	**Wallkill River.**		0.3
8.2	**Oil City Rd. (State Line Rd.)**, turn R (E) on road; no parking.		0.5
8.0	**Carnegie Rd.** (no parking); follow road to L (N).	400/122	0.7
7.4	Cross **Lower Rd.**, day parking.	500/152	1.3
6.9	Cross **NJ 284**, day parking.	400/122	1.8
5.9	Cross **Lott Rd.**, day parking.		2.8
5.2	Cross **Quarry Rd.**, day parking.		3.5
4.9	Cross **Unionville Rd.**, day parking. This and the next 4 road crossings to N are early exit options.		3.8
4.5	Cross **Goldsmith Lane**, private, no parking.	600/183	4.2
4.2	**Vernie Swamp.**	550/168	4.5
4.1	Cross **Goldsmith Rd.**, day parking.	600/183	4.6
3.9	**Wolf Pit Hill**, view of High Point Monument.	700/213	4.8
3.6	Cross **Goodrich Rd.**, day parking.	600/183	5.1
2.6	Cross **Gemmer Rd.**, day parking.	750/229	6.1
2.0	Cross **Ferguson Rd.**, day parking.	900/274	6.7
0.8	Cross **Courtwright Rd.**, day parking. This and the next 4 road crossings to N are early exit options.	1000/305	7.9
0.0	**Start:** County Rte. 519, day parking, 2.9 mi. N of High Point SP headquarters at NJ 23.	1100/335	8.7

SOUTH

Wallkill and Vernon Valleys

Maps: ATC N.Y. & N.J. Map 4; NY-NJTC North Jersey Trails Wawayanda SP Map

Route: From Oil City Rd. through the Wallkill River valley, over Pochuck Mt., along County Rte. 517, through Vernon Valley to NJ 94

Recommended direction: S to N

Access trail name & length: Oil City Rd. (State Line Rd.), 0.3 mi.

Distance: 10.1 mi. total; 9.8 mi. on AT

Elevation +/-: 400 to 1150 to 450 ft.

Effort: Moderate

Day hike: Yes

Overnight backpacking hike: Optional

Duration: 7½ hr.

Early exit options: At 2.1 mi., Liberty Corners Rd. (Wallkill Rd.); at 3.9 mi., Banks Pond Rd.; at 5.2 mi., County Rte. 565; at 6.8 mi., County Rte. 517; at 8.9 mi., Canal Rd.

Natural history features: Wallkill River valley (part of the Great Valley of the Appalachians); Pochuck Mt. (some of the oldest bedrock along the AT); Pochuck Quagmire (a mile-long swamp walk)

Social history features: Wallkill National Wildlife Refuge; Lehigh & New England Railroad bed; Great Wall of Pochuck; Glenwood Schoolhouse; Pochuck Quagmire Suspension Bridge; Native American rock shelter; Lehigh & Hudson River Railroad

Trailhead access: *Start:* From NJ 23 N or S take NJ 284N toward Unionville, NY. Just before the center of town, make a R onto Oil City Rd. (State Line Rd.). Follow for 1.4 mi. over the Wallkill River Bridge. In another 0.6 mi. look for parking lot of Wallkill River National Wildlife Refuge. Room for 6 cars (daytime parking only). Do not block gate. *End:* Take NJ 94S from the NY state line for 2.0 mi. to the AT parking area on L. Or take NJ 94N for 2.2 mi. from Vernon stoplight to AT parking area on R. There is over-night parking for 5 to 6 cars (with permit from Wawayanda SP office).

Camping: Pochuck Shelter

It would be hard to find a New Jersey AT hike offering greater variety than this one. While most of the state's trail hugs the ridgelines, this 9.8-mi. walk crosses the eastern half of the Wallkill River valley as well as Vernon Valley, fertile bottomlands rich in natural and cultural history. It also traverses Pochuck Mt., a rugged, multipeaked ridge of billion-year-old stone that long ago became isolated from the main body of the New Jersey Highlands to the east.

River valleys are traditionally characterized as being the cradles of civilization, and in their own small way, the Wallkill and Vernon valleys fit that description. For 12,000 years these two lowlands have been traveled over, hunted, fished, farmed, grazed, logged, mined, and quarried; the land has been used, reused, and abused repeatedly, first by Native Americans, then by colonial and early American settlers, and now by the residents of the bedroom communities at the farthest edge of the New York City suburbs.

The valleys' plant and animal populations have adapted to the constant human presence, as has the AT. This AT section is in transition; it is the last piece of the trail in New Jersey to be removed from roads and is benefiting from the purchase and preservation of hundreds of wild acres by the state and federal governments. Trail relocations are presently common here, so this hike description and mileage may vary somewhat from your actual experience. When in doubt, follow the white blazes. You can also call the NY-NJTC for up-to-the-minute trail routes.

The hike begins at the Oil City Rd. (State Line Rd.) parking lot for the Wallkill River National Wildlife Refuge. Walk west (left) from the lot for 0.3 mi. to the AT, which goes south (left) through a gate and follows a dirt road atop an earthen dike into the Wallkill River National Wildlife Refuge, through which you will travel for 1.5 mi.

Ahead stretches a vast open plain of pitch-black ground, what locals call "the black dirt." These rich soil deposits were born out of the area's unique geology. The Wallkill valley is bounded on the east by erosion-resistant Precambrian Pochuck Mt., and on the west by the slate hills of Wantage township. Thousands of years ago, the softer Kittatinny limestone of the valley itself was eroded away and became the lowland pathway for the river. When the Wisconsin glacier descended on the area it blocked the Wallkill's flow, creating a great glacial lake. When the glacier finally receded 15,000 years ago, it left behind a stony moraine, just north of the AT's present location. This moraine acted as a dam, causing the Wallkill to back up behind it and to flood annually, allowing for the build-up of a deep layer of fertile "black dirt." In some places, the black dirt has been laid down to a depth of several hundred feet.

Native Americans used the Wallkill River as a major trading route and established campsites up and down it. Arriving European settlers were eager to capitalize on the rich bottomland soils but were stymied by the repeated flooding. The frustrated farmers called this the "Drowned Lands" and sought ways to claim it back from the thick marsh grasses and waterfowl. In the 1870s a canal was dug through the glacial moraine, draining the Drowned Lands and opening them to farming. Onions, celery, and sod became major crops.

Today nature is being allowed to reclaim this lush valley. The Wallkill River National Wildlife Refuge, established in 1990, will eventually encompass 7500 acres of fish and wildlife habitat along the river. Cultivated fields of black dirt are being flooded and allowed to revert back to their marshy condition, growing up again with cattails, pondweed, and duckweed. Short-eared owls, barred owls, red-shouldered hawks, snow geese, bobolinks, coyotes, deer, otters, mink, bog turtles, and wood turtles are again making this area their home. Raptors and songbirds again are plentiful. Sometime soon the AT may be rerouted through the heart of the refuge, allowing hikers to enjoy some of the best bird- and animal-watching found anywhere in New Jersey.

Presently the trail is located at the north end of the preserve, running along a dike of what was once the Liberty Sod Farm; it turns left along another dike and heads toward the base of Pochuck Mt. At 1.2 mi. the AT turns left again onto the abandoned Lehigh & New England Railroad bed. There are plans in the works to convert this old rail line into a wildlife refuge trail.

The AT turns right at 1.5 mi., leaves the old sod farm and railroad bed, enters the woods, and for the next 0.4 mi. crosses a red maple swamp. In springtime this is a magical place, one of the first spots in northern New Jersey to come alive. Skunk cabbages, with their unfurling purple hoods, show themselves in March. These plants generate their own heat (they can be up to 20 degrees hotter than their surroundings), melting up through the last layers of snow and ice. With winter's disappearance, fluorescent green mosses coat every downed tree and stump. Then, the marsh marigolds make their appearance. They offer a stunning spring display, a bright spray of golden flowers dotting the swampy earth. The wetland can be just as beautiful in autumn, when swamp maples turn scarlet red.

On the far side of the swamp, the AT passes a freshwater pump (2.0 mi.). This is the place to stock up on water if your plans include an overnight stay at the Pochuck Shelter. The trail immediately crosses Liberty Corners Rd. (also called Wallkill Rd.), and begins to climb through abandoned fields covered in red cedar up the steep western slope of Pochuck Mt. There are fine views back over the black dirt toward Wolf Pit Hill and High Point Monument.

"Pochuck" is a Lenape (Delaware) word for "out-of-the-way place," maybe so named for the annual valley floods that cut the ridge off from the surrounding region. Today Pochuck Mt. remains a secluded enclave. As new housing developments spring up like mushrooms in the lowlands, its 1140-ft. height resists civilization, remaining mostly forested. The trail grows steeper, switchbacking across a thickly wooded hillside.

A blue-blazed side trail goes left (2.4 mi.) and leads in a short distance to the Pochuck Shelter, nicknamed Fort Pochuck. Volunteers carried it piece by piece on their

The Ghosts of Lenapehoking

As we pass through New Jersey's urban sprawl of highways, gas stations, and fast-food joints, it is hard to remember that this culture's arrival in North America is extremely recent, and that everywhere we look the pavement literally has been laid down over a far older culture. On the AT in the forest, however, it is much easier to imagine that we are walking in Lenapehoking, the land of the Lenape.

Native Americans crossed out of Siberia on a land bridge into North America as much as 40,000 years ago. They lived in the mid-Atlantic region for at least 12,000 years before the first European explorers arrived less than 400 years ago. Every spring, Vernon Valley farmers dig up direct evidence of this fact as their plows uncover a fresh crop of Native American artifacts. Large Clovis spearheads, evidence of Paleo-Indian habitation (10,000 to 8000 B.C.), have been found in cornfields just north of the AT.

These first nomadic peoples entered Vernon Valley 7500 years before the Egyptians built the Great Pyramid, at a time when the region still stood in the cold shadow of the Wisconsin glacier. Hardy tundra plants—lichens, mosses, dwarf birch, and arctic willow—thrived in frigid conditions. The last saber-toothed tigers, woolly mammoths and mastodons, musk ox, caribou, and elk roamed the countryside.

Over thousands of years the glacier disappeared and the climate warmed, with plants and animals becoming those we recognize today. Meanwhile, wave after wave of Native Americans settled and resettled mid-Atlantic valleys and hunted Appalachian mountains. Small family groups traded actively with each other, and shifted from hunting with spear and bola to bow and arrow. They learned how to make pottery and, eventually, to farm.

backs up the hillside you just climbed. The shelter has no water, but does have a chum, an outhouse without walls. In warm, sunny weather, a chum is a fine spot from which to contemplate all of nature; it is less so in cold rain or a north wind.

Typically it is difficult to guess the exact age of forests along the AT but this area can be dated precisely. A forest fire ravaged this part of the mountain in October 1910. The maturing forest of oak and ash has grown back since then.

The AT continues climbing, crossing the mountain's first summit (2.7 mi.), then rises up over a steep boulder scramble to a second summit and a very good western overlook (3.3 mi.). The Drowned Lands and the Great Valley of the Appalachians stretch out before you. The Great Valley is a vast lowland that parallels the Appalachian ridges from Ala-

More recent Native American artifacts from the Archaic Period (8000 to 1000 B.C.), the Woodland Period (1000 B.C. to A.D. 1600), and the Contact Period (A.D. 1600 to 1750) abound in Vernon Valley. Flint chips, spear and arrow heads, hammer stones (used to pound acorns and grind grains), scrapers (used on hides), fishing net sinkers, a stone hatchet, and even human remains have been found at scattered prehistoric rock shelters, villages, and campsites.

When Europeans first arrived, they were horrified by what they found here. New Jersey was occupied by a culture that called itself the Lenape, a society that appeared both wild and pagan. Lenape men tattooed their bodies with colorful animal, snake, and bird shapes. They greased their hair with bear fat and oiled their bodies against the cold and insects with fish oil, eagle fat, and raccoon grease. Men and women went nearly naked in summer and donned animal furs during winter. Their shamanistic beliefs demanded strange talismans: neck pendants and necklaces, sacred tobacco pouches, and medicine bags.

What most Europeans failed to see was that the Woodland Lenape lived a peaceful, communal life. Food and hunting grounds were shared in good times and bad. The old and infirm were cared for by all. The small family bands never felt much need for government, never erected great fortresses, monuments, or temples, and spent no time building arsenals and armies.

When Europeans invaded, with their devastating diseases, alcohol, and the seduction of superior technology, the Lenape quickly succumbed. Cotton Mather echoed the arrogance of most colonists. "We must either convert these tawny serpents or annihilate them," he declared. The Lenape were swept away in a mere 150 years, but they have left their stony legacy for us to discover and interpret in the fields and forests along the AT.

bama to southern New York state (see Hike #30).

Over the next 3.5 mi. the AT continues to hump its way over the little peaks of Pochuck Mt., going through small stony passes, by rhododendron bogs, and over small streams. At 3.7 mi. the trail leaves a mostly deciduous forest and enters a grove of hemlocks. A hundred feet off the AT to the left (and invisible from the trail) is the most spectacular farmer's stone wall we have ever seen. It's worth detouring a short distance along the "Great Wall of Pochuck" and to wonder at the work ethic (or divine madness) that could have driven some anonymous farmer to construct it. The wall is monumental: wide and level enough to drive a compact car along, as it doggedly follows an arrow-straight course, completely ignoring the topography's abrupt ups and downs.

Just beyond the Great Wall, the AT intersects dirt Banks Pond Rd. A detour left along the road brings hikers in about 0.2 mi. to two beautiful forest ponds. These secluded bodies of water have attracted partying teenagers for years, some of whom nicknamed this hard-to-reach wild spot the "Pochuck Republic." Waterfowl love the ponds for the same reason. We have come upon great blue herons here, and watched them lift up gracefully from the water on outspread wings. Volunteers recently worked with the government to purchase this 450-acre tract, preserving it as part of the AT corridor and protecting it from a proposed housing development.

After crossing the third major Pochuck Mt. summit (4.0 mi.) with its limited view west, the AT begins to descend. It traverses open woods, crosses a wooden bridge over Millbrook Creek (5.1 mi.), and reaches County Rte. 565 at 5.2 mi. To the right is the former Glenwood School. Built in 1864, this two-room schoolhouse continued to operate until 1958.

The trail continues rising and falling over hilly terrain, passing through forest glens and over wide-open fields until it eventually descends into Vernon Valley and intersects County Rte. 517 (6.8 mi.). A detour for 1.0 mi. north along Rte. 517 brings you to one of the most acclaimed B & Bs of the AT: the Apple Valley Inn. Built in 1831, this colonial-style mansion is owned by John and Mitzi Durham. The couple, originally

from Alabama, has brought real Southern hospitality to their New Jersey inn. A popular AT thru-hiker stopover, it offers six antiques-furnished bedrooms, a sunroom, pool, and trail shuttles. Mitzi's only requirement of hikers is that they write a little rhyming poem in the Apple Valley's trail register.

At the time of this book's publication, the AT still turned right on Rte. 517 and followed it for 0.8 mi, turned left onto Maple Grange Rd. for 0.8 mi., then turned left onto Canal Rd. for 0.5 mi. While Rte. 517 is an unpleasantly busy highway, both Maple Grange Rd. and Canal Rd. offer hikers a sampling of the quiet country roads that formed much of the AT's route in the 1920s and 1930s.

If plans continue on schedule, however, this AT road walk (the last in New Jersey) will be eliminated by autumn 1998. It will be replaced by one of the largest building projects ever undertaken by AT volunteers, a mile-long hike over an elevated treadway crossing the Pochuck Quagmire. Fifteen thousand years ago, the quagmire lay at the bottom of a 200-ft.-deep glacial lake. Today, after torrential rains, the area seeks to become a lake again. Pochuck Creek (at the heart of the quagmire) jumps its banks, submerges fields of goldenrod and cattails, and rushes downstream, carrying tree limbs and other refuse in its path. In winter, floating ice cakes glide through the valley, colliding with swamp maples. During drier parts of each year, the waters recede and the quagmire becomes a knee-deep, leg-sucking sea of black muck.

This floodplain was decidedly *not* the ideal place to put a trail, but it was the only undeveloped section of Vernon Valley left available in the 1970s when the State of New Jersey sought to buy land for the AT's passage. The partial solution to the quagmire problem was to build an 110-ft. suspension bridge across Pochuck Creek. The elevated walkway of this immense wooden bridge had to be placed 14 ft. above the ground, putting it 5 ft. above the 100-yr. flood level. The bridge's approaches on both sides will run through a wide, open floodplain, presenting equally difficult engineering problems. The treadway must not float away during high water but must also avoid acting as a dam, blocking the water's flow.

The resulting hike will take walkers straight across Rte. 517 and into a uniquely beautiful wetland ecosystem. In late summer, clumps of buttery yellow sneezeweed, white asters, yellow goldenrod, and deep purple ironweed fill the open meadows with color. Scarlet cardinal flowers grow near the banks of the Pochuck, and cattails fill the marshy areas. Phoebes swoop over the swamp, catching insects in midflight. Northern harriers dive low over the tall grasses, hunting small rodents.

After crossing Pochuck Creek on the suspension bridge, the newly relocated AT will cross another wide wetland, then enter woods, swinging along the edge of impressive limestone bluffs. A Native American rock shelter at this spot was a campsite for Woodland Period Lenapes, and it has yielded a male skeleton plus many artifacts to archeologists (see "The Ghosts of Lenapehoking"). Unfortunately, this rock shelter has been badly looted in recent years, as has a large Lenape village site just a half mile north of here. The reason for such heavy prehistoric habitation can be found in the dark black veins of chert in the limestone cliffs. This material was shaped into a wide variety of useful stone tools, including knives, scrapers, and spear and arrow heads. This prehistoric rock quarry has been nominated for inclusion in the National Register of Historic Places. The limestone terraces also support an unusual proliferation of plants: chinkapin oak, columbine, may-apple, wild ginger, lady's-slipper, bloodroot, and three varieties of jack-in-the-pulpit grow here.

The relocated trail rejoins the old AT at the Canal Rd. bridge (8.9 mi.), where it crosses the Wawayanda-Pochuck Drainage Canal. What appears to be a creek is actually a ditch dug by farmers and later deepened and widened by the Civilian Conservation Corps in an unsuccessful attempt to drain the surrounding wetlands. From here, the AT strikes off across a series of gently rolling pastures, dotted by glacial erratics (large boulders left behind by the receding Wisconsin glacier). A small wooden bridge over the original

Wawayanda Creek (9.1 mi.) is a good spot to look for brilliantly plumaged scarlet tanagers.

The trail crosses the Lehigh & Hudson River Railroad at 9.6 mi. Built in 1882, this line once transported agricultural products to New York City and weary New Yorkers (including F. Scott Fitzgerald) to the quaint resort village of Warwick, New York.

The AT passes through one last pasture, usually filled with amiable cows, before reaching the overnight hiker parking area at NJ 94 (9.8 mi.) and ending this walk. NJ 94 was a "King's Highway," laid out by the British Crown in 1735 and used to move colonial troops during the Revolution. Looming up to the east are the 1400-ft. heights of the Wawayanda Escarpment and the start of the New Jersey Highlands.

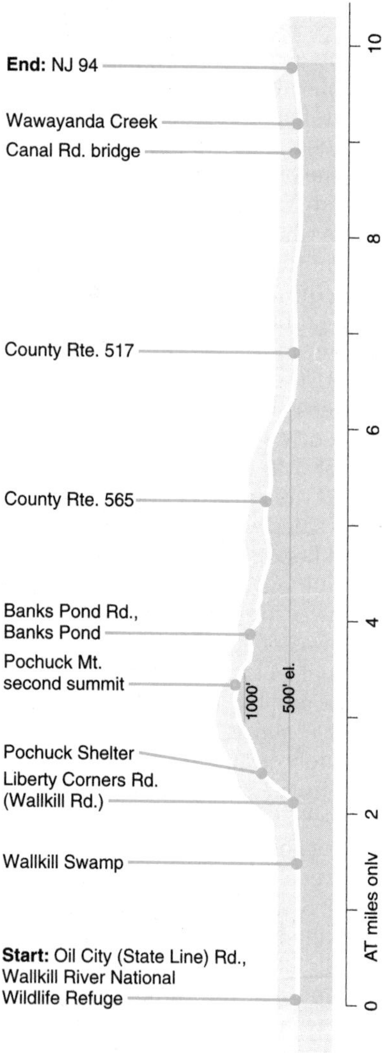

End: NJ 94 — 10

Wawayanda Creek

Canal Rd. bridge

County Rte. 517 — 8

County Rte. 565 — 6

Banks Pond Rd., Banks Pond — 4

Pochuck Mt. second summit

1000' el.   500' el.

Pochuck Shelter

Liberty Corners Rd. (Wallkill Rd.) — 2

Wallkill Swamp

Start: Oil City (State Line) Rd., Wallkill River National Wildlife Refuge — 0

AT miles only

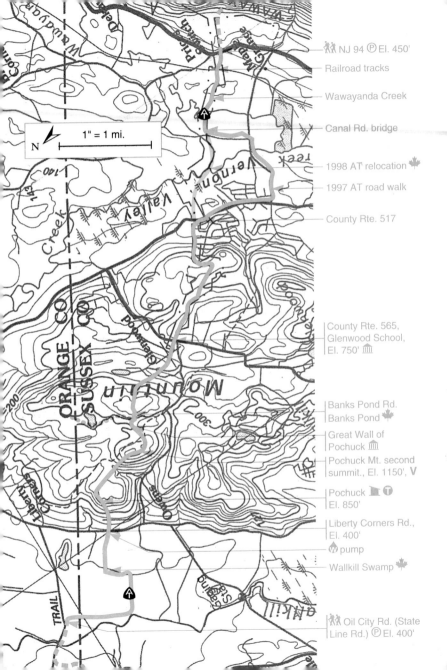

🚶 NJ 94 Ⓟ El. 450'

— Railroad tracks

— Wawayanda Creek

— Canal Rd. bridge

— 1998 AT relocation 🍁

— 1997 AT road walk

— County Rte. 517

County Rte. 565,
Glenwood School,
El. 750' 🏛

Banks Pond Rd.
Banks Pond 🍁

Great Wall of
Pochuck 🏛

Pochuck Mt. second
summit., El. 1150', V

Pochuck ▰ ⊤
El. 850'

Liberty Corners Rd.,
El. 400'

💧 pump

— Wallkill Swamp 🍁

🚶 Oil City Rd. (State
Line Rd.) Ⓟ El. 400'

1" = 1 mi.

N

ORANGE CO.
SUSSEX CO.

Vernon Valley

Mountain

Miles N	NORTH	Elev. (ft./m)	Miles S
	Total: 10.1 mi. with access on Oil City Rd. (State Line Rd.)		
9.8	**End:** NJ 94, overnight parking, 2.2 mi. N of Vernon.	450/137	0.0
9.6	**Lehigh & Hudson River Railroad,** built 1882.		0.2
9.1	**Wawayanda Creek bridge.**		0.7
8.9	**Canal Rd.** bridge and early exit option.		0.9
6.8	**County Rte. 517;** start of 1998 Pochuck Quagmire AT relocation, follow blazes. Early exit option.	450/137	3.0
5.2	**County Rte. 565;** Glenwood School (built 1864) to R (S); early exit option.	750/229	4.6
5.1	**Millbrook Creek bridge.**	700/213	4.7
4.0	Eastern summit, **Pochuck Mt.**	1100/335	5.8
3.9	**Banks Pond Rd.,** leads L (N) 0.4 mi. to Banks Pond (no camping). Early exit option.	850/259	5.9
3.7	**Great Wall of Pochuck,** massive farmer's stone fence.	900/274	6.1
3.3	Second **Pochuck** summit, view.	1150/351	6.5
2.7	Western summit, **Pochuck Mt.**	950/290	7.1
2.4	**Pochuck Shelter** side trail leads L (N) to shelter and privy (0.2 mi.).	850/259	7.4
2.1	**Liberty Corners Rd. (Wallkill Rd.),** early exit option.	400/122	7.7
2.0	**Water pump.**		7.8
1.9	**Wallkill Swamp;** AT leaves swamp.		7.9
1.5	**Wallkill Swamp;** AT turns R (E) into swamp over bog bridges.		8.3
1.2	Abandoned **Lehigh & New England Railroad** bed.		8.6
0.0	**Start AT miles:** Oil City Rd. (State Line Rd.), Wallkill River National Wildlife Refuge day parking (1.6 mi. SE of Unionville, NY); follow trail along old sod farm dikes.	400/122	9.8
0.3	Access: Go straight on Oil City Rd. to parking lot on S side of road.		0.3

SOUTH

Wawayanda Mt. to Warwick Tpk.

Maps: ATC N.Y. & N.J. Map 4; NY-NJTC North Jersey Trails Map 21

Route: From Warwick Tpk. to Luther's Rock, Wawayanda Escarpment, Pinwheel's Vista, and NJ 94

Recommended direction: N to S

Distance: 6.0 mi.

Elevation +/-: 1150 to 1350 to 450 ft.

Effort: Easy

Day hike: Yes

Overnight backpacking hike: Optional

Duration: 4 hr.

Early exit options: At 0.8 mi., Wawayanda Rd.; at 1.9 mi., Iron Mt. Rd.

Natural history features: Billion-year-old Wawayanda Escarpment; Pinwheel's Vista; glacial erratics; spring wildflowers; glacial kame terrace

Social history features: Pullis Hotel foundation; iron-mining exploratory pit; Kasmar house foundation; Wawayanda and Green iron mines; Baldwin Gravel Quarry

Trailhead access: *Start:* Take NJ 94 for 2.2 mi. N of NY state line. Turn R onto Moe Rd. (Warwick Tpk.). Follow for 2.7 mi. to AT daytime pull-over spots just N of Wawayanda SP entrance. *End:* Take NJ 94S from the NY state line 2.0 mi. to the AT parking area on L. Or take NJ 94N 2.2 mi. from Vernon stoplight to AT parking area on R. There is overnight parking for 5 to 6 cars (with permit from Wawayanda SP office).

Camping: Wawayanda Hilton Shelter

Wawayanda State Park extends across 13,000 acres of wild land. It is a remote plateau covered by rhododendron bogs where bears forage, craggy cliffs where coyote and bobcat make their dens, and hemlock ravines through which fast-moving streams surge and plummet. This mountain boasts some of the oldest bedrock along the entire AT and a history of habitation that stretches back 12,000 years.

This 6.0-mi. day hike provides one of the most far-reaching vistas in the state, a preserved 19th-century mountain farm, and even the promise of buried treasure. Begin at one of the two pull-off spots on either side of Warwick Tpk. Follow the white blazes west into an open but abandoned farm field that in summer grows thick with goldenrod and red clover. Wawayanda State Park surrounds you. The unusual name is not, as asserted in Samuel Eager's 19th-century *History of Orange County*, a corruption of "way, way yonder." It is actually a Lenape (see Hike #31) phrase meaning "winding, winding motion," a good description of the meandering streams that twist through the valley on the west side of the mountain.

If you take a detour into the field 100 ft. or so off the trail to your right (north), you will find the stone foundation of the Pullis Hotel hidden in brush, and thereby hangs a tale. The twelve-room inn, boardinghouse, and tavern was built in 1829. It served a roughneck clientele, men who worked the local iron mines and furnace. In the late 1800s, legend has it, an old woman took a job here. She was paid in silver coin, but cunningly hid her earnings in the forest to prevent theft. Then she suffered a stroke and was paralyzed and unable to speak. As she lay dying, co-workers begged her to reveal the whereabouts of her secret stash. All she could manage was a feeble gesture toward a window. Many have come since, with pick and shovel, to search for the lost treasure. All have gone away empty-handed. The Pullis Hotel was still serving guests into the 1920s, and early AT guidebooks say you could get a bed and meal here for $2. It was torn down in 1959, leaving only the mystery of the lost treasure.

Return to the trail and cross a small bridge over the outlet of what was once Parker Pond, now returning to wetland. The AT then joins an ancient, sunken country lane with high stone fences on either side. This byway has been a road since the 1790s and once carried heavy wagon traffic moving iron ore to Chester, New York. It was used by vehicles into the 1940s, and is probably the only original section of the AT in the park. The rest of the trail has since been relocated away from more public areas.

At 0.3 mi. the blue-blazed Hoeferlin Trail leads left in 0.3 mi. to the Wawayanda SP headquarters, which has a public telephone, rest rooms, parking, and water. Bill Hoeferlin was a NY-NJTC volunteer who from 1934 to 1964 created detailed hiking maps for the entire New York metropolitan area. "Father Bill" also penned folksy newsletters, chock-full of poetry in the style of Burma Shave ads and cornball prose, that spread the Good News about trails. Early in life Bill had found the cure for his tuberculosis. He wrote:

> What's the sport that legs were made for,
> What's the purpose trails were laid for?
> Well or ill, in debt or paid for,
> Troubles burden you, just walk them off.

Just 0.1 mi. farther along, another blue-blazed side trail leads left uphill to the Wawayanda Hilton, the newest shelter in New Jersey. It was built in 1990 by volunteers from Vernon High School, St. Thomas Episcopal Church, and local Boy Scout troops. There is a privy, but no fires are allowed. The closest water is at the park office. A tall shagbark hickory stands just in front of the lean-to. This tree is distinguished by its shaggy, vertically peeling bark. Early settlers pulverized and boiled hickory nuts to produce a sweet, oily hickory milk used in the cooking of corn cakes and hominy.

In its early days the Hilton's overnight guests received disconcerting wake-up calls, as this 1991 shelter register entry relates: "I just came down off the roof. Do you want to know why? 'Cause while I was unpacking breakfast, Yogi Bear came waddling up, looking as if he was hungry enough to eat Boo Boo. I hauled myself and my pack up on the shelter roof. He ain't gettin' my food!—Hey, he's leavin'. I'm makin' a break for it. —Woody (proud member of the coalition to remove Yogis from AT shelters)."

A hiker education program and the relocation of a nearby park trash can have solved the bear problem, but quiet walkers still may spot the animals on the trail at twilight (see "The Black Bear Comeback"). Remember, when tent camping, always to hang your food high in the trees, or when staying at New Jersey shelters, store it in the metal bear-proof boxes provided. Wander downhill and to the right of the shelter and you will find an iron mine test pit, a hole dug a few feet into the ground. Nineteenth-century prospectors walked the iron-rich hills with compasses. When the needle went crazy, pointing away from true north, they dug pits to test for iron. The low-grade quality of the ore found here prevented this spot from being turned into a mine.

At 0.6 mi., the AT turns left and follows dirt Wawayanda Rd. for a short distance (this trail section may be relocated slightly in 1998). The filled-in shafts of the W[...] Green iron mines lie here, and the ruins of th[...] Furnace are 2 mi. to the [...] cinating detour). Opened [...] first years of the Revolutio[...] [...]r, the mines were worked intermittently, and produced ore for swords and shovels in the Civil War. The mines were over 100 ft. deep and could produce up to 5000 tons of ore a year. The Wawayanda Furnace, built in 1846, ran for eighteen months at a stretch, requiring one acre of forest per day just to keep it burning. The denuded plateau, roaring blast furnace, and towering column of soot and smoke must have made this area hell on earth. The furnace shut down in 1867, the last of the mines closed in 1891, and gradually the forest reclaimed the battered land.

The AT turns right into the woods, leaving dirt Wawayanda Rd. at 0.8 mi. Wawayanda Rd. provides an early exit opportunity for this hike: if you continue straight ahead on the road, leaving the AT, you will reach the state park's paved main road in about half a mile. A left turn on the paved road brings you to the park office in another 0.6 mi.

After leaving Wawayanda Rd., the AT climbs gently to the crest of a rise, then descends to intersect and turn left onto dirt Iron Mt. Rd. (1.3 mi.). The stone foundation and chimney of the Kasmar house (built in 1815) are on the left. Local legend claims this farm was a training camp for Max Schmeling, world heavyweight

The Black Bear Comeback

Approaching the Wawayanda shelter at twilight, a friend and I heard a soft snort. We looked up in surprise to see a massive black bear galloping away from us at top speed. As it fled, the powerful animal looked back over its shoulder, giving us an irate look, as if to say, "What business do you have here?" We stood in awe, watching as it vanished in the gloom.

Black bears have made an extraordinary comeback in New Jersey. Native bears were hunted nearly to extinction in the 1800s, but with the restoration of forest habitat they have returned, migrating east from Pennsylvania's Pocono Mts. Today approximately 500 of these animals make their homes in the Garden State's densely thicketed, swampy uplands.

When you hike the AT through oak and hemlock forests or mountain laurel thickets or near rhododendron or blueberry bogs, you're in prime bear country. About 60 percent of the state's black bears live in the highlands between Wawayanda Mt. and Greenwood Lake, with 40 percent residing in the Kittatinnies.

Black bears do not hibernate. They den for the winter, taking cover in hollow trees, rock cavities, or holes in the ground. While their metabolisms slow by over 50 percent, they don't fall into a sound sleep, and can be awakened easily. During denning, the animals eat and drink nothing, nor do they relieve themselves. Their bodies have the unique ability to reabsorb the toxic by-products of metabolism, a fact that has spurred intense interest among researchers studying human kidney disease.

boxing champion in the 1930s. Despite the house's historic value, the state leveled it in 1991.

The trail continues through abandoned farm fields that are slowly growing up with saplings. It crosses the Double Kill over an iron truss bridge (1.5 mi.) installed in the 1890s. After crossing the bridge, the AT leaves Iron Mt. Rd. (1.9 mi.). You can use Iron Mt. Rd. as an early exit opportunity, following it away from the AT for approximately 1 mi. to the Wawayanda SP beach and parking area. After leaving Iron Mt. Rd., the trail continues through young forest until it comes to a woods road, which skirts the edge of the upper fields of High Breeze Farm (2.5 mi.). Views stretch north to the Shawangunk and Catskill mountains.

Cross dirt Barrett Rd. at 2.7 mi. (no parking) and think about stopping for lunch. The fields, with their Currier and Ives vista, make a great spot for a picnic (but watch out for poison ivy). High Breeze Farm stretches out below you. Established in the 1820s by the Barrett family, it is one of the last surviving 19th-century

New Jersey's bears have adapted well to living near people. They are shy, elusive creatures, and would really rather not meet humans. Their diet is mostly vegetarian: nuts, berries, roots, tubers, and grasses, with meat coming from insects and carrion. They are rarely aggressive, though they are opportunists, and will grab a free meal when offered. Backpacks filled with food and left unattended or stowed in a shelter or tent overnight are top targets, as are garbage cans.

If you come face to face with a bear, use common sense. Treat these large animals with the same respect you would a sumo wrestler. Always yield the right-of-way to bears. Most will flee from you. If a bear doesn't flee, take a nonaggressive stance. Do not make eye contact. Talk in a quiet voice. If the animal continues to approach, talk louder, bang pots, whistle, wave your arms, or shoot the flash of a camera. Never run. A bear can hit speeds of up to 35 mph, and can easily overtake the fastest human sprinter. Most of all, never come between a mother bear and her cubs.

When camping, neatness counts. Never cook or eat where you will be sleeping. Avoid spilling food. Never pour grease drippings into a firepit; that attracts wildlife. Finally, no matter how unlikely a bear visit seems, always hang your food from a rope high in a tree or store it in the bear-proof metal boxes provided at New Jersey shelters. Hang anything that has a strong scent, such as food, greasy cooking utensils, and toiletries, including toothpaste and soap.

Regard these magnificent animals with healthy respect. View them from a distance with the awe and wonder they deserve.

---

highlands farms in New Jersey. It was rescued from demolition in 1989 through the concerted efforts of Ron Dupont, Jr., and the Vernon Historical Society. Dupont gave dozens of slide shows and rallied schoolchildren in a campaign to save the landmark. Its farmhouse, barns, outbuildings, and fields are slated to become a living history museum.

Four generations of Barretts pursued a now nearly forgotten rural lifestyle here, raising horses, cows, and chickens, harvesting hay, corn, turnips, and rutabagas, cultivating apples, peaches, pears, and plums, bottling honey and maple syrup, hunting game, and renting rooms. Even after the railroads bypassed the Appalachians for the rich croplands of the Midwest, the Barretts kept farming. Luther Barrett, the last in the line, still used a horse-drawn mower to cut his hay fields in the late 1980s. The mowers, sickle bars, and other farm equipment, their wrought-iron wheels colored by a chocolate-brown patina of rust, still litter the fields and draw hikers' thoughts back into the 19th century.

The trail leaves the fields and slowly climbs, reaching a narrow vista at Luther's Rock, a glacial erratic (3.1 mi.). It continues downhill through hemlocks, then descends steeply on stone steps to a stream, which it crosses. The trail now begins a steep ascent on more stone steps. Look for a new blue-blazed trail to the left (south) leading to a small waterfall (this side trail opens in late 1998). The AT continues ascending, though at a lesser grade, until it reaches the crest of Wawayanda Mt. at a register box (4.6 mi.). The blue-blazed Wawayanda Ridge Trail (formerly the AT) goes left for 0.8 mi. past several good viewpoints.

The AT now begins a steep, 900-vertical-ft. descent of the Wawayanda Escarpment, a highly erosion-resistant, billion-year-old formation of crystalline rock. These Grenville Time formations are some of the oldest in the Appalachians, created before the first land plants had evolved. The continent this bedrock originally belonged to was located well below the equator before it split into fragments that eventually drifted north to their present positions.

A blue-blazed side trail (4.7 mi.) leads right (north) in 0.1 mi. to Pinwheel's Vista. Just before reaching the overlook, the side trail passes to the left of a 20-ft.-tall limestone glacial erratic that blooms with drooping red columbine every spring. Pinwheel's Vista, offering one of the best views in the state, looks north to the Catskills and south toward the

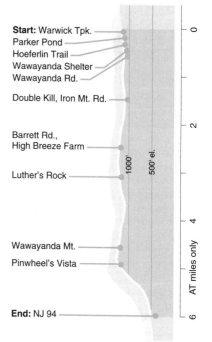

Delaware Water Gap. The entire length of the Kittatinny Ridge, topped by High Point Monument (see Hike #29), stretches along the far horizon. Vernon Valley, with its patchwork quilt of farms and forests, lies immediately below.

Settled in the early 1700s, rural Vernon Valley resists development despite intense pressure from home and golf course builders. Sadly, the view from Pinwheel's Vista could be very different fifty years from now. As old-time farmers give up their lands, the narrow AT corridor may see strip malls and subdivisions closing in

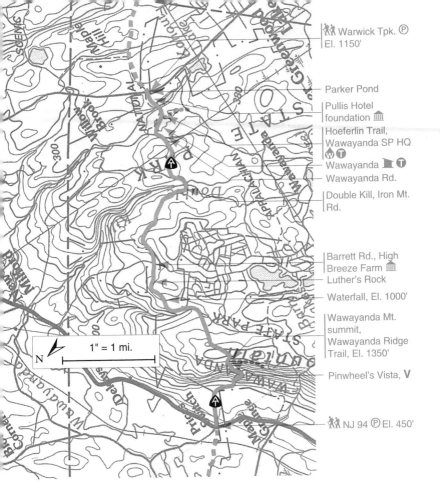

🚶🚶 Warwick Tpk. Ⓟ
El. 1150'

— Parker Pond

Pullis Hotel
foundation 🏛

Hoeferlin Trail,
Wawayanda SP HQ
🐾Ⓣ

— Wawayanda 🖼 Ⓣ

— Wawayanda Rd.

Double Kill, Iron Mt.
Rd.

Barrett Rd., High
Breeze Farm 🏛

— Luther's Rock

— Waterfall, El. 1000'

Wawayanda Mt.
summit,
Wawayanda Ridge
Trail, El. 1350'

— Pinwheel's Vista, **V**

🚶🚶 NJ 94 Ⓟ El. 450'

1" = 1 mi.

N

around it. As in many other AT communities, the battle to protect these lands against uncontrolled development is being fought by concerned citizens in local town council and planning board meetings.

The AT steeply descends the boulder-strewn escarpment on a trail relocation built between 1988 and 1990. It replaces a treacherous, washed-out gully trail that had been in use since the 1920s. The new trail consists of switchbacks, over 400 stone steps, rock cribbing, and drains placed by local volunteers and the Mid-Atlantic ATC work crew. The Stairway to

Heaven (4.8 mi.) alone has over sixty monstrous steps, dug into a 60-degree dirt slope. Each stone weighs about 300 lb., in keeping with the rule of thumb that if two people can move a rock, it is too small. The purpose of the relocation was not only to protect hikers but also to prevent erosion of the mountain. In springtime, the rugged terrain blooms with little clusters of Virginia saxifrage, Solomon's-seal, Solomon's-plume, and small, nodding, pale yellow wild oats. At the base of the escarpment, the AT winds through a moonscape of fallen boulders and then passes through open woods. In spring, the forest floor is dotted by jack-in-the-pulpit, white baneberry, cranesbill (a species of wild geranium), and may-apple.

The AT crosses a stone wall and exits onto a gently sloping hillside (5.5 mi.). This is what geologists call a "kame terrace," a long gravel slope deposited by the sideways pressure of the retreating Wisconsin glacier 15,000 years ago. Views look west across Vernon Valley to Pochuck Mt. The last 0.5 mi. of the hike descends gradually through a gravel quarry to the AT parking area at NJ 94.

Miles N	**NORTH**	Elev. (ft./m)	Miles S
6.0	**Start:** **Warwick Tpk.** day parking; 0.6 mi. S on AT and side trail to Wawayanda SP headquarters.	1150/351	0.0
5.9	**Pullis Hotel** foundation 100 ft. to R (N).		0.1
5.8	**Parker Pond.**		0.2
5.7	**Hoeferlin Trail** to Wawayanda SP headquarters, parking, telephone, water, rest rooms, information (0.3 mi.).	1200/366	0.3
5.6	**Wawayanda Hilton,** side trail to shelter and privy (0.1).		0.4
5.4	Turn L (S) onto **Wawayanda Rd.**		0.6
5.2	Turn R (E) off **Wawayanda Rd.** Early exit option.	1100/335	0.8
4.5	**Double Kill** stream crossing on **Iron Mt. Rd.**		1.5
4.1	Leave **Iron Mt. Rd.** Early exit option.		1.9
3.5	**Barrett Rd.;** High Breeze Farm, 19th-century subsistence farm.		2.7
2.9	**Luther's Rock,** glacial erratic and view.	1250/381	3.1
2.4	Trail to **waterfall** opens in 1998.	1000/305	3.6
1.4	**Wawayanda Mt.** summit, register box, and Wawayanda Ridge Trail (0.8 mi.).	1350/412	4.6
1.3	**Pinwheel's Vista** side trail leads past large glacial erratic to view (0.1 mi.).		4.7
1.2	**Stairway to Heaven,** massive stone steps built by volunteers.	1200/366	4.8
0.5	Base of **Wawayanda Mt.**	550/168	5.5
0.0	**End:** **NJ 94** overnight parking, 2.2 mi. N of Vernon.	450/137	6.0

SOUTH

HIKE #33
Warwick Tpk. to Mt. Peter, NY

Maps: ATC N.Y. & N.J. Maps 4 & 3; NY-NJTC North Jersey Trail Map 21

Route: From Warwick Tpk. over Bearfort Mt. to Greenwood Lake and NY 17A atop Mt. Peter

Recommended direction: S to N

Distance: 9.5 mi.

Elevation +/-: 1150 to 1433 to 1130 ft.

Effort: Strenuous

Day hike: Yes

Overnight backpacking hike: No

Duration: 7 hr.

Early exit options: At 1.0 mi., Long House Rd. (Brady Rd.); at 3.6 mi., State Line Trail

Natural history features: Puddingstone summits and hemlock hollows atop Bearfort Mt.; Greenwood Lake vistas

Social history features: Welling Iron Mine; Long Pond Iron Works; proposed site of metropolitan jetport

Other feature: View of New York City skyline

Trailhead access: *Start:* Take NJ 94 for 2.2 mi. N of NY state line. Turn R onto Moe Rd. (Warwick Tpk.). Follow for 2.7 mi. to AT daytime pull-over spots just N of Wawayanda SP entrance. *End:* From NJ/NY 94 or NY 17 take NY 17A to Continental Rd.; at crest of Mt. Peter go approximately 100 yd. to parking area.

Camping: None

T his 9.5-mi. hike begins in New Jersey and ends in New York. It is strenuous, but well worth the effort, providing more stunning views per mile than just about any other walk on the AT in this region. The far-reaching vistas along windswept Bearfort Ridge (also called Mt. Peter) look out over the full sweep of the New York and New Jersey highlands, down to Greenwood Lake, east to the Ramapo Mts., and off to a horizon marked by the shimmering towers of New York City skyscrapers.

One warning: Bearfort Ridge's AT section runs along miles of exposed bedrock and on a blistering hot,

sunny day, makes hikers feel like bugs scurrying across a sizzling griddle. Avoid the ridge in very hot weather. The bedrock can also be slippery and dangerous in wet weather.

The walk begins at a pull-over on Warwick Tpk. Follow the white blazes east into the woods and over bog bridges through a small swamp. In early April you will be welcomed on your way by a wild chorus of spring peepers. These are the region's tiniest frogs, just an inch in length. But there is nothing small about the song these critters sing. Male peepers, advertising for a mate, distend their throats into a bubble almost as big as their entire bodies, and then let out a joyful birdlike whistle that can be heard half a mile away. This attention-getting maneuver is understandable; the peepers must attract a mate and see their tadpoles turned into frogs before the spring swamps dry up in the July heat.

Climbing gently, the AT follows a farm road along the edge of a former field covered in a riot of young saplings, all fighting to rise above each other into the sunlight. Old-timers called these young trees "hoop poles" because the pliable wood could easily be shaped into barrel hoops.

At the top of this field (0.3 mi.), the AT crosses a level patch of bedrock stained with dark black and rust-colored streaks, a sure sign of iron ore. This fact didn't go unnoticed by 19th-century prospectors. Just 0.3 mi. northeast of this spot (but not along the AT) are the ruins of the Welling Iron Mine. Opened in 1855, the operation failed to be profitable, and was closed by the 1880s. Ed Lenik's book *Iron Mine Trails* provides directions to this and forty other highlands mines. If you decide to bushwhack to the mine site, stay out of its deep vertical shafts. They are unstable and dangerous.

The trail descends very steeply over stone steps (0.4 mi.), then crosses a small brook whose waters sparkle golden brown with tannic acid produced by the surrounding hemlock trees.

For the next 2.9 mi., footing is tricky as the AT repeatedly ascends small hillocks over loose rock and descends into swampy spots. AT thru-hikers "lovingly" refer to this rugged sort of terrain as PUDs: "Pointless Ups and Downs." You can take your mind off the PUDs by noting forest diversity. Here, the New Jersey Highlands supports hemlocks, young sycamores, chestnut oaks, red oaks, black birches, and beeches. When the leaves are off the trees, Bearfort Ridge can be seen dramatically looming up ahead.

The trail crosses paved Long House Rd. (also called Brady Rd.) at 1.0 mi., and then passes over Long House Creek on a bridge at 1.5 mi. Located a few miles downstream was Lawrence Scrauley's iron forge, built in 1745 at Bellvale, New York. Scrauley made a fatal business error in 1750 when he thumbed his nose at a royal decree ordering American colonists to ship their iron ore directly to England and forbidding the local manufacture of finished goods. In response, English Redcoats seized and wrecked the forge. It was one of many incidents leading to the American Revolution. After the trail crosses a grassy woods road (2.7 mi.), mountain laurel begins to appear on both sides of the path as it makes a steady and purposeful ascent toward the summit of Bearfort Ridge.

At 3.1 mi. the AT arrives at a high ledge composed of strikingly beautiful puddingstone. This erosion-resis-

Giant oyster mushroom

tant conglomerate, laid out in long parallel, pavementlike sections, forms the spine of Bearfort Ridge. Puddingstone is a geological concoction composed of red sandstone beds shot through with intrusive white quartz veins and dotted with a mix of pebbles and rock chips of many sizes and hues. It is named after a thick mealy pudding served in the 18th century. This boldly colored bedrock was formed in the Devonian Age (350 to 380 million years ago), when coarse pebbles and fine sands were washed down from the heights of ancient mountains into a river delta and then compressed. An extra dash of living color is provided to Bearfort's puddingstone by the bright green patches of lichen clinging to it. A little way off the trail to the right along the ledge, where a lone pitch pine stands, a vista looks west, back over Taylor Mt. to Vernon Valley.

A short but very steep climb through a shallow, rocky pass brings the AT to a junction with the yellow-blazed Ernest Walter Trail (3.3 mi.) and to a windblown, east-facing crag at the crest of Bearfort Mt. (3.4 mi.). This is a great spot for a snack and water break.

The view looks down over glacial Surprise Lake, which is encircled by the 1.4-mi.-long Ernest Walter Trail. Further east is the Wanaque Reservoir (a Native American name pronounced "wa-na-ki" and meaning "land of sassafras"). Still farther east are the ridges of the Ramapo Mts., and on the far horizon rise New York City's skyscrapers. On a clear day the World Trade Center towers can be seen above and to the right of the reservoir; the very top of the Empire State Building is harder to spot where it peeks over a ridge, just beyond the reservoir's waters. By late afternoon, the tall buildings sparkle with reflected sunlight and are transformed in the mind's eye into upright quartz crystals.

Turning to the left and following the windblown ridgeline, the AT runs atop a long series of puddingstone ledges. While there are smooth, sidewalklike sections, the mountain gives walkers a knee-jarring workout with its continuous stony ups and downs. At 3.6 mi., a painted sign on a puddingstone slab tells you that you are crossing out of New Jersey into New York. The blue-blazed State Line Trail descends right for 1.2 mi. to NY 210 and the Greenwood Lake Marina. There is parking at the intersection of

NY 210 and Lake Shore Dr. north of the marina.

This seemingly tranquil ridgetop location marks the peaceful settlement of a 100-year-long war between the states. The diagonal state line running between the Hudson River just south of Nyack and Port Jervis on the Delaware River was fought over from 1664 until the 1770s. Survey inaccuracies started the disagreement and land greed propelled it. At one point, New York claimed all property as far south as Easton, Pennsylvania (a claim that put most of North Jersey inside their boundary). The Boundary Wars, as they were known, were fought with lawsuits, angry words, and even bullets. A survey completed in 1774 brought a lasting peace.

Just 0.5 mi. past the border, at 4.1 mi., the AT reaches Prospect Rock (elev. 1433 ft.). This lookout, with its 360-degree view, is the highest and best of the hike. From here, seams of puddingstone flow as far as the eye can see along Bearfort Ridge. Taylor Mt. rises to the west; New York's skyscrapers rise to the southeast. The entire south end of Greenwood Lake is visible below. Once called Long Pond, this body of water was dammed and enlarged to provide water power to the ironworks at its southern end. There, large waterwheels (one of which has been painstakingly restored) powered great bellows that superheated the raging charcoal fires of the Long Pond iron furnace, which operated from 1766 to 1882.

Greenwood Lake was doubled in size in 1825 to provide water for the Morris Canal, an engineering marvel that raised coal-laden barges from the Delaware River, floated them through the highlands, and lowered them to Newark on the Atlantic coast. By the mid-19th century, Greenwood Lake was a popular resort with rambling Catskill-style hotels and steamboats delivering their urban guests. Hudson River school artist Jasper Cropsley vacationed and painted here. Yesterday's grand hotels and steamers have been replaced by today's highway motels and motorboats.

Beyond Prospect Rock, the AT plunges steeply into a secluded hemlock ravine through which Furnace Brook runs (4.9 mi.). This stream provided water to the Queensboro iron furnace in the valley to the east. A very steep, short climb leads out of the ravine over immense fallen boulders, along vertical slabs, and up a wooden ladder to the top of a wind-and-glacier-sculpted puddingstone castle-fortress. This climb is rewarded with another sweeping view of Greenwood Lake (5.2 mi.).

For the next 1.7 mi., the trail leapfrogs from one rugged, exposed puddingstone sidewalk to the next, offering many great views. It also occasionally turns away from the ridge into sheltered hemlock hollows. The puddingstone bedrock shows clear evidence of the smoothing and polishing effects of glacial action.

Lest we take the preservation of this magnificent spot for granted, it is important to remember that planners in the 1960s saw Bearfort Mt. as a potentially viable jetport site. How to bring a jumbo jet down safely atop this jagged mountain? No problem. The experts proposed controlled thermonuclear explosions to level the entire ridge. Luckily for hikers, the scheme was scrapped.

At 7.3 mi., the AT cuts sharply left away from the ridgeline, and the knee-pounding puddingstone pavements are, thankfully, replaced by a level earthen treadway through open hardwood forest. The last 2.2 mi. reward walkers with easy terrain.

The trail passes to the left of a vista that looks over the resort town of Greenwood Lake and then passes to the right of a wetland (8.7 mi.). This swamp is filled with spring peepers every April. For those taking this hike in springtime, the little critters that welcomed you at the start of your walk also conclude it. At 9.5 mi., the trail exits the woods at an overnight parking area on Continental Rd. (just opposite NY 17A).

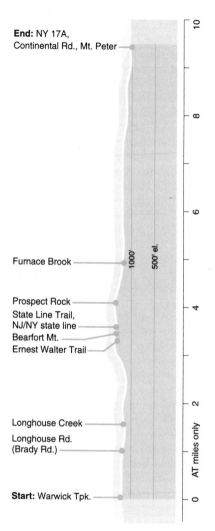

🚶 Continental Rd. Ⓟ
NY 17A, El. 1130'

El. 1200', **V**

Bearfort Ridge,
El. 1300', **V**

Prospect Rock, **V**

State Line Trail,
NJ/NY state line

Bearfort Mt. summit,
El. 1460', **V**

Ernest Walter Trail,
Surprise Lake

V

Longhouse Rd. (Brady
Rd.) Ⓟ

🚶 Warwick Tpk. Ⓟ
El. 1150'

1" = 1 mi.

Miles N	NORTH	Elev. (ft./m)	Miles S
9.5	**End:** In NY, **Continental Rd.** overnight parking at **Mt. Peter** summit, 2.0 mi. N of Greenwood Lake and 1.6 mi. E of Bellvale.	1130/344	0.0
8.7	**View** over town of Greenwood Lake, swamp.		0.8
7.3	Trail leaves ledges.	1200/366	2.2
5.2	Climb to **Bearfort Ridge** view.	1300/396	4.3
4.9	Descend to **Furnace Brook** hemlock hollow.	1100/335	4.6
4.1	**Prospect Rock,** 360-degree view.	1433/437	5.4
3.6	**NJ/NY state line; State Line Trail** descends steeply to NY 210 and Greenwood Lake (1.2 mi.). Early exit option.		5.9
3.4	**Bearfort Mt.** summit and east view.		6.1
3.3	**Ernest Walter Trail** to Surprise Lake (1.4 mi.).		6.2
3.1	Ledge with **views** west.	1350/412	6.4
2.7	Cross grassy **woods road.**		6.8
1.5	**Long House Creek bridge.**		8.0
1.0	**Long House Rd. (Brady Rd.)** day parking, early exit option.	1200/366	8.5
0.4	**Steep descent** on stone steps and brook crossing.		9.1
0.0	**Start:** In NJ, **Warwick Tpk.** day parking; 0.6 mi. S on AT and side trail to Wawayanda SP headquarters.	1150/351	9.5

SOUTH

Sterling Forest

Maps: ATC N.Y. & N.J. Map 3
Route: From NY 17A on Mt. Peter to Mombasha High Point, Buchanan Mt., NY 17, and Arden Valley Rd. (Elk Pen).
Recommended direction: S to N
Distance: 12.3 mi.
Elevation +/-: 1130 to 1294 to 550 ft.
Effort: Moderate
Day hike: Yes
Overnight backpacking hike: Optional
Duration: 8½ hr.
Early exit options: At 3.7 mi., Lakes Rd.; at 7.0 mi., W. Mombasha Rd.; at 8.8 mi., E. Mombasha Rd.; at 10.2 mi., Orange Tpk.
Natural history features: Mt. Peter birding station; Sterling Forest; Eastern Pinnacles; Cat Rocks; Fitzgerald Falls; Mombasha High Point; Buchanan Mt.; Little Dam Lake
Social history features: Sterling Forest; Peter Buck plaque
Trailhead access: *Start:* From NJ/NY 94 or NY 17 take NY 17A to Continental Rd. at crest of Mt. Peter; go approximately 100 yd. to parking area. *Midpoint:* From Rte. 17N in Southfields, turn L onto Orange Tpk. for 0.8 mi., then L onto W Mombasha Rd. for about 2.4 mi. Look for AT daytime pull-over spot on L. *End:* Take NY 17 1.9 mi. N of Southfields or 0.7 mi. S of Arden to Arden Valley Rd. and go 0.3 mi. E to Elk Pen parking area (overnight).
Camping: Wildcat Shelter

The top of Mt. Peter, where this hike begins, is one of the prime birding spots of the northeastern United States. In autumn 1995, hawk watchers tallied 8142 raptors headed south from here. These migrating birds know what casual AT hikers may not: they are overlooking the best-preserved natural landscape in the entire New York metropolitan area, 17,500-acre Sterling Forest.

Imagine a wild landscape where black bears freely roam, where red-shouldered hawks soar against cumulus clouds, where the small-footed bat makes its home in abandoned 19th-century iron mines, and where the threatened northern cricket frog and golden-winged warbler sing. Sterling Forest, supporting the largest diversity of flora and fauna in the region, is such a place.

Now imagine the same landscape scarred by shopping centers, office parks, golf courses, and 13,000 homes. A planned city of 35,000 people is the fate that developers prepared for Sterling Forest starting in 1980. But by 1985, a coalition of environmentalists had begun a fight to preserve this vital watershed and nearly pristine habitat. Although conservationists are winning the battle, the last chapter in the controversy is yet to be written (see "The Fight to Save Sterling Forest").

The protection of Sterling Forest would also mean the protection of the AT viewshed (the pristine green valleys seen from mountaintops). The trail follows high ridges, curving around the western edge of Sterling Forest and cutting through its northern section. This 12.3-mi. hike can be walked as a long summertime day hike, or may be divided at W. Mombasha Rd. into two day hikes of 7.0 mi. and 5.3 mi. Whatever your plan, give yourself time to enjoy the unique natural scenery, and bring binoculars and a bird identification book.

The hike begins at the overnight AT parking area on the crest of Mt. Peter (also sometimes called Bearfort Ridge). Follow the white blazes east along Continental Rd. and turn right at its intersection with NY 17A. In 150 ft. the trail leaves the highway, turning left into the woods. The AT meets a blue-blazed side trail within a few hundred yards. This short detour left (100 yd. or so) takes you to a breathtaking view and the Mt. Peter birding station. From this lookout birders trace the Atlantic flyway migration of osprey, bald and golden eagles, and sharp-shinned, Cooper's, red-shouldered, broad-winged, and red-tailed hawks. The best time to watch is from September 1 to November 15.

Follow the blue-blazed trail back to the AT and continue along the ridgetop, passing amid dense mountain laurel thickets. The trail is relatively level here, except for very brief, steep climbs over two impressive rock outcrops: the Eastern Pinnacles (1.3 mi.) and Cat Rocks (1.8 mi.). These crags are composed of a boldly colored conglomerate called puddingstone that consists of red and white quartz pebbles mixed with other rock chips (see Hike #33). Blue-blazed trails lead around the rock formations and should be used in wet weather or by the less agile. Both crags rise above the trees and give views east over Sterling Forest.

The AT crosses a small brook at 2.1 mi. and reaches a blue-blazed trail, left, to the Wildcat Shelter. Built in 1992, this fine lean-to has a water pump that has never failed, thanks to NY-NJ Trail Conference volunteer Liz Levers, who led the effort to get the AT off New York roads and onto protected land in the 1970s. She also hired a dowser to find water for this shelter. Though many doubted the sanity of this move, the dowser's hickory rod pinpointed a reliable underground spring within 5 min. (Remember that even pumped water should be purified.)

Wildcat Shelter also has a privy, a fire ring, and three tent sites, and offers an opportunity for a weekend adventure: backpack in the 2.1 mi. from NY 17A to the shelter on a Friday night, then complete the rest of this hike (10.2 mi.) to NY 17 the following day.

The AT continues along the ridgeline of Bellvale Mt., then descends gradually (from 2.5 mi.) and then steeply (from 3.2 mi.) into a valley, where it crosses paved Lakes Rd. (also called Monroe Rd.) at 3.7 mi. There is a pull-over spot for a few cars. The trail soon goes over Trout Brook and reaches Fitzgerald Falls (3.9 mi.). A blue-blazed trail runs from Trout Brook to the falls (0.1 mi.), and may be used if the AT is flooded during high water times.

Pretty Fitzgerald Falls is 25 ft. high and marked by pink feldspar. Proximity to Lakes Rd. has made this a popular party spot, and its beauty is often marred by trash. Please help keep the AT clean: carry a plastic bag and pack out any trash you find. Local volunteers will appreciate your thoughtfulness.

The trail climbs above the falls, passing old stone walls that indicate that this tableland may have once been used for grazing. This area is frequently filled with birdsong. Approximately ninety bird species regularly breed in Sterling Forest, compared to twenty or thirty species in urban parks. They include eighteen species of warblers, plus wild turkey and the endangered barred owl.

The AT steadily ascends, and at 5.1 mi. intersects the blue-blazed Allis Trail, named for J. Ashton Allis, New York banker and AT trailblazer. This trail and a short section of the AT are presently used as part of the 150-mi. Highlands Trail, a woodland path running between the Hudson and Delaware rivers. If conservationists get their way and Sterling Forest is fully protected, the Highlands Trail will one day be routed through the heart of the new preserve.

At 5.9 mi. the trail reaches Mombasha High Point (1280 ft.). Fifteen thousand years ago the Wisconsin glacier shaved off the tops of this and other Hudson Highland ridges, leaving behind the polished, pavementlike bedrock surfaces found here. On a clear day, New York City skyscrapers are visible, due magnetic south on your compass, rising above the treeline.

From here the trail descends, and at 6.9 mi. it emerges from woods into an overgrown field. This remarkable 4-acre clearing, known as Butterfly Meadow, was discovered in 1992 by John Yrizarry, who identified twenty-five butterfly species here on a single summer morning. The field, with its common milkweed (very important to monarch butterflies), dogbane, knapweed, thistle, and many other nectar-producing flowers, perfectly suits butterflies with evocative names like mourning cloak, red admiral, painted lady, and the very rare northern hairstreak. Butterfly counts have declined, but volunteers maintain the field as open space to encourage their return. Over sixty-six varieties of butterfly are found in Sterling Forest.

At 7.0 mi. the AT crosses W. Mombasha Rd. There is pull-off daytime parking for several cars to the left. This is a good point at which to break up this 12.3-mi. hike into two shorter day hikes. The odd name "Mombasha" is believed to be a

The Fight to Save Sterling Forest

While most mid-Atlantic AT maps are crisscrossed by roads, the Sterling Forest section is nearly empty of pavement and marked only by rugged topography lines. Therein lies its value. This Hudson Highlands region is a vast, largely intact, unfragmented forest, protected from development in this century by its dramatic relief. Elevations peak at 1300 ft., while sheer, rocky talus slopes fall away into sheltered valleys dotted by secluded marshes, brooks, and lakes just 550 ft. above sea level. Remarkably, just 400 homes break up this 17,500-acre property sitting 50 mi. from Manhattan.

William Alexander, Lord Stirling, a general in Washington's army, was an early owner of the property and its namesake. In the 18th and 19th centuries these hills were deforested for charcoal and lumber, grazed, and mined. The Sterling Iron and Railway Company sold the land in 1893 to the Harriman family, which absorbed it into their vast estate.

Hikers were among the first to recognize the value to outdoor recreation of the recovering woodlands. In the 1920s, NY-NJTC founder Raymond Torrey routed the AT through Sterling Forest, dubbing it "a real skyline trail" and worthy of protection under public ownership.

The Harrimans offered the land to New York as a gift in 1947, and in an incredible blunder the state refused, declaring it already owned enough park land! The parcel was offered for sale to a developer for just $975,000. It was resold several times, ending up in

corruption of the Native American "mombaccus," meaning "the place of death," possibly referring to a prehistoric burial site or battleground.

The trail reenters the forest, continuing north and passing through mature stands of oak, ash, and shagbark, pignut, and mockernut hickory. It continues with small ups and downs, goes past a dense mountain laurel thicket and a hemlock grove, and then ascends steeply over jumbled rocks (7.7 mi.). At the top of this small cliff the trail turns to the right, following along the edge of a 30-ft.-high escarpment.

At 7.9 mi., a bronze plaque embedded in stone and surrounded by leathery, olive drab rock tripe (a lichen) is a tribute to trail maintainer Peter Buck. Born in Vienna, Austria, in 1894, Buck worked with Joseph Bartha's Trail Patrol (see Hike #36) to keep the AT open during World War II. He died on the trail in 1962 and his ashes were spread at this high spot.

A hundred yards past the plaque, at 8.0 mi., is the first Buchanan Mt. vista (elev. 1142 ft.), from a rocky outcrop looking west to Sterling Mt. and southwest to Tiger, Cedar, and Hogback mts. If the Zurich Insur-

the hands of investors who mapped out a 35,000-person planned community for Sterling Forest.

In 1985, NY-NJTC Executive Director JoAnn Dolan and her husband, Paul, took grassroots action. They organized local citizens, land preservation groups, state and federal authorities, and the ATC into a powerful coalition to save Sterling Forest. By the early 1990s the fight had reached the halls of Congress. In her testimony Dolan declared, "If Sterling Forest is developed . . . the highlands region will be severed in half. Habitat will be fragmented and watershed areas compromised. A dream for future generations will be destroyed."

The property's owners finally agreed to sell about 90 percent of the forest for $55 million, but a Republican Congress wrestling with draconian budget-balancing measures repeatedly blocked needed appropriations until, in 1996, they authorized $17.5 million. Added to New York and New Jersey's pledge of $26 million each, and several million in private donations, the coalition was able to secure 15,300 acres in December 1997. John Gebhards, director of Sterling Forest Resources, hopes to purchase the remaining property as well: "The real sticking point is that the developers still want to keep 2,200 acres [and] build 3,000 homes and 2.7 million square ft. of commercial and light industry." That's a concession many environmentalists are unwilling to make. The jury is still out on Sterling Forest's ultimate fate. But if it is preserved, it will be largely because hikers recognized the value of this unique area.

ance Group, foreign owners of Sterling Forest, had been successful with their development plans, these green heights would have been capped by suburban sprawl.

The trail makes a steady descent into a deep, shady hollow where Christmas ferns and red-back salamanders live. It then makes a stiff climb up a rock face, requiring a little hand-over-hand climbing. This short slope, draped in moss and covered in lichen, rises 100 vertical ft. and is the steepest ascent of the hike. Lichens are actually two plants living in perfect symbiotic harmony. A fungus composed of filaments roots itself firmly to rocks and trees, and an alga clings to the fungus and photosynthesizes food for itself and the fungus. Lichens can withstand great extremes in temperature and are found worldwide, from polar regions to deserts.

A second summit of Buchanan Mt. is reached at 8.6 mi. A vista looks east past a large pitch pine and down to Little Dam Lake. The trail descends steeply, reaching and crossing paved E. Mombasha Rd. at 8.8 mi. (daytime parking). Thriving on this steep mountainside are Christmas fern (named because it stays green all year), wood aster, spotted wintergreen, and witch's butter, an orange-yellow fungus found in globs at the ends of rotting logs.

The AT continues on a winding woods road, providing the perfect habitat for trailing arbutus, a spring-blooming creeper with sweet-scented pink or white flowers. This ground-hugging, light-loving plant grows right in the middle of the treadway. Try not to step on it with your hiking boots! Trailing arbutus is disappearing as people (unsuccessfully) try to transplant it to their gardens. Reindeer lichen, looking like a tangle of hundreds of tiny, entwined antlers, also grows here.

At 9.1 mi., the trail crosses the waters of the Mombasha Kill (*kil* is a Dutch word for "stream") on a bridge. We viewed this creek the day after a nor'easter dumped 4 in. of rain. It ran crystal clear and unmuddied, proving the power of wetlands to purify groundwater naturally. This clean stream is a powerful argument for preserving Sterling Forest. The 17,500-acre watershed supplies drinking water to millions of people in northern New Jersey and southern New York State. Development would destroy the land's natural cleansing power and force construction of expensive municipal purification systems.

Little Dam Lake (9.3 mi.) is half-encircled by the AT. This former marsh was dammed to provide water to local industry in the 19th century.

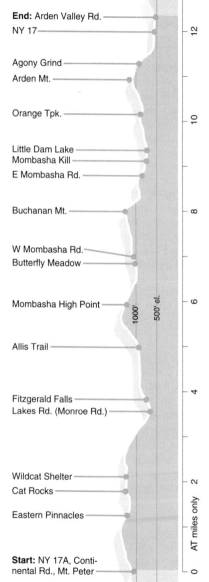

End: Arden Valley Rd.
NY 17
Agony Grind
Arden Mt.
Orange Tpk.
Little Dam Lake
Mombasha Kill
E Mombasha Rd.
Buchanan Mt.
W Mombasha Rd.
Butterfly Meadow
Mombasha High Point
Allis Trail
Fitzgerald Falls
Lakes Rd. (Monroe Rd.)
Wildcat Shelter
Cat Rocks
Eastern Pinnacles
Start: NY 17A, Continental Rd., Mt. Peter

1000' el.
500' el.
AT miles only

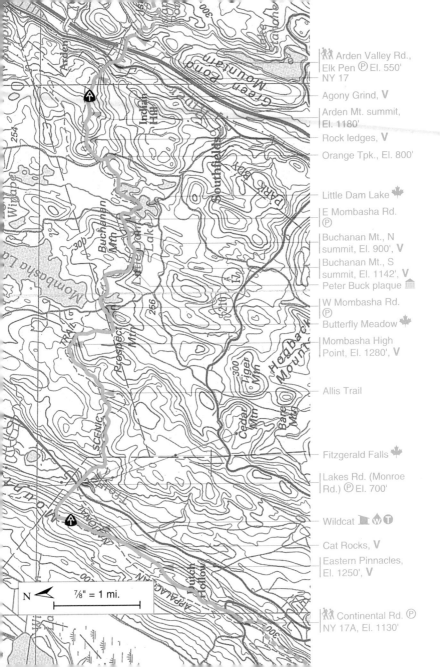

Arden Valley Rd., Elk Pen Ⓟ El. 550', NY 17

Agony Grind, **V**

Arden Mt. summit, El. 1180'

Rock ledges, **V**

Orange Tpk., El. 800'

Little Dam Lake 🍁

E Mombasha Rd. Ⓟ

Buchanan Mt., N summit, El. 900', **V**

Buchanan Mt., S summit, El. 1142', 🏛
Peter Buck plaque 🏛

W Mombasha Rd. Ⓟ

Butterfly Meadow 🍁

Mombasha High Point, El. 1280', **V**

Allis Trail

Fitzgerald Falls 🍁

Lakes Rd. (Monroe Rd.) Ⓟ El. 700'

Wildcat 🏕 🚰 🚻

Cat Rocks, **V**

Eastern Pinnacles, El. 1250', **V**

Continental Rd. Ⓟ NY 17A, El. 1130'

N ◄ ⅞" = 1 mi.

Several miles from here, beside Orange Tpk., stand the ruins of the Southfield and Sterling iron furnaces (both are on private property). The Sterling Furnace burned night and day for four months during the American Revolution to forge a great chain that was stretched across the Hudson River to block British men-of-war at West Point. This chain replaced an earlier one destroyed by the English at Bear Mt. in 1777 (see Hike #36). The Sterling Furnace chain, each link 2 ft. long and weighing 180 lb., was never broken by the invaders.

The fiery days of the iron furnace are all but forgotten on the peaceful shore of Little Dam Lake. This is a Class I Wetland (the highest New York state designation). It supports the rare northern cricket frog and nesting red-shouldered hawk. The shallow lake also supports pickerel, bass, abundant aquatic plants, and waterfowl. Pepperbush, highbush blueberry, winterberry, and wild rose grow here, in the shadow of alders, black oak, pin oak, and sweetgum. Wood duck, osprey, great blue heron, and flocks of mergansers pass through. A pair of playful otters has been sighted. In spring 1995 Sterling Forest preservation supporters gathered with four indigenous Native American tribal chiefs on the lake's shore to offer a blessing to the land. A perfectly clear blue sky and a flock of Canadian geese provided a backdrop to drum and flute music, chants and songs. It was the first time these hills had echoed with such music in 250 years but, we hope, not the last.

Beyond the lake, the trail ascends 100 ft., then descends to Orange Tpk. (daytime parking) at 10.2 mi. Entering the woods, the AT begins ascending Arden Mt., crossing rock ledges at 10.4 mi. with views west to Mombasha High Point and north to the Catskill Mts. The trail reaches the scrub oak–covered summit of Arden Mt. (1180 ft.) at 10.9 mi., which offers only limited views. It continues another 0.7 mi. to a vista east over the Ramapo Valley, where the sounds of the NYS Thruway and NY 17 rush up to meet you. "Ramapo" is the name of a Native American tribe that once lived here.

The AT descends extremely steeply for 550 vertical ft. to the valley, intersecting NY 17 at 12.0 mi. Be thankful that you're *descending* this slope, lovingly dubbed "Agony Grind" by southbound AT hikers.

Cross NY 17 and go east on Arden Valley Rd. for 0.3 mi. to the Elk Pen parking area (overnight). This name is all that survives of an unsuccessful attempt by Harriman State Park to reintroduce elk to the region. Arriving at your car, you may want to consider the value of what you have just seen and perhaps become involved in the preservation of Sterling Forest. Groups such as the NY-NJTC and Sterling Forest Resources need volunteers to help protect this sprawling greenway stretching from the Hudson River into northern New Jersey.

Miles N	**NORTH**	Elev. (ft./m)	Miles S
12.3	**End:** **Arden Valley Rd.,** Elk Pen overnight AT parking, 1.0 mi. SE of Arden.	550/168	0.0
12.0	**NY 17,** no parking.	565/172	0.3
11.6	**Agony Grind;** view; begin steep, 550-vertical-ft. descent.		0.7
10.9	**Arden Mt.** summit.	1180/360	1.4
10.4	Rock ledges and **view.**	1000/305	1.9
10.2	**Orange Tpk.,** parking, early exit option.	800/244	2.1
9.3	**Little Dam Lake.**		3.0
9.1	**Mombasha Kill,** stream crossing.	750/229	3.2
8.8	**E Mombasha Rd.,** day parking, early exit option.	800/244	3.5
8.6	**Buchanan Mt.** north summit, view; begin steep descent.	900/274	3.7
8.0	**Buchanan Mt.** south summit, view.	1142/348	4.3
7.9	**Peter Buck plaque.**		4.4
7.7	Begin **steep ascent** to ledge.	1000/305	4.6
7.0	**W Mombasha Rd.,** day parking, early exit option.		5.3
6.9	**Butterfly Meadow.**		5.4
5.9	**Mombasha High Point,** view.	1280/390	6.4
5.1	**Allis Trail,** connects with NY 17A and Highlands Trail.	900/274	7.2
3.9	**Fitzgerald Falls,** 25-ft. high waterfall.		8.4
3.8	**Trout Brook** bridge.		8.5
3.7	**Lakes Rd. (Monroe Rd.),** day parking, early exit option.	700/213	8.6
3.2	Begin **steep descent.**	1100/335	9.1
2.1	**Wildcat Shelter** side trail leads to shelter, privy, and water pump (600 ft.).		10.2
1.8	**Cat Rocks** view.	1294/395	10.5
1.3	**Eastern Pinnacles** view.	1250/381	11.0
0.0	**Start:** **Continental Rd. (Mt. Peter summit)** overnight parking, 2.0 mi. N of Greenwood Lake and 1.6 mi. E of Bellvale. AT follows road to R (E) for 150 ft., then follows NY 17A for 150 ft. and turns L (N) into woods.	1130/344	12.3

SOUTH

HIKE #35
Bear Mt.–Harriman State Parks — West

Maps: ATC N.Y. & N.J. Map 3; NY-NJTC Harriman Map North

Route: In Bear Mt.–Harriman SP, from Arden Valley Rd. (Elk Pen) to Island Pond, Surebridge Mt., and Arden Valley Rd. at Tiorati Circle

Recommended direction: S to N

Distance: 5.7 mi. total; 5.5 mi. on AT

Access trail name & length: Arden Valley Rd./Ramapo-Dunderberg Trail, 0.2 mi.

Elevation +/-: 550 to 1328 to 1050 ft.

Effort: Moderate

Day hike: Yes

Overnight backpacking hike: Optional

Duration: 3½ hr.

Early exit option: At 4.1 mi., Hurst Trail

Natural history features: Green Pond Mt.; Island Pond; Lemon Squeezer; Surebridge Mt.; Fingerboard Mt.

Social history features: Clove Furnace; Civilian Conservation Corps spillway; Long Path; Ramapo-Dunderberg Trail; Surebridge Mine Rd.; Greenwood Mine; first miles of AT ever built

Trailhead access: *Start:* Take NY 17 1.9 mi. N of Southfields or 0.7 mi. S of Arden to Arden Valley Rd. and go 0.3 mi. E to Elk Pen parking area (overnight). *End:* Continue past Elk Pen parking area on Arden Valley Rd. 3.5 mi to Tiorati Circle parking area (overnight).

Camping: Fingerboard Shelter

The less-traveled western section of Bear Mt.–Harriman SP offers an ideal introduction to the history, flora, and fauna of the Hudson Highlands. The land here comes alive with signs of the dynamic 12,000-year relationship between human beings and nature. You will travel through secluded forest once occupied by Native Americans, walk along the shores of pretty Island Pond, slip through the Lemon Squeezer (an unusual rock formation), and explore the ruins of a 19th-century iron mine. Most notably, this hike follows the approx-

imate route of the very first 5.5 mi. of Appalachian Trail ever blazed.

The hike begins at the bottom of the deep, narrow Ramapo Valley, once a north-south wagon route for hardy 18th- and 19th-century pioneers (the same route followed by the NYS Thruway, NY 17, and tired commuters today). Here a 700-ft.-deep gorge and the Ramapo River neatly divide the Hudson Highlands in two, marking the western edge of Bear Mt.–Harriman SP. These two adjoining parks (part of the Palisades Interstate Park) were founded in 1910 and are among the oldest in New York. In the 1920s they served as a model for the design of state parks across the nation.

From the Elk Pen parking area (the name "Elk Pen" is all that remains of a failed 1915 attempt by park personnel to introduce elk to the Hudson Highlands), turn right onto Arden Valley Rd. and immediately look for the AT's white blazes along the road. In 0.1 mi. the trail turns right onto a chained-off woods road (old Arden Rd.). The flowering meadow at right and forest-cloaked hills to the left may seem like a pastoral setting untouched by human hands. In reality, you are seeing how thoroughly nature has healed itself over the past 125 years. The town of Arden, on NY 17 just a mile north of this spot, was a mini-Pittsburgh in the 1800s, inhabited by 2000 industrious citizens all dedicated to ironmaking. Arden's Clove Furnace (now headquarters for the Orange County Historical Society and open to visitors) produced thousands of tons of iron between 1854 and 1871. The three-story-tall blast furnace, fed with iron ore dug from these hills, roared like a deafening rocket at liftoff and ran twenty-four hours a day. It belched soot, covering the green hills with a layer of gray ash. The Parrott brothers, who owned the furnace and the surrounding mines and mountains, made a fortune manufacturing cannon and shot for the Union Army in the Civil War.

At 0.3 mi. the trail turns left off the road and ascends Green Pond Mt.

Dale Gelfand

Mountain laurel

Notice how young the mixed hardwood forest of oak, ash, and maple is here. These hills were stripped clean of trees to provide charcoal for the Clove Furnace. The charcoal makers, a reclusive breed of men, scoured these hills, selected smaller trees, cut them, and built tight tepees of wood, which they set afire. In a slow, controlled burn lasting several days, the mounds smoldered and the wood inside turned to charcoal. The charcoal mounds required constant attention, giving the soot-covered workers little time for a social life. They were generally viewed as outsiders and little welcome in more polite 19th-century society.

The trail ascends steeply on switchbacks and reaches the rocky summit of Green Pond Mt. (0.8 mi.). Some archeologists believe that the

From Dream to Reality: The AT Is Born

In October 1921 regional planner and visionary Benton MacKaye first proposed the building of the AT in an article for the *Journal of the American Institute of Architects*. MacKaye called for the creation of a million-person volunteer army to "walk the skyline and develop its varied opportunities . . . for recreation, recuperation and employment in the region of the Appalachian[s]." MacKaye's dream did not fall on deaf ears. A fledgling hiking club confederation whose charter it was to build trails in Bear Mt.–Harriman State Parks met in 1922. They established the New York–New Jersey Trail Conference and went to work creating the very first miles of the 2100-mi. Maine-to-Georgia trail.

Led by New York journalist and conservationist Raymond Torrey and by J. Ashton Allis (a New York banker who helped engineer Vermont's Long Trail in 1916), the first section of the AT quickly took shape. Years later, Torrey described in the *New York Evening Post* how his crews made it happen. "The working parties were divided according to experience and ability into scouting, clearing, and marking squads. The scouts were those who knew how to lay out a trail to include the highest scenic qualities: directness of route, supplies of water . . . and occasional ledges and cliff climbs to make the routes interesting. They went out ahead of the rest and made temporary small blazes or rock cairns. When everyone had agreed to the best route, it was primarily marked with a line of cotton string looped over the bushes and trees."

Next came the "elephant squads," who followed the white string, clearing the way with hatchets and pruning shears. Lastly, specially made metal AT markers were affixed to the trees. Torrey's elephant squads couldn't work fast enough for a public eager to enjoy the new trail. He tells of a group of conference volunteers "laying string along the top of the cliffs on West Mountain in Harriman Park. The string had not been up two hours when eleven persons came along it."

In October 1923 MacKaye, Torrey, Allis, and trail club members from Maine to Georgia met at the Bear Mountain Inn (see Hike #37) to celebrate the completion of the first 6 mi. of AT, running from the Ramapo River to Fingerboard Mt. By January 1924, 20 mi. of continuous trail were complete, all the way across Bear Mt.–Harriman State Parks. Trail Conference volunteers then struck off to the north and the south, completing New York's and New Jersey's AT sections by 1931. Other hiking clubs stretched the trail farther north and south, and the entire AT was finished by 1937.

extreme stoniness of Harriman SP's peaks was caused by 19th-century clear-cutting of forests for charcoal, lumber, firewood, railroad ties, and ship masts. The resulting erosion left a rocky, acidic soil where stone-clinging lichen, carpets of moss, sedges, and grasses work resolutely to rebuild lost layers of topsoil. Open rocks here provide views west over the Ramapo Valley.

At 1.0 mi. the trail descends, then turns left onto Island Pond Rd. This carriage road was built by 19th-century railroad magnate and self-made millionaire Edward Harriman. By the 1880s the discovery of vast iron ore deposits in Minnesota had caused the collapse of Eastern iron making. So when the Parrott brothers decided to sell their 7863-acre Hudson Highlands holdings, Harriman bought the land for $52,500, absorbing it into his estate. This property was later sold to New York State and formed the core of Bear Mt.–Harriman SP.

When not on the balding ridgetops, the AT in Harriman SP passes through a maturing oak forest, rich with life. A deluge of autumn acorns supports a vast army of squirrels and chipmunks who regularly scold passing hikers. Jays (who also feed on the acorns), flickers, crows, and nuthatches flit from branch to branch of understory maples. Deer can often be spotted among the trees or browsing at the edges of clearings. The forest floor is littered with rotting logs and leaves, home to millions of insects, fungi, and bacteria that digest these materials, breaking them down into natural fertilizer.

The trail leaves Island Pond Rd. (1.3 mi.), climbs log steps, and crosses a gravel road that provides vehicle access to Island Pond for fishing (by permit only). The trail then crosses a bridge over the pond's outlet. The outlet is channeled into a cut stone spillway, the work of the Civilian Conservation Corps, who in the early 1930s transformed the face of Bear Mt.–Harriman SP by building dams, lakes, roads, and camps (see "With the Boys of the CCC" in Hike #29).

Shortly the trail crests a rise with a lovely view of Island Pond. At 1.7 mi. the AT reaches, briefly follows, then turns left off of Crooked Rd., an old woods road, then starts to ascend. The trail reaches the Lemon Squeezer at 1.9 mi. This narrow passage slices upward through the center of a split rock ledge composed of coarse gneiss, the result of eons of glacial or frost action. The 300-ft.-long climb to the top can be a tight squeeze and tricky work with a wide backpack. It can also be difficult for small children or the less agile. A bypass trail to the left snakes easily around the Lemon Squeezer. Early in 1922, members of the NY-NJTC scouted out the first 6 mi. of the AT ever blazed, looking for interesting historical and geological features for the trail within Bear Mt.–Harriman parks (see "From Dream to

Reality: The AT Is Born"). The much-photographed Lemon Squeezer may have been one of their best finds. The Arden-Surebridge Trail (red-triangle-on-white blazes) also passes through this geological feature; be sure to stay on the white-blazed AT.

Over the next 0.3 mi. the trail gradually ascends Island Pond Mt. (1303 ft.) through a mixed oak forest. At 2.6 mi. the AT crosses the turquoise-blazed Long Path. This long-distance trail was first proposed by Vince Schaefer, a self-taught General Electric meteorologist and trail builder, in the 1920s. The Long Path presently extends 300 mi. from the George Washington Bridge nearly to the Mohawk River, and will, when finished, go another 200 mi. to the Adirondack Mts. But you needn't walk that far to enjoy nature. The forest floor in Bear Mt.–Harriman SP is dotted with wildflowers. Beginning with coltsfoot in early April, a long parade of flowers follows: bloodroot, Dutchman's-breeches, dwarf ginseng, rue anemone, wood anemone, wild geranium, and Solomon's-seal, to name just a few. By September, the many varieties of aster dominate.

The AT descends, crosses an intermittent stream, then ascends steeply, reaching a shoulder of Surebridge Mt. The trail crosses Surebridge Brook at 3.4 mi. and turns left onto Surebridge Mine Rd., passing the water-filled pit of Greenwood Iron Mine on your right. Take a look at the immense tailings piles to your left and you'll begin to get an idea

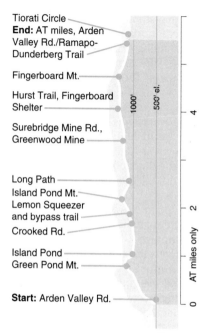

Tiorati Circle
End: AT miles, Arden Valley Rd./Ramapo-Dunderberg Trail
Fingerboard Mt.
Hurst Trail, Fingerboard Shelter
Surebridge Mine Rd., Greenwood Mine
Long Path
Island Pond Mt.
Lemon Squeezer and bypass trail
Crooked Rd.
Island Pond
Green Pond Mt.
Start: Arden Valley Rd.
1000'
500' el.
4
2
0
AT miles only

of just how deep this mine goes. Tailings are the worthless rock left behind by the miners (though these stony heaps still contain enough magnetite ore to deflect a compass needle). While the Greenwood Mine's actual depth is not recorded, Hudson Highland iron mines typically dove several hundred feet underground. They were dug out largely by hand, using black powder, picks, and shovels. The mine road beneath your feet once carried wagons loaded with tons of ore headed for the Clove Furnace.

Tiorati Circle Ⓟ
El. 1050'

🚶 Arden Valley Rd./
Ramapo-Dunderberg
Trail 🏛

Fingerboard Mt.
summit, El. 1328'

Seven Lakes Drive

Hurst Trail,
Fingerboard ◼️🐾

Surebridge Mine Rd.,
Greenwood Mine,
El. 1100' 🏛

Long Path 🏛

Island Pond Mt.
summit, El. 1303'

Lemon Squeezer 🍁

Crooked Rd.

Island Pond 🍁

Green Pond Mt.,
El. 1200', V

🚶 Arden Valley Rd.,
Elk Pen Ⓟ El. 550'

N 1" = 1 mi.

In another 0.1 mi. the trail turns right, leaving the mine road. It ascends through hemlocks, climbing to the ridge of Fingerboard Mt. (4.0 mi.). Here, the red-on-white-blazed Ramapo-Dunderberg Trail (R-D) co-aligns with the AT. The R-D was the first trail constructed by volunteers of the NY-NJTC and one of the first built in the New York metropolitan area. Bear Mt.–Harriman SP Superintendent Major William Welch recruited the volunteers to blaze this 24-mi. path in 1920, the start of a trail-building-and-maintenance relationship between the public and private sector lasting to the present day. In another 0.1 mi. the blue-blazed Hurst Trail goes 350 ft. right to Fingerboard Shelter. The

Hurst Trail continues past the shelter, reaching Seven Lakes Dr. on Lake Tiorati in 0.4 mi. (a water source, but purify). Closeness to the road makes this a less-than-private camp spot with big weekend crowds. The shelter has no privy.

At 4.7 mi. the AT reaches the summit of Fingerboard Mt. (1328 ft.) and begins a gradual descent over sloping rock that in some places seems nearly as smooth as pavement. Veins of pegmatite crystals, a combination of quartz and feldspar, glitter like white ice permanently frozen in the exposed Hudson Highlands bedrock. These crystals were formed millions of years ago, deep underground, under intense heat and tremendous pressure.

There are views of Lake Tiorati (best when leaves are off the trees) from Fingerboard Mt. The large lake, once two small ponds, was dammed in 1915 by Major Welch as part of his plan to provide outdoor recreation for New York City residents. At 5.5 mi. the trail arrives at paved Arden Valley Rd. Turn right, leaving the AT but still following the R-D, and walk 0.2 mi. to the Tiorati Circle parking area (overnight).

Miles N	NORTH	Elev. (ft./m)	Miles S
	Total: 5.7 mi. with access on Arden Valley Rd./Ramapo-Dunderberg Trail		
0.2	Access: **Tiorati Circle** in Bear Mt.–Harriman SP, overnight parking; go W from circle following Arden Valley Rd./Ramapo-Dunderberg Trail.	1050/320	0.2
5.5	**End AT miles:** Arden Valley Rd. Leave AT, turning right (E) on road, still following Ramapo-Dunderberg Trail.	1196/365	0.0
4.7	**Fingerboard Mt.** summit.	1328/405	0.8
4.1	**Hurst Trail** to Fingerboard Shelter (350 ft.) and to Seven Lakes Drive (0.4 mi.); water from lake; early exit option.		1.4
4.0	Ridge of **Fingerboard Mt.;** Ramapo-Dunderberg Trail joins AT.		1.5
3.4	**Surebridge Brook;** Surebridge Mine Rd.; Greenwood Mine.	1100/335	2.1
2.6	Cross **Long Path,** 300-mi. trail between George Washington Bridge and Mohawk River.		2.9
2.2	**Island Pond Mt.** summit.	1303/397	3.3
1.9	**Lemon Squeezer** rock formation with bypass trail.		3.6
1.7	**Crooked Rd.** woods road.		3.8
1.3	Leave **Island Pond Rd.**		4.2
1.0	Descend to **Island Pond.**	1100/335	4.5
0.8	**Green Pond Mt.** summit.	1200/366	4.7
0.3	Turn L (E) into woods and **begin climbing.**	600/183	5.2
0.1	Turn R (S) onto chained-off **Old Arden Rd.**		5.4
0.0	**Start:** Arden Valley Rd., Elk Pen overnight parking, 1.0 mi. SE of Arden.	550/168	5.5

SOUTH

HIKE #36

Bear Mt.–Harriman State Parks—East

Maps: ATC N.Y. & N.J. Map 3; NY-NJTC Harriman North

Route: From Arden Valley Rd. at Tiorati Circle over Letterrock Mt. and Black Mt. to Bear Mt.

Recommended direction: S to N

Distance: 12.7 mi.; 12.5 mi. on AT

Access trail name & length: Arden Valley Rd./Ramapo-Dunderberg Trail, 0.2 mi.

Elevation +/-: 1196 to 700 to 1305 to 178 ft.

Effort: Moderate to strenuous

Day hike: Optional

Overnight backpacking hike: Yes

Duration: 9½ hr.

Early exit option: At 9.1 mi., Perkins Drive

Natural history features: Precambrian bedrock; evidence of glacial action; views of Hudson River gorge

Social history features: Revolutionary War troop routes; Perkins Memorial Tower; Joseph Bartha Plaque; Bear Mt. suspension bridge views; Bear Mt. Inn

Trailhead access: *Start:* Take NY 17 1.9 mi. N of Southfields or 0.7 mi. S of Arden to Arden Valley Rd.; go 3.8 mi. to Tiorati Circle parking lot (overnight). *End:* From Bear Mt. Bridge Circle on US 9W go S 0.4 mi. and take R fork onto access road to Bear Mt. Inn. Turn R into parking lot (fee for day and overnight parking; call 914-786-2701).

Camping: William Brien Memorial Shelter; West Mt. Shelter

This overnight trip (or long day hike) has it all: a great diversity of Hudson Highlands landscape, including mountain vistas, lake shore, open fields, swamps, hemlock forests, and hardwood ridges. Exit Tiorati Circle parking area and walk west on Arden Valley Rd. (contiguous here with the red-on-white-blazed Ramapo-Dunderberg Trail) for 0.2 mi. to its intersection with the AT at the crest of a hill. Turn right, following the white blazes north into the woods. Over the next mile you'll hike through a maturing forest dominated by oak and maple, crossing several woods roads that once served the farms and mines of the Hudson Highlands.

The quiet of the mixed oak forest is deceiving. In summer, each chestnut oak and red maple is actually an intensely active factory, sucking tons of water up into its roots, pumping it through the trunk and branches to the leaves, which use the water, sunlight, and carbon dioxide from the atmosphere to create food for the tree, and eventually for every living thing in the forest. The leaves also give off vast amounts of water vapor. A tree "sweats out" 100,000 pounds of water to the surrounding air just to make 100 pounds of cellulose (the main ingredient of wood). This ex-plains the stifling forest air through which AT hikers must walk on the hottest, most humid days of summer.

At 1.2 mi. the trail comes out onto a small, rocky promontory with a limited view south over Lake Tiorati. In the early 1900s many of the park's newly constructed lakes were given picturesque Native American names. "Tiorati" is Algonquin for "skylike."

The trail continues through woods until it bridges a stream at 2.1. mi. and crosses Seven Lakes Dr. at 2.2 mi. (no parking). This scenic road traverses Harriman Park from south to north. It actually passes nine lakes in total, provides access to several major Harriman Park trailheads, and is worth exploring by car.

The trail ascends gradually through open forest and at 3.4 mi. reaches a wooden bridge in the saddle between Letterrock and Goshen Mts. A tall tale about 16th-century Spaniards and buried sacks of coins atop Letterrock Mt. resulted in its being significantly "reshaped" in 1934. Four treasure hunters dynamited deep gouges in the mountainside for several months before finally being apprehended by park police. The treasure seekers never found a single doubloon.

The Ramapo-Dunderberg (R-D) Trail comes in from the right (west) and joins the AT for the next 3.3 mi. The 24-mi. R-D is the oldest trail in the parks and covers some fascinating landscape.

At 4.2 mi. the AT arrives at the William Brien Memorial Shelter, a three-sided stone lean-to with a wooden floor and a small fireplace—your home for the night. A blue-blazed trail goes right for 250 ft. to a spring-fed well; this water source may fail in dry weather. Vandalism, unfortunately, has forced the removal of the site's privy. Naturalist William Brien was founding president of the New York Ramblers, one of many hiking clubs in the NY-NJTC. These clubs not only provided volunteers who built the first trails and shelters in the New York metropolitan area; they also pioneered the spirit of adventure and camaraderie that is so much a part of today's AT community. The Ramblers, like most other conference clubs of the time, hailed from New York City. A contemporary account describes the hiking clubs' weekend sorties from Manhattan: "On Sundays and holidays, from September to June, rucksack-laden stalwarts assemble at ferry-houses and railroad stations, bound for the Hudson Highlands. . . . No fair-weather strollers these, but seasoned hikers, knights of brush and brier, modern Bayards, without fear and above reproach. It would be superfluous to add that they are enthusiasts, and perhaps they are slightly tinged with madness."

In the 1920s there were clubs to appeal to every outdoor adventurer's taste. The Fresh Air Club was an all-male group of speed hikers who averaged 30 mi. of walking per outing, the Inkowas were young professional women, the Young Men's Hebrew Association launched a group of Jewish hikers, the Naturfreunde were German Socialist trampers, and the All-Tramp Soviet recruited Communists from Greenwich Village. The most eclectic of them all, the Yosians, gathered "at Pan's Altar" to listen to their self-proclaimed Druidic high priest, J. Otis Swift, who invited "the sorely puzzled, tired, automobile-dazzled, pleasure-weary folk of the modern towns and cities . . . to sit like children on the lichened stones and listen as the story of Creation is retold." As you bed down at the shelter, you may want to think of the thousands of backpackers (slightly tinged with madness!) who have bunked here before you, and of the good work they have done to build and maintain the trails and lean-tos over the decades (see Glenn Scherer's *Vistas and Vision,* a seventy-five-year history of hiking and conservation in the metropolitan area).

The next day, continue north along the AT. At 0.9 mi. from the William Brien shelter (5.1 mi. into this two-day hike), you will cross a fire road now used as a cross-country-skiing trail. Bear Mt.–Harriman SP offer terrific winter recreation opportunities, with many miles of trail (including the AT) perfect for cross-country skiing and snowshoeing. We've spent many a snowy afternoon tracking deer, coyote, squirrels, and mice in the parks.

The AT ascends steeply, arriving at the first vista atop Black Mt. (5.3 mi.).

But the best view is another 0.2 mi. farther up the trail, where it crosses open rocks facing south with views to the Hudson River and, on a clear day, all the way to New York City. This is an ideal spot for an early morning snack and water break. In summer, we've seen hawks gliding the updrafts, scouting for rodents living in the dry grass of this summit.

Descend steeply and reach the 1779 Trail at 6.0 mi. This trail (blazed with blue numerals inside a white diamond) marks the route of the Continental Army in its Revolutionary War attack on the British Army at Stony Point on the Hudson. When Commander George Washington asked General "Mad" Anthony Wayne if he would lead this difficult overland assault, he responded, "I would storm hell if Washington would prepare the plan." The march and attack, conducted under cover of darkness, took the British by surprise and gave the colonists a stunning victory. Although it was a big morale booster, the fight had no lasting effect; the English retook the fort a few days later.

At 6.3 mi., the AT crosses the Palisades Interstate Pkwy. (no parking; be cautious of the high-speed traffic), goes over Beechy Bottom Brook (6.5 mi.), a fairly reliable water source (purify), and begins a steep ascent of West Mt. The trail arrives at the open rock ledges of West Mt. at 7.5 mi. Here the blue-blazed Timp-Torne Trail (T-T) comes in from the right (east) and aligns with the AT.

The trail is named for two of Bear Mt.–Harriman's most interesting summits, the bald top of the Timp and the open crest of Popolopen Torne. The West Mt. shelter is 0.6 mi. to the right on the T-T Trail; this shelter has no water or privy, but offers good views out over the Hudson River's Haverstraw Bay.

For the next 0.7 mi. the AT runs along the cliffs of West Mt. with many opportunities to stop and enjoy the view or have lunch. The Hudson Highlands stretching westward before you are made of the most ancient of bedrock, Precambrian in age. These heights once towered over 10,000 ft., rivaling the American Rockies. Seven hundred million years of steady erosion have reduced them to a mere 1200 ft. Look for the banded gneisses across the open rock faces, clearly displaying the flow of hot, invading molten rock. Also look for polished, scratched, and grooved stone surfaces, evidence of the last glacial epoch, which ended 15,000 years ago. The parks' ridges are topped with many glacial erratics, boulders dropped by the receding glaciers like so many abandoned marbles. You'll see some large erratics to your left just as you begin to descend West Mt.

Enjoy a last West Mt. vista toward Bear Mt. and then begin descending steeply at 8.3 mi. As the T-T Trail goes straight ahead, the AT bears right. The AT intersects the woods road route of the 1777 W Trail at 9.0 mi. and parallels it briefly. This trail follows the march of British troops in

Michael Warren

Day hikers, Bear Mt. State Park

their successful attempt to capture Revolutionary War forts Clinton and Montgomery at Bear Mt. and to destroy the Continental Army's great chain blocking British warships on the Hudson River (see Hike #37). This attack was part of a sweeping British campaign meant to split the American colonies in half at the Hudson, a plan foiled by Gen. "Gentleman Johnny" Burgoyne's disastrous defeat at Saratoga.

At 9.1 mi. the trail crosses Seven Lakes Dr. (no parking), reenters the woods, and begins ascending Bear Mt. It briefly parallels and crosses Perkins Drive several times during the strenuous climb. Here, on the side of Bear Mt., we learned to appreciate the value of hiking in bad weather. A cold rain had just stopped falling on a damp October morning when a herd of white-tailed deer broke from cover and shot uphill through columns of mist suddenly illuminated by bright rays of sunlight penetrating the autumn canopy. This was a stunning reminder of the wealth of wildlife living in Bear Mt.–Harriman SP. Black bear, coyote, bobcat, beaver, and deer roam freely over these 51,000 acres.

The trail attains the top of Bear Mt. (1305 ft.) and Perkins Memorial Tower at 10.6 mi. This landmark offers sweeping 360-degree views of all the Highlands and down to New York City 50 mi. away. The tower was built in 1934 and named after George W. Perkins, first president of the Palisades Interstate Park Commission. In

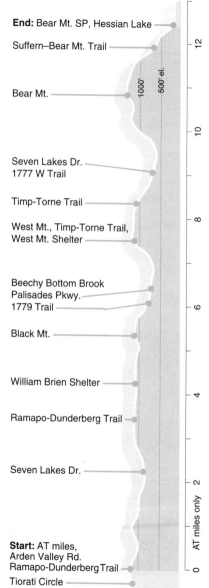

End: Bear Mt. SP, Hessian Lake

Suffern–Bear Mt. Trail

Bear Mt.

Seven Lakes Dr.
1777 W Trail

Timp-Torne Trail

West Mt., Timp-Torne Trail,
West Mt. Shelter

Beechy Bottom Brook
Palisades Pkwy.
1779 Trail

Black Mt.

William Brien Shelter

Ramapo-Dunderberg Trail

Seven Lakes Dr.

Start: AT miles,
Arden Valley Rd.
Ramapo-Dunderberg Trail

Tiorati Circle

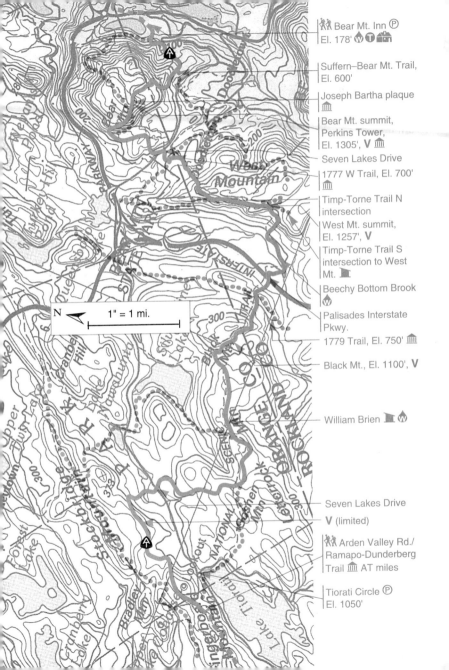

Bear Mt. Inn Ⓟ
El. 178' Ⓦ Ⓣ 🏨

Suffern–Bear Mt. Trail,
El. 600'

Joseph Bartha plaque
🏛

Bear Mt. summit,
Perkins Tower,
El. 1305', V 🏛

Seven Lakes Drive

1777 W Trail, El. 700'
🏛

Timp-Torne Trail N
intersection

West Mt. summit,
El. 1257', V

Timp-Torne Trail S
intersection to West
Mt. ▰

Beechy Bottom Brook
Ⓦ

Palisades Interstate
Pkwy.

1779 Trail, El. 750' 🏛

Black Mt., El. 1100', V

William Brien ▰ Ⓦ

Seven Lakes Drive

V (limited)

Arden Valley Rd./
Ramapo-Dunderberg
Trail 🏛 AT miles

Tiorati Circle Ⓟ
El. 1050'

N ← 1" = 1 mi.

another 0.2 mi. there is a plaque commemorating Joseph Bartha, a NY-NJTC volunteer who proved that fresh air and hard work make for a long life. Bartha is credited with almost single-handedly keeping the AT open in the New York metropolitan area during World War II. At age ninety-five, the Austrian immigrant was honored with this plaque, and became miffed when a reporter offered him a walking stick. Pointing to his knees, Bartha responded, "These are still in perfect walking condition. . . . As long as they're not wobbling, I go up in my mountains. I feel absolutely like a youngster!"

On the way down Bear Mt., the AT repeatedly crosses and parallels Scenic Drive, and provides magnificent views over the Hudson River. As you descend, thank Mary Harriman for the forest around you and for the pristine river views. In 1908 the New York State legislature could find no better purpose for this spectacular river gorge than as the site for what was to become Sing Sing Prison. When convicts began constructing a stockade, public outrage exploded. In 1910 Mary Harriman, widow of railroad magnate Edward Harriman, offered a deal: she would donate 10,000 acres of her Hudson Highlands estate as a park if the state would move their prison elsewhere. New York agreed; Ossining, New York, got Sing Sing and the public got Bear Mt.–Harriman SP.

The view below includes Iona Island, a one-time navy munitions depot, now a wildlife refuge visited by migrating bald eagles. The suspension cables of the Bear Mt. Bridge, possibly the most amazing road walk along the entire AT, shine in the sun. This magnificent bridge was privately built and maintained by the Harriman family until 1940, when they sold it to New York State. Across the river loom the heights of Anthony's Nose.

At 11.5 mi. the trail reaches the dead-end turnaround of Scenic Drive, then leaves the road and descends steadily through the woods. In another 0.4 mi. it parallels the yellow-blazed Suffern–Bear Mt. Trail. At 12.1 mi. the AT crosses a stream and joins a crushed-stone road coming in from the left. It soon passes the Bear Mt. ski jump, where, at the end of a winter hike, it's not unusual to see airborne competitors.

The trail intersects several paved paths at the south end of Hessian Lake at 12.5 mi. The Bear Mt. Inn lies straight ahead. This rustic stone structure, built in the style of the Yellowstone National Park lodge, was host to the first major powwow between Benton MacKaye and other AT planners in 1923. It now offers hikers rest rooms, phones, and meals. Leave the AT on one of the paved paths. The parking lot is a few hundred feet to your right.

Miles N	**NORTH**	Elev. (ft./m)	Miles S
	Total: 12.7 mi. with access on Arden Valley Rd./Ramapo-Dunderberg Trail		
12.5	**End:** South end **Hessian Lake** at Bear Mt. Inn, in Bear Mt.–Harriman SP; walk 100 yd. R (E) to overnight parking.	178/54	0.0
12.1	Cross **stream** and join **crushed-stone road.**	300/91	0.4
11.9	**Suffern–Bear Mt. Trail.**	600/183	0.6
11.5	**Scenic Drive** dead-end turnaround.	1000/305	1.0
10.8	**Joseph Bartha plaque**; begin descent of Bear Mt.		1.7
10.6	**Bear Mt. summit, Perkins Memorial Tower,** view.	1305/398	1.9
9.1	**Seven Lakes Drive**; begin ascent of Bear Mt.; cross **Perkins Drive** several times in ascent. Early exit option.		3.4
9.0	**1777 W Trail,** marks route of Revolutionary War British troops.	700/213	3.5
8.3	**Timp-Torne Trail** goes L (N) to Seven Lakes Dr.	1100/335	4.2
7.5	**West Mt.** summit and **Timp-Torne Trail** R (E) to **West Mt. Shelter,** no water (0.6 mi.); trail aligns with AT.	1257/383	5.0
6.5	**Beechy Bottom Brook,** water.		6.0
6.3	Cross **Palisades Interstate Pkwy.**	700/213	6.2
6.0	**1779 Trail,** marks route of Revolutionary War Continental troops.	750/229	6.5

(continued on next page)

Miles N		Elev. (ft./m)	Miles S
5.5	**Black Mt.** view.		7.0
5.3	**Black Mt.** summit.	1100/335	7.2
5.1	Cross **fire road**.	900/274	7.4
4.2	**William Brien Memorial Shelter** fireplace, well.		8.3
3.4	Wooden bridge in saddle between **Letterrock and Goshen Mts.; Ramapo-Dunderberg Trail** aligns with AT next 3.4 mi.	1100/335	9.1
2.2	**Seven Lakes Drive.**		10.3
2.1	Cross **stream** on bridge.	850/259	10.4
1.2	**Rocky promontory** with limited view.	1150/351	11.3
0.0	**Start AT miles:** **Arden Valley Rd.** Leave road and turn R (N), following AT into woods.	1196/365	12.5
0.2	Access: **Tiorati Circle** in Bear Mt.–Harriman SP, overnight parking. Go W from circle following Arden Valley Rd./Ramapo-Dunderberg Trail.	1050/320	0.2

SOUTH

Bear Mt. Bridge and Anthony's Nose

Maps: ATC N.Y. & N.J. Maps 2 & 3; NY-NJTC Harriman Map North & East Hudson Trails Map 1

Route: From Bear Mt. Inn across Bear Mt. Bridge to Anthony's Nose, South Mt. Pass, Canada Hill, and US 9

Recommended direction: S to N

Distance: 6.7 mi. total; 6.6 mi. on AT

Access trail name & length: US 9, 0.1 mi.

Elevation +/-: 178 to 900 to 400 ft.

Effort: Moderate

Day hike: Yes

Overnight backpacking hike: Optional

Duration: 5 hr.

Early exit options: At 3.1 mi., Manitou Rd.; at 4.2 mi., Osborn Loop Trail

Natural history features: Hessian Lake; Hudson River crossing; spectacular views of Hudson Highlands

Social history features: Bear Mt. Inn; Bear Mt. Trailside Museum and Zoo; Walt Whitman statue; Bear Mt. Suspension Bridge; old military road to Anthony's Nose

Trailhead access: *Start:* From Bear Mt. Bridge Circle on US 9W go S 0.4 mi. to R fork onto access road to Bear Mt. Inn. Turn R into parking lot (fee for day and overnight parking; call 914-786-2701). *End:* From E side of Bear Mt. Bridge, go 4.7 mi. N on NY 9D, then R on NY 403 for 2.2 mi. to intersection with US 9. Day-use parking on unnamed connector road 0.1 mi. N on US 9.

Camping: Hemlock Springs Campsite

A great river offers the focus for this walk. Powerful mountain-building forces first molded the stark relief of this Hudson River gorge, then glacial action carved a 15-mi.-long fjord here. Human beings shaped the land too: Native American encampments, colonial exploration, Revolutionary War combat, 19th- and 20th-century commerce, and the conservation movement all made their mark. This 6.6-mi. AT hike is one of the most varied and inspiring in New York. Allow lots of time for exploring and for the 1.2-mi. round-trip to Anthony's Nose.

Leave the Bear Mt. Inn parking lot (fee) by heading west (away from US 9W) to the paved path at the south end of Hessian Lake. Follow the AT's white blazes north along the lake's right (eastern) edge. This pretty little lake was gouged by glacial action and named for human violence. The corpses of Hessian soldiers found floating in its waters after the Revolutionary War battle of Fort Clinton inspired the name.

To your right, at the start of the hike, is the Bear Mt. Inn, a rambling structure built from native stone in 1915 and a fine example of Yellowstone

Park–style construction. The inn has accommodations, a restaurant, and rest rooms and hosts activities including a crafts fair, Oktoberfest, and Christmas festival. In 1923, it was the site of the first major meeting of Appalachian Trail founders.

The AT soon veers right, away from the lake shore, passes a food concession, and descends a concrete staircase to a pedestrian tunnel under US 9W. This underpass gives many hikers the eerie feeling of entering a New York City subway station, and in a few moments you may imagine you've walked straight into Central Park. After passing another refreshment stand (with great hot dogs in summer), the AT enters the Bear Mt. Trailside Museum and Zoo (0.5 mi.). This is a terrific spot for kids. It is also the only place along the AT where you're likely to see a coyote, river otter, and black bear all on the same day. This is an old-style zoo, built in the 1920s, and animal lovers may feel indignant over the close quarters in which these critters are kept. The entrance fees are $2 for adults and 50 cents for children (prices subject to change; call 914-786-2701 for the latest). You can bypass the zoo and fee by staying alongside Hessian Lake, then turning right and walking beside US 6E around the traffic circle to the Bear Mt. Bridge.

At the heart of the zoo is a statue of Walt Whitman, the free spirit and graybeard poet adopted by many AT thru-hikers as their patron saint. Look for a quote from Whitman's "Song of the Open Road" chiseled into a nearby boulder:

Afoot and light-hearted I take to the open road,
Healthy, free, the world before me,
The long brown path before me leading wherever I choose.
Henceforth I ask not good-fortune, I myself am good-fortune,
Henceforth I whimper no more, postpone no more, need nothing,
Done with indoor complaints, libraries, querulous criticisms,
Strong and content I travel the open road.

The Trailside nature, geology, and history museums make another fascinating stopping point. Exhibits span the history of the valley from its geological origins to Native American settlement, the Battle of Fort Clinton, and the founding of Bear Mt.–Harriman SP. Try to get to the zoo and Trailside Museum early in the day. On summer afternoons backpackers share this paved AT section with women carrying designer handbags and men pushing baby strollers. The zoo closes at 5:00 p.m.

At the Trailside Museum, you have reached the lowest point along the entire AT (just 124 ft. above sea level). A very small ascent brings you up to the Bear Mt. Bridge (0.8 mi.). AT hikers were once charged 15 cents to cross, but no more; pedestrians now cross for free. When built, in 1924, this 1600-ft. suspension bridge was the longest in the world. Remarkably, it was financed privately by the Harriman family and other investors (railroad magnate E. H. Harriman once held all of Bear Mt.–Harriman SP as his private estate; see Hikes #35 and #36). The new bridge was opposed by some, who saw it as an ugly scar upon the Highlands. Others saw its Victorian-style tollhouse and the graceful sweep of its cables as complementing the landscape. You can make your own judgment as you cross the river and watch ocean-going ships plying the waters below. Bear Mt. (1305 ft.) rises behind you and the heights of Anthony's Nose (900 ft.) loom ahead.

The view from the bridge is nothing less than spectacular. To the north, the Hudson River twists toward West Point and its source at Lake Tear of the Clouds in the Adirondack Mts. To the south, it flows toward New York City and the Atlantic Ocean. In truth, the river at Bear Mt. is an estuary, an arm of the sea, and experiences tidal fluctuations. Fresh water mixing with salt water creates a unique natural environment. Ocean fish such as shad, alewives, bay anchovies, herring, and striped bass swim up the brackish river to spawn. Commercial fishing thrived until recent years, when it was discovered that the fish were contaminated with deadly PCBs, chemicals dumped into the river at upstream industrial sites. However, efforts to clean up the Hudson have met with considerable success, though there is still much to do.

Glenn Scherer

Walt Whitman statue, Bear Mt.

At the far end of the bridge (1.3 mi.), the trail goes left (north) along NY 9D for 0.2 mi. It then crosses the road, enters the woods, and climbs steeply over fine, natural-stone steps placed there by NY-NJTC volunteers. The trail climbs 500 vertical ft. over the next 0.5 mi., the toughest part of the day, then levels off on a dirt road (2.0 mi.). When the AT turns left along the road, follow the blue blazes right. This short side trail leads in 0.6 mi. to one of the most beautiful vistas in all of the Hudson Highlands, the view from the crest of Anthony's Nose, an overlook composed of erosion-resistant gneisses and granites (see "The View from the Nose: A Hudson River History").

The View from the Nose: A Hudson River History

From Anthony's Nose it is possible to imagine the entire history of the Hudson Highlands unfolding. The same 300-million-year-long series of mountain-building episodes that created the Appalachians also raised the surrounding summits. Erosion has softened the contours of these ridges, which may have once rivaled the American Rockies in height. Over 15,000 years ago, the Wisconsin glacier tore the top off Anthony's Nose and gouged a deeper channel for the Hudson River, creating one of the eastern states' only fjords, a drowned tidal river valley. At Bear Mt. the river is over 165 ft. deep.

In 1609, Native Americans sitting atop the Nose could have watched Dutch explorer Henry Hudson and his ship, the *Half Moon*, penetrating this narrow gorge. The first colonial sailors to come upriver called this spot the Devil's Horse Race because of its swift, treacherous currents and fickle winds. Anthony's Nose would have also provided a bird's-eye view of the British attack on Fort Clinton during the Revolutionary War. The earthen redoubt (located where the Bear Mt. Zoo now sits) guarded the colonists' great chain (an iron barrier stretched across the river), which was meant to stop British shipping on the Hudson. The 1777 battle ended in American defeat and the shattering of the chain. The British sailed on north, burning Poughkeepsie and Kingston, before retreating to New York City. Gen. "Gentleman Johnny" Burgoyne's de-

---

On a clear day, the tiny silhouetted skyscrapers of Manhattan can be seen from here, far off to the south, beyond the Hudson River's widening at Haverstraw Bay. To the southwest is little Iona Island, once a navy ammunition depot, now a nature preserve that hosts migrating bald eagles. On the far side of the river, the Hudson River escarpments rise. From south to north, there's the loaf-shaped Dunderberg Mt., the sharp profile of the Timp and Timp Pass, Bear Mt. (topped by Perkins Tower), and Crown Ridge. Below are the Bear Mt. Bridge and Popolopen Gorge, spanned by a graceful highway bridge.

For those unable to arrange a shuttle hike, return the way you came to your car at Bear Mt. This makes for a splendid 5.2-mi. out-and-back hike. For those taking the shuttle hike, return via the blue-blazed trail to the AT and follow it straight ahead, north, along the woods road. On a 1996 walk here we noticed hundreds of tiny, perfectly round holes in the packed earth. A quick listen to the surrounding woods told us that we were in the midst of a cicada coming-out party. Cicadas have the

feat at Saratoga foiled British plans to gain full control of the river.

Nineteenth-century visitors to the Nose would have seen a brisk river trade; Robert Fulton's brainchild, the steamboat, tamed the Hudson's perilous currents. Quarry stone, blasted out of Hudson Highlands mountainsides, was one commodity that shaped the future of the valley. By the late 1800s outraged conservationists fought to end the blasting and to preserve the spectacular river scenery. In a fight that began in the 1890s and went on into the mid-1900s, the Palisades to the south, Anthony's Nose, and Mt. Taurus to the north were saved one by one from the dynamite of the stonecutters. The fight continues today, upriver near Fishkill. Atop Anthony's Nose, observers can again see graceful sailing ships pass by. Pete Seeger's Hudson River sloop, *Clearwa-* *ter,* fighting for the river's cleanup, makes frequent passages through the Devil's Horse Race.

A final note on the Nose: the origin of the slope's unusual name is lost in myth, though the most fanciful explanation is the most entertaining. Writer Washington Irving declared that it was named for the large beak of one of Henry Hudson's crewmen. "It must be known then that the nose of Anthony the trumpeter was of a very lusty size, strutting from his countenance like a mountain," Irving wrote. It was so large, in fact, that a sunbeam reflected off of this great "schnoz" shot out from the deck of the *Half Moon* into the river, killing a monstrous sturgeon, which the crew promptly ate. One wonders if Irving's own nose grew in the telling of his tale.

longest life cycle of any insect. Various broods of 17-year cicadas live underground for most of their lives, feeding on sap in deep soil roots. In late spring and early summer, at the end of each 17-year cycle, millions of the insects emerge from the earth to sing and mate. The long gap between breeding cycles, followed by the en masse mating frenzy, is thought to be a survival strategy. Predators are unable to feed upon the insect during its dormant period, and when the bugs do come forth and are most vulnerable, their numbers are vast and it is not likely that all will be eaten. The next anticipated Hudson Highlands 17-year cicada sing-alongs are scheduled for the years 2004 and 2013 (when two different broods come aboveground). Of course one-year cicadas, in smaller numbers, serenade us each summer.

At 2.2 mi. the AT leaves the woods road (an old military road that served the signal towers atop Anthony's Nose in the Revolutionary War) and continues on a narrow footpath. In another 0.5 mi., the trail passes to the left of the massive stone embankment of another abandoned road. The trail then descends into a hollow and at 3.0 mi. reaches a blue-blazed path leading right to the Hemlock Springs Campsite. This site has a reliable spring (purify) but is within a few hundred feet of the crossing of Manitou Rd. in South Mt. Pass. The garbage sometimes strewn here proves our pet theory that beer bottles rarely migrate much farther than a half mile from trailheads. Packing out trash from this spot will help local maintainers and other hikers.

A brief but steep climb puts you atop Canada Hill (4.1 mi.), where a few large chestnut oaks and many smaller red oaks and shagbark hickories grow. The understory is very sparse, with scattered mountain laurel and grasses. Shallow soils and hard winters allow only the hardiest plants to grow here.

In another 0.1 mi., the Osborn Loop Trail comes in from the left (west). This trail descends in about 0.7 mi. to intersect with one of the Manitoga Nature Preserve's trails, then goes over Sugarloaf Mt. and reconnects with the AT at 5.6 mi. The Manitoga Nature Preserve (914-424-3812) provides an interesting alternate destination for this AT hike. Open year-round, Manitoga holds summertime outdoor musical and theatrical events. Home-furnishing designer Russel Wright purchased this property in 1942 with the intent of restoring an ideal northern forest to land that had been abused by 150 years of logging and quarrying. His gentle sculpting of the grounds (which include nature trails, native

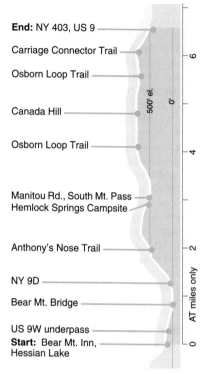

End: NY 403, US 9

Carriage Connector Trail

Osborn Loop Trail

Canada Hill

Osborn Loop Trail

Manitou Rd., South Mt. Pass
Hemlock Springs Campsite

Anthony's Nose Trail

NY 9D

Bear Mt. Bridge

US 9W underpass

Start: Bear Mt. Inn,
Hessian Lake

500' el.   0'

AT miles only

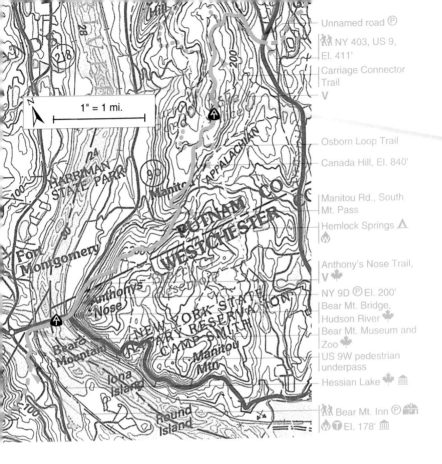

Unnamed road Ⓟ

𝕏𝕏 NY 403, US 9,
El. 411'

Carriage Connector
Trail
V

Osborn Loop Trail

Canada Hill, El. 840'

Manitou Rd., South
Mt. Pass

Hemlock Springs △
ⓦ

Anthony's Nose Trail,
V 🍁 ⓦ

NY 9D Ⓟ El. 200'

Bear Mt. Bridge,
Hudson River 🍁

Bear Mt. Museum and
Zoo 🍁

US 9W pedestrian
underpass

Hessian Lake 🍁 🏛

𝕏𝕏 Bear Mt. Inn Ⓟ 🏠
ⓦ 🍴 El. 178' 🏛

trees, ferns, mosses, and wildflower plantings) mirrors the care with which he once designed furniture, dishes, bowls, and flatware. The trails utilize natural materials in their construction, reflecting Wright's love of organic shapes and curves. "Manitoga" is the Algonquin word for "place of the great spirit," and Wright's preserve is a place where many come to experience a gentle kinship with the land.

The AT continues to the north end of Canada Hill, where a short blue-blazed trail leads left (west) to a small vista (5.5 mi.), best in autumn and winter. This rocky spot provides views of the U.S. Military Academy at West Point (see Hike #38) and Bare Rock Mt. Trains can be heard whistling and speeding along the Hudson River far below.

At 5.6 mi. the Osborn Loop Trail reconnects with the AT. The Osborn Loop Trail goes straight ahead on a woods road, while the AT turns sharply to the right (east). The AT now begins an easy descent of about 450 vertical ft. over the next mile. At 6.1 mi. it intersects with the yellow-blazed Carriage Connector Trail, part of the Hudson Highlands State Park trail system. At 6.6 mi. the trail crosses puncheons (bog bridging) through a pasture and intersects NY 403. Cross the road and a cement island to reach US 9 and the end of the hike. To reach trail parking, walk 0.1 mi. north on US 9 and turn left onto the small unmarked road.

Miles N	NORTH	Elev. (ft./m)	Miles S

Total: 6.7 mi. with access on US 9

Miles N		Elev. (ft./m)	Miles S
0.1	Access: Turn L (N) on **US 9**, and in 0.1 mi. turn L (E) on unnamed road to reach day parking.	400/122	0.1
6.6	**End AT miles:** NY 403 and US 9.	411/125	0.0
6.1	**Carriage Connector Trail.**	500/152	0.5
5.8	Begin **450-ft. descent.**	850/259	0.8
5.6	**Osborn Loop Trail**, N junction.		1.0
5.5	Unnamed side trail to **view** (30 yd.).	800/244	1.1
4.8	**Canada Hill** summit.	900/274	1.8
4.2	**Osborn Loop Trail**, S junction, descends to Manitoga Nature Preserve (0.7 mi.; early exit option) then climbs Sugarloaf Mt. and reconnects with AT.	800/244	2.4
3.1	**Manitou Rd., South Mt. Pass,** no parking, begin steep 250-ft. ascent. Early exit option.	550/168	3.5
3.0	Side trail to **Hemlock Springs Campsite** and spring (100 yd.).	600/183	3.6
2.2	Leave woods road.		4.4
2.0	**Anthony's Nose Trail** goes uphill R (S) to Hudson River view (0.6 mi., elev. 900 ft.), AT goes L (N) on woods road.	700/213	4.6
1.5	**NY 9D,** turn R (E) off road, enter woods and begin 500-ft. ascent.	200/61	5.1
1.3	**Bear Mt. Bridge east end,** day parking, turn L (N) following NY 9D.		5.3
0.8	**Bear Mt. Bridge west end.**		5.8
0.5	**Bear Mt. Trailside Museum and Zoo** main entrance; Walt Whitman statue.		6.1
0.3	**US 9W pedestrian underpass.**		6.3
0.2	AT turns R (E) away from **Hessian Lake.**		6.4
0.0	**Start:** In Bear Mt.–Harriman SP, **Bear Mt. Inn** overnight parking. Walk 100 yd. W to paved walkway at S end of Hessian Lake, follow AT along lake.	178/54	6.6

SOUTH

HIKE #38
US 9 to Dennytown Rd.

Maps: ATC N.Y. & N.J. Map 2; NY-NJTC East Hudson Trails Maps 1 & 3

Route: From US 9 to Old West Point Rd., Little Fort Hill, Denning Hill, Old Albany Post Rd., Canopus Hill Rd., South Highland Rd., and Dennytown Rd.

Recommended direction: S to N

Distance: 8.9 mi.; 8.8 mi. on AT

Elevation +/-: 400 to 900 to 750 ft.

Effort: Moderate

Day hike: Yes

Overnight backpacking hike: No

Duration: 6 hr.

Early exit options: At 3.3 mi., Old Albany Post Rd.; at 5.0 mi., Canopus Hill Rd.

Natural history features: Little Fort Hill; vista of Storm King Mt.; vistas of Haverstraw Bay and New York City from Denning Hill

Social history features: Graymoor Monastery; Revolutionary War–period Old West Point Rd. and Old Albany Post Rd.; Fahnestock State Park

Trailhead access: *Start:* Take NY 403 2.3 mi. E of Garrison to intersection with US 9. Day-use parking on unnamed connector road 0.1 mi. N on US 9. *End:* From intersection of NY 403 and US 9, go N on US 9 for 6.8 mi. to McKeel Corners; turn R onto NY 301 and go E for 2.7 mi.; turn R onto Dennytown Rd. and go 1.1 mi. to hiker day-use parking on R.

Camping: Group campsite on Dennytown Rd.

This 8.8-mi. hike offers the pleasant illusion of wilderness. The AT here is heavily wooded and less traveled than through Bear Mt.–Harriman State Parks to the south or Fahnestock State Park to the north. But these seemingly peaceful Hudson Highlands hills are far from wild. They were farmed and fought over at least as far back as the American Revolution.

You will find parking for a few cars on the short unnamed road that connects US 9 and NY 403 0.1 mi. north

of where these two highways and the AT intersect. Walk from the parking area 0.1 mi. south on US 9 and turn left, following the white blazes into the woods.

The trail almost immediately crosses a swamp on puncheons (bog bridging). In summer there is a showy display of purple loosestrife here. Don't be fooled by the natural beauty of this plant. It is the "Boston Strangler" of eastern swamps. Purple loosestrife is an exotic species brought from Europe to America in colonialists' seed bags. It strangles out native wetland plants such as the broad-leaved arrowhead (whose tubers feed waterfowl), as well as seventy-five native varieties of goldenrod (a prime food for birds). Loosestrife has absolutely no nutritional value, and so starves out wetland animals. At the edge of the swamp, the trail crosses a massive stone wall, the first of many crossed on this hike. Each wall was handstacked by 18th- and 19th-century farmers. Try hefting one of the rocks in order to better visualize the "sweat equity" earned in their construction.

The AT crosses Highland Tpk. (0.2 mi.) and Old West Point Rd. (0.6 mi.), a vital supply route for Continental troops defending the impregnable Revolutionary War fortress at West Point. Old West Point Rd. also led to Gen. Benedict Arnold's headquarters in the town of Garrison, and was used to transport Arnold's traitorous spying accomplice, Maj. John André, to his trial and hanging.

Pay close attention to the blazing through this area as the trail weaves among the grassy, open fields and gravel and paved roads of Graymoor Monastery's grounds. The Friars of Atonement are famous for hospitality to thru-hikers. In most past years, the friary has offered rooms and meals to long-distance hikers in summer and a campsite with running water at a covered picnic pavilion in spring and fall. Hikers were also welcomed to daily mass. Call the NY-NJTC (212-685-9699) to see if the friary is offer-

ing lodging before stopping there for the night.

The trail begins ascending Little Fort Hill at 0.7 mi. This small rise was named for the earthen redoubt that once stood here. When American troops were routed in a 1777 battle at Peekskill and Continental Village, some of them retreated to these hills, where they established rough-hewn fortifications. These little forts served as the outermost defense positions for the Continental stronghold at West Point.

The rest of the day's hike passes through a typical Hudson Highlands forest of chestnut oak, red oak, hickory, ash, sweet birch, and white oak. These trees, along with shrubs such as mountain laurel and highbush and lowbush blueberry, thrive in the very rocky, acidic, nutrient-poor soils of these mountains.

A blue-blazed side trail (1.3 mi.) leads right (east) to a short, steep rock scramble and the shrine of Graymoor Monastery. This rustic meditation spot comes complete with a statue of the Virgin Mary, a bench, and a trail register and New Testament stuffed inside a mailbox. Thankful Christians have left their entries here. Some offer formal prayers: "Holy Mother, thank you for seeing us through these past few days of hiking safely. Thank you for your constant guidance and our good health. We ask that you bless our family and friends, and help them in their time of need." Others are a little more pragmatic in their requests: "Dear God, please let it clear. Aren't three days of rain enough?"

Atop Little Fort Hill (1.6 mi.) there is a stand of hemlocks that offer perches to birds of prey. On one hike we repeatedly found the tiny, regurgitated bones and fur of rodents (which can't be digested by the large birds). We were suddenly startled by a huge, utterly silent shape lifting from an overhead branch and winging away. A great horned owl disappeared in an instant, before we could utter a word or point to the sky.

Far underground, beneath Little Fort Hill, runs the Catskill Aqueduct Tunnel. Completed in 1917, it gravity-feeds 500 million gallons of water daily from the Catskill Mts. to thirsty New Yorkers. An extraordinary engineering feat, the tunnel often plunges through mountain bedrock, and it passes invisibly beneath the Hudson River at Storm King Mt.

At 1.7 mi. the AT passes through the site of a 1991 forest fire. The gray shafts of skeletal trees stand guard over a tangled green understory. Boulders and tree trunks are still scorched black, but it is remarkable to see how fast the forest is recovering.

Near the top of Denning Hill (2.2 mi.), a blue-blazed trail leads left (west) 650 ft. to the best view of the day. This sweeping vista, framed by tall trees, looks north to West Point, Constitution Island, and the North Gate of the Hudson Highlands. Here, Storm King Mt. and Breakneck Ridge form a 1000-ft.-deep gorge through which the Hudson River flows. Were

it not for the efforts of one man, Leo Rothschild, this vista would be marred today by an immense power plant cut into the bowels of Storm King Mt. In 1962 the Consolidated Edison public utility announced plans to build the 2-million-kilowatt Storm King power plant, complete with huge transmission lines that would cross the river on ten-story-high towers. Rothschild and other members of the NY-NJTC and The Nature Conservancy formed the Scenic Hudson Coalition and led a fourteen-year battle to stop construction. Con Edison characterized these environmentalists as "misinformed bird watchers, nature fakers, land grabbers, and militant adversaries of progress." The courts didn't see it that way. They banned the plant in a decision that declared that such building projects "must include as a basic concern the preservation of natural beauty and of national historic shrines." This landmark case first established the need for obtaining environmental impact statements in large construction projects, and its precedent was used to help defeat the Delaware River's Tocks Island Dam project (see "A Pox Called Tocks" in Hike #27) and to fight the logging of old-growth forests in the Pacific Northwest.

At 2.5 mi. the trail crosses the rocky outcrop marking the crest of Denning Hill. This vista looks south to Haverstraw Bay, and on a clear day offers the northernmost point at which AT hikers can catch a faint glimpse of

Manhattan skyscrapers. The trail crosses the Old Albany Post Rd. at 3.3 mi. (day parking). This former Native American trail was widened during the French and Indian War as a means of providing supplies to colonial troops. Designated a Queens Highway in 1703, this Albany-to-New York City coach road is worth exploring by car. Milestones still line its way, as do ancient apple trees, stone walls, the remnants of cleared fields, and colonial-era stone houses, some of which served as inns.

After you cross Old Albany Post Rd., thick forest quickly closes in, though there is a good, open viewpoint atop Canopus Hill (4.3 mi.). An easy 300-vertical-ft. descent leads into a small pass and to Canopus Hill Rd. at 5.0 mi. (there is pull-off room for one or two cars near the trail). The AT crosses the road and begins a slow, steady climb, weaving amid the largest series of foundations and stone walls we've seen on the trail. The stone fences interconnect in complex patterns, forming varied geometrically shaped enclosures. These may have been animal holding pens, the walls topped with fence posts (now long since rotted) and the openings between pens closed off with wooden gates. Whatever their purpose, these massive walls provide proof of the 19th-century work ethic. They also provide great photo opportunities, especially during autumn leaf time.

The trail continues a steady but

Michael Warren

The Hudson River and Hudson Highlands from Denning Hill

easy climb over the next 3 mi., with one or two small dips. At 6.0 mi. the AT crosses South Highland Rd., also called Philipse Brook Rd. (no parking). At 6.5 mi. the trail enters Fahnestock SP, and at 7.5 mi. crosses the red-blazed Catfish Trail. This rugged, fairly level area is covered in thickets of mountain laurel (with showy white and pinkish blossoms in early June) and lowbush blueberries (especially beautiful in autumn when the reddening leaves form a brilliant scarlet carpet on the forest floor).

The AT intersects and then parallels the Three Lakes Trail for a short distance before reaching paved Dennytown Rd. (8.8 mi.), where there is a hiker parking area and water pump, and where this hike ends. There is a group campsite along the Three Lakes Trail just north of Dennytown Rd. Day hikers can create a variety of interesting loop hikes utilizing the Dennytown hiker parking area, the AT, Three Lakes Trail, Catfish Loop Trail, and various woods roads. This is a great way to explore the southernmost section of Fahnestock SP (see Hike #39), a Hudson Highlands landscape that was shaped by farming, iron mining, and the vast Fahnestock estate.

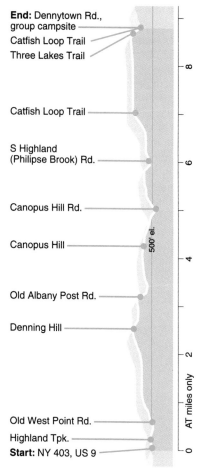

Dennytown Rd. Ⓟ
Group ⛺ 🚻 El. 750'

Three Lakes Trail

Catfish Trail

S boundary
Fahnestock SP 🏛

S Highland (Philipse
Brook) Rd. Ⓟ

Canopus Hill Rd. Ⓟ
El. 400'

Canopus Hill,
El. 700', **V**

Old Albany Post Rd.
Ⓟ 🏛

Denning Hill, El. 900',
V
Side trail to **V**

Little Fort Hill,
El. 700' 🍁 🏛

Old West Point Rd.
🏛

Highland Tpk.

US 9, NY 403 Ⓟ
El. 411'
Unnamed road Ⓟ

N
1" = 1 mi.

Miles N	NORTH	Elev. (ft./m)	Miles S
Total: 8.9 mi. with access on US 9			
8.8	**End:** Dennytown Rd., day parking, 1.2 mi. S of NY 301; water pump, group campsite; Catfish Trail northern terminus is 0.2 mi. N.	750/229	0.0
8.7	**Three Lakes Trail** forms loop with AT (5.5 mi.).		0.1
7.0	**Catfish Trail** southern terminus forms loop with AT (3.4 mi.).	900/274	1.8
6.5	**Fahnestock SP** southern boundary.	600/183	2.3
6.0	Cross **S Highland Rd. (Philipse Brook Rd.).**	550/168	2.8
5.0	Cross **Canopus Hill Rd.;** day parking, early exit option.	400/122	3.8
4.3	**Canopus Hill** summit, view; begin easy 300-ft. descent.	700/213	4.5
3.3	**Old Albany Post Rd.,** day parking, early exit option.	607/185	5.5
2.5	**Denning Hill** summit, view.	900/274	6.3
2.2	**Storm King vista,** side trail leads 220 yd. L (W) to view.	850/259	6.6
1.7	**Site of 1991 forest fire.**	800/244	7.1
1.3	**Graymoor Monastery shrine** side trail leads R (E) 100 yd. to shrine.	700/213	7.5
0.7	**Begin ascent of** Little Fort Hill.	500/152	8.1
0.6	**Old West Point Rd.;** Graymoor Monastery grounds.		8.2
0.2	**Highland Tpk.;** Graymoor Monastery grounds.	500/152	8.6
0.0	**Start:** US 9 and NY 403, turn L (E) onto AT into woods.	411/125	8.8
0.1	Access: From day parking on unnamed road turn R (S) onto **US 9** for 0.1 mi.	400/122	0.1

SOUTH

HIKE #39
Fahnestock State Park

Maps: ATC N.Y. & N.J. Map 2; NY-NJTC
   East Hudson Trails Map 3
Route: From Dennytown Rd. through
   Fahnestock SP to Canopus Lake,
   Looking Mt., and Hortontown Rd.
Recommended direction: S to N
Distance: 10.4 mi.
Elevation +/-: 750 to 1282 to 300 ft.
Effort: Moderate
Day hike: Moderate
Overnight backpacking hike: No
Duration: 7 hr.
Early exit options: At 3.6 mi., NY 301; at
   8.1 mi., Long Hill Rd.
Natural history features: Mud Pond wet-
   land; Canopus Lake vista; Looking Mt.
   vista
Social history features: Fahnestock SP;
   stone chapel ruins; Sunk Mine nar-
   row-gauge railroad; farm building
   foundations and stone walls

Trailhead access: *Start:* From the intersection of NY 403 and US 9, go N on US 9
   for 6.8 mi. to McKeel Corners; turn R
   onto NY 301 and go E for 2.7 mi.; turn
   R onto Dennytown Rd. and go 1.1 mi.
   to hiker day-use parking on R. *End:*
   From the intersection of NY 301 and
   Taconic State Pkwy., go 4.3 mi. N on
   parkway and make L onto Miller Hill
   Rd. In 0.3 mi. turn L onto Hortontown
   Rd., and intersect AT in 0.2 mi. Fifty ft.
   past the trail, turn R at "RPH" mailbox
   into unnamed lane. Limited hiker day-
   use parking is located at RPH Shelter
   0.1 mi. down lane between garage
   and shelter.
Camping: Group campsites on Dennytown Rd. and N of Long Hill Rd.; RPH
   Shelter

C larence Fahnestock State Park
straddles rugged, boulder-
strewn hills where highbush
blueberry and mountain laurel com-
pete in thin, acidic soils atop glacier-
scraped bedrock. This 10.4-mi. hike
cuts through the heart of the park,
from south to north, touches ponds
and marshes, and explores hemlock
ravines and the massive stone
remains of a 19th-century mine railroad line. Everywhere there are cellar holes, stone fences, old roads,

mine tunnels, pits, and ore dumps,
reminders of the tough, hardscrabble
mountain life led by Hudson Highlands farmers and miners.

These uplands resisted settlement
long after the lowlands of the Hudson Valley were heavily populated.
Only in the 1800s, after the discovery
of iron deposits and with the growing
urban need for farm produce, did
people lay claim to the land. Later,
with the coming of the railroads, the
opening up of midwestern agricul-

Building an AT shelter

Terry Karkas

ing area on the north side of Dennytown Rd. But before setting off, take a
quick detour to your left, across the
open field, following the blue blazes
of the Three Lakes Trail. At the edge
of the meadow, hidden by vines and
trees, are the picturesque ruins of
what appears to have been a small
chapel. In early spring, the four stone
and masonry walls, gracefully
arched windows, and entranceway
are draped in yellow forsythia blossoms. The true use of this building
seems lost to history, though some
claim it was never a chapel at all, but
a chicken coop. The Dennytown Rd.
group campsite is located nearby.

Retrace your steps and follow the
white blazes of the AT north into the
woods. The trail winds around the
swampy remains of a beaver pond,
intersects with the red-blazed Catfish
Loop Trail (to your right, or south),
and then makes a stiff ascent of
about 390 vertical ft. to the top of a
ridge (0.9 mi.). Similar short, rocky
climbs will give you a great aerobic
workout throughout this hike.

Over the next 0.6 mi. the trail
descends on a deeply eroded woods
road until it crosses Sunk Mine Rd.
(1.5 mi.), and then goes over a small
stream and waterfall on a log bridge.
Step to your left and look out over
the remains of a pond, now a peaceful, cattail-covered swamp. In winter,
the mine openings of Sunk Mine
may be seen faintly through the trees
on the steep hillside opposite the
wetland. In the 19th century this area
was an industrial wasteland. Five

ture, and the discovery of iron ore in
Minnesota, Highlands farming and
mining collapsed and the hills returned to forest. Clarence Fahnestock, a New York City doctor and big
game hunter, built his mountain
estate here in 1915. He died of pneu-
monia while serving as a major in
World War I. His brother, Ernest,
donated the 2000-acre estate to the
Taconic State Park Commission in
1929, as a memorial. Today Fahnestock SP totals over 6530 acres and is
adjoined by the 4000 pristine acres
of the Hubbard-Perkins Conservation
Area (site of many miles of new hiking trails).

You can pick up the AT at the park-

massive mine shafts penetrated 300 ft. into the hillside. Explosive blasts of black powder, and later dynamite, reverberated over the mountains. Steam boilers powered noisy hoists that lifted the ore out of the mines. The surrounding slopes were stripped of forest to make charcoal for the nearby West Point Foundry at Cold Spring. A narrow-gauge railroad hauled ore away from the site.

Prospectors Jacobus Ter Boss and John Burnet were the first to discover iron ore here, in 1756, and were paid just "two fowls" for their trouble. That was a real bargain for finding an 8-mi.-long iron ore vein that eventually earned mine owners millions of dollars and made New York State the nation's biggest iron producer. The Sunk Mine provided iron for Civil War cannon, steamship boilers, and the first locomotive built in the United States. Many smaller mines were located nearby, some owned and operated by farmers to supplement their incomes. The Denny Mine, for example, was just 60 ft. deep and run by "two men, a boy and mule."

What was once an industrial wasteland is a state park today. The Sunk Mine shafts, being so close to water, teem with life. Hundreds of little brown bats spend their days snoozing, suspended from mine ceilings. Brooding females and their young hang together, while males hang alone. Phoebes nest on narrow ledges along mine walls, and pickerel frogs hop about in the groundwater that

has seeped into the mines. Mosquitoes are the most prolific mine fauna, and they help keep humans out of the unsafe depths of the tunnels.

The AT climbs a short, steep cliff, then levels out, passing through a dense hemlock grove. Hemlocks, like other evergreens, grow best in cold hollows and on sun-starved, north-facing ridges. Their waxy needles, stems, and roots are filled with resinous chemicals that work like a botanical antifreeze, protecting them from subzero temperatures. Hemlocks can survive harsh winter temperatures without frost damage (they have been found resistant down to -112°F). In early spring, with their needles already in place, they get a head start on deciduous trees, starting photosynthesis as soon as the thaw begins. Healthy hemlocks grow so thickly that they create their own microclimate, always several degrees cooler than surrounding forests.

The AT again crosses the blue-blazed Three Lakes Trail, at 2.7 mi. These two trails can be combined into an easy 5.3-mi. loop hike, leaving from and returning to the Dennytown Rd. parking area.

In another 0.2 mi., the AT turns right onto the Sunk Mine narrow-gauge railroad bed (2.9 mi.); the yellow-blazed Old Mine Railroad Trail is on the left. The railroad line is a remarkable engineering feat, passing between cuts blasted in solid rock, and running along freestanding stone causeways that rise 20 ft. from the forest floor. The railroad, built in

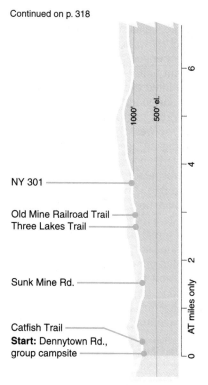

Continued on p. 318

1861, hauled ore to the Cold Spring–Paterson Tpk., where it was dumped out of the rail carts and loaded onto wagons for transport to the Cold Spring Foundry. Each wagon held 6 to 8 tons of ore and was pulled by six to seven mules, horses, or oxen. Some of the iron hauled along this little railway was probably thrown at rebelling Confederate troops as cannonballs during the Civil War. The mines went silent in the 1870s, going bankrupt as more accessible sources of iron were found in the Mesabi Range of Minnesota.

The AT leaves the railroad bed (3.6 mi.) and turns left along NY 301, where there is parking. It follows the highway along the crest of a dam holding back the waters of Canopus Lake, the largest of the Civilian Conservation Corps' 1930s Fahnestock SP building projects. In 0.1 mi., the AT reaches another parking area and reenters the woods, ascending steeply on a narrow path through dense mountain laurel. This gnarled evergreen, with shiny, leathery leaves, grows best in uplands with well-drained acidic soils. Its showy display of white and pink chalice-shaped flowers is one of the finest forest spectacles of early June. While mountain laurel flowers provide safe nectar to bees and the seed capsules are meals to flickers, chickadees, and ruffed grouse, the plant is deadly to humans and livestock. Even honey made from the nectar is poisonous to people.

The trail continues through thick underbrush along high white rock ledges, which offer fleeting glimpses of the lake below. At 6.0 mi. the AT abruptly opens onto a cliff of billion-year-old white quartzite and thinly layered schist. The inspiring view looks south along the length of Canopus Lake and back at the territory you have already walked. Swimming beaches and concession stands are visible on the left side of

Looking Mt., El. 1282', **V**

247

stone walls, cellar holes 🏛

El. 1100', **V**

301

Canopus Lake

NY 301 Ⓟ

Old Mine Railroad Trail 🏛

Three Lakes Trail

Sunk Mine Rd. 🏛

Catfish Trail

🚶 Dennytown Rd. Ⓟ
💧 El. 750'

N

1" = 1 mi.

CLARENCE FAHNESTOCK MEMORIAL STATE PARK

Canopus

Pelton Pond

Jordan Pond

Mudoure Pond

Clear Lake

Wiccopee Reservoir

Dennytown

Duck Pond

Christian Corners

SCENIC

WALL

200

the lake. Fahnestock SP attracts thousands for summer swimming, boating, fishing, and hiking. In wintertime snow can be deep in these Highland hills and the cross-country skiing excellent. The Taconic Outdoor Education Center (914-265-3773) rents cross-country skis in winter at the park swimming area and has maple-syrup-making demonstrations in springtime, nature walks in summer, and daylong family programs.

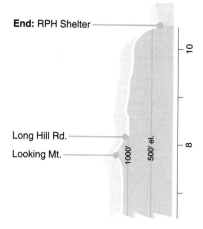

The trail descends steeply from the vista and crosses a small stream at 6.4 mi., where cardinal-flowers bloom in early autumn. These brilliant scarlet flowers, named for the robes of Roman Catholic clergy, are chiefly pollinated by hummingbirds, who can hover while reaching up into the drooping tubular blossoms. Over-picking has made these flowers scarce. Please look, but don't touch.

The trail soon turns left, joining an old woods road that climbs very gradually uphill toward the summit of Looking Mt. The road is paralleled by a particularly fine stone wall, and if you look closely in the thick underbrush you will spot several old stone-lined cellar holes just a few feet off the AT to your right (east). Farming was never as important to this section of the Highlands as was iron mining. Spring came late to these hills; snows often stayed well into April, while the fertile Hudson Valley to the west was coming into bloom. The subsistence farms here were known for their potatoes, with 3- to 4-acre plots of spuds

feeding farmers and livestock. In the late 1800s dairy cows offered another source of income.

Many of these stone walls, important in keeping animals away from crops, were carefully constructed. Farmers first dug out the loam, down to the frost line or subsoil. Next, a bed of small stones topped by boulders was placed, and this foundation was allowed to settle. Then smaller stones were selected according to size and shape, and carefully fitted together to form a stone fence jigsaw puzzle. A hardworking farmer could build about 8 ft. of stone wall per day.

Leaving the woods road, the AT climbs a little more steeply now to the bare summit of Looking Mt. (1282 ft.) at 7.8 mi. The view east of green

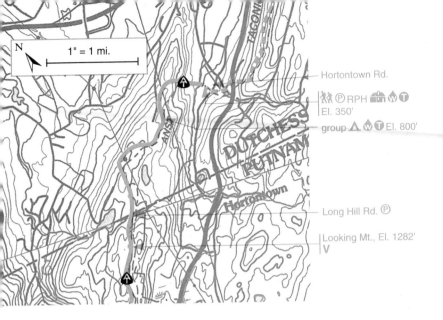

Hortontown Rd.

🚶🅿 RPH 🏕 Ⓦ 🚻
El. 350'

group 🔺 Ⓦ 🚻 El. 800'

Long Hill Rd. 🅿

Looking Mt., El. 1282'
V

hills is somewhat spoiled by electrical transmission towers. From this point, the trail descends 300 vertical ft. to Long Hill Rd. (8.1 mi.), where there is parking. The road leads right (east) in a few miles to the Taconic State Pkwy.

After two brief, easy ascents, the AT reaches a blue-blazed side trail that leads left (west) to a new group campsite, well, and privy (9.4 mi.). Within 0.1 mi. the trail begins a long, steady 500-vertical-ft. descent through hemlocks, traversing many stone walls, until the Taconic comes within earshot.

After crossing a stream, the trail levels out, and at 10.4 mi. it reaches a side trail leading in 130 yd. to the RPH Shelter (RPH stands for Ralph's

Peak Hikers, a walking group led by Ralph Ferrusi). This is no rustic lean-to, but deluxe accommodations. The cinder-block hut has real glass windows and is painted in shades of pink and salmon. It is furnished with church pews, a rocking chair, a large table, and three bunks. There is even a scale with which you can see how many pounds you've shed over the past 10.4 mi. There is a privy, and water is available from a pump. Although the shelter is open only in summer, there is a garage where hikers can stay in winter. There is parking for several cars between the garage and the shelter, and this is where this hike ends. A short driveway leads in less than 0.1 mi. out to Hortontown Rd.

Miles N	NORTH	Elev. (ft./m)	Miles S
10.4	**End:** RPH Shelter side trail leads R (E) 130 yd. to shelter, water, privy, parking; 1.1 mi. SW of Shenandoah	350/91	0.0
9.5	Begin long, steady **500-ft. descent.**	800/244	0.9
8.1	**Long Hill Rd.,** day parking, early exit option.	980/299	2.3
7.8	**Looking Mt.** summit, view; begin steep 300-ft. descent.	1282/391	2.6
6.7	AT follows **old woods road** lined by stone walls.	1000/305	3.4
6.4	**Descend steeply** and cross small stream.	1100/335	3.7
6.0	**Canopus Lake** view.	1100/335	4.4
3.7	**NY 301** day parking; AT turns R (N) off road, into woods, and ascends steeply.		6.7
3.6	**NY 301,** day parking, early exit option; AT turns L (W) on road for 0.1 mi. (Fahnestock SP Campground is 1.0 mi. R (E) along road).		6.8
2.9	**Sunk Mine narrow-gauge railroad bed;** Old Mine Railroad Trail goes L.	900/274	7.5
2.7	Cross **Three Lakes Trail.**		7.7
1.5	**Sunk Mine Rd.,** a woods road.	800/244	8.9
0.9	Top of steep **390-ft. ascent.**	1190/363	9.5
0.2	Cross **Catfish Trail,** forms loop with AT (3.4 mi.).	800/244	10.2
0.0	**Start:** Dennytown Rd., day parking, 1.2 mi. S of NY 301; water pump, group campsite; Three Lakes Trail intersection.	750/229	10.4

SOUTH

Hosner Mt. to Cat Rocks

Maps: ATC N.Y. Maps 2 & 1

Route: From Hortontown Rd. past Hosner Mt., over Stormville Mt., Mt. Egbert, Depot Hill, and West Mt., to Cat Rocks and County Rte. 20 (W Dover Rd.)

Recommended direction: S to N

Distance: 16.8 mi.

Elevation +/-: 350 to 1329 to 550 ft.

Effort: Moderate

Day hike: Optional

Overnight backpacking hike: Yes

Duration: 11½ hr.

Early exit options: At 5.1 mi., NY 52; at 12.6 mi., NY 55

Natural history features: Hosner Mt. vista; Mt. Egbert vista; upland swamps; beaver pond; Cat Rocks vista; second-largest oak tree in Duchess County

Social history features: Ralph's Peak Hikers Supermarket Spring; Mt. Egbert U.S. Geodetic Survey marker; Morgan Stewart Shelter; Nuclear Lake

Trailhead access: *Start:* From the intersection of NY 301 and Taconic State Pkwy., go 4.3 mi. N on parkway and make L onto Miller Hill Rd. In 0.3 mi. turn L onto Hortontown Rd. and intersect AT in 0.2 mi. Fifty ft. past the trail, turn R at "RPH" mailbox into unnamed lane. Limited hiker day-use parking is located at the RPH Shelter 0.1 mi down lane between garage and shelter. *End:* Go N from Pawling on NY 22, making L at light by Harlem Valley State Hospital. At T make a L, then immediate R onto County Rte. 20 (West Dover Rd.). AT overnight parking area is in 3.5 mi. on L.

Camping: Morgan Stewart Shelter; Telephone Pioneers Shelter

The rounded Hudson Highland hills north of the Taconic State Pkwy. offer a kinder and gentler hiking experience than their rugged cousins to the south. This area, with two AT shelters, is perfect for beginning backpackers or for those just returning to the trail after too many winter weekends in front of the TV. This overnight trip is accomplished in a 9.0-mi. day and a 7.8-mi. day. Numerous road crossings make a variety of day hikes possible in this forested hill country where 19th-century mountain farms once flourished.

Today the mountains traversed by this section of the AT thrive as lush woodland oases, surrounded by lowland highways, suburbs, and agricultural lands. These green Appalachian islands are reminders of the vast mixed deciduous forest that once stretched uninterrupted from the Atlantic Ocean to the Mississippi River.

This forest land harbors remarkable biodiversity. Hardy chesnut oaks grow on the driest, rockiest heights,

When completed in 1937, much of the AT ran across private property and was protected merely by a landowner's handshake. Its wildlands were safe for the time being because they were remote. But by the mid-'60s suburban highways and homes reached into the mountains and threatened the trail. Nowhere was the danger greater than in New York State. Only 20 percent of its AT was protected on public lands, while more and more sections were being pushed from private property onto roads. To the trail community it appeared as if the AT wilderness experience would soon become a tiptoe through urban backyards.

In 1968 the federal government stepped in, passing the National Trails System Act, designating the AT a National Scenic Trail and authorizing the states to acquire land for a protected trail corridor. When New York's Governor Rockefeller refused to respond, the Feds took action. They called on AT volunteers to take to the New York hills and look for an ideal trail route. "They gave us a bundle of topographic maps," remembers Liz Levers, who organized volunteers, "and said, 'You go out and figure where you want to put [the trail]. If we approve, we'll begin buying the land.'" The volunteers had just one month to map their route.

Hurried route selection led to lengthy town meetings and negotia-

while red, white, and black oaks, hickory, ash, and maple thrive on more protected slopes. Every year, these trees lay down a nutrient-rich blanket of natural fertilizer: estimates say that 10 million leaves annually fall over each acre of eastern deciduous forest. This decaying foliage supports a varied understory of mountain laurel, blueberries, common violets, asters, Virginia creeper, Solomon's-seal, wild ginger, viburnums, may-apple, plus many other shrubs and wildflowers. The forest also offers shelter and abundant food to warblers, woodpeckers, tanagers, raptors, and other birds, plus large mammals: white-tailed deer, raccoon, rabbit, squirrel, and elusive coyote and bobcat. Tree, wildflower, and bird field guides will enrich your walk.

The hike begins at the small parking area at the RPH Shelter (see Hike #39) just off Hortontown Rd. Follow the blue-blazed trail from the shelter for 400 ft. to the AT and turn right, following the white blazes. The AT crosses Hortontown Rd. (0.1 mi.), heading north through shadowy hemlocks, and reaches the Taconic State Pkwy. (0.3 mi.). Cross this high-speed highway carefully (no parking). On the far side of the Taconic, the AT follows Miller Hill Rd. and

tions with landowners. While many locals welcomed the AT, some did not. "Some worried that 'trail weirdos and hippies' would threaten their children," recalls Don Derr, a volunteer leader. One family feared the AT would be used for a secret Communist invasion from Canada. Despite the obstacles, an AT route east of the Hudson River was finally selected. But then the trail itself had to be built. The long grind of backbreaking work by over 400 volunteers lasted from 1982 to 1986. Similar work went on over the entire length of the Appalachians. You may want to remember these gung-ho volunteers as you ascend rock steps, descend over water bars (used to divert rain water off the trail), or sleep at shelters.

While the trail presently sits almost entirely within a publicly owned corridor, it will never be fully protected from development. It is the job of local AT management committees, government and volunteer partnerships that serve as watchdogs to see that these wildlands are forever preserved against encroachment. The first such committee to be organized was in Dutchess County, New York. "We had to invent the whole AT land management process as we went along," remembers committee chair Ron Rosen. Today similar committees from Maine to Georgia confront corridor encroachments by builders, loggers, and all-terrain vehicles. It is these land managers who launch spring work trips to clear away blowdowns, who negotiate with town zoning boards, and who address all the complex issues that assail a primitive, 2100-mi.-long national park.

Rock Ledge Rd. for 0.1 mi., then turns right, into the woods. It takes you steadily upward, away from traffic noise and through a young forest of maple, ash, and oak. This beautiful trail section is cut into the western shoulder of Hosner Mt. The climb is long and steady, but it is never overly steep. The ankle-twisting rocks of New Jersey and lower New York have, mercifully, been replaced by a smooth dirt treadway.

Legend has it that Hosner Mt. was purchased from local Native Americans by James J. Thompkins. Old Dutch families had already occupied the Hudson Valley flatland below, so Thompkins settled on the rocky hillside, paying for it with a keg of gunpowder, a powder horn, a musket, a blanket, and a dog. Some say he sweetened the deal with a contraband keg of whiskey. Thompkins's descendants cut the mountains' timber, and by the mid-19th century most of Hosner Mt. was in cultivation, though a few isolated woodlots remained. The land produced hundreds of bushels of potatoes and inspired the legend of a lost cave once used by Native Americans. Today most of the ridge has returned to forest, and only old stone walls remain to remind you that this steep hillside was once farmed and grazed.

There is a good viewpoint at 1.3 mi., but there is an even better one 0.6 mi. farther on (just past the first intersection with the blue-blazed Hosner Mt. Loop Trail at 1.7 mi.). This second vista, reached by a set of masterfully placed natural-stone steps, looks out from an open ledge to the Hudson Valley, over lush farm fields and toward the town of Fishkill (a Revolutionary War supply depot for Washington's army). The Catskill and Shawangunk mountains border the far western horizon. The sound of traffic at the Taconic Parkway and I-84 interchange below detract from the view. A birdsong audiocassette played over headphones can soften this noisy intrusion. From the vista, the trail descends a short way and intersects the blue-blazed Hosner Mt. Loop Trail (2.2 mi.) a second time. For those seeking an easy day hike (recommended for families with children), this loop trail can be coupled with the AT. Total round-trip mileage from the Hortontown Rd. parking area to the Hosner Mt. vista and back is about 4.5 mi.

After passing another view, the trail climbs through hemlocks. Near here, Bailey Spring once served AT hikers with fresh water and a camping spot. A local AT maintainer told us that a very old man "loved that spring like a wife, cleaning it of leaves and debris, and keeping the water clear year round." When the old man died, no one took over his task; the campsite and spring became choked with weeds. A new "spring" has since replaced it: Ralph's Peak Hikers' Supermarket Spring. Right on the AT, it consists of a 5-gal. jug of water set on a boulder above a bed of gravel. It may not be Perrier, but it's a welcome sight, being the only water on the mountain.

The AT circles to the right, providing relief from the traffic noise below and offering a fine view east over farm country. It then descends to Hosner Mt. Rd. (3.5 mi.). From this shallow gap, the trail ascends 550 vertical ft. to the top of Stormville Mt. (4.1 mi.), then descends slightly to NY 52 (5.1 mi.), where there is overnight parking.

Begin an easy climb through a young forest of sweet birch, white ash, and shagbark hickory. The trail skirts the edges of unused farm fields that are mowed regularly to provide an impressive view west over the Hudson Valley. Now back in the woods, the AT climbs briefly past rocky dens before descending to Stormville Mt. Rd. and winding through a small housing development (6.1 mi.). When we came through here, we were greeted by a raucous chorus of woofers; thankfully, all of the dogs were tied. Although this noisy, short stretch of "trail" passing along paved roads between homes may be jarring, it acts as a reminder of just how close adjacent forests came to being suburban developments rather than the AT corridor (see "The Race to Protect the AT in New York").

The AT crosses over I-84 on Mountain Top Rd. (6.3 mi.) and reenters the woods (6.5 mi.). The I-84 road cut provides a geology lesson for those able to read the land. The flow of the once molten, soft, and flexible gneiss is plainly visible in its curving, layered, light and dark bands.

A rustic wooden AT sign directs hikers back into the woods. The sign is one of hundreds carved and painted by Vernon, New Jersey, developmentally disabled high school students. Similar signs, made by these children who have trouble walking even a short distance, guide hikers on their way at road crossings up and down the AT.

The trail now begins a steady ascent of Mt. Egbert (1329 ft.), passing many old stone walls and several foundations. It seems amazing that Native Americans lived on this land for 12,000 years and never felt the need to construct a single stone fence, while 300 years of European colonization have left every last ridge top crisscrossed with these barriers. The view from Egbert (8.6 mi.) looks south toward Hosner Mt. and the way you've come.

A U.S. Geodetic Survey marker graces the summit of Mt. Egbert (8.8 mi.) Such markers dot Appalachian ridgetops and provide elevation reference points for the complex network of topographical lines that swirl over our hiking maps. It is startling to realize that every last square mile of the United States has been

Michael Warren

The Harlem Valley from high on the AT

meticulously mapped by teams of surveyors who, beginning in the 19th century, tromped over difficult, often trail-less terrain carrying heavy survey equipment on their backs. This mapping effort, begun as a means of settling boundary questions, was completed during World War II, when the threat of invasion added a military urgency to the project. Today most mapping is done from airplanes, using a technique called aerial stereo photogrammetry.

The Morgan Stewart lean-to (8.9 mi.) marks the end of the first day's backpack. A shelter sign tells ambitious hikers that they are only 734 mi. short of Mt. Katahdin, Maine, and 1376 mi. away from Springer Mt., Georgia. But for now, forget the miles ahead and enjoy the amenities: a dry shelter, fireplace, water pump, privy, and designated overflow campsites.

Leaving the shelter on your second day out, continue along the ridge to a north-facing view from the top of Depot Hill (9.2 mi.). The AT then descends slightly to unpaved Depot Hill Rd. (10.0 mi.). The road and hill are named for a railway station built by the New York & New England Railroad in 1912 at the foot of the ridge. Back in the 1850s, Depot Hill Rd. was named Negro Hill Rd., and the surrounding area called Freemanville. Charles Freeman, a freed slave, lived here, and may have invited other freed slaves to share his hilltop. An 1856 map shows a double row of houses along the road, but unlike for the "white folk" communities shown

Continued on p. 328

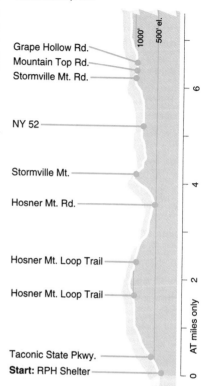

Grape Hollow Rd. Ⓟ

I-84
Mountain Top Rd.

V

NY 52 Ⓟ

Stormville Mt.
El. 1056'

Hosner Mt. Rd. Ⓟ
El. 550'

Ⓦ V

El. 1050', V

Hosner Mt. Loop Trail

Taconic State Pkwy.
El. 600'

Ⓟ RPH Ⓦ Ⓣ
El. 350'

N   1" = 1 mi.

on the map, the home owners' names are not marked.

The AT continues through woods, passes a small swamp and stream, and begins to descend toward NY 55. At 11.4 mi., it passes a balanced glacial erratic, 30 ft. around and 5 ft. high. The boulder was dumped here by retreating glaciers about 15,000 years ago. A steep 450-vertical-ft. descent leads into a mountain pass long used by local transportation.

The AT crosses railroad tracks at 11.9 mi. Next it crosses picturesque Whaley Lake Stream on a bridge, Old Rte. 55, and NY 55 (overnight parking is available via a short blue-blazed side trail 0.3 mi. north of the NY 55 crossing, making an early exit option possible here). It then begins climbing out of the valley (12.6 mi.).

The AT soon crests, and for the next 1.5 mi. does something it almost never does: it provides a nearly level, rock-free treadway. This little plateau allows for what a friend calls "choogling," striding along at top speed. But don't go too fast—there's plenty to see. Chestnut oak, red oak, sweet birch, and mountain laurel cluster around small hillocks, rock outcrops, old farm foundations, and stone walls.

The AT makes a long, looping half circle to the west here to avoid going anywhere near Nuclear Lake. The lake, former site of a nuclear test facility, was purchased as part of the AT corridor by the National Park Service in 1979 and immediately became a major headache to the vol-

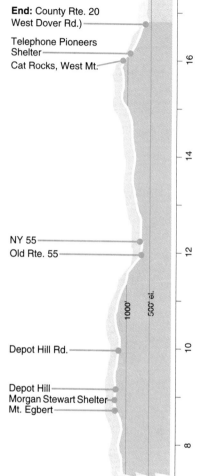

End: County Rte. 20 West Dover Rd.)

Telephone Pioneers Shelter

Cat Rocks, West Mt.

NY 55

Old Rte. 55

Depot Hill Rd.

Depot Hill
Morgan Stewart Shelter
Mt. Egbert

1000'

500' el.

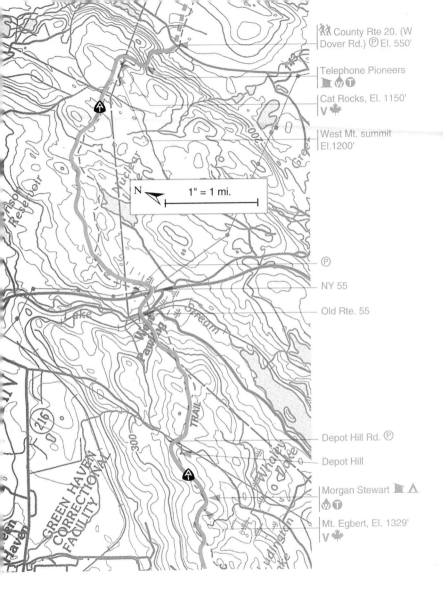

County Rte 20. (W Dover Rd.) Ⓟ El. 550'

Telephone Pioneers

Cat Rocks, El. 1150'
V

West Mt. summit El.1200'

N
1" = 1 mi.

Ⓟ

NY 55

Old Rte. 55

Depot Hill Rd. Ⓟ

Depot Hill

Morgan Stewart ▲

Mt. Egbert, El. 1329'
V

GREEN HAVEN CORRECTIONAL FACILITY

216

unteer committee that manages this portion of the AT. "Rumor had it that 55 gallon drums of radioactive waste had been dumped by rowboat into the water, and people reacted with a lot of fear," relates Ron Rosen, chair of the local AT management committee. "After much testing, we learned that the high radioactivity rumors were false. Ultimately, the government spent more money for testing and cleanup than they ever did for the property." Today, Nuclear Lake has been given a clean bill of health, and plans call for the AT to be rerouted along its western shore. This relocation (which will begin 0.6 mi. north of NY 55) could open as early as 1998, so watch blazes closely.

You are more likely to be shot at on this part of the AT than you are to die from radiation poisoning. AT corridor lands are not open to hunting, but we heard shots ringing out uncomfortably close by on a recent hike. During autumn hunting seasons, hikers anywhere on the AT should take the precautions of wearing blaze orange, red, or yellow. A friend hangs bells from his day pack, though we've warned him that he may be mistaken for one of Santa's reindeer. Some hikers avoid the woods entirely during these times.

The level section of trail goes by too fast, and soon you are climbing again, but only briefly. A small hollow holds a long, narrow swamp, cupped between two hillocks. Puncheons (bog bridging) cross this wet area with its drowned gray ghosts of trees.

The AT crosses Penny Rd. (15.4 mi.), a sunken dirt road lined by stone walls. A little farther on there is evidence of recent beaver activity. A small pond is backing up behind a tightly woven dam of sticks. There were over 60 million beavers in pre-colonial America. Trapped for their pelts, the beavers also provided food to early settlers. In the 1700s French Catholics ate beaver on holy fast days, since the Pope (the ultimate authority on all matters scientific!) had classified this toothy mammal as a *fish,* due to the scales on its tail. Protected in 1930, the beaver has gained in numbers and can be found up and down the AT.

The trail ascends slightly, crossing rock sheets at the summit of West Mt. (15.9 mi.), then begins descending. In 0.1 mi. it comes to a side trail leading in 100 ft. to Cat Rocks and the best view of the day. A narrow farm valley far below is dotted with barns and trim white farmhouses. Straight ahead, Corbin Hill and Hammersly Ridge can be used to trace the route of the AT north.

The descent from here is steep, one of those climb-downs that make you feel as if your toes are going to shoot right out of the fronts of your boots. At 16.2 mi., a blue-blazed side trail leads right for 0.1 mi. to the Telephone Pioneers Shelter. Built in 1988 by AT&T employees and retirees, the lean-to has a privy and fireplace and supplies water from a stream that frequently goes dry in summer (purify). The descent now gets even steeper. A friend grimly remembers a hike up this mountain one hot August day. He and two buddies miraculously discovered a hot dog vendor near the base of the mountain. "The cold soda was a blessing," he said. "The two chili dogs I ate before climbing were *not*."

The trail switchbacks down through hemlocks and red cedars over rock slabs to County Rte. 20, also known as West Dover Rd. (16.8 mi.). There is overnight parking here beside a great old oak. From 1981 to 1991 this beautiful specimen grew from 18 ft. 10 in. around to 19 ft. 7 in. —a real granddaddy of a tree. Some speculate that it is the largest oak on the entire AT.

Miles N	NORTH	Elev. (ft./m)	Miles S
16.8	**End: County Rte. 20 (W Dover Rd.)** day parking; second-largest oak tree in Dutchess County; 2.3 mi. N of Pawling.	550/168	0.0
16.2	**Telephone Pioneers Shelter,** side trail to shelter, stream, fireplace, privy (0.1 mi.).	900/274	0.6
16.0	**Cat Rocks** side trail to view (33 yd.); begin steep 600-ft. descent.	1150/351	0.8
15.9	**West Mt.** summit.	1200/366	0.9
15.4	**Penny Rd.,** woods road.	1070/326	1.4
12.9	Upcoming AT relocation to Nuclear Lake begins.		1.7
12.6	Side trail to overnight parking on NY 55 (0.3 mi., early exit option), begin 150-ft. ascent to level plateau.	800/244	4.2
12.3	Cross **NY 55.**	700/213	4.5
12.0	Cross **Old Rte. 55.**	700/213	4.8
11.9	Cross railroad tracks and **Whaley Lake Stream.**	650/198	4.9
11.4	Balanced **glacial erratic** at top of 450-ft. descent.	1100/335	5.4
10.0	**Depot Hill Rd.,** day parking.	1250/381	6.8
9.2	**Depot Hill** summit, view.	1300/396	7.6
8.9	**Morgan Stewart Shelter,** side trail to shelter, fireplace, water pump, privy, designated overflow campsites (25 yd.).	1300/396	7.9
8.8	**Mt. Egbert** summit.		8.0
8.6	**Mt. Egbert,** view.	1329/405	8.2

Miles N		Elev. (ft./m)	Miles S
6.5	Cross **Grape Hollow Rd.,** go straight ahead into woods and down stone steps, begin ascending (day parking).	950/290	10.3
6.3	**Mountain Top Rd.,** turn L (N) and follow road across I-84 overpass (no parking).	950/290	10.5
6.1	**Stormville Mt. Rd.,** turn R (E) and follow road (no parking).	978/298	10.7
5.7	Open field **view** W into Hudson Valley.	875/267	11.1
5.1	**NY 52,** overnight parking, early exit option.	800/244	11.7
4.1	**Stormville Mt.** summit; begin short descent.	1056/322	12.7
3.5	**Hosner Mt. Rd.** day parking; begin moderate 500-ft. climb.	550/168	13.3
3.3	E-facing **view.**	700/213	13.5
2.7	W-facing **view.**	900/274	14.1
2.2	**Hosner Mt. Trail** northern terminus forms loop with AT (0.5 mi.).	950/290	14.6
1.9	**Hosner Mt. vista,** view from ledges.	1050/320	14.9
1.7	**Hosner Mt. Trail** southern terminus forms loop with AT (0.5 mi.).	1000/305	15.1
1.3	Unnamed view over Hudson Valley.	1050/320	15.5
0.3	**Taconic State Pkwy.,** no parking, cross to Miller Hill Rd., follow for 16 yd., turn L (N) onto Rock Ledge Rd., follow for 0.1 mi., turn R (E) into woods and begin climbing Hosner Mt.	600/183	16.5
0.0	**Start:** RPH Shelter, 1.1 mi. SW of Shenandoah; parking, water, privy. Follow blue-blazed trail 130 yd. from shelter to AT, turn R.	350/91	16.8

SOUTH

HIKE #41
Corbin Hill and Pawling Nature Reserve

Maps: ATC N.Y. & N.J. Map 1

Route: From County Rte. 20 (W Dover Rd.) over Corbin Hill, through the Great Swamp, into Pawling Nature Reserve, over Hammersly Ridge to Duell Hollow Rd. and Hoyt Rd.

Recommended direction: S to N

Distance: 9.5 mi.

Elevation +/-: 550 to 1053 to 450 ft.

Effort: Easy

Day hike: Yes

Overnight backpacking hike: No

Duration: 6 hr.

Early exit options: At 2.3 mi., NY 22; Pawling Reserve Trail system; at 8.5 mi., Duell Hollow Rd.

Natural history features: Second-largest oak in Dutchess County; Corbin Hill; the Great Swamp; Hammersly Ridge (Pawling Nature Reserve)

Social history features: Metro-North Railroad (historic rail line); Davidson Tattoo Parlor; Pawling Nature Reserve trail system; Gates of Heaven potters' field, Wiley (Webatuck) Shelter; Duell Hollow; Hoag family cemetery

Trailhead access: *Start:* Go N from Pawling on NY 22, making L at light by Harlem Valley State Hospital. At T make a L, then immediate R onto County Rte. 20 (W Dover Rd). AT overnight parking area is in 3.5 mi. on L. *End:* Take NY 55E (toward the CT state line), making a R onto Hoyt Rd. AT crosses road at NY–CT line in 0.3 mi. Limited day parking in pull-off.

Camping: Wiley (Webatuck) Shelter

The AT covers relatively easy terrain on this 9.5-mi. hike as it provides sweeping vistas of gently rolling farmlands, offers a walk through New York's second largest freshwater wetland, the Great Swamp, and traverses the secluded forest lands of the 1000-acre Pawling Nature Reserve.

The walk begins at the overnight AT parking area at County Rte. 20. The huge oak at the trailhead deserves a look; it is the second-largest oak in Dutchess County.

The AT climbs quickly up over stone steps and away from the road, rising easily along the edge of a hillside field, then descending through a pasture and small wetland over bog bridging. On a recent winter hike we discovered that hikers weren't the only ones keeping their feet dry on the raised planking. Mice had left their tiny paw prints there, too.

The trail climbs gently again, curving around the northern slope of Corbin Hill (a billion-year-old formation of quartz and feldspar). There are beautiful views north to the little bump of Waldo Hill and the loaf-shaped Sharp Hills. Look back the way you came to see West Mt. and Cat Rocks. When the leaves are off the trees, the AT's Telephone Pioneers Shelter can be seen three-quarters of the way up the mountain.

These wide-open fields, with their wealth of sunlight, support wildflowers that were both beautiful and useful to old-time farmers and Native Americans. Coltsfoot (named for its horse-hoof-shaped leaves) is among the first flowers to bloom here after the snow melts. The fresh leaves of this dandelion-like plant were once combined with sugar and boiled to make cough drops or syrup. The leaves can also be dried, then burned, with the resulting ash making a good salt substitute. As spring turns to summer, common mullein shoots up into 4-ft. stalks, each topped by a lance of bright yellow flowers. Mullein's soft, velvety leaves were once used as moccasin insoles by Native Americans. They were also applied to the skin to help soothe sunburn and other inflammations. Fringed gentians, with their showy blue trumpet-shaped flowers, bloom here in September. The ancient Roman naturalist Pliny recommended the roots of this plant as a laxative and tonic. But please don't pick them. The fringed gentian's striking beauty has made it popular with collectors, making it a rare find.

The AT twists south, slabbing steeply down along the side of Corbin Hill through thick hemlocks and black birch (0.9 mi.). A small spring bubbles up along a stone wall. You can always identify a spring during cold times because even at sub-zero temperatures the water refuses to freeze where it seeps from the ground. Be sure to purify all trailside water before drinking it.

At the base of Corbin Hill, the AT goes over Swamp River on a bridge (2.0 mi.) and then crosses the Great Swamp on a long stretch of raised bog bridging. This is New York's second-largest freshwater wetland, and in summer it grows up thickly with cattails, offering a habitat to red-winged blackbirds and muskrats. Cattails were the equivalent of a grocery store to early settlers and Native Americans: the starchy roots were ground into meal, young shoots were eaten like asparagus, and immature flower spikes were boiled and eaten like corn on the cob.

In another 0.3 mi. you will come to the AT Metro-North station (2.3 mi.). This sleepy little spot was once a vital rail hub for the New York & Harlem Railroad. During the early 19th century, transportation stalled when the Hudson River became clogged with ice. The New York & Harlem rail line solved that problem by 1851. It hauled feed, fertilizer, farm machinery, lumber, hay, milk, cider, ice, hogs, sheep, cattle, and limestone up and down the valley. The freight houses, stock pens, dairies, and ice ponds are long gone, but hikers today can still catch weekend trains out of New

AT / Metro North train stop, Pawling

York City and be on the AT within two hours. Check the timetable at Grand Central Terminal or call 212-532-4900 or 800-638-7646.

Turning left onto NY 22 briefly, the trail passes the Davidson Tattoo Parlor. A sign invites passers-by to walk in and "Live 'n Skin." To our knowledge, this is the only place along the AT where you can get a good tattoo. A hot dog vendor sometimes parks his truck beside NY 22, offering hungry hikers a balanced diet of cold soda and hot chili dogs.

The AT crosses NY 22, then Hurd's Corner Rd (2.6 mi.), climbing gently through an open sheep meadow. It passes an old wooden water tower, then enters a hayfield that provides sweeping views of the surrounding hills and valley. When crossing the wooden stiles, be careful not to touch the farmer's electric fences.

Also watch for a small wooden sign in the middle of the hayfield, which reads "Ap Trail" and directs you sharply left.

At the woods line (3.2 mi.), the trail enters the Pawling Nature Reserve, 1000 acres of Nature Conservancy –protected forest land and part of the watershed for the Great Swamp. The reserve is interlaced with hiking trails that pass through hemlock ravines, birch groves, a red maple swamp, alder swamps, and abandoned apple orchards. Deer, turkey, coyotes, bobcats, and beaver have been spotted here. The reserve's main entrance is on Quaker Lake Rd. For maps and information call 914-244-3271.

Over the next 0.7 mi., the AT climbs steeply to the crest of Hammersly Ridge (1053 ft.), the most challenging ascent of the day. For the next 4.5 mi. the path makes many slight descents and ascents as it crosses a rugged highland that was scoured and gouged by glacial action. The top of Hammersly Ridge offers many fun little rock scrambles, up over lichen-covered boulders and down to bog bridging through marshy areas. The highland is landscaped in dense thickets of mountain laurel. In June, the laurel's stiff, crooked branches bloom with delicate starlike chalices of white and pink blossoms. Native Americans called this evergreen "spoonwood" because its branches could be carved into eating utensils. Don't let the smallness of the shrub fool you; mountain laurel can outlive most human beings, with plants surviving for over one hundred years. Another showy flower of Hammersly Ridge is the pinxster flower, or pink azalea. Blossoming in May or June, its tubular vase-shaped flowers often burst forth ahead of its late-blooming leaves.

The AT intersects the Pawling Nature Reserve's red-blazed trail at 4.1 mi, and again at 4.9 mi. It intersects a yellow-blazed trail at 4.6 mi. (leading east to the reserve's main entrance), a green-blazed trail (5.0 mi.), a second red-blazed trail at 5.1 mi., and a second yellow-blazed trail at 5.9 mi. (leading to the reserve's north entrance). All of these trails can be used in combination with the AT to make interesting loops and side trips.

The AT leaves the Pawling Nature Reserve at 6.0 mi., continuing atop Hammersly Ridge to the Gates of Heaven Cemetery (7.1 mi.). The cemetery's brick and wrought-iron gate opens to a potters' field overgrown in milkweed and brambles. This forlorn spot is the final resting place for patients of the now-defunct Harlem Valley Psychiatric Hospital. Only three tipped-over headstones from the 1930s and '40s show above the grass, though it is said that many are buried here without grave markers.

The trail now passes through what was once contested ground. This is the Oblong, a strip of land 60 mi. long and 1.8 mi. wide, once claimed by both New York and Connecticut. The dispute, beginning in the 1700s, was not settled until 1881. The AT crosses dirt Leather Hill Rd. (7.9 mi.), then descends to the Wiley (Webatuck) Shelter at 8.3 mi. Built over 50 years ago, the lean-to got a freshwater well in 1995. It also has a fireplace and a new privy.

Descending another 0.2 mi., the AT crosses Duell Hollow Rd., named for a Quaker family who were among the first settlers of this region during the 1730s. A detour right, away from the trail, leads in about 0.1 mi. to the Hoag Cemetery. Shaded by large overhanging hemlocks, this family burial ground dates back to at least 1779. Some of the stones have been weathered clean of words and are covered in orange and yellow lichen. Gravestone rubbings can often bring out the seemingly illegible lettering.

Backtrack to the AT, and after a brief ascent, descend using switchbacks deeper into Duell Hollow. Tall hemlocks close in until you cross two small streams that cascade down to meet Duell Hollow Brook (8.8 mi.). The bridge, built on log pilings, stands high above the brook and is a fine place to stop, relax, and enjoy the solitude. The AT now climbs away from the hemlocks and enters abandoned farm fields in an advanced stage of forest succession. Old red cedars are being choked out by younger but taller deciduous trees. The lavender blossoms of wild bergamot bloom here in summer. These aromatic blossoms can be dried and made into tea. Oil from the leaves was once used to treat respiratory illnesses.

Just before reaching Hoyt Rd. (9.5 mi.), the trail passes a large standing dead tree that has provided many a meal for hungry woodpeckers and other bug-loving birds. Hoyt Rd. roughly marks the Connecticut state line. For "completists," those who wish to finish absolutely every last inch of the AT in New York, there is a small piece of the trail a few mi. north of this spot that weaves out of Connecticut and briefly back into New York. For a description of this trail section, see Volume 4 of *Exploring the Appalachian Trail*.

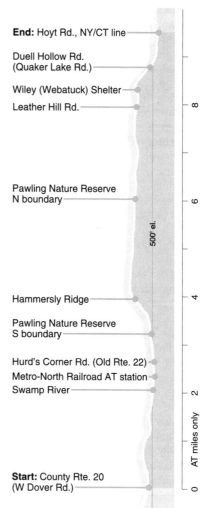

Hoyt Rd. ℗ NY/CT line, El. 450'

Duell Hollow Rd. ℗, Hoag Cemetery 🏛
Wiley (Webatuck) 🛏 ⛺ ⓣ

Leather Hill Rd., El. 700'

Gates of Heaven Cemetery 🏛

Pawling Nature Reserve, N boundary 🍁

Hammersly Ridge summit, El. 1053' 🍁

Pawling Nature Reserve, S boundary 🍁

Hurd's Corner Rd. (Old Rte. 22)

NY 22 ℗ Metro-North R.R. AT station

Swamp River, Great Swamp 🍁

Corbin Hill, **V**

🚶🚶 County Rte. 20 (W Dover Rd.) ℗ El. 550'

Miles N	**NORTH**	Elev. (ft./m)	Miles S
9.5	**End:** Hoyt Rd. parking, NY/CT state line, 3.3 mi. E of Wingdale.	450/137	0.0
8.8	**Duell Hollow Brook.**	400/122	0.7
8.5	Cross **Duell Hollow Rd. (Quaker Lake Rd.)** Hoag Cemetery is about 0.1 mi. R (E) on road. Early exit option.	750/229	1.0
8.3	**Wiley (Webatuck) Shelter,** fireplace, privy, water pump.	850/259	1.2
7.9	**Leather Hill Rd.**	700/213	1.6
7.1	**Gates of Heaven Cemetery.**	850/259	2.4
6.0	**Pawling Nature Reserve N boundary.**	850/259	3.5
5.9	**Pawling Nature Reserve second yellow-blazed trail** goes to reserve's N trailhead on Duell Hollow Rd. (Quaker Lake Rd.) in 0.25 mi.	900/274	3.6
5.1	**Pawling Nature Reserve second red-blazed trail** goes R (E) to intersect Yellow Trail near reserve's main entrance on Duell Hollow Rd. (Quaker Lake Rd.) in 0.7 mi.	900/274	4.4
5.0	**Pawling Nature Reserve green-blazed trail** goes L (W) to intersect with orange-blazed trail near reserve's trailhead on Deer Ridge Rd. (0.75 mi.).	950/290	4.5
4.9	**Pawling Nature Reserve red-blazed trail** forms loop with AT and also leads to Duell Hollow Rd. (Quaker Lake Rd.) at the reserve's S trailhead (1.75 mi.).	1000/305	4.6
4.6	**Pawling Nature Reserve yellow-blazed trail** goes R (E) to reserve's main entrance on Duell Hollow Rd. (Quaker Lake Rd.) in 0.5 mi.	1000/305	4.9
4.1	**Pawling Nature Reserve red-blazed trail** forms loop with AT and also leads to Duell Hollow Rd. (Quaker Lake Rd.) at the reserve's S trailhead (1.75 mi.).	1000/305	5.4

Miles N		Elev. (ft./m)	Miles S
3.9	**Hammersly Ridge** summit.	1053/321	5.6
3.2	**Pawling Nature Reserve S boundary** information board; begin climbing steeply.	575/175	6.3
2.9	AT turns L (N) at small sign in middle of field.	575/175	6.6
2.6	**Hurd's Corner Rd. (Old Rte. 22).**	475/145	6.9
2.3	**NY 22,** parking; **Metro-North R.R. AT Station;** early exit option.	450/137	7.2
2.0	**Swamp River** bridge and long stretch of bog bridging through NY's second-largest wetland.	430/131	7.5
0.9	**Corbin Hill,** view; AT skirts L (N) around summit and begins descending.	750/229	8.6
0.0	**Start:** County Rte. 20 (W Dover Rd.) day parking, 2.3 mi. N of Pawling; second-largest oak tree in Duchess County; begin climbing rock steps into series of fields.	550/168	9.5

SOUTH

Useful Information

US Geological Survey Topographical Maps

USGS maps used in this series are scaled at 1:100,000 (1 cm = 1 km), but in this book we have converted the scale generally to 1 in. = 1 mi. or a close fraction thereof. The maps listed below, which cover all the AT miles in this volume, are quadrangles covering the area surrounding the named town (approximately 50 mi. E-W and 35 mi. N-S).

> Waterbury
> Bridgeport
> Middletown
> Scranton
> Allentown
> Sunbury
> Harrisburg
> Carlisle
> Hagerstown
> Frederick
> Washington West

To order USGS maps, see "Web Sites" and the Bibliography.

Appalachian Trail Conference Maps

ATC sells its own 4-color topo hiking maps and some maps published by regional hiking clubs. Together these maps cover the entire AT. Generally

ATC maps are scaled at 1:62,500 (1 in. = 1 mi.). Maps referred to in this volume are listed here.

ATC New York-New Jersey, Map 1
(N.Y./CT. Line to N.Y. Route 52)

ATC New York-New Jersey, Map 2
(N.Y. Route 52 to Hudson River)

ATC New York-New Jersey, Map 3
(Hudson River to Greenwood Lake)

ATC New York-New Jersey, Map 4
(Greenwood Lake to High Point)

ATC New York-New Jersey, Map 5
(High Point to Mid-Kittatinny)

ATC New York-New Jersey, Map 6
(Mid-Kittatinny to N.J./PA. Line)

Keystone Trails Association

KTA Pennsylvania Section 1
(Delaware Water Gap to Wind Gap)

KTA Pennsylvania Section 2
(Wind Gap to Lehigh Gap)

KTA Pennsylvania Section 3
(Lehigh Gap to PA 309)

KTA Pennsylvania Section 4
(PA 309 to Port Clinton Gap)

KTA Pennsylvania Section 5
(Port Clinton Gap to PA 183)

KTA Pennsylvania Section 6
(PA 183 to Swatara Gap)

KTA Pennsylvania Sections 7 & 8
(Susquehanna River to Swatara Gap)

KTA Pennsylvania Sections 9 & 10
(Susquehanna River/US 322 to Boiling Springs/PA 174)

KTA Pennsylvania Sections 11 & 12
(Boiling Spring/PA 174 to Pine Grove Furnace S.P./PA 233)

KTA Pennsylvania Section 13
(Pine Grove Furnace S.P./PA 233 to Caledonia S.P./US 30)

KTA Pennsylvania Section 14
(Caledonia S.P./US 30 to Penmar)

Potomac Appalachian Trail Club

PATC Map 5
(Maryland, North Half)

PATC Map 6
(Maryland, South Half)

Many ATC maps are double maps on one sheet (a map on each side); for example, the KTA maps for Section 1 & 2 appear on one sheet.

To order ATC maps, see "Address & Telephone" and "Web Sites."

DEGREE OF DIFFICULTY

Definitions

Easy: gentle ups and downs, fairly smooth path, few obstacles

Moderate: elevation gain or loss of up to 1000 ft.; narrower, rocky path; some obstacles (for example, brook crossings with no bridge)

Strenuous: elevation gain or loss of more than 1000 ft.; steep ups and downs; difficult, challenging path; numerous obstacles; possibly unsuitable for young children or the infirm.

Hikes

EASY

- #2, Crampton Gap, Fox Gap, and Turners Gap
- #4, Pen Mar County Park, MD, to Old Forge Picnic Grounds

- #7, South Mt. Ridge to Pine Grove Furnace State Park
- #9, Center Point Knob and Boiling Springs
- #10, Boiling Springs to Scott Farm Trail Work Center
- #13, Peters Mt. Ridge to Clark Creek
- #23, Smith Gap Rd. to Wind Gap
- #25, Fox Gap to Delaware Water Gap
- #27, Catfish Mt. to Flatbrookville Rd.
- #30, The Great Valley of the Appalachians
- #32, Wawayanda Mt. to Warwick Tpk.
- #41, Corbin Hill and Pawling Nature Reserve

EASY TO MODERATE
#17, Blue Mt. Ridge to Port Clinton

SEE PAGE 14 for general notes about shelters and campsites on or close to the AT. We list here the shelters (a.k.a. lean-tos) and named campsites (a.k.a. tent sites) described in this book. When shelters have officially designated tent sites, we indicate "campsite" below. Consult the narrative of each hike for information on unofficial tent sites at some shelters and on shelters that are farther off the AT.

Hike #	Shelter	Campsite	Lodge/Cabin	Name
1		x		Weverton Primitive Camp
2	x			Crampton Gap
			x	Bear Spring Cabin
	x			Rocky Run
		x		Dahlgren Back Pack Campground
3	x			Pine Knob
		x		Pogo Memorial
	x			Hemlock Hill
	x			Devils Racecourse
4	x			Deer Lick
	x	x		Antietam
5	x			Tumbling Run
			x	Hermitage Cabin
	x			Rocky Mt.
		x		Caledonia SP
6		x		Caledonia SP
	x			Quarry Gap
			x	Milesburn Cabin
	x			Birch Run
7			x	Anna Michener Memorial Cabin
	x			Toms Run
		x		primitive campsites
8		x		Pine Grove Furnace SP Campground
		x		Mt. Creek Campground
	x			Tagg Run
9	x			Alec Kennedy
11	x			Thelma Marks Memorial
12	x			Clarks Ferry
13	x			Peters Mt.
14	x			Rausch Gap

Hike #	Shelter	Campsite	Lodge/Cabin	Name
15	x			William Penn
		x		Blue Mt.
16	x			501
		x		Pilger Ruh
		x		Hertlein
17	x			Eagles Nest
18		x		YMCA Blue Mt. Camp
		x		Pocohontas Spring
		x		Hamburg Reservoir
	x	x		Windsor Furnace
19	x	x		Eckville
	x			Allentown
20		x		New Tripoli
21	x			Bake Oven Knob
	x			George W. Outerbridge
23	x			Leroy Smith
25	x			Kirkridge
26		x		Backpacker Campsite
		x	x	AMC Mohican Outdoor Center
		x		Delaware Water Gap National Recreation Area (+ #27, #28)
27		x	x	AMC Mohican Outdoor Center
28			x	Brink
29	x			Gren Anderson
	x			Mashipacong
	x			Rutherford
		x		High Point
31	x			Pochuck
32	x			Wawayanda
34	x			Wildcat
35	x			Fingerboard
36	x			William Brien Memorial
	x			West Mt.
37			x	Bear Mt. Inn
		x		Hemlock Springs
38		x		Dennytown Rd. group site
39		x		Dennytown Rd. group site
	x			RPH
40	x			Morgan Stewart
	x			Telephone Pioneers
41	x			Wiley (Webatuck)

Day Hikes

Depending on your starting time, physical condition, ambition, and the weather, the following hikes can be manageable day hikes. Check "Duration" and "Distance" in the information block at the beginning of the hike before starting. Many of these work well as sections of longer backpacking hikes, and some appear in the "Overnight Hikes" list as well.

#1, Crampton Gap to Harpers Ferry, WV

#2, Crampton Gap, Fox Gap, and Turners Gap

#3, Pine Knob to Pen Mar County Park

#4, Pen Mar County Park, MD, to Old Forge Picnic Grounds

#5 Old Forge Picnic Grounds to Caledonia State Park

#6, Caledonia State Park and Big Pine Flat Ridge

#7, South Mt. Ridge to Pine Grove Furnace State Park

#8, Pine Grove Furnace State Park to Sheet Iron Rd.

#9, Center Point Knob and Boiling Springs

#10, Boiling Springs to Scott Farm Trail Work Center

#11, Cove Mt. to Duncannon

#12, Clarks Ferry Bridge to Peters Mt. Ridge

#13, Peters Mt. Ridge to Clark Creek

#14, Clark Creek to Swatara Gap

#15, Swatara Gap and Blue Mt. Ridge

#16, Along Blue Mt. Ridge

#17, Blue Mt. Ridge to Port Clinton

#18, Port Clinton to Pine Swamp Rd.

#19, Hawk Mt. to PA 309

#20, The Cliffs and Bear Rocks

#21, Bake Oven Knob to Lehigh Gap

#22, Lehigh Gap to Smith Gap Rd.

#23, Smith Gap Rd. to Wind Gap

#24, Wind Gap to Fox Gap

#25, Fox Gap to Delaware Water Gap

#26, Sunfish Pond and Mt. Mohican

#27, Catfish Mt. to Flatbrookville Rd.

#28, Rattlesnake and Bird Mts.

#29, Sunrise Mt. and High Point

#30, The Great Valley of the Appalachians

#31, Wallkill and Vernon Valleys

#32, Wawayanda Mt. to Warwick Tpk.

#33, Warwick Tpk. to Mt. Peter, NY

#34, Sterling Forest

#35, Bear Mt.–Harriman State Parks—West

#36, Bear Mt.–Harriman State Parks—East

#37, Bear Mt. Bridge and Anthony's Nose

#38, US 9 to Dennytown Rd.

#39, Fahnestock State Park

#40, Hosner Mt. to Cat Rocks

#41, Corbin Hill and Pawling Nature Reserve

Overnight Hikes

These are overnight backpacking trips. Segments of some overnight hikes can also be manageable day hikes.

#2, Crampton Gap, Fox Gap, and Turners Gap

#3, Pine Knob to Pen Mar County Park

#6, Caledonia State Park and Big Pine Flat Ridge

#14, Clark Creek to Swatara Gap

#15, Swatara Gap and Blue Mt. Ridge

#17, Blue Mt. Ridge to Port Clinton

#18, Port Clinton to Pine Swamp Rd.

#19, Hawk Mt. to PA 309

#26, Sunfish Pond and Mt. Mohican

#27, Catfish Mt. to Flatbrookville Rd.

#28, Rattlesnake and Bird Mts.

#29, Sunrise Mt. and High Point

#31, Wallkill and Vernon Valleys

#32, Wawayanda Mt. to Warwick Tpk.

#34, Sterling Forest

#35, Bear Mt.-Harriman State Parks-West

#36, Bear Mt.-Harriman State Parks-East

#37, Bear Mt. Bridge and Anthony's Nose

#40, Hosner Mt. to Cat Rocks

OTHER TRAIL SYSTEMS

THERE ARE SCORES of trails connecting to the Mid-Atlantic AT, many of which offer vistas and facilities similar to those found on the AT itself. Numerous short connecting side trails are noted in the hike narratives in this book. Avid hikers and those wanting to avoid crowded conditions on popular sections of the AT may enjoy exploring some of these more extended trail systems.

Maryland

Maryland offers a remarkable trail system for such a small state. The Chesapeake & Ohio (C&O) Canal Towpath stretches for 184.5 flat miles between Washington, D.C., and Cumberland, Maryland, and includes Potomac River–side campsites all along the trail's length (for information contact C&O Canal Headquarters, P.O. Box 4, Sharpsburg, MD 21782; 301-739-4200). The C&O also co-aligns with the 6,357-mi. coast-to-coast American Discovery Trail (contact the American Hiking Society).

Catoctin Mt. Park and Cunningham Falls State Park (with its magnificent 78-ft.-tall cascade) lie in mountainous areas just east of the AT and boast fine trail systems, including the 27-mi.-long Catoctin Trail maintained by the PATC (contact Catoctin Mt. Park,

6602 Foxville Rd., Thurmont, MD 21788; 301-663-9388; or the PATC). The Elk Ridge Trail is a short but spectacular path that climbs Maryland Heights near the AT, giving the best views of historic Harpers Ferry (contact Harpers Ferry National Historical Park, P.O. Box 65, Harpers Ferry, WV 25425; 304-535-6223).

Pennsylvania
The Keystone State offers thousands of beautiful trail miles, many of which are little known and underused. State parks and Game Lands boast the most miles, including highlights within State Game Lands 210 and 211 and St. Anthony's Wilderness (remote, wild territory on Peters Mt., Stony Mt., Sharp Mt., and Second Mt.), Michaux State Forest, and Caledonia State Park (where a dozen AT side trails make a variety of interesting day hikes and loops possible).

The Delaware Water Gap National Recreation Area also features several trails linking with the AT, offering circuit hike possibilities. The Horse-Shoe and Tuscarora trails are two long-distance paths that intersect Pennsylvania's AT. The 105-mi., orange-blazed Tuscarora Trail runs south from the AT near Dean's Gap and ends at the C&O Canal in Hancock, MD. The 130-mi., yellow-blazed Horse-Shoe Trail is a hiker and horse trail that runs from Valley Forge west to its terminus on the AT at Stony Mt.

For information on Pennsylvania hiking trails, contact the Keystone Trails Association. This association's book, *Pennsylvania Hiking Trails,* offers detailed information on the state's trail network.

New Jersey and New York
The mountainous regions surrounding the AT in these states claim over 1000 mi. of trails maintained by volunteers of the NY-NJ Trail Conference. Most of these trails lie within the state and federal parks that border the AT, offering many day-hiking and backpacking opportunities. Some highlights are the trails within the Delaware Water Gap National Recreation Area (hikes to Blue Mt. Lakes and Buttermilk Falls are especially noteworthy), and within Worthington State Forest (the views of the Delaware Water Gap from the Blue Dot Trail are spectacular), Stokes State Forest, High Point State Park (the Monument Trail and Shawangunk Ridge Trail offer great hiking), Wawayanda State Park, Bear Mt.-Harriman State Parks (there are over 200 mi. of trail within the park, plus the Long Path, a 300-mi. trail stretching from the George Washington Bridge to the Mohawk River), Hudson Highlands State Park, and Fahnestock State Park. The NY-NJTC sells maps for all of these trail systems and publishes the *New York Walk Book* and *New Jersey Walk Book.*

For information on contacting the trail organizations mentioned, see "Address & Telephone," below.

General Hiking Clubs

American Hiking Society, 1422 Fenwick La., Silver Spring, MD 20910; 301-565-6704

Appalachian Mountain Club, 5 Joy St., Boston, MA 02108; 617-523-0636. For their hiking guides: Box 298, Gorham, NH 03581; 800-262-4455

Appalachian Trail Conference, P.O. Box 807, Harpers Ferry, WV 25425-0807; 304-535-6331; fax 304-535-2667

Mid-Atlantic Regional Hiking Clubs

Allentown Hiking Club, P.O. Box 1542, Allentown, PA 18105-1542

AMC-Delaware Valley Chapter, 1180 Greenleaf Dr., Bethlehem, PA 18017

AMC-New York/North Jersey Chapter, 5 Tudor City Place, New York, NY 10017

Batona Hiking Club, 514 Inman Terr., Willow Grove, PA 19090

Blue Mountain Eagle Climbing Club, P.O. Box 3523, Reading, PA 19605

Brandywine Valley Outing Club, P.O. Box 134, Rockland, DE 19732

Cumberland Valley A.T. Management Association, 43 Walnut Trail, Carroll Valley, PA 17320

Keystone Trails Association, P.O. Box 251, Cogan Station, PA 17728-0251

Mountain Club of Maryland, Rte. 1, Box 1436, Harpers Ferry, WV 25425

New York-New Jersey Trail Conference, 232 Madison Ave., New York, NY 10016

Philadelphia Trail Club, 741 Golf Dr., Warrington, PA 18975

Susquehanna Appalachian Trail Club, P.O. Box 61001, Harrisburg, PA 17106-1001

Wilmington Trail Club, P.O. Box 1184, Wilmington, DE 19899

York Hiking Club, 2684 Forest Rd., York, PA 17402

NOTE: ALMOST ALL WEB SITE addresses begin with http:// , preceding www. Most Web sites are updated periodically. Some listed here were still in development when we visited them.

Major Organizations

American Hiking Society   www.orca.org/ahs/

Dedicated to promoting hiking and to protecting and maintaining America's trails, AHS offers programs, publications (newsletter), legislative updates, volunteer vacations, and links to many clubs and resources.

Appalachian Long Distance Hikers Association   www.connix.com/~aldha/

Aimed primarily at thru-hikers. Savvy advice, networking, forums, volunteering opportunities.

Appalachian Mountain Club   www.outdoors.org/

Granddaddy of the eastern hiking clubs, AMC covers not only the northeastern AT but activities and trail reports on many other trails. AMC Books, AMC Outdoors (magazine), adult and kids' activities (trips and workshops year-round), conservation initiatives, hiking trip planning, AMC hut reservations, and much more.

Appalachian Trail Conference   www.atconf.org/

This site is comprehensive, with many lists of and links to regional trail clubs. ATC's "Ultimate Trail Store" has arguably the biggest selection of AT books and maps anywhere (member discounts). Updated trail conditions, permit regulations, and other helpful subjects.

AT Regional Trail Maintaining Clubs

Many regional hiking clubs have their own Web sites, and most of them can be found easily by way of links from the Appalachian Trail Conference Web site listed above. Here are some Web sites concerned with the AT in the states covered by this book.

Allentown Hiking Club   www.enter.net/~dch/

AMC — Delaware Valley Chapter   www.enter.net/~dvamc/

AMC — New York-North Jersey Chapter   www.gti.net/amcny/

Batona Hiking Club   www.seas.upenn.edu/~mahesh/batona/batona.html

Keystone Trails Association Home Page   www.reston.com/kta/KTA.html

Mountain Club of Maryland   pw2.netcom.com/~sburket/mcm.html

New York-New Jersey Trail Conference   www.nynjtc.org/

Other AT Web sites

America's Roof—High Point   www.inch.com/~dipper/nj.html

Click on the state map and up comes a home page for the state's highest mountain. This site covers New Jersey's High Point, on the AT. The highest points in New York (Mt. Marcy), Pennsylvania (Mt. Davis), and Maryland (Backbone Mt.) are not on the AT. Mountain information is not extensive here, however.

The Appalachian Trail Home Page   www.fred.net/kathy/at.html

The official-sounding name belies the fact that this is a personal home page built by a thru-hiker, Kathy Bilton. Nonetheless, it's one of the better general sites for miscellaneous information about the AT and for connecting with AT people. Links to AT maintaining clubs (also to the AT organizations and to other National Scenic Trails), forums for AT issues discussions, advice from thru-hikers, and more.

Appalachian Trail Place   www.trailplace.com

Center for Appalachian Trail Studies. Hosted by Dan "Wingfoot" Bruce, a thru-hiker who maintains a hostel by the trail in Virginia. A spin-off from Wingfoot's *Thru-Hiker's Handbook.* Dozens of searchable databases on AT subjects, many especially helpful to long-distance hikers or those with natural history interests. "Mailing lists" of former and would-be thru-hikers, women hikers, teenage hikers, others. Chat rooms. Bibliography. One of the better sites.

Commercial and Government Web sites

GENERAL

GORP   www.gorp.com

Great Outdoor Recreation Pages. From various purveyors of travel and outdoor adventure information, services, and supplies. The AT is one small part of this huge, diverse site. Rewarding for those with time to fill.

MAGAZINES

Backpacker   www.bpbasecamp.com

Extensive, well-researched information about hiking worldwide. Many articles on either the AT specifically or on hiking skills and equipment useful to AT trekkers. "Trail Talk Forums" bring hikers together on-line. An "Encyclopedia" includes a section on "Backcountry Jargon." "Gearfinder" is a searchable database of hiking/camping products. The site is fueled by links to *Backpacker*'s advertisers, a convenience or a distraction depending on your disposition.

Outside   outside.starwave.com

Most of the magazine, on-line. Hiking per se and the AT specifically are only occasionally featured in *Outside* (whose travel beat is worldwide), but the treatment is usually in-depth and colorful. Generally aimed at the under-forty crowd. Good articles on fitness and training. Excellent book reviews.

BOOKSTORES

Adventurous Traveler Bookstore   www.adventuroustraveler.com

If you are anywhere near Burlington, Vermont, go to this store. Short of that, visit on-line. Over 4000 travel-related titles await you. Extensive AT and other North American hiking book inventory. Maps too. Paper catalogue available.

Amazon   www.amazon.com

The leader in on-line bookstores. Search the database on the words "Appalachian Trail" for a long list of titles.

Barnes & Noble   www.barnesandnoble.com

They're everywhere and they carry almost everything. If the local store doesn't have it, search on-line under the subject "Appalachian Trail."

Borders Books & Music   www.borders.com

Not quite as widespread as Barnes & Noble, but by spring 1998, Borders expected to have an extensive Web site, offering their entire inventory on-line.

MAPS

Delorme Map Co.   www.delorme.com

Detailed atlases for the following AT states: North Carolina, Tennessee, Virginia, Maryland, Pennsylvania, New York, Vermont, New Hampshire, Maine.

Perry-Castaneda Library Map Collection
www.lib.utexas.edu/Libs/PCL/Map_collection/Map_collection.html

An extensive collection of links to on-line map resources around the world. Including not only topographic maps but also historical and weather maps.

United States Geologic Survey (USGS)
www.usgs.gov/pubprod/products.html

A giant site for both the general public and scientists. This address is for ordering maps. A database facilitates finding the correct map, at the desired scale, for the area you're hiking.

WEATHER

National Oceanic & Atmospheric Administration
www.nws.noaa.gov/weather

NOAA offers continuously updated weather reports and forecasts all across the country on dedicated radio channels (a lightweight weather-only radio is worth carrying on extended backpacking trips). Or access NOAA's weather report Web site at the address above (expected to be fully functional in spring 1998).

The Weather Underground   www.wunderground.com

Up-to-the-hour weather reports and forecasts for many cities in the U.S., including numerous smaller cities near the Appalachian Trail.

Bibliography

Hiking Guides

Chase, Jim. *Backpacker Magazine's Guide to the Appalachian Trail.* Stackpole Books, 1989.

Chazin, Daniel D. *Appalachian Trail Guide to New York-New Jersey, Thirteenth Edition.* New York-New Jersey Trail Conference, 1994.

Forrester, Jr., Maurice J., ed. *Guide to the Appalachian Trail in Pennsylvania.* Keystone Trails Association, 1994.

Golightly, Jean C., ed. *Appalachian Trail Guide to Maryland and Northern Virginia, Fifteenth Edition.* Potomac Appalachian Trail Club, 1995.

New York Walk Book. New York-New Jersey Trail Conference, 1998.

Logue, Victoria and Frank. *The Best of the Appalachian Trail: Day Hikes.* Menasha Ridge Press, 1994.

Logue, Victoria and Frank. *The Best of the Appalachian Trail: Overnight Hikes.* Menasha Ridge Press, 1994.

Maps & Atlases

U.S. Geological Survey, Topographic maps available in printed versions and on CD-ROM. Call 800-HELP-MAP; write to USGS, Map Distribution, Box 25286, Denver, CO 80225; or access their Web site (p. 355).

Field Guides & Natural History

Alden, Peter. *Peterson First Guide to Mammals of North America.* Houghton Mifflin, 1987.

Bull, John and John Farrand Jr. *National Audubon Society Field Guide to North American Birds, Eastern Region.* Chanticleer Press, 1994.

Chew, V. Collins. *Underfoot: A Geologic Guide to the Appalachian Trail.* Appalachian Trail Conference, 1993.

Collins, Beryl Robichaud and Karl Anderson. *Plant Communities of New Jersey.* Rutgers University Press, 1994.

Lawrence, Eleanor, and Cecilia Fitzsimons. *An Instant Guide to Trees.* Longmeadow Press, 1991.

Newcomb, Lawrence. *Newcomb's Wildflower Guide.* Little, Brown, 1977.

Peterson, Lee Allen. *A Field Guide to Edible Wild Plants of Eastern and Central North America.* Houghton Mifflin, 1977.

Peterson, Roger Tory. *Peterson First Guide to Birds of North America.* Houghton Mifflin, 1986.

Peterson, Roger Tory. *Peterson First Guide to Wildflowers of Northeastern and North-central North America.* Houghton Mifflin, 1986.

Raymo, Chet and Maureen E. *Written in Stone: A Geological History of the Northeastern United States.* The Globe Pequot Press, 1989.

Rezendez, Paul. *Tracking and the Art of Seeing: How to Read Animal Tracks and Signs.* Camden House Publishing, 1992.

Rue, Leonard Lee, III. *New Jersey Out of Doors: A History of its Flora and Fauna.* Hicks Printing Co., 1964.

Serrao, John. *Nature's Events: A Note-book of the Unfolding Seasons.* Stackpole Books, 1992.

Sutton, Ann, and Myron Sutton. *Eastern Forests* (Audubon Field Guide). Alfred A. Knopf, 1993.

Watts, May Theilgaard. *Tree Finder.* Nature Study Guild, 1986.

General Books: Appalachian Trail

Appalachian Trail Conference. *Walking the Appalachian Trail Step by Step,* Appalachian Trail Conference, 1993.

Bruce, Dan "Wingfoot." *The Thru-Hiker's Handbook.* Center for Appalachian Trail Studies, 1997. (Updated annually)

Chazin, Daniel D. *Appalachian Trail Data Book 1996.* Appalachian Trail Conference, 1997. (Updated annually)

Emblidge, David, ed. *The Appalachian Trail Reader.* Oxford University Press, 1997.

Fisher, Ronald M. *The Appalachian Trail.* National Geographic Society, 1972.

O'Brien, Bill, ed. *Appalachian Trail Thru-Hikers' Companion.* Appalachian Trail Conference, 1997. (Updated annually)

Scherer, Glenn D. *Vistas and Vision: A History of the New York-New Jersey Trail Conference.* New York-New Jersey Trail Conference, 1995.

Scherer, Glenn D. "Bridge to 'Somewhere.'" *Appalachian Trailway News* (March/April, 1996): 13-16.

Scherer, Glenn D. "The Making of a Park." *AMC Outdoors* vol. 60, no. 3. (April 1994): 28-35.

Whalen, Christopher. *The Appalachian Trail Workbook for Planning Thru-Hikes.* Appalachian Trail Conference, 1995.

Practical Advice: Hiking & Camping

Berger, Karen. *Hiking & Backpacking: A Complete Guide.* W. W. Norton, 1995.

Cary, Alice. *Parents' Guide to Hiking & Camping.* W. W. Norton, 1997.

Fletcher, Colin. *The Complete Walker.* Alfred A. Knopf, 1984.

Hampton, Bruce, and David Cole. *Soft Paths: How to Enjoy the Wilderness Without Harming It.* Stackpole, 1995.

McManners, Hugh. *The Backpacker's Handbook.* Dorling Kindersley, 1995.

Meyer, Kathleen. *How to Shit in the Woods: An Environmentally Sound Approach to a Lost Art.* Ten Speed Press, 1994.

Staffs of the Pittsburgh *Post-Gazette,* Hartford *Courant,* Atlanta *Journal-Constitution,* Raleigh *News and Observer,* and Maine *Sunday Telegram. Appalachian Adventure.* Longstreet Press, 1995.

Viehman, John, ed. *Trailside's Hints & Tips for Outdoor Adventures.* Rodale Press, 1993.

Wood, Robert S. *The 2 Oz. Backpacker.* Ten Speed Press, 1982.

Background Reading

Allport, Susan. *Sermons in Stone: The Stone Walls of New England and New York.* W. W. Norton, 1994.

Bertland, Dennis N., Patricia M. Valence, and Russell J. Woodling. *The Minisink.* Four-County Task Force on the Tocks Island Dam Project, 1975.

Dunwell, Frances F. *The Hudson River Highlands.* Columbia University Press, 1991.

Dupont, Ronald J. Jr. *Hiking with History.* Unpublished manuscript, 1994.

Dupont, Ronald J. Jr. *Vernon 200: A Bicentennial History of the Township of Vernon, New Jersey 1792–1992,* Friends of the Dorothy E. Henry Library, 1992.

Dupont, Ronald J. Jr. and Kevin Wright. *High Point of the Blue Mountains.* Sussex County Historical Society, 1990.

Durham, Michael. Ed. Roger G. Kennedy. *Smithsonian Guide to Historic America: The Mid-Atlantic States: New York, New Jersey, Pennsylvania.* Stewart Tabori & Chang, 1989.

Flato, Charles and American Heritage Publishing Co., eds. *The Golden Book of the Civil War.* Golden Press, 1961.

Goller, Robert R. and Harper's New Monthly Magazine. *Artist-Life in the Highlands and Among the Nail Makers—An 1859 Visit to Northern New Jersey's Iron Industry and the Morris Canal.* Canal Society of New Jersey, 1994.

Lenik, Edward J. *Iron Mine Trails.* New York-New Jersey Trail Conference, 1996.

Strain, Paula M. *The Blue Hills of Maryland.* Potomac Appalachian Trail Club, 1993.

Schlesinger, Arthur M., Jr., ed. *The Almanac of American History.* Perigee Books, 1983.

Waterman, Laura and Guy. *Forest and Crag: A History of Hiking, Trail Blazing, and Adventure in the Northeast Mountains.* Appalachian Mountain Club, 1989.

Index

Page numbers in *italic* refer to topographic maps and itineraries.

GLENN SCHERER is a NY-NJTC volunteer who moves rocks and mountains of paperwork to support the AT. Scherer has hiked the AT in Maryland, New Jersey, and New York, plus Vermont's Long Trail and Maine's 100-Mile Wilderness. His writing has appeared in *Backpacker, Outside, AMC Outdoors, Appalachian Trailway News, American Hiker,* and *New Jersey Country Roads.* In 1995 he wrote *Vistas and Vision: A History of the New York-New Jersey Trail Conference.* His *Nature Walks in New Jersey* is forthcoming from AMC. Glenn Scherer lives in Highland Lakes, New Jersey.

DON HOPEY is the Pittsburgh *Post-Gazette* environmental reporter. He has hiked 700 miles of the AT in Pennsylvania, Virginia, Maryland, West Virginia, Georgia, and Maine. Hopey contributed to *Appalachian Adventure,* about a 1995 AT relay hike by reporters from five newspapers. He has also hiked in the Grand Canyon (Yellowstone River), Black Canyon (Gunnison River), Never Summer Mountains (Colorado), Great Smoky Mts. (Tennessee), and on Mt. Rainier (Washington), all with a fly rod poking from his backpack.

The Exploring the Appalachian Trail™ series

Hikes in the Southern Appalachians: Georgia, North Carolina, Tennessee
by Doris Gove $19.95   432 pages

Hikes in the Virginias: Virginia, West Virginia
by David Lillard and Gwyn Hicks $19.95   432 pages

Hikes in the Mid-Atlantic States: Maryland, Pennsylvania, New Jersey, New York
by Glenn Scherer and Don Hopey $19.95   372 pages

Hikes in Southern New England: Connecticut, Massachusetts, Vermont
by David Emblidge $19.95   292 pages

Hikes in Northern New England: New Hampshire, Maine
by Michael Kodas, Andrew Weegar, Mark Condon, Glenn Scherer $19.95   368 pages

Available from your favorite bookseller or outdoor retailer, or from the publisher.

STACKPOLE
BOOKS
5067 Ritter Road
Mechanicsburg, PA 17055
1-800-732-3669
www.stackpolebooks.com